Elizabeth II

In Private. In Public. The Inside Story.

Also by Robert Hardman

Queen of the World
Our Queen
Monarchy: The Royal Family at Work
Queen of Our Times
Charles III

Elizabeth II

In Private. In Public. The Inside Story.

ROBERT HARDMAN

MACMILLAN

First published 2026 by Macmillan
an imprint of Pan Macmillan
The Smithson, 6 Briset Street, London EC1M 5NR
EU representative: Macmillan Publishers Ireland Ltd, 1st Floor,
The Liffey Trust Centre, 117–126 Sheriff Street Upper,
Dublin 1 D01 YC43
Associated companies throughout the world

ISBN 978-1-0350-9730-2

Copyright © Robert Hardman Limited 2026

The right of Robert Hardman to be identified as the
author of this work has been asserted in accordance
with the Copyright, Designs and Patents Act 1988.

The picture credits on pp. 419–22 constitute an extension of this copyright page.

All rights reserved. No part of this publication may be reproduced,
stored in a retrieval system, or transmitted, in any form, or by any means
(including, without limitation, electronic, mechanical, photocopying, recording or
otherwise) without the prior written permission of the publisher.

Pan Macmillan does not have any control over, or any responsibility for,
any author or third-party websites (including, without limitation, URLs,
emails and QR codes) referred to in or on this book.

1 3 5 7 9 8 6 4 2

A CIP catalogue record for this book is available from the British Library.

Typeset by Palimpsest Book Production Limited, Falkirk, Stirlingshire
Printed and bound in the UK using 100% Renewable Electricity
by CPI Group (UK) Ltd

This book is sold subject to the condition that it shall not, by way of
trade or otherwise, be lent, hired out, or otherwise circulated without
the publisher's prior consent in any form of binding or cover other than
that in which it is published and without a similar condition including this
condition being imposed on the subsequent purchaser. The publisher does not
authorize the use or reproduction of any part of this book in any manner
for the purpose of training artificial intelligence technologies or systems.
The publisher expressly reserves this book from the Text and Data Mining
exception in accordance with Article 4(3) of the European Union
Digital Single Market Directive 2019/790.

Visit **www.panmacmillan.com** to read more
about all our books and to buy them.

For Marion Cowley

Contents

Preface		1
1	A Personal View: 'Oh, really?'	3
2	1926–39: Number Three	27
3	1939–47: 'People will say we're in love'	39
4	1947–52: Duchess Days	57
5	1952–55: A Reluctant Gloriana	75
6	1955–60: Rifts	89
7	1960–69: Mountbatten-Windsor	101
8	1970–79: Walkabouts and Monsters	117
9	1979–82: 'Don't look back'	137
10	1983–91: 'Let's have him'	155
11	1992–95: 'Horribilis'	171
12	1996–97: 'These are for you'	195
13	1998–2002: 'We must speak of change'	213
14	2003–11: The Winners' Enclosure	231
15	2012–16: Diamond Days	253
16	2016–18: 'My sincere wish'	273
17	2019: 'One hell of a lady'	291
18	2020–21: Recollections	307
19	2021–22: The 'Too Difficult' Folder	331
20	Sunset: 'Very peaceful'	347
21	Legacy: 'Fresh air'	363

Acknowledgements	383
Notes	389
Selected Bibliography	411
Sources	417
Picture Credits	419
Index	423

Preface

This is the fifth book I have written about Elizabeth II over two decades. Ahead of each one, people close to her – and, in some cases, related to her – have said to me: 'Is there anything new to say?' To which, as it has turned out, I have always been able to reply: 'A very great deal.' This book is no exception. It also differs from the others in one fundamental regard. This is my first book on our longest-reigning monarch that is written in the past tense. Elizabeth II was very much alive – and, in many ways, at the height of her powers – when I was writing my previous study, *Queen of Our Times*. Any 'living' biography will, inevitably, be open-ended, with a different mood and tone, in contrast to a retrospective portrait of a full life.

Though many of us may feel that Elizabeth II has only just left the stage – as we still stumble over the national anthem; as we ask 'which one?' when someone makes mention of 'the Queen' – the fact remains that she is now an historic figure. The reign of Charles III has been firmly established, as I have examined in my biography of the King, *Charles III: The Inside Story*. We can begin to view Elizabeth II through a different lens as Britain, and much of the world, grapples with the challenge of 'memorializing' her. A monarch feted with more

Elizabeth II

jubilees than any other is now starting to accumulate posthumous milestones, starting with her centenary.

That is why this book is an entirely new undertaking, written from scratch, and not a compilation. It does not supersede the others, but complements them. While they all sought to answer the eternal question: 'What is she really like?', I am confident that this book takes us nearer than ever to answering a slightly different question: 'What *was* she really like?' Inevitably, some facts, anecdotes and quotations have appeared previously, not least because many earlier interviewees are no longer available or because a good story deserves another airing. However, there is much new material that has only emerged since her death. Many of those who have spoken in the past have also spoken afresh with new perspectives and interpretations. If this book feels more personal, that's probably because it is.

That is all reflected in the fact that this book contains more material on the latter stages of the life and reign of Elizabeth II than on her earlier years. It is quite deliberate. Her youth, her 'Gloriana' era and her very gradual transition to a matriarchal agelessness are a vivid and essential part of this great story. However, it is her later years which are still most keenly debated and to which there are still many eyewitnesses. They are also years I have seen for myself. More than a third of a century has passed since I started writing on this subject – for what was only supposed to be a few days. It was, in fact, the calm before one of the greatest storms in modern royal history. At the end of that same year, I was at London's Guildhall to hear a croaky but insistent voice speak of an 'annus horribilis'. So much for a celebration to mark the past forty years of Queen Elizabeth II. It felt like a turning point for her monarchy, but in which direction? This is the remarkable story of her life prior to that question – and the even more extraordinary story of how she answered it.

Chapter One

A Personal View

'Oh, really?'

The new Lord Chamberlain, Earl Peel, was not having the easiest start to his first Buckingham Palace garden party as the head of the Royal Household. It was his duty to escort the Queen among the 8,000 guests and introduce her to the handful picked out by the team of Gentlemen Ushers. As she approached the first couple, Lord Peel was given the handwritten note with their names at the very moment it started to rain. The ink promptly ran all over the card. The next couple he introduced turned out to be a Royal Canadian Air Force officer with his Polish girlfriend. As they were in mid-chat with the monarch, the woman's mobile telephone suddenly burst noisily into life. Courtiers' toes curled inside gleaming brogues. Smiles froze in rictus grins as everyone pretended to ignore the noise. With commendable sangfroid, the woman calmly slid her hand into her bag without averting her gaze and instantly tossed the phone over the heads of the crowd, continuing the conversation as if nothing had happened. The Queen did not blink either.

'What was that all about?' she asked Lord Peel afterwards. 'I wasn't sure what was going on.' She was highly amused – and

Elizabeth II

rather impressed – when the Lord Chamberlain explained this brief comedy of manners. It was an interesting snapshot of an ordinary day of royal duties. Here was an illustration of the extent to which people would go to avoid doing anything embarrassing in front of Elizabeth II. It also highlights the way she enjoyed it when things did not go entirely according to plan, her capacity to be unshocked by almost anything and her tendency, in any tricky situation, to defer to the most practical solution. She was also pleased to hear that, minutes later, someone in the crowd had reunited the flying phone with its owner.

Of all the character traits attributed to Elizabeth II, common sense is the one that would recur most often. There was, of course, the ingrained, almost hefted, sense of duty; the stoicism, modesty, kindness, shyness, Herculean self-restraint, self-deprecation and periodic parental myopia (especially when it came to the flaws of her second son), all seasoned with occasional flashes of humour, anger, acerbity and exasperation. After thirty years of encountering the late Queen as a journalist, author, commentator and film-maker, however, I would argue that pragmatism was her default setting. 'She more or less invented the word,' says Lord Peel.

As one former private secretary put it: 'I discovered that, given the choice between practicalities and protocols, the choice between an argument for doing something, because that's how we've always done it, or an argument for doing something different, because it would actually work better, then that was always the best way of arguing it.' In this regard, we see an instructive temperamental difference between the Queen (together with Prince Philip) and her parents, along with her eldest son. The Queen, the private secretary added, would 'metaphorically roll her eyes' at some of the more

A Personal View: 'Oh, really?'

pedantic elements within the Lord Chamberlain's Office, the Palace department in charge of ceremonial. 'She was happy to puncture the balloons of the sort of people who were obsessed about things like collar days or being immaculately dressed at a dress rehearsal.'

Seating plans were often a battleground between common sense and precedence. As we shall see in a later chapter, the Queen had to overrule her own officials at a multinational banquet to stop the presidents of the USA and France being placed at the wrong end of the table because they were, in theory, outranked by Euro-royalty.[1] When all the world's monarchs came to Windsor for a lunch to mark the Queen's Diamond Jubilee in 2012, her staff fretted about how to arrange two dozen majesties for the official photograph. She had a simple solution. She would sit in the middle and the others would be seated according to their date of accession. It meant that she was flanked by King Michael of Romania (who first came to his throne in 1927) and King Simeon of the Bulgarians (1943). This raised fresh questions of protocol, since both had long since lost their thrones. It was no problem for the Queen, though. Neither had abdicated of his own volition so, in her view, both were still members of the club. On another occasion, ahead of the state visit of Nelson Mandela in 1996, the Queen learned that the South African president liked to be in bed by 10 p.m. – a legacy of his long years in prison. State banquets run to a strict and well-established format, but in this instance she asked her staff to ignore it and ensure that proceedings were all over by ten o'clock.

At the grandest events, her eye would usually be drawn to the prosaic detail, the bandsman with the curious cap badge or the photographer in the wrong position. Watching private film footage of her own wedding nearly seventy years later for a BBC film to mark her ninetieth birthday, she was particularly struck by shots of the honeymoon departure from Buckingham Palace. 'This is quite funny, look! Oooh,' she exclaimed. It was not the shots of herself and Prince Philip that had caught her eye, however. Instead, she was glued to the edge of the screen, where one of the horses in the procession was clearly spooked by the confetti. 'The Household Cavalry not used to this sort of thing!' she chuckled.[2]

It was a reminder of another character trait of Elizabeth II: she was rigorously unsentimental. This is in marked contrast to King Charles III, who has always been an incurable romantic. During that same film, he could be heard sighing nostalgically as he spotted some old Balmoral crockery or lamenting the passing of HMS *Vanguard* – 'that wonderful battleship, the last one'. The Queen, in contrast, could be bracingly matter-of-fact. 'Look at the size of her!' she gasped, transfixed by the sight of Queen Sālote of Tonga.

The Queen's old friend, Prue Penn, recalled staying at Sandringham not long after the death of Diana, Princess of Wales. Some of the housemaids had reported sensing a mysterious and unhappy spiritual presence in one of the rooms. There were even mutterings about having an exorcism. The Queen decided the simplest solution was to invite the local rector to investigate. 'She got the parson in and he agreed to have a communion service – just Her Majesty, Princess Margaret and me,' Lady Penn recalled. 'He sensed a troubled soul unable to leave and he thought it was Diana.' The Queen had an answer to that. 'I shouldn't think so,' she told the rector briskly. 'Diana didn't like Sandringham much.'[3]

To hear a candid, straight-talking Queen in private could surprise those used to the reticent public figure. Former foreign secretary Douglas Hurd lamented the Queen's 'very cautious' approach to speechmaking and would often find himself

A Personal View: 'Oh, really?'

'wishing she'd let go' in public. She was happy to do so in private. 'She could be very frank with her opinions. They weren't party political, of course, but I was very struck by how forthcoming she could be about people – past and present,' said one former (Labour) minister.[4] A former (Tory) Cabinet minister described her outlook as 'rooted in hard work and not much sympathy for people who don't work hard, but very definitely supportive of people who are unfortunate through no fault of their own'. Hers, he added, were 'not the views of an aristocrat, or a very rich, out-of-touch person'.[5]

In her later years, particularly, there could be occasional flashes of Queen Victoria. When a Cabinet minister found himself talking to her over drinks in Windsor Castle's Grand Reception Room, he pointed to the distant sight of urban sprawl to the north. 'I know this area very well. I spent many years living in Slough,' he remarked. 'Oh, you poor thing,' the Queen replied.[6] On another occasion, when a guest remarked brightly that she must be looking forward to an upcoming Commonwealth summit in Uganda, she replied crisply: 'No one looks forward to going to Uganda.'

It was not rudeness. She would simply prefer to be frank than to prevaricate; she hated even the most innocuous, well-meaning insincerity. The journalist and biographer Charles Moore found himself seated next to the Queen at a dinner and half-apologetically started to explain his next book. 'Oh, don't worry,' she assured him. 'I shan't read it.' Lord Peel well remembered her first words when she appointed him as her Lord Chamberlain: 'Do you really want this job?' she asked with a big smile.[7] She expressed similar sentiments to Boris Johnson when he arrived to be appointed as prime minister in 2019. A senior clergyman awaiting a royal verdict on a carefully prepared sermon was both amused and bemused by her parting remark: 'So many long words, bishop!' Having won the 2015 election by a tiny margin, David Cameron arrived at the Palace to be greeted with a blunt assessment: 'You haven't got a very big majority.' To which he instantly replied (much to the Queen's amusement): 'But it's getting bigger all the time.'[8]

Though she was much more in tune with cultural norms and societal shifts than most of her contemporaries, there was still some terminology that could make the younger generation wince. 'She would talk about someone being "dotty" for all sorts of reasons,' one close aide observed, recalling that it could span everything from mild eccentricity to severe mental impairment. In 2006, I heard her describe an extremist preacher as a 'beardyweirdy'.

Her candour reflected an essential quality of the Queen, namely her authenticity. It also underpinned her sense of humour. She was said to be much amused by the orderly who remarked mournfully on the death of Pope John Paul I in 1978, barely a month after that of Paul VI: 'I see the Pope's dead again, Ma'am.' During his days as Secretary of State for Scotland, Sir Malcolm Rifkind witnessed similar royal amusement on many occasions. He remembered her delight, after asking when restoration work at Stirling Castle would be completed, on being told: 'It won't be in your time, Ma'am.'[9] She was equally entertained, during a media reception at a Commonwealth summit, when the late Fleet Street journalist Chris Buckland confessed that he had defaced a piece of her property. Pressed by her to confess, he explained it had been his passport. Pressed further, he explained that when entering communist Albania, he had carefully tweaked the box citing his occupation (then included in a British passport) from 'writer' to 'waiter'. She would recount that one for years afterwards. It worked the other way, too. A senior courtier was invited for a weekend at Balmoral but had to explain

A Personal View: 'Oh, really?'

that he was already hosting a house party at home. 'Well, I won't be asking you again,' the Queen replied.[10]

It was a dry, regal humour that she had inherited from her parents. Prue Penn, lady-in-waiting to the Queen Mother, fondly recalled the day that they both appeared at an event wearing similar brooches from Cartier. 'Snap!' said Lady Penn, adding: 'Yours is slightly bigger than mine.' To which the Queen Mother replied: 'I should hope so.'[11]

Elizabeth II might always have been conscious of her position; when Tony Blair was airing various plans for the 2002 Golden Jubilee, he was politely reminded: '*My* Golden Jubilee.'[12] Yet she would not take herself too seriously. A close aide fondly remembered how, late in life, she had a fit of giggles trying (and failing) to help a butterfly out of the window of her study at Balmoral. We need only look back to her Olympic appearance with James Bond in 2012 and her Paddington Bear Jubilee encounter in 2022 to realize how few, if any, world leaders would stoop to taking part in a comedy skit, let alone pull it off.

The Queen neither would nor could go as far as the Duke of Edinburgh when it came to barbed remarks, but she could still be amused by such moments. During the installation of one new Knight of the Garter, the senior herald, Garter King of Arms, was being particularly punctilious about where the Duke should stand. Eventually, he cracked. 'Piss off, Garter!' he exclaimed. 'The family were in stitches,' one of them confided afterwards.[13]

She disliked cruel humour, but the Queen was always tickled by stories of innocent mistakes and of things going wrong. A long-running favourite was the tale of Sylvi Kekkonen, wife of the president of Finland. Having muddled her medication on the morning of their state visit to London, the Finnish first lady swallowed sleeping pills instead of heart pills and had to be propped upright by Prince Philip and Princess Anne as she snoozed through the carriage procession to Buckingham Palace. Mishaps at investitures were always eagerly retold. Sometimes it would be a man so overcome with nerves that he followed the person in front and performed a curtsey to the Queen. On one occasion, an eminent figure from the fashion world, having just received her MBE,* was so flustered that, instead of curtseying to the Queen, she turned round and bowed to the audience.

An investiture in 2004 brought out both her pragmatism and another much-quoted quality: her thoughtfulness. Midway through the ceremony, the Lord Chamberlain, Lord Luce, blacked out and collapsed at the very moment he was reading out the citation for the MBE being presented to the weather forecaster, Michael Fish. As the first-aid team rushed to stretcher Luce off to an ambulance, the Queen pressed on regardless, whispering that it couldn't matter less who received which decoration as it could all be sorted out later. When Luce eventually returned to work, the Queen told him that she was happy to bend the rules. By tradition, the monarch and her entourage remain standing throughout investitures. However, she had arranged for him to have a high chair behind a screen so that he would appear to be standing, even if he was sitting down. 'It was thoughtful in the extreme,' he said later.[14] It was an echo of the words of her father's private secretary, Sir Alan 'Tommy' Lascelles, more than fifty years earlier: 'She has got an astonishing solicitude for other people's comfort; such unselfishness is not a normal characteristic of that family.'[15]

Douglas Hurd experienced this when he was feeling

---

* Member of the Order of the British Empire.

A Personal View: 'Oh, really?'

particularly under the weather on board the royal yacht at the end of the Queen's historic state visit to Russia in 1994. 'The Queen sent me to bed using the royal prerogative,' he said. 'I was suffering and she said: "I think your place is in bed, Foreign Secretary." She prescribed the equivalent of Lemsip and I quickly recovered. I thoroughly enjoyed it all.' From a young age, the Queen had absorbed the fact that the greater the enthusiasm for a royal event, the greater the disappointment if you then let people down. When sudden back pain forced her to pull out of opening Arsenal Football Club's new stadium at a few hours' notice in 2006, she did not forget the sadness caused by her no-show. Within days, the squad, management and board had been invited to the Palace for tea with her at a later date.

In 2007, a trailer for a BBC royal documentary cost senior executives their jobs when it turned out clips had been re-edited to show the Queen storming out of a portrait shoot after a row with the American photographer Annie Liebovitz. The monarch had actually been cross with an aide and had been expressing her displeasure on the way in, but it blew up into a story which greatly upset Leibovitz and caused her considerable professional loss of face. Almost ten years later, she was suddenly contacted by the Palace to see if she would like to take another set of photographs, this time for the Queen's ninetieth. A tearful Leibovitz was thrilled to accept. The resulting images were widely acclaimed, especially a tender shot of the Queen and Princess Anne (showing the depth of an often overlooked relationship). It may have been nearly a decade since her previous encounter with the photographer, but the Queen had not forgotten.

The late Chris Martin, private secretary to David Cameron as prime minister, liked to define the essence of the British

Elizabeth II

constitution as the weekly audience between the prime minister and the monarch. He would then distil the essence of Elizabeth II herself down to two core qualities underpinning her role: her sense of duty and a sense of kindness.[16] That, however, did not prevent even the grandest and the bravest from quaking in front of her. As she was about to present the Victoria Cross to Australian warrant officer Keith Payne on board the royal yacht in 1970, the Vietnam war hero was nowhere to be seen. The Queen's equerry, Jock Slater, finally found the fearless jungle warrior on another deck puffing furiously on a cigarette. 'Sir,' he explained, 'I have never been so nervous in all my life.'[17]

Outright fury was rare and only vented in-house. No less dreaded was a silent signal of displeasure towards those who crossed an invisible line, one usually involving overfamiliarity, culpable incompetence or plain rudeness. Staff would call it, with some trepidation, 'the look'. 'If the Queen ever feels affronted about something, she has the perfect answer,' the diarist and biographer Kenneth Rose told this author. 'She just stares at the person with open eyes, absolutely no expression.' Former Foreign Secretary Douglas Hurd witnessed it at the annual Diplomatic Reception, where all the members of the diplomatic corps from more than 150 embassies and high commissions are lined up according to the international diplomatic order of precedence. One ambassador arrived late and missed his slot. 'He was very anxious not to lose the opportunity of bowing to the Queen, and he shoved himself into position out of line and he got the stare,' said Hurd. 'The courtiers escorted him away to the right position. Nothing would be said.'[18]

The courtiers and staff were certainly not immune themselves. 'When I went over the top, her eyebrows would go up and I'd apologize. She hoped you'd sort out the distance you needed to

A Personal View: 'Oh, really?'

keep,' the former captain of *Britannia*, Sir Robert Woodard, once explained.[19] Tony Blair warned that 'she can be matey with you, but don't try to reciprocate, or you get "The Look".'[20]

One prime minister on the receiving end of it was New Zealand's Helen Clark, during the Queen's Golden Jubilee tour of the Pacific in 2002. The centrepiece was Clark's black-tie banquet at the New Zealand Parliament. The Queen duly arrived in a full-length white evening gown of lace and pearl, plus tiara. She was met by her hostess wearing trousers. This was a time when female members of staff at Buckingham Palace were still quietly reminded that skirts and dresses were appropriate office day clothes, while trousers were not. 'The poor Queen turned up as planned in a full ballgown and tiara, and Helen Clark tried to score points,' recalled a member of the entourage. 'It was just rude and rather embarrassing. The Queen did not get angry or say anything. But she understood very well when people were point-scoring. She was quite sanguine about it.'[21]

Innocent blunders, however, rarely bothered her at all. During a Balmoral shooting weekend in her later years, the guns stopped for lunch. One of the younger members of the party, the heir to a famous nearby estate, was so busy tucking into his plate of venison stew that he had not noticed a new arrival take a seat at the table. 'How are you getting on?' asked the Queen brightly. The young earl was so shocked to look up and see the monarch that his garbled attempt at a reply resulted in a small piece of meat landing in her face. 'She didn't flinch,' said one of those present.[22] She was similarly unfussed when a young Guards officer was dragooned into an after-dinner game of charades and handed a favourite family phrase to mime. Pointing to the Queen and pulling an imaginary chain, he was suddenly terrified that he might have committed *lèse-majesté*. He need not have worried. 'Royal Flush!' she replied instantly, delighted to be the first to get the clue. The perennial problem of the rogue mobile phone, mentioned earlier, would always mortify the owner more than it irked the Queen, who had a ready response. 'You'd better answer it, Lord Chancellor,' she told Robert Buckland when he started to emit ringing noises during a Privy Council meeting. 'It might be someone important.' He was neither the first nor last to do that.

In 2011, David Cameron was worried that he and his wife, Samantha, might have inadvertently overstepped the mark at the private Downing Street lunch they gave for the Queen and Duke of Edinburgh to celebrate the Duke's ninetieth birthday. At the end, their ten-month-old daughter, Florence, was introduced to the Queen, who was paying her first visit inside Number Ten in a decade. 'It was a small lunch in the small drawing room on the first floor, just the four of us. We brought Florence in at the end as we thought it would be a sweet moment,' Cameron recalled. 'And she literally grabbed the Queen's pearl brooch and was not going to let go. We really had to prise it off her. The Queen took it well, but there was that slight look in her eyes of "What the hell is this child doing? Why isn't she in the nursery?" There was a time and a place for children, but grabbing her brooch was not that place.'[23]

Her former private secretary, Martin Charteris, would say that while the Queen was a woman of her times and generation, her constancy actually made change easier for others to bear. 'We became a very, very different country,' he said, looking back on her reign after more than four decades. 'I don't think that she ever felt despairing about it. She has done a great deal to keep a balance in the country during all this change. She's never really wavered. She has steel in her spine.'

Her tastes in both food and drink were unexotic, her

consumption careful. Her mother and sister were both famously thirsty; the clergyman diarist Victor Stock was present at a 1988 City luncheon where the Queen Mother had worked her way through two glasses of gin and Dubonnet, followed by champagne, white wine and claret before being offered a closing glass of Chateau d'Yquem. 'Oh no, I really couldn't drink any more,' she told her hosts. 'I'll just have a glass of champagne.' Elizabeth II would have stopped after the first or possibly second gin and Dubonnet. Similarly, Prince Philip seldom advanced from a single bottle of beer (a local one when on his travels). The Queen liked simple food, prepared to the highest standard, though the Duke was more adventurous (his extensive library contained a whole section devoted to cookery books and, in 2010, he took all his staff to Heston Blumenthal's Fat Duck to try the snail porridge and other delicacies). Again, though, both of them exercised a steely self-restraint. It was something which they passed on to all of their children, all of whom eat sparingly while the middle two are also teetotal. A guest invited to tea with the Queen at Balmoral in the early 2000s was impressed by the size of the spread. 'An enormous table was laden with scones and cakes, so my wife and I were expecting at least a dozen people to turn up,' he recalled. 'And then we sat there for about an hour, just us and the Queen.' Yet she would still eat carefully. In 2014, she was seated next to a newly elected lady mayor at a civic lunch in Belfast. According to a fellow guest, the Queen advised her: 'You're only a month in and you are going to have to eat many lunches and dinners like this, so this is what you do.' Whereupon she gave a demonstration of moving food around the plate. 'She showed how you push the food into the corners so it looks like you've eaten a lot,' added the guest. 'She was almost being maternal about it.'[24]

It would often be said by female spouses that, outside her

immediate circle, the Queen was more comfortable in male company. 'She definitely had a different smile for men. The women just had to make much more of an effort,' recalled the female half of a couple regularly invited to stay. 'But once you broke through, she would be sweet, almost conspiratorial. "You're not on those heels again" – that sort of thing. And once you were accepted, she might invite you to come and look at some of her photo albums.'[25]

She was especially reserved when it came to mourning. For the most part, she avoided overt commiseration and non-family funerals, sending a representative instead. Were she to start attending, so the thinking went, she would soon find herself doing little else. However, she always liked to know of bereavements among staff and friends so that formal condolences could be sent. On receiving a note from a private secretary saying that a retired member of the Balmoral staff had died and had no next of kin, the Queen wrote back: 'Oh yes she has. She has a niece; her name is Bunty and I met her when I was last in New Zealand.'[26]

It was often said that she found it easier to discuss emotions through animals. Martin Charteris, her former private secretary, told author Graham Turner that he had written many personal letters to her without reply, but received an anguished missive after the death of a much-loved Labrador killed by rat poison. A former lady-in-waiting received no response to a letter about a seriously ill child, but a six-page outpouring on the subject of a dead corgi.[27] Those who knew her well were neither offended nor surprised. They had no doubt that she cared deeply but preferred to keep her emotions in check. 'She thought a sobbing Queen was no use to anyone,' said one, 'whereas Charles is the opposite. He's always writing letters of condolence. It's the pragmatist versus the romantic.'[28] Animals could be that

A Personal View: 'Oh, really?'

pressure valve for the Queen. During his days as Lord Chamberlain, Lord Peel had a much-loved gundog called Dixie that his wife, Charlotte, had bought as a puppy from the royal kennels at Sandringham. Dixie later had a litter of her own, from which the Peels reared a puppy called Panda. As he recalled: 'When Dixie died, I did say to the Queen: "I'm sorry to say, Ma'am, but we lost Dixie the other day." And she said straight away: "I'm so sorry to hear that. The end of an era. How's Panda taken it?" Can you imagine her remembering that?'[29]

This capacity for remembering small, personal details would often surprise even those who knew her very well. The Labour MP and Privy Councillor Sir Gerald Kaufman recalled a meeting where the clerk was reading out a long list of new high sheriffs for royal approval. Suddenly, at one name, the Queen interjected: 'But he's dead.'[30] As, indeed, he turned out to be.

Though privy to the greatest state secrets and the first copy of the minutes of every Cabinet meeting, she was capable of viewing any issue through the other end of the telescope. Professor Sir Vernon Bogdanor liked to say that she understood what some might call 'the soul of the British people', a quality which Lord Salisbury had attributed more than a century before to Queen Victoria.[31] Even when Elizabeth II was accused of being 'out of touch', as happened when she was attacked for staying at Balmoral after the death of Diana, Princess of Wales, her primary motives were those of a worried grandmother, not an ivory-towered Marie Antoinette. 'You have to remember that she would start each day listening to Terry Wogan, not the *Today* programme,' said one of her most senior aides, recalling her preference for chatty BBC Radio 2 breakfast banter as opposed to the meatier current affairs on Radio 4. 'She always had all the papers on her table, including the red-tops. She liked to start with the *Daily Mail* and end with *The Daily*

Elizabeth II

Telegraph – and do the crossword.'³² 'The fact that all the newspapers were always laid out at Balmoral made you think: "they do really care what's being said about them",' said David Cameron.³³ It is another small contrast with King Charles III, whose mornings invariably involve Radio 4 and a need-to-know press digest rather than a pile of papers.

As the Queen grew older, she increasingly preferred the company of younger people. In the last twenty years of her reign, the age range of invitees at royal receptions was consciously lowered, with an emphasis on youth and a reduction in greeting lines of civic worthies in mayoral regalia (known as 'chain gangs'). But that Downing Street lunch was a reminder for Cameron that the Queen was a product of her generation. 'She very much reminded me of my two grandmothers,' he reflected. 'They were of a similar age and similar values. You just got on with it; no complaining; you remembered nettle soup and feeling lucky if you could eat rabbit in the war. It was about cracking on, being stoical. But there were ways of doing things and there were certain standards. So you didn't think twice about changing clothes six times in a day at Balmoral. It's just what you did.'³⁴

In later life, the Queen was virtually unshockable, though that was not the case as a princess. Having been created a Counsellor of State at the age of eighteen (King George VI had lowered the minimum age from twenty-one on the grounds that, in wartime, she might become monarch at any minute), she had to sign a reprieve for a murderer. It entailed some gruesome details. 'What makes people do such terrible things?' she asked her governess, Marion Crawford. 'I have so much to learn about people!'³⁵ She was similarly innocent when it came to the opposite sex. Before Prince Philip became the love of her life, she was fond of the young Duke of Rutland – until she

A Personal View: 'Oh, really?'

was not. Years later, Martin Charteris summoned up the courage to raise the matter. 'He was certainly very fond of her but evidently made a pass at her, which greatly offended her,' Charteris told Graham Turner. 'I once asked her whether he had done so and there was no answer, which tells its own story.' To a family friend, asking the same question, she had confided: 'There are passes – and passes.'[36]

Over her long years as Queen, however, she soon became familiar with every facet of human life. Being married to a forthright Royal Navy officer certainly helped. She did not wish to be shielded from any cases of inappropriate behaviour among her own staff (although her children could be a different matter). An aide had been nervous of appraising her of disciplinary action against a senior footman who had been molesting a subordinate at Balmoral. 'I was astonished to discover that she was in no way fazed by such an incident and agreed with the action I had taken,' he recalled.[37]

In the days when homosexuality was still illegal in the armed forces and problematic in public service, the Queen's default response when any examples came to her attention was one of sympathy. Staff noticed that she was much more likely to be judgemental when adultery was involved. In the early years of the reign, divorce had been a taboo topic, to the point that she asked Harold Wilson's government to give her formal advice before she was prepared to give her cousin, the Earl of Harewood, permission to remarry. That was in 1967. By the time her sister and three of her children had been through the divorce courts, she had simply accepted it as a fact of modern life. Earl Peel remembered being called by a very nervous senior Establishment figure who was about to seek a divorce and who asked him to alert the Queen before she read about it in the papers. 'I found myself sitting next to her at a lunch very shortly afterwards,' the

Elizabeth II

former Lord Chamberlain recalled. 'So I said: "Ma'am, by the way, did you know that so-and-so is getting divorced?" She just said: "Oh, really?" And carried on. In other words: "Fine."'

Successive generations of courtiers would speak of the Queen's unerring negative judgement; her innate sense of knowing when not to do or say something. It was not in her nature, nor indeed part of her constitutional role, to be wildly enthusiastic about anything. Hers was a temperament well-suited to her times, a period of managed decline. Her father and all his predecessors had been duty-bound to hold and reign over existing territories, if not expand them. In 1947, however, the 'Empire' had ceased to be and, five years later, she came to the throne as the first monarch whose destiny was not to accumulate parts of the planet, but to relinquish, to withdraw and to shrink, helping former imperial possessions morph into independent members of the Commonwealth. Her role was to ensure it happened as amicably as possible. A cautious, non-confrontational monarch would find that process much easier than a bombastic reactionary like, say, George V.

However, some wished that she could be more proactive. As her biographer, Elizabeth Longford, memorably observed, while the Queen had 'not put a foot wrong, she never put a foot forward'.[38] Over time, her staff would learn to interpret the sliding scale of responses. 'Oh, really?' was a qualified indifference which, while not conferring approval, did not denote disapproval. In other words, it was, as Lord Peel noted, 'fine'. Next came the raising of an eyebrow – a mark of caution. A 'double eyebrow' would make it clear that she had found fault. Next came 'Are you sure?', which was tantamount to 'No'. Martin Sullivan, a dean of St Paul's, told Kenneth Rose that he had once asked the Queen if she would ever contradict one of her ministers and express open disagreement. 'I never put it as strongly as that,' she had replied. 'What I say is that I should like further information about it and that is an indication to the minister I am talking to that I don't agree.'[39]

She was sparing with plaudits, including for her own children, but also with criticism. 'She was so regulated that very rarely did anything rile her,' said one close aide. 'She had a few facial expressions. You could tell if something wasn't going well as there'd be a slight down in the mouth. But she did not heap praise and nor did she admonish. She'd say: "I think that was alright" or "I think we got through that". You can't heap praise all the time when you have so many people trying to ingratiate themselves.'[40]

Whenever her office was recruiting senior staff, a prerequisite for headhunters was 'low ego': a capacity to perform without constant praise or validation. 'It was essential because she was a low ego person, too,' said a former private secretary. 'She would avoid a tricky situation by saying something like "no one tells me anything". When you are monarch, that's canny but it also requires a great deal of confidence – and a low ego.'[41]

It was a great royal paradox that an inherently shy and non-competitive person should end up as the most famous woman in the world. There was precious little of either the diva or the recluse. 'It always used to fascinate me watching her take a normal train, as she liked to in later years,' said one senior staffer. 'She'd walk across a concourse and people would be pointing and taking pictures. She just wouldn't react in the way a celebrity would.' The essential difference between the public and the private Elizabeth II was her vivacity. On duty and in almost all dramatic depictions, including the Netflix series *The Crown*, she was so often seen as aloof, contained, put-upon, well-meaning but chilly, even when smiling. In private, she was so much warmer, engaged, intriguing, relatable.

Elizabeth II

The diarist Kenneth Rose liked to call her 'exhilarating'.[42] Surroundings had much to do with it, as I learned from my own experience, whether as a journalist or as an occasional guest at state occasions and receptions or behind the scenes with a tiny film crew. I always found her at her most animated and easy-going in those off-camera moments in her happiest places – with her horses in the Royal Mews at Windsor or in her study overlooking the sunken garden at Balmoral. The smile would be slightly different, the conversation lighter.

She was undeniably brave. As will be noted later, she was fearless in the face of almost anything except helicopters (for which she had a deep mistrust all her life, despite seeing two sons and two grandsons qualify as helicopter pilots). Her reign was peppered with occasions when politicians and the military were urging her not to visit places due to a plausible risk of assassination. In 1961, many MPs warned her not to go to Ghana after a spate of bombings.[43] In 1964, her British ministers were suggesting that she should cancel a tour of Quebec, where violent protests against the Crown were expected.[44] In 1979, there were credible intelligence reports of a plan to shoot her plane out of the sky as she flew in for the Commonwealth summit in the Zambian capital, Lusaka.[45] In 1993, two years after an IRA mortar attack on Downing Street, she received intelligence reports of a plot to launch a similar attack on Buckingham Palace.[46] The security advice was to move out. On every one of those occasions, she was unmoved.

During the 1980s and '90s, bomb scares were an occupational hazard. In 1981, a bomb exploded at the Sullom Voe oil terminal in Scotland while the Queen was opening it (the device had been planted in a different building). One month later, a gunman opened fire as she was riding down the Mall (she wasn't to know he was firing blanks and, as will be revealed

A Personal View: 'Oh, really?'

later, actually thought that the Duke of Edinburgh had just been assassinated). The Queen was well aware of the risks but more concerned about the outcome. As she told the writer Sir Antony Jay at a luncheon: 'I'm not afraid of being killed. I just don't want to be maimed.'[47]

She never dwelt on her close shaves or even mentioned them. Many people still have to be reminded of events like that 1981 incident in the Mall. 'I didn't know about that,' said Donald Trump, a fellow member of that fortunate but unenviable club of world figures who have survived being fired upon in public.* It is yet another reason why Mr Trump admired the Queen so much. 'She was unbelievable,' the US president told me. 'She was in her nineties and she'd call me a lot and I'd call her a lot. She liked me, I liked her and we talked.'[48] She would, no doubt, have been quick to console Mr Trump (as King Charles did) after the attempt on his life by an assassin in Pennsylvania in 2024. Throughout the Queen's life, she would come to know several heads of state who did not survive these moments, including John F. Kennedy and Indira Gandhi. Her attitude was that one could only follow one's instincts, hope for the best and trust in the Almighty.

The epicentral importance of her faith cannot be overstated. Clergy aside, she was the only major national figure who was entirely comfortable discussing God in public, as she would do each Christmas Day at 3 p.m. Her faith was, in the words of Nigel McCulloch, former bishop and Lord High Almoner, 'very straightforward, consistent and sincere'. She was a devoted 'low church' Anglican of a generation who liked a service of

---

* The Queen, Ronald Reagan and the Pope all came under fire in 1981 (she from blanks, while they were both hit by bullets); Prince Charles was attacked in 1994 (also with blanks) and Donald Trump was hit in the ear by a sniper in 2024.

matins every Sunday and Holy Communion on special occasions, usually in private. She loved the annual Royal Maundy service which she took more seriously than any monarch since the Reformation, holding it in different cathedrals all over her kingdom for the first time in its 800-year history. She took an uncomplicated view of her role as Supreme Governor of the Church of England. It was the same with her role as head of the armed forces and as head of the Commonwealth. None of these could ever be taken for granted. As David Cameron observed: 'She was very conscious that consent for the royal family is permanently being earned.'[49]

It is why the charge sheet of errors at the end of her record-breaking reign would be a short one and consist mainly of sins of omission, of things which might have been said or done but were not. The lack of a royal representative at the service for victims of the 1988 Lockerbie plane bombing or at matches during England's progress through the 1996 European football championships (on home turf) are examples. They might have been blunders, but they hardly amounted to a constitutional crisis.

Some, like the historian David Starkey, repeatedly accused Elizabeth II of being unbending, uneducated, incurious and dull. She had no intellectual or bookish leanings, unlike her successor. Culturally, she was content to be remembered as a curator rather than a connoisseur. When asked which ballet she might like to see on a foreign tour, the reply would usually be 'a short one'. Others argued that these were precisely the qualities one should welcome in a hereditary monarch. 'Everybody likes to be interesting,' said the former Foreign Secretary, Lord Owen. 'You have to be disciplined to be boring or to run the risk of being boring.' Even her staunchest defenders would accept that her weak spot was her dislike of confrontation,

A Personal View: 'Oh, really?'

especially on family matters. 'She just wasn't good at family meetings. Those were a struggle,' conceded a senior aide of her later years. In particular, her indulgence of Prince Andrew* and failure to heed warnings about his judgement, his expenditure and his arrogance would ultimately prove to be damaging for the institution and catastrophic for the prince himself.

However, her place at or near the top of any ranking of English and British monarchs is assured, and not just because of her longevity. No one (with the possible exception of Charles I) reigned through more change, be it social, technological or geopolitical. It helped greatly that, even in dark times, and all through the worst of the crises and scandals which she had to navigate in the fifties, the nineties and the last three years of her life, she still loved being Queen. That her monarchy and her authority were as solid at the end as they had been at the beginning, seventy years before, is why she will always be ranked among the greats. Luck and genetics may have played their part, but it was chiefly down to character. It was because of 'what she was really like' that she reigned the way she did.

---

* Prince Andrew, later the Duke of York, was stripped of both titles and became Andrew Mountbatten-Windsor in 2025, as will be recorded later in this book.

Chapter Two

1926–39

Number Three

The new arrival was never meant to rise above number three. She was born on 21 April 1926, not in a castle or a palace but in a house with a number on the door: 17 Bruton Street, London. The baby's father, the Duke of York, known in the family as Bertie, was the second son of King George V, making the baby a princess and third in line to the throne behind her father and his elder brother, the Prince of Wales. Every expectation was that the child would slowly make her way down the line of succession, as was the natural order of things.

It was generally assumed that the Prince of Wales, then the most glamorous man on the planet (with a playboy lifestyle to match), would do his duty in due course, marry and produce an heir. Even if he did not, it seemed likely that the Duke and Duchess of York would produce several more children. Bertie was one of six. The baby's mother, the Duchess of York, formerly Lady Elizabeth Bowes-Lyon, was the tenth of the eleven children of the Earl of Strathmore (in whose London home the child had been born). It was possible, if not probable, that a York boy would appear in due course and nudge the baby girl down to number four. That was the prevailing view in April

Elizabeth II

1926. Even so, those with their ear to the Court sensed that something historic had just happened. 'I have a feeling the child will be Queen of England,' wrote diarist, socialite and aristocratic anthropologist Henry 'Chips' Channon.[1]

A month later, the baby was christened Elizabeth Alexandra Mary at Buckingham Palace, taking the names of her mother, great-grandmother and grandmother. In those days, all such matters still had to be cleared with the King. 'We are so anxious for her first name to be Elizabeth as it is such a nice name & there has been no one of that name in your family for a long time. Elizabeth of York sounds so nice too,' Bertie wrote to his father.[2] Including 'Mary' in the mix had been a shrewd move. The King and Queen Mary approved. By now, George V was a much happier man. When Elizabeth had been born, Britain was days away from a general strike which would have crippled the country and, some feared, might lead to violent disorder. Bolshevik revolution, recently triumphant in Russia, was the middle- and upper-class phobia of the day. Having followed every gory detail of the imprisonment and slaughter of his cousin, Tsar Nicholas II, eight years earlier, George V was anything but complacent. In the event, the strike had petered out and life returned to normal.

The King had been an ogre of a father to his own children, adopting a similar disciplinary philosophy to the one he had learned in the Royal Navy. However, he came to dote on his new granddaughter. When the Duke and Duchess of York were sent away on a long royal tour of Australia and New Zealand just months after Elizabeth's birth, the baby came to live with the King and Queen. Even imperious Queen Mary would melt each day upon being presented with the grandchild she called 'the bambino'. In December 1928, the King nearly died of an abscess on the lung. During his convalescence in Bognor, Elizabeth was despatched to help boost his spirits, which, by all accounts, she did. Like the rest of the family, he came to know her as 'Lilibet' – a variation on her own name for herself: 'Tillabet'. In 1930, a younger sister arrived. Because it was August, Princess Margaret Rose was born at the Strathmores' Scottish seat, Glamis Castle. It was the first time in 300 years that a child in the direct line of succession had been born in Scotland.

It was now starting to look as though Chips Channon might have been on to something, after all. There had been a four-year gap between the births of Lilibet and Margaret. The Yorks, now both in their thirties, were clearly not going to be emulating their parents in terms of filling the nursery. More worryingly, the private life of the Prince of Wales, whom the Princesses knew as Uncle David, was now a serious cause for concern. At the onset of the King's grave illness in 1928, he had been on tour in Africa and was told to head home. 'I don't believe a word of it,' the Prince told his assistant private secretary, Alan 'Tommy' Lascelles, who wrote that the heir to the throne then 'went out without a word and spent the remainder of the evening in the successful seduction of a Mrs Barnes, wife of the local commissioner. He told me so himself, next morning.'[3] When Lascelles subsequently resigned, his boss had the honesty to admit: 'I'm quite the wrong person to be Prince of Wales.'[4]

Life for the two Princesses centred on the nursery at 145 Piccadilly, a grand – though not palatial – south-facing property overlooking Green Park and Buckingham Palace beyond. The Yorks had leased the eighteenth-century house in 1927, though it had required substantial work to make it a family home.* Running the nursery was the Duchess's former nanny, Clara

---

* Damaged by a bomb in 1940, it was demolished in 1959. Part of the site is now road, while the rest is occupied by the InterContinental Hotel.

Knight, known as 'Alah' (Lilibet's attempt at 'Clara'). Following the arrival of Margaret, they were joined by a new Scottish nursery maid, Margaret MacDonald, whom the Princesses called 'Bobo'. She would become a formidable royal fixture for the best part of a century. Though the set-up was much like that in any other aristocratic family, the Yorks were not as aloof as many. Some parents might only see their children for formal presentations between bath and bedtime, whereas the Yorks liked to start the day with the children running into their bedroom for 'high jinks'.[5]

The King gave them the use of Royal Lodge in Windsor Great Park, to which the family would decamp at weekends. It had once been a Georgian folly (and would become very much associated with the folly of another Duke of York in years to come). The children loved it there, especially when they received a spectacular gift to mark Princess Elizabeth's sixth birthday. The people of Wales had commissioned a child-size Welsh thatched cottage, with running water, electricity and loving attention to detail. It was installed in the Royal Lodge garden, where it still stands, and the girls adored it.

Despite such adulation, the family – and, above all, Queen Mary – appreciated the need for rules and some sort of engagement with the real world. This was still a time when royal children, especially girls, did not go to school, but were taught by a governess. In 1933, a fresh face arrived in the nursery. Marion Crawford, a twenty-three-year-old newly graduated teacher from Scotland, came for a one-month trial and stayed for the next seventeen years. Swiftly renamed 'Crawfie', she introduced a timetable and a curriculum. The King had given her a more rudimentary instruction: 'For goodness' sake, teach Margaret and Lilibet to write a decent hand, that's all I ask you. Not one of my children can write properly.'[6] Thanks to the

1926–39: Number Three

indiscretions of Crawfie in later life, when she wrote a best-selling but career-ending memoir of her time in royal service, we have an engaging portrait of these years; of precocious Margaret with her imaginary friend, 'Cousin Halifax', and her made-up words (any sort of mushed-up food was a 'hoosh-mi'); orderly Lilibet, lining up her toy ponies in neat lines and tidying up with a dustpan and brush. In fights, Lilibet was a hitter, Margaret more of a biter. Margaret was also much more interested in clothes and shoes, whereas her elder sister simply couldn't care less. A biddable, reserved girl, Lilibet's only known act of rebellion was upending an inkpot over her own head in revolt against a French teacher, who swiftly moved on. As well as Crawfie, there was another arrival in the Princesses' lives in 1933, one which made an even longer-lasting impact than their Scottish governess: their first Pembroke Welsh corgi, Dookie. Another, Jane, would come soon afterwards, cementing a lifelong love of the breed.

There was much excitement when the girls were invited to be bridesmaids at the 1934 wedding of their father's younger brother, the Duke of Kent, to Princess Marina of Greece. The occasion was notable for several reasons. It was the first time that Lilibet was at the same royal event as the bride's first cousin, Prince Philip of Greece. It was also the first time that the King and Queen were in the same room as Uncle David's new girlfriend, Wallis Simpson. The King was appalled. With one divorce behind her already, the American socialite was now cheating on her second husband, Ernest Simpson, with the Prince of Wales. It was becoming an open secret in society circles, and the King was later heard to rage: 'That woman in my own house!'[7]

In private, George V was starting to accept that the future lay not with the Prince of Wales, but with his granddaughter. 'I pray to God that my eldest son will never marry and that

Elizabeth II

nothing will come between Bertie and Lilibet and the throne,' he said at the end of 1935.⁸

It had been an emotional year for the ailing King Emperor after twenty-five years as monarch. Celebrating his Silver Jubilee, the first jubilee since Victoria's sixtieth anniversary in 1897, he had discovered just how fond the public had become of him. In some ways, he was a caricature of a curmudgeonly squire, despising high art, 'abroad', cocktails and jazz music, while devoting his days to shooting and stamp-collecting. Yet, unlike so many of his continental counterparts, he had appointed good advisers and listened to public opinion. He had steered his monarchy through the First World War and Britain's first Labour government. Dictatorships were on the rise across much of Europe, yet Britain remained democratic, imperial, grumpy, stable and reasonably prosperous.

During his reign, five emperors and eight kings had lost their thrones.* George V had come through. But the death of his sister, Princess Victoria, at the end his jubilee year had hit him hard, and the selfishness of his heir troubled him deeply. 'After I am dead, the boy will ruin himself in twelve months,' he told the prime minister, Stanley Baldwin.⁹

That clock would start ticking on 20 January 1936, when the King breathed his last just before midnight, sent on his way by a regicidal overdose of morphine. He had been fading slowly, but his doctor, Lord Dawson of Penn, had wanted him dead in time for the last edition of *The Times*.¹⁰ Were he to soldier on into the early hours, the demise of the Sovereign would be announced by the downmarket evening papers the following

---

* Emperors of Russia, Germany, Austria-Hungary, the Ottoman Empire and China, plus kings of Portugal, Spain, Bavaria, Saxony, Württemberg, Montenegro, Greece (later restored) and Bulgaria (replaced by his son).

1926–39: Number Three

day, which would never do. Lilibet went to see her grandfather lying in state and was transfixed by the sight of Uncle David during what was called 'the Vigil of the Princes'. 'He never moved at all,' she told Crawfie. 'Not even an eyelid. It was wonderful. And everyone was so quiet. As if the King were asleep.'[11]

Lilibet had now moved up to number two in the line of succession, and yet the Princesses were largely insulated from the dramas of that year, as were most of the British public. 'All we at 145 Piccadilly knew in the schoolroom was that of a sudden we saw much less of handsome golden-headed Uncle David,' Crawfie noted.[12]

Throughout that year, the new King spent increasing amounts of time with Mrs Simpson as their relationship gathered pace. She began appearing in the Court Circular, and the pair embarked on a Mediterranean cruise together. Considerable umbrage was taken in Scotland when the King pulled out of opening a new hospital in Aberdeen, claiming to be in mourning, only to be photographed driving to the city to collect Wallis from the station. The Yorks saved the day by cutting the ribbon instead.

When Wallis began divorce proceedings from her husband in the autumn, it was clear where things were heading, and, on 16 November, the King informed the prime minister of his intention to marry her. Stanley Baldwin, along with church leaders and most of the governments of the King's other realms, told him that the people would not tolerate a monarch married to a double divorcee. A story which had been widely covered abroad for weeks finally arrived on British front pages in December, and the entire country could have a view on the matter. Forced to decide between his throne and his heart, Edward chose the latter, and on 10 December, he signed the Instrument of Abdication. A day later, his last act as monarch was to approve it, after which he went into voluntary exile, downgraded from 'His Majesty' to

Elizabeth II

'His Royal Highness the Duke of Windsor'. Instantly elevated to the throne, Bertie found the whole experience traumatic. 'I broke down & sobbed like a child,' he wrote in his abdication memorandum.[13] It would leave a lifelong impression on Lilibet, too. 'The girls were not supposed to see the papers, but she never forgot finding a front page of the *Evening Standard*,' a senior aide of her later years recalled. 'That was how she learned she was heir presumptive. That was a shock.'[14]

Though he had been known as Bertie all his life, the new King would reign as George VI. After the shock of the abdication, it was important to shunt all trappings of Edward VIII to one side as swiftly as possible and re-establish a sense of continuity from George V. For the same reason, there would be no change to the date fixed for the Coronation. They would just need to change the cyphers from 'E' to 'G'.

'I'm afraid there are going to be great changes in our lives, Crawfie,' the new Queen Elizabeth told the governess, who, in turn, had to explain to the children that they would shortly be moving house. The girls were less than thrilled. 'But I have only just learned to write "York",' Margaret replied crossly. They would also have to learn to curtsey to their parents. 'Try not to topple over,' Crawfie told the girls as they prepared to welcome Papa home.[15] It was the one sight that cheered him up on that momentous day.

The Princesses did not enjoy the move from 145 Piccadilly to Buckingham Palace any more than their parents. 'People here need bicycles,' Lilibet told Crawfie, who likened palace life to 'camping in a museum'.[16] The governess organized a Buckingham Palace company of Girl Guides, drawn from suitable families nearby, to introduce Lilibet to a wider circle of friends. A Brownies pack was created for Margaret.

Chips Channon's bold prediction a decade earlier now

looked a certainty. She might be styled 'Heir Presumptive' rather than 'Heir Apparent' – the law still leaving room for that elusive male heir – and denied the rights and revenues of the Duchy of Cornwall that she would have enjoyed had she been a boy; yet, at number one in the line of succession, it now had to be assumed that she would one day be Queen.

Crawfie's schoolroom sessions would be more important than ever for a future monarch, and there would need to be extra tuition in constitutional history in due course. Queen Elizabeth organized lessons for Lilibet with Henry Marten, Vice Provost of Eton, while the girls' grandmother, Queen Mary, arranged edifying excursions to appropriate landmarks. The dowager queen had been horrified by the behaviour of her eldest son and was thrilled that Bertie and his young family were now in charge. 'What a joy it has been to me to feel that the beloved old Home is in such good hands,' she wrote to Bertie and Elizabeth shortly before the Coronation.[17]

The Princesses sat with their grandmother throughout the ceremony at Westminster Abbey, eleven-year-old Lilibet later writing an enchanting account of it for her parents. 'The arches and beams at the top were covered with a sort of haze of wonder as Papa was crowned, at least I thought so,' she observed.[18] The Princesses had still not quite grasped the sequence of events, however. 'Why isn't Uncle David here?' Princess Margaret whispered during the service. 'He abdicated,' Lilibet replied. 'Why?' asked Margaret. Lilibet whispered back: 'He wanted to marry Mrs Baldwin.'[19] Hence the need for those lessons with Henry Marten.

With the new King crowned, Stanley Baldwin (still firmly attached to Mrs Baldwin) retired and the King appointed the obvious candidate, longstanding Chancellor of the Exchequer Neville Chamberlain, as the new prime minster. The Coronation,

Elizabeth II

like the postage stamps and coins, had established the new reign at home, but the King would have to make his mark internationally, especially with his elder brother on manoeuvres overseas. Three weeks after Bertie's crowning, the Duke of Windsor married Wallis in France, with none of the Royal Family present (both the King and the prime minister had made it clear that family should not attend). What angered Uncle David even more than the boycott by his relations was the King's decision to issue letters patent specifically denying Wallis the style of HRH. Four months later, the Windsors were touring Nazi Germany, meeting Adolf Hitler and performing Nazi salutes. As the prospect of another great conflict in Europe grew closer, the King and Queen would need to bolster old alliances. In July 1938, they left Britain for their first state visit, to France. Two months later, talk of war briefly receded as Neville Chamberlain returned from Munich having signed a non-aggression pact with Hitler. To the eternal regret of the Royal Family, the King invited him onto the Buckingham Palace balcony to receive the cheers of the gathering crowds (a brazenly political royal decision, given that Winston Churchill was already condemning the deal as 'an awful milestone in our history'). It soon proved to be a false dawn. A year later, the King became the first reigning monarch to visit his largest realm, Canada, and paid the first state visit in history to the USA (it was also the first recorded royal encounter with fast food: 'HOT DOGS too!' the Queen wrote excitedly to her daughters).[20]

The Princesses had remained at home, but did set sail with their parents later in the summer of 1939 for a coastal cruise in the royal yacht, *Victoria and Albert*. Along the way, they visited Dartmouth, where the King took his family to see his alma mater, Britannia Royal Naval College. While the grown-ups went in one direction, the Princesses were entrusted to the care of eighteen-year-old Cadet Captain Prince Philip of Greece, who had been given the task of entertaining them. Very distantly related (he was also a great-great-grandchild of Queen Victoria), he now looked very different from the schoolboy cousin of the bride at that Kent wedding five years earlier. This time, Crawfie noted, he made a proper impression, especially with thirteen-year-old Lilibet. The Prince was later invited back to the royal yacht, where he embraced the opportunity to wolf down large quantities of decent food, including a banana split. As Crawfie recorded: 'Lilibet sat, pink-faced, enjoying it all very much.'[21] She would always remember that introduction to Philip at Dartmouth. Many years later, the King's official biographer would write (with her approval) that Princess Elizabeth had been 'in love from their first meeting.'[22] It would be a few years before the Prince felt the same.

Just six weeks later, Britain was at war following Germany's invasion of Poland, with which the United Kingdom and France had signed defence pacts. On 3 September 1939, the King and Queen were at Buckingham Palace listening to the wireless as the prime minister grimly announced that Britain was at war. It was followed almost immediately by the first air-raid warning – a false alarm, as it turned out (it would be another year before bombs started falling on London). However, a decision was taken that the Princesses should remain at Balmoral, where they were still on holiday. They moved from the main castle to Birkhall, the less conspicuous home which the family had rented from George V in their days as the Yorks. It was deemed less of a target, and Crawfie soon ensured a return to regular lessons in the makeshift schoolroom. The Princesses were not shielded from the news, though Lilibet was characteristically protective of her little sister. 'I don't think people should talk about battles and things in front of Margaret,' she told Crawfie. 'We don't want to upset her.'[23]

Elizabeth II

After a relatively quiet start to the war, Britain was suddenly shaken five weeks in by the loss of the battleship *Royal Oak*. A German U-boat had sneaked past the anti-submarine defences at Scapa Flow in the Orkney Islands to sink this grand old warhorse of the previous war, at a cost of 835 lives, a third of them teenagers. Lilibet was distraught on hearing the news. The King was equally upset. Not only had he served as a midshipman in the First World War, but he had met the crew of the *Royal Oak* during a trip to Scapa Flow just the week before. 'It reminded me so much of my time in the Gr. Fleet in the last war,' he had confided to his war diary.[24] Never published but lodged in the Royal Archives, it provides an illuminating insight into the mind of a reluctant monarch thrown into the gravest existential crisis in British history. Its punctilious, modest and unvarnished entries – never boastful but never defeatist – give us a good idea of the thought processes of Elizabeth II by the time she embarked on the task of being monarch. Through these darkest years, she would be observing and learning. Throughout her life, her family, friends and staff would be struck by her consideration for what her father would have done in any given situation. 'Anything in the way of a dictum her father had left her was very important,' observed Sir William Heseltine, who had served as her press and then private secretary over three decades long after the reign of George VI.[25] Even later, as Lilibet was marking her ninetieth birthday, her cousin Margaret Rhodes reflected that her entire reign had been a homage to King George VI: 'She did it with such dedication because she wanted to make her father proud of her.'[26] To a greater extent than with any other pair of monarchs in the course of British history, to understand George VI is to understand Elizabeth II.

Chapter Three

1939–47

'People will say we're in love'

For the first four months of the war, Princess Elizabeth did not see her father at all. Those who wondered why and how, in later life, she could go for long periods without seeing her own children, need only look at her childhood for illumination. During the war, many children would not see their fathers for years, if indeed ever again. The Princesses were overjoyed when they were reunited with their parents at Sandringham in December. Even so, the loss of the *Royal Oak* was still weighing heavily on Lilibet's mind. 'Perhaps we were too happy,' she wrote to her governess who was spending Christmas with her own family. 'I kept thinking of those sailors, Crawfie, and what Christmas must have been like in their homes.'[1]

The King and Queen were so pleased to have the children with them that they decided not to send them back to Scotland. Though there had been no enemy attacks on London, it was still deemed off-limits, so the girls were relocated to Royal Lodge, their pre-war weekend retreat on the Windsor estate. Crawfie set up the schoolroom once again, along with a new company of Girl Guides. Lilibet celebrated her fourteenth birthday with a screening of Walt Disney's *Pinocchio*.

Elizabeth II

Then, suddenly, in May 1940, everything changed as Hitler's forces charged through the Low Countries, bound for France, while Britain's attempt to defend Norway ended in failure and withdrawal. As the erstwhile architect of appeasement, Chamberlain's position was untenable. With the 'Phoney War' now at an end, the King sent for Winston Churchill. Royal Lodge was now deemed too dangerous for his daughters. There was not only the risk of bombing, but of kidnap by enemy paratroopers, a fate which nearly befell the Dutch royal family. 'I was woken by the police sergeant at 5.00 a.m. who told me Queen Wilhelmina of the Netherlands wished to speak,' the King wrote in his diary on 13 May. 'It is not often one is rung up at that hour, and especially by a Queen. But in these days anything may happen.'[2] The King told Crawfie to move the Princesses inside Windsor Castle. They would remain there for most of the next five years. 'The feeble barbed wire wouldn't have kept anybody out, but it kept us in,' Princess Margaret told the BBC's *Desert Island Discs* in 1981.[3] A special royalty protection unit, known as the Coats Mission, was formed by Major 'Jimmy' Coats of the Coldstream Guards, along with secret plans to move the family between a series of 'safe' houses in the event of invasion.*

By now, many wealthy families were evacuating their children not just from big cities but from Britain altogether. It has become received wisdom that the Royal Family refused to countenance such defeatist behaviour. 'The children could not go without me,' Queen Elizabeth famously said (though to whom is unrecorded), 'I could not possibly leave the King, and the King would never go.'[4] In fact, the King's war diary reveals that he did explore

---

* Madresfield Court in Worcestershire, Pitchford Hall in Shropshire and Newby Hall in North Yorkshire.

1939–47: 'People will say we're in love'

evacuation options for his daughters and twice raised the matter with Winston Churchill. On both occasions, it was the prime minister who was against the idea, not the King and Queen. By July, it was confirmed to the press that 'the Princesses will stay in Britain'. From then on, any mention of them would merely refer to them living 'in the country'. Churchill was equally adamant that another national asset should not be despatched overseas out of harm's way. There had been a plan to send the Crown Jewels to Canada, but it was vetoed by the prime minister. These national treasures were placed in an old siege tunnel beneath Windsor Castle. It made for a very exciting little adventure when the Royal Librarian took the Princesses down for a look.[5]

By late summer, the bombs started raining down on London, just twenty-five miles to the east. In the space of just one week, two incidents revealed how dangerous the situation had become – and how close Lilibet came to becoming Queen. On 9 September, a bomb landed outside the King's study and failed to explode. With so much unexploded ordnance scattered over London, he had continued to work there, unaware that it was equipped with a time-delayed fuse. He had gone home to Windsor when the thing went off late at night, destroying much of that wing of the palace. Three days later, he was with the Queen in a small sitting room overlooking the Quadrangle when they saw two bombs come down in front of them. 'We looked at each other and then we were out into the passage as fast as we could get there. The whole thing happened in a matter of seconds. We all wondered why we weren't dead.'[6] The royal couple put on a brave face in public, but, privately, they were in deep shock. The King thought twice before confessing as much in his diary: 'I should not put it down in writing but I did feel the reaction after the bombing last Friday (13th) & I quite disliked sitting in my room in BP. I found myself unable to read, always in a hurry & glancing out of the window.'⁷ His real fear, however, was not being killed but becoming 'dugout-minded'. In short, he could not bear the thought of letting the side down.

The next month, the first bombs were landing on Windsor. Crawfie had harsh words with Lilibet and Alah after they had failed to appear in the designated castle dungeon when the sirens sounded. 'We're dressing, Crawfie. We must dress,' the Princess explained when the frantic governess found them in the nursery in Lancaster Tower. Alah was still putting on her regulation nursery uniform. It would not be allowed to happen again. The two Princesses soon grew used to bunking down for the night in the dungeons, which were eventually equipped with beds and basic plumbing.⁸ At the height of the Blitz, it was agreed that Lilibet would make her first broadcast. Her message to child evacuees as part of the BBC's *Children's Hour* radio programme was a very public foretaste of the role that lay ahead. 'We know, every one of us, that in the end all will be well,' she declared on 13 October, 1940. It would be best remembered for its sign-off: 'Come on, Margaret,' she said at the end. 'Goodnight, children. Goodnight, and good luck to you all.'⁹ Such was the impact of the speech that it was later released as a record in the USA. Even if the phrase would not be identified for another fifty years, here was an early indicator of the way in which Lilibet could wield 'soft power' – influencing through persuasion, not coercion – on behalf of her country.*

For the Princesses, life at Windsor would consist of long periods of boredom interspersed with the momentary alarm of an air raid. The family could still be slow to respond, despite

---

* The term 'soft power' entered common usage after it was defined by Professor Joseph Nye in his 1990 book, *Bound to Lead*.

1939–47: 'People will say we're in love'

that early scare. The Queen's cousin, Margaret Rhodes, liked to recall a Windsor lunch with the family during which the King was telling a lengthy anecdote while his page was politely coughing. Finally the coughing reached the point where the King paused, a little irritated. 'What is it?' he asked. 'Air raid, Your Majesty,' came the reply.[10] One high point would be the occasional party for whichever group of young officers were garrisoned at the local barracks prior to being despatched elsewhere. A close contemporary and wartime friend of the Princesses, Alathea Fitzalan Howard, spent the war at an uncle's house on the Windsor estate. 'Lilibet finds making conversation very difficult like me; but she did very well,'[11] Fitzalan Howard noted in her diary after one reception for young Guards and Royal Air Force officers. A favourite Lilibet tactic was to bring in the royal dogs as a conversation starter.

By July 1941, she was attending her first party, a 'small dance' organized by the King and Queen. Among the guests was a handsome young Guards officer, Viscount Euston, heir to the Duke of Grafton. He was among those discreetly spoken of as potential suitor material for Lilibet and regularly invited to the castle by the King and Queen. 'They're so pointedly nice to him that one wonders if there's anything behind it,' wrote a beady-eyed Fitzalan Howard, who also noticed that Lilibet was 'rather hurt' when Euston only asked her for one dance at the party. As noted earlier, a young Duke of Rutland was another eligible name in the frame.

Soon afterwards, however, another visitor started to recur more frequently in everyone's diaries. 'Philip of Greece came to stay. He is doing his courses at Portsmouth & is an acting Sub Lt.,' the King recorded without fanfare in October 1941.[12] By now, some were already referring to Philip as Lilibet's 'beau', though the Princess was not giving much away. 'She is the most ungossipy person I know. If only she could be drawn out of her shell,' observed Fitzalan Howard, unwittingly spotting character traits which would bode well for the monarchy. Lilibet 'never needs companionship of others,' she wrote, adding: 'Margaret is far and away more the type I would like for the future queen. She has that frivolity and irresponsibility that L lacks.'[13]

Philip was back at the castle again shortly before Christmas to watch the annual play. This year it was a pantomime, *Cinderella*, produced by the headmaster of the local school, with Margaret in the title role and Lilibet as Prince Charming. At fifteen, the heir to the throne was in an adolescent limbo. Queen Elizabeth was still dressing both Princesses in matching outfits, and their idea of a fun evening's entertainment in February 1942 was a screening of *Dumbo*.

That same month, however, following the death of the elderly Duke of Connaught (the third son of Queen Victoria), Lilibet received her first military appointment. The King decided that she should succeed 'Uncle Arthur' as Colonel of the Grenadier Guards. By now, she was also writing letters of condolence to the families of all those officers who, having been stationed at the castle, had been killed in action. On 21 April, on her sixteenth birthday, she was in uniform and undertaking her first official engagement at a parade of the Grenadiers. For the first time, she had her own full entry in the Court Circular, the formal log of royal engagements. A year later, she was accepting her first patronages (including the National Society for the Prevention of Cruelty to Children). Yet Lilibet remained as shy and diffident as ever.

In late 1942, the US first lady, Eleanor Roosevelt, on a tour of the UK, was struck by the deplorable food, a lack of heating and a 'very attractive, quite serious' heir to the throne.[14] The

1939–47: 'People will say we're in love'

following year, Crawfie was still asking hostesses not to invite both Princesses to parties, because Margaret would always try to be the centre of attention and, as a result, seventeen-year-old Lilibet would retreat into her shell again. She was not terribly interested in meeting new, eligible young officers, however, since by now it was clear to all that Prince Philip was the firm favourite. He came to Windsor again on 18 December 1943 to watch the Princesses in another Christmas pantomime, *Aladdin*. 'He seems so suited to PE [Princess Elizabeth] and I kept wondering today whether he is her future husband,' observed Fitzalan Howard from her seat in the second row. 'She would like it and though he could not be in love with her, I believe he is not averse to the idea.'[15] Crawfie had similar thoughts about the 'grave and charming young man' who 'looked more than ever like a Viking, weather-beaten and strained'. While there was no shortage of those, like Prince Philip's uncle, Lord Louis Mountbatten, who would be thrilled by such a match, it was starting to take its own course unaided. 'The pantomime went off very well. I have never known Lilibet more animated,' wrote Crawfie. 'There was a sparkle about her none of us had ever seen before. Many people remarked on it. From then on, the two young people began to correspond. She took an immense interest in him, where he was and on what ship.'[16]

Philip had been accompanying his first cousin, the Duchess of Kent, the former Princess Marina of Greece, who, as Fitzalan Howard observed, 'looked a dream all in black'. It was no fashion statement: she was still mourning her husband. The Duke of Kent, the King's younger brother, had been killed in a flying accident the year before, leaving behind three small children, including two-month-old Prince Michael. It was the gravest tragedy of the war for the Royal Family.

Elizabeth II

At this point, Prince Philip was having what would be termed a 'good war'. He had been mentioned in despatches for his quick thinking during the Battle of Cape Matapan, and had become one of the youngest first lieutenants in the Royal Navy. However, had it not been for his uncle, Lord Louis Mountbatten, he would probably have been wearing a different uniform – if indeed he were still alive. 'I really wanted to go into the Air Force,' he later told biographer Basil Boothroyd. 'Oh yes. Left to my own devices, I'd have gone into the Air Force without a doubt.'[17] Mountbatten – known by his family as 'Dickie' – had prevailed. 'He may have persuaded me. I just sort of accepted it.' Given wartime life expectancy in the air – almost half of those who served in Bomber Command never returned – it is not unreasonable to say that the RAF's loss was Lilibet's gain.

It had been a lively end to 1943. After dinner and charades at Windsor Castle on Boxing Day, the King's private secretary, Sir Alan Lascelles, wrote that Prince Philip had been among the young crowd who had 'frisked and capered away till near 1 a.m.'[18]

It was still too early to talk of romance, however. In 1944, Philip was on his way to the Far East for over a year as second-in-command of the destroyer, HMS *Whelp*. Lilibet was turning eighteen, but the King was playing down any idea of a serious relationship. He told Queen Mary that Lilibet was 'too young for that now, as she has never met any young men of her own age.'[19] The Princess was still alternating between childhood and the grim realities of war. One week, she was accompanying her parents to watch the 6th Airborne Division preparing for D-Day and the liberation of France. The next, she was winning a junior carriage-driving competition at the Windsor Horse Show on Queen Victoria's open pony chaise. 'They won entirely on merit,' the King noted proudly in his diary after both Princesses

1939–47: 'People will say we're in love'

picked up trophies. Not long afterwards, Lilibet would be back on duty in Bedfordshire, naming a US Air Force B-17 Flying Fortress 'Rose of York'. The Americans had wanted to call it 'Princess Elizabeth', but the proposal was rejected on the grounds that it would be a coup for the enemy propaganda machine if it were to be shot down (which, sadly, it was, with no survivors, in February 1945).

Historians like to point to 6 June 1944, D-Day, as the turning point in the war. The King and Churchill were so excited that both had initially been determined to join the great Allied invasion of Normandy.[20] The King's private secretary, the astute Tommy Lascelles, managed to head off this reckless idea by simply asking the monarch what advice he was supposed to give Lilibet on appointing her first prime minister, in the event that both men ended up on the seabed. For the population of southern England, however, the thrill of D-Day was soon eclipsed by a ghastly apparition. Within days, a new type of pilotless flying bomb, the V1 'Doodlebug', started to cross the Channel. Since the dark days of the Blitz, the Royal Air Force had gained the upper hand in the sky, so air raids had started to tail off. The new weapons wreaked instant terror. Crawfie recorded that she had thrown herself on top of Princess Margaret when a flying bomb came buzzing over their heads while they were out in the park. The girls lost several friends when another V1 landed on the Guards Chapel in London during Sunday morning service. The King's weekly lunches with Winston Churchill were relocated to the blast shelter. The Queen felt the time had come for precautionary farewell letters to the Princesses. 'Let's hope this won't be needed, but I know that you will always do the right thing, & remember to keep your temper & your word,' she wrote.[21]

With Philip in the Far East, there was no 'beau' in the audience

Elizabeth II

for the 1944 pantomime, *Old Mother Red Riding Hood*, but Alathea Fitzalan Howard wrote that he had sent Lilibet a photograph. According to Margaret, she had 'danced around the room with it for joy.'²²

Now well past her eighteenth birthday, and with the direction of the war clearly moving towards a close, Lilibet had been pressing to do her bit. In early 1945, the King relented and No. 230873 Second Subaltern Elizabeth Windsor joined the Auxiliary Territorial Service (ATS), learning to drive and maintain an army lorry. It was not her first exposure to 'ordinary people', since the Windsor Girl Guides and pantomimes had involved local children and evacuees. Unlike her fellow ATS recruits, she was not expected to live in barracks, but she received no special treatment when it came to the training. As a result, and to her lasting delight, she was in uniform on the night of 8 May 1945, as Britain celebrated Victory in Europe or VE Day.

After the Princesses had appeared with their parents on the balcony of Buckingham Palace, the King agreed that they could venture out into the jubilant crowds accompanied by a cohort of trusted Guards officers. Also with them was their cousin, Margaret Rhodes (then Margaret Elphinstone), and their French teacher, Antoinette 'Toni' de Bellaigue. They danced through the streets, joined a conga through the Ritz Hotel, and blended in with the multitude crying 'We want the King!' at the palace railings. Margaret Rhodes later recorded the episode in her memoir, and was also given permission to quote from the diary that Lilibet herself had been keeping through the war. 'PM announced unconditional surrender,' the Princess wrote. 'Sixteen of us went out in crowd, cheered parents on balcony. Up St J's St, Piccadilly, great fun.'²³ The King's own diary concluded one of the great days in British history, a proper

1939–47: 'People will say we're in love'

moment of national salvation, on a protective and sombre note about his daughters: 'Poor darlings, they have never had any fun yet.'[24]

The King would be equally wistful when Britain finally held a general election two and a half months later, even as the war continued to grind on in the Far East. To his astonishment, the British people turned against Winston Churchill's Tories and elected Clement Attlee's Labour Party. In private, the monarch was 'very sad', and said as much to Churchill when he came to resign. 'I told him I thought the people were very ungrateful after the way they had been led in the war,' the King wrote in his diary.[25] His canny private secretary, Tommy Lascelles, reassured him that it might turn out to be 'the best thing that could have happened.'[26] Churchill was tired; the old warhorse needed to let someone else shoulder the task of building and shaping a post-war Britain while he enjoyed some respite on the Opposition benches. That was not an option for the King.

With peace came a return to ordinary pleasures, not least horse racing. Just a fortnight after VE Day, the King introduced his eldest daughter to a sport which would give her more pleasure than any other during her long life. 'I took Lilibet racing at Ascot,' he recorded in his diary. 'Her first race meeting. We watched 3 races.'[27] From that moment on, she would be hooked. The family resumed life at Buckingham Palace, where Lilibet was given a handful of staff – two ladies-in-waiting, a housemaid and a footman – plus her own set of rooms, including an office. A photograph of Prince Philip sat in pride of place on her desk. When Crawfie remarked that people might talk, the Princess did not shyly take it down, but swapped it for a picture of a bearded Philip. 'There you are, Crawfie. I defy anyone to recognize who that is,' she said proudly. 'He's completely incognito in that one.'[28]

Elizabeth II

Her infatuation with Philip was clearly helping her self-confidence. By 1946, he was finally back from the Far East and a regular visitor at the palace. He took Lilibet to see *Oklahoma!*, a much-needed splash of excitement on the West End stage, and 'People Will Say We're In Love' became 'their' song. Invited to Balmoral as a house guest that summer, Philip was now as keen on Lilibet as she had long been on him. 'It was probably then that we began to think about it seriously and even talk about it,' Prince Philip later told Basil Boothroyd.[29]

In September, Philip proposed. Lilibet's acceptance, he wrote to Queen Elizabeth, had done 'more for me than anything else in my life.'[30] He had finally found the sort of stability and contentment which had been woefully absent from his childhood. The only son of a younger son of the King of Greece and Princess Alice of Battenberg, he had grown up in exile in Paris. The family had resettled there after Philip's father, Prince Andrew, was made the scapegoat for a Greek military disaster and was forced to flee Greece in 1922. The marriage fell apart and Philip's mother eventually had a nervous breakdown. Locked away in a sanatorium when Philip was eight, she scarcely saw him during the first two years of her confinement and would then not set eyes on him for another five. His sisters were all married off to German nobility, while he was sent abroad to prep school in Berkshire and then to Gordonstoun in Scotland after a brief unhappy interlude at school in Germany. Young Philip would occasionally see his father in the school holidays but would otherwise depend on the hospitality of his cousins, the Mountbattens (as the Battenbergs had been renamed in 1917).* His first family reunion would be in

---

* Prince Philip's mother was from the German princely house of Battenberg. Her father had risen to the top of the Royal Navy by the out-

1939–47: 'People will say we're in love'

horrific circumstances following the death of his favourite sister, Cecile, along with her family, in a 1937 plane crash.

'He had the most appalling childhood, which would explain a lot about him in later life,' said one who worked closely with him for many years. 'It was why he could be so brisk but also very sensitive to people from troubled homes.'[31] During the Second World War, all his surviving sisters had been on the enemy side while his mother had been living as a nun in occupied Athens. His father had died in the arms of his mistress in a hotel room in enemy-controlled Monte Carlo in December 1944, his body interred in a cemetery in Nice (until repatriation to Greece after the war). Philip received the news, in a telegram from Lord Louis Mountbatten, while at sea on the other side of the world in HMS *Whelp*. Whatever the challenges and drama involved in marrying the most eligible woman on Earth, life, in Philip's case, was about to become refreshingly normal.

The couple were told not to say a word about their engagement until the Royal Family had paid a long-awaited visit to the King's southern African realms in early 1947. As well as wanting to thank them for their support during the war, George VI also wished to support the English-speaking government of the Union of South Africa and its leader, Jan Smuts, an heroic figure in both world wars. There were to be no distractions.

The family sailed south in the battleship HMS *Vanguard* (which happened to be the first ship launched by Lilibet, back in November 1944). Their grand arrival in the blazing heat of Cape Town was the very first time that the Princesses had set foot on foreign soil. The royal party were then taken all over the country in an air-conditioned palace-on-wheels known as the White Train.

---

break of the First World War and, in 1917, the British branch of the family changed their name to Mountbatten to counter anti-German sentiment.

Elizabeth II

Back at home, Britain was enduring the worst winter in living memory, with parts of the countryside cut off for days. Crawfie wrote to the girls that she had cut her face on an icicle. 'Margaret wrote with her usual gaiety,' the governess noted, 'all about the fun they were having, how beautiful the White Train was, how warm the sun, how wonderful the food. Lilibet wrote, immensely distressed by all that was going on in England in the bitter weather. It bothered her to feel she was far away having a good time, in a land so full of everything. She felt she ought to be at home.'[32] It was a telling observation by the former governess, another small reminder that, when the time came, Britain would end up with the right Queen.

There was an added subtext to the tour. Since it would coincide with Lilibet's coming of age, this would be a moment to remind and reassure the dominions and colonies of the British Empire that their future was in safe hands. The tour branched off into Northern and Southern Rhodesia (destined to become Zambia and Zimbabwe), and in the latter, on Sunday 13 April, Lilibet sat down to record one of the most celebrated speeches of her life. 'Princess Elizabeth read her 21st Birthday speech for the newsreel photographer,' the King's equerry noted in the official tour diary, adding that she then recorded the audio version later on the same day.[33] One section, in particular, has entered royal history: 'I declare before you all that my whole life whether it be long or short shall be devoted to your service and the service of our great imperial family to which we all belong . . .' The speech had been written by Dermot Morrah, a *Times* journalist and herald at the College of Arms, and tweaked by a very grateful Tommy Lascelles. 'Dusty old cynic that I am, it moved me greatly,' the King's private secretary told Morrah.[34] The Princess actually cried when she read it through for the first time. Lascelles was delighted, telling her: 'If it makes you cry now, it will make 200 million cry when

1939–47: 'People will say we're in love'

they hear you.'[35] As the speech was broadcast at 7 p.m. on 21 April 1947, one of those listeners who would indeed be in tears was Winston Churchill. Historians have faithfully recorded that it was delivered from South Africa. Documentaries always show film of an earnest Princess reciting her speech in the dappled sunlight of what is presumed to be a Cape Town garden. In fact it was night-time when the world heard those words. The Princess was indeed in Cape Town but, at that precise moment, she was getting ready for her birthday ball. Her speech and that historic footage had actually been pre-recorded in the grounds of the Victoria Falls Hotel in what is now Zimbabwe.

Three months later, the British Empire ceased to exist following the partition of newly independent India into two nations with the creation of Pakistan. Jan Smuts would lose the next South African election to the Nationalists, who would go on to create the white supremacist system of apartheid and abandon the link with the Crown. The tour had been the forlorn, final foray of a weary monarch who was about to become very ill. It had also been the launch of Lilibet. 'She has come on in the most surprising way,' Lascelles wrote home to his wife. 'Not a great sense of humour, but a healthy sense of fun. Moreover, when necessary, she can take on the old bores with much of her mother's skill . . . When necessary – not infrequently – she tells her father off to rights.' Prescient as ever, he added: 'My impression, by the way, is that we shall be subscribing to a w-p [wedding present] before the year is out.'[36]

On 9 July 1947, the Palace announced the engagement. Philip had by now renounced his Greek nationality to become a British citizen. In doing so, he had lost his royal status as Prince Philip of Greece and Denmark* to become plain Lieutenant

---

* The Greek monarchy was imported from Denmark in 1863.

Elizabeth II

Philip Mountbatten RN. It did not stop him presenting his bride-to-be with an impeccably royal ring. His mother had given him some diamonds from a family tiara which had been a gift from the last Tsar, and he went to jeweller Philip Antrobus in Old Bond Street to have them made into a ring of his own design. Much as it might run counter to his image in later life, Philip would be an enthusiastic jewellery designer in the early days of marriage. The wedding ring itself would be made from a nugget of Welsh gold. Like the little thatched cottage she had received for her sixth birthday, it was a gift from the people of Wales. There was a similar – and typical – generosity of spirit from Lilibet herself. 'There is enough for two rings,' she told Crawfie. 'We can save a piece for Margaret.'[37]

The wedding was the first burst of proper royal excitement since VE Day. Although Britain was in the throes of austerity bordering on bankruptcy and still very much on rations, many ordinary people wanted a royal spectacle to be proud of on 20 November 1947. Women around the country sent the Princess their clothing ration coupons, which, by law, had to be returned. There were no such restrictions on gifts like sugar and crystallized fruit, which the Girl Guides of Australia sent in for the wedding cake. The King and Queen gave Lilibet a string of pearls, which went on public display alongside most of the other 2,583 gifts, with the notable exception of a racehorse from the Aga Khan. Just before the wedding, Philip received the Dukedom of Edinburgh and the Order of the Garter from the King. After four months as Lt Mountbatten RN, he was titled once more, and the popular ditty of that summer – 'Oh come to my arms/Thou bundle of charms/Philip Mountbatten RN' – was now out of date.

There were plenty of last-minute glitches on the morning of the wedding, including a snapped tiara plus a frantic hunt for

1939–47: 'People will say we're in love'

both the string of pearls and the bridal bouquet (the former had to be retrieved from the exhibition of wedding gifts while the latter had been carefully locked away in a cold storage cupboard). There had also been some difficult moments with the guest list. It was decided that there could be no invitations for the groom's sisters, since they were all married to former German officers; just two and a half years on from VE Day, forgiveness had only come so far. Philip's family group consisted of just his mother, plus his Mountbatten cousins.

On the bride's side, there was one notable uninvited member of the Royal Family. All through the war, the Duke of Windsor had behaved appallingly. Regularly bombarding his brother with complaints about money and the non-HRH status of his wife, he had initially been posted to France in a liaison role until the collapse of the French forces forced him to flee with the Duchess to neutral Spain and then Portugal. There he would airily talk down Britain's chances of victory within earshot of German agents who were under orders to recruit him as some sort of intermediary. Winston Churchill and the King wanted him as far removed from Britain, Europe and Nazi interlopers as possible. He would spend the rest of the war – free of tax, bombs and freezing winters – serving as Governor of the Bahamas. Even then, he had the nerve to complain to his brother about the heat. Though he expected an invitation to his niece's wedding, none was forthcoming. Instead, Queen Mary would send him a long account of the happy day by post.

A grimy London, still pockmarked with bomb sites, was dazzled by it all. Churchill called the wedding 'a flash of colour on the hard road we have to travel'. Some of that colour came from the Household Cavalry escorts who were commanded to wear full dress – their finest scarlet tunics and breastplates – for the first time since the outbreak of war. Ever the traditionalist, Lilibet chose to 'love, cherish and obey' her husband. However, she also set a new musical trend. It had been her choice to set the words of Psalm 23, 'The Lord's My Shepherd', to the little-known Scottish tune, 'Crimond'. It soon caught on and would be a firm favourite for the rest of her life.

After a wedding breakfast of 'filet de sole Mountbatten', 'bombe glacée Princess Elizabeth' and a shy balcony appearance (there would be no newly-wed balcony kiss until 1981), the couple departed for a honeymoon at Broadlands, the country estate of Earl Mountbatten.* Unseen by the public was a third passenger in the open carriage: beneath the piles of confetti and a blanket was the Princess's corgi, Susan, the successor to Dookie and Jane. Even in rural Hampshire, there was no escaping the crowds. When the couple arrived for Sunday morning church at Romsey Abbey, they were greeted by a crowd of 10,000.

---

* Formerly Lord Louis Mountbatten, he had been created Viscount and then Earl Mountbatten of Burma in 1947 following his role as the last Viceroy of India.

Chapter Four

1947–52

Duchess Days

The King would miss Lilibet very much. 'When I handed your hand to the Archbishop I felt that I had lost something very precious,' he wrote to her.[1] But he was also confident for the future. 'I have watched you grow up all these years with pride under the skilful direction of Mummy, who as you know is the most marvellous person in the World in my eyes, & I can, I know, always count on you, & now Philip.'[2] Lilibet felt much the same. 'I think I've got the best mother and father in the world,' she wrote to her mother, 'and I only hope that I can bring up my children in the happy atmosphere of love and fairness which Margaret and I have grown up in.'[3]

There would hardly be a great parting of the ways. The marital home was due to be Clarence House, but it had sustained bomb damage in the war and required extensive repairs. For now, the young couple would keep their offices at Buckingham Palace and live in an apartment at Kensington Palace. At weekends, they would decamp to Windlesham Moor. This stockbroker-belt Victorian rental with five bedrooms and a tiny staff, set in 58 acres on the Surrey/Berkshire border, would be the first home they could really call their own. One of the Duke's early innovations was to mark out a cricket pitch.

The couple were in high demand at home and overseas, causing a sensation as they toured Paris the following spring. The French press saluted the style and slim figure of the Princess, whom they liked to call 'Zizette'. Unbeknown to anyone except the Duke, she was already three months' pregnant, and so had to smile and soldier on through the champagne receptions and banquets, one of which left the Duke of Edinburgh with food poisoning.

As the due date approached, the King had to do some urgent eleventh-hour constitutional tinkering. Under the rules laid down by George V, the baby would be neither HRH nor strictly speaking royal, since those letters patent from 1917 restricted royal status to grandchildren in the male line. George VI issued the appropriate amendments.

What alarmed courtiers much more, however, were reports that the Duke had been seen revelling into the early hours at a nightclub. His friend, the society photographer Stirling Nahum, known as Baron, had invited Philip and an equerry to come with him to see the musical actress Pat Kirkwood, appearing at the Hippodrome. Afterwards, Baron had invited Kirkwood to join them all at a nightclub where the Duke of Edinburgh asked her to dance. The party then adjourned for scrambled eggs at Baron's flat before the Duke and his equerry returned to the Palace. There had been nothing furtive about the encounter; Kirkwood later recalled that Philip had pulled faces at disapproving 'courtiers' in the nightclub, which would suggest he felt he had nothing to hide.[4] However, word reached the King, and we can therefore assume that it also reached the Princess. The monarch, Baron later told Kirkwood, gave Philip a ferocious dressing down and nothing more was said. The story also reached the gossip

1947–52: *Duchess Days*

columns, and 'Prince and the Party Girl' rumours would dog Pat Kirkwood for the rest of her life. Decades later, having married a fourth time to a prominent lawyer, she threatened legal action when a new biography of the Queen alleged that there had been an actual affair (the publisher retracted the claim). 'A lady is not normally expected to defend her honour. It is the gentleman who should do that,' Kirkwood later told a journalist. 'I would have had a happier and easier life if Prince Philip, instead of coming uninvited to my dressing room, had gone home to his pregnant wife on the night in question.'[5] At the time of the proposed legal action, she had asked the Duke, via the Palace, to offer a robust denial, but he declined to get embroiled. 'Short of starting libel proceedings,' he told her, 'there is absolutely nothing to be done. Invasion of privacy, invention and false quotations are the bane of our existence.'[6] Elizabeth II would always prefer the old royal doctrine of 'never complain, never explain', in tandem with the old motto of the Order of the Garter, '*Honi soit qui mal y pense*' ('shame on him who thinks evil of it'). Even so, it would not make such rumours any easier to bear for a shy young mother-to-be.

The incident would not be the last of its kind. At various stages of the Duke's life, through early married years, middle age and right up to his retirement, there would be gossip and speculation about a handful of the Duke's friendships. It was always accepted among royal staff and friends that the Duke liked the company of attractive women, and they of him. While that could easily translate into rumour, it remains the case that none of those rumours ever materialized into cast iron fact. The Duke himself would protest on several occasions that the demands of royal security meant that there had been 'a detective in my company night and day since 1947'. He was a good dancer and enjoyed spinning a partner across the dance floor

Elizabeth II

at a wedding or a party or the Royal Yacht Squadron Ball. Thanks to him, the disco and dance band would replace the waltz and the gavotte as the musical entertainment at palace events. But his right-hand man through his more youthful years, his former shipmate and equerry Mike Parker, was emphatic: 'Philip has been one hundred per cent faithful to the Queen.'[7]

In later life, another rumour would circulate that the Duke had been especially close to the Duchess of Abercorn, with whom he shared an interest in the Swiss analyst, Carl Jung. 'It was a passionate friendship, but the passion was in the ideas. It was certainly not a full relationship,' the Duchess told Gyles Brandreth. 'I did not go to bed with him. It probably looked like that to the world. I can understand why people might have thought it, but it didn't happen. It's complicated and, at the same time, it's quite simple. He needs a playmate and someone to share his intellectual pursuits.'[8] In later life, there would be much media focus on Viscountess Romsey (later Countess Mountbatten). Married to the Duke's younger kinsman, Norton, she would often accompany the Duke to carriage-driving events and became a regular companion in his final years. She would be the only member of the Mountbatten family at the Duke's funeral and at the coronation of Charles III. Much as it might baffle or intrigue the press, the Duke was not going to curtail a platonic friendship which was accepted as a given by the Queen and the rest of the family. One neighbour remembered Sandringham shooting weekends in the Duke's later years where a house party (without the Queen) might include Lady Romsey – who always referred to him as 'Cousin Philip' – along with family members including her own daughter, Alexandra, Prince William and Prince Harry.[9] Just as he did in that nightclub in October 1948, the Duke would always be ready to make faces at any disapproving prude who 'might think evil of it'.

The Edinburghs became parents at 9.14 p.m. on 14 November

1947–52: *Duchess Days*

1948. Princess Elizabeth gave birth to a healthy boy weighing seven pounds and six ounces after four hours of labour. Thanks to a further reform by George VI, there were no politicians hovering around the Buhl Room, the Buckingham Palace guest room used as a delivery suite.

By tradition, the home secretary had always been in attendance for a royal birth (though not in the actual room) to vouch for the legitimacy of the child – a curious throwback to the days when a scheming courtier might smuggle a baby into the bed. In recent years, the King's other kingdoms had become increasingly vocal about their rights under the 1931 Statute of Westminster, which declared that all realms were equal under the Crown. If a British minister was to attend, then Canada, Australia and the rest would be within their rights to send one too. Rather than clutter the palace with superfluous strangers waiting awkwardly for news, the King simply abolished the rule. Normally, his conservative instincts would incline him to protect such traditions, but he was happy to break this one for Lilibet's sake. As a result, only the medical team were present.

The Duke of Edinburgh would not attend a birth until the arrival of his youngest child in 1964 (a royal child would not be born in a hospital until Princess Anne had Peter Phillips in 1977). In those days, expectant fathers had to be kept preoccupied elsewhere, so the Duke had been playing squash with Mike Parker. As news spread, the fountains of Trafalgar Square ran blue and the crowds gathered outside Buckingham Palace were so boisterous that Parker was sent out to ask them to keep the noise down. A month later, the Archbishop of Canterbury used water from the River Jordan to christen Charles Philip Arthur George at Buckingham Palace.

In the summer of 1949, the young family could finally move into Clarence House. Completely refurbished, with central heating and a palette of white, pale blues and greens and lighter woods for panelling, it had an atmosphere described as 'bright, fresh and full of energy' compared to the royal quarters at Buckingham Palace.[10] A small, youthful household was bolstered by the presence of Jock Colville, formerly of Churchill's Downing Street, as private secretary and Lieutenant-General 'Boy' Browning, the wartime hero of the Battle of Arnhem and husband of novelist Daphne du Maurier, who had the wide-ranging title of 'Comptroller'. His appointment had been suggested by Philip's ever-attentive uncle, Lord Mountbatten, who had served with Browning, with the close involvement of the King. George VI wanted Lilibet and Philip to feel a sense of independence with recourse to a wise old consigliere of their own and had insisted on interviewing Browning first. 'He is not a "yes man" or even a courtier and never will be,' Mountbatten, the arch-courtier, assured his nephew. 'Frankly, Philip, I do not think you can do better.'[11]

The couple could now unpack all those wedding presents. The handsome mahogany table from the Royal Warrant Holders Association went into the dining room. A second television set, a gift from Lord Mountbatten, was directed to the servants' hall. The Duke loved having a place where he could make decisions, and the Princess was happy to let him do so, right down to choosing the pictures on the wall (including plenty of portraits of his own family) and even the menus. Philip also liked to carry his own luggage and drive his own cars – though the latter was a source of mounting concern. Shortly before the wedding, Philip had flipped a car into a ditch. As Crawfie noted, Lilibet was 'very upset and anxious' – feelings shared by Palace officials. 'They did not feel that Philip should be allowed to drive the heir to the throne about London as he had been doing,' wrote Crawfie.[12] 'It was surprising to all

1947–52: Duchess Days

of us that the King did not forbid him, but I have no doubt whatever that Philip was gravely cautioned by His Majesty.' Palace chauffeurs were reluctant to let the Duke anywhere near their vehicles for fear of dents and scratches. One day, Philip was driving through London with the Princess when he collided with a taxi at Hyde Park Corner. 'Oh, Crawfie, how am I to make Mummie and Papa realize that this time it really wasn't Philip's fault. It was the taxi. They will never believe it.'[13]

The Duke was fascinated by vehicles and would soon become a very active president of the Automobile Association. However, if the Establishment were worried enough about him driving the Princess, they were even more concerned when the infant Prince Charles was on board too. In early 1949, the diplomat Sir Gladwyn Jebb and his diarist wife, Cynthia, were staying at Sandringham with the King and Queen. The Edinburghs had also been there for the weekend and there was palpable nervousness when the time came for Philip to drive his family home. 'It was a drizzling day,' Cynthia recorded in her diary. 'Gladwyn and I felt some alarm at seeing the Duke, who has the reputation of being rather a wild driver, starting off on the long journey of about 140 miles to Windlesham with the responsibility of driving the two immediate heirs to the throne.'[14]

The Jebbs, sharp-eyed observers of the royal scene, had been struck by how close and deferential Lilibet remained to her parents. Marriage to Philip had only changed her so much. 'Pretty light brown curly hair, worn short,' wrote Cynthia Jebb. '[With a] most charming mixture of eagerness to please and yet seriously aware of her rank,' Lilibet exhibited 'the touch of genuine gravity which separates royalty from the common herd & warns them no liberty can be taken.' There was also 'a certain gaucheness in her walk, showing her to be still just a growing girl.'[15] The Duke of Edinburgh, on the other hand, was now a veteran Royal Navy officer, ascending the upper reaches of the promotional ladder. After postings in and around London in the early years of the marriage, Philip was finally sent overseas again in October 1949. He was to join the Mediterranean Fleet in Malta where his uncle, Lord Mountbatten, had conveniently just been appointed commander of the 1st Cruiser Squadron. Philip was to be First Lieutenant of the destroyer HMS *Chequers*.

Princess Elizabeth was not far behind, accompanied by the eternal Bobo MacDonald. Prince Charles was left in the care of the King and Queen, along with his nannies, Helen Lightbody and Mabel Anderson. In Malta, the couple enjoyed a sort of extended second honeymoon, living in a wing of the eighteenth-century Villa Guardamangia that had been rented by Lord Mountbatten. There were picnics, boat trips, waterskiing, afternoons at the polo and evening dances with other naval couples at places like the Phoenicia Hotel – where the band were always ready to strike up 'their' song from *Oklahoma!* For the Princess, this was as near to a 'normal' life as she would ever lead, driving her small sports car to social events, to the hairdresser and to the shops. Having to handle cash or to reverse up a narrow lane to make way for a horse and cart was all part of the fun. Two years into married life, her priority was to be alongside her husband rather than her baby son, who was safely in the care of two doting grandparents. Indeed, Lilibet loved Malta so much that she stayed for Christmas before coming home. Even then, her first port of call on returning home was not to rush to Prince Charles at Sandringham. She went to see her racehorse, Monaveen, in action at Hurst Park. It is a sign of the prevailing times that there was not a whisper of criticism in the media. The Princess also had a more important appointment – with her doctors. For she was now expecting her second child.

These were trying times for the Royal Medical Household, as

1947-52: Duchess Days

the family's doctors are known. The King had developed serious arteriosclerosis in his leg in 1948, making walking increasingly difficult. At one point, there was a fear of gangrene and even talk of amputation. Nothing was said until after the birth of Prince Charles for fear of upsetting Lilibet, whereupon the Palace announced that the King's forthcoming tour of Australia and New Zealand – an even more ambitious journey than his great South African tour of 1947 – would have to be postponed.

In March 1949, the palace became a hospital once again as the King underwent a lumbar sympathectomy to improve the circulation in his leg. It was a success – so much so that the King was well enough to attend the 1949 conference of the prime ministers of all his realms. Long before anyone would talk of 'summits', this was a meeting convened to address the schismatic implications of Indian independence and the end of the British Empire, culminating in a landmark agreement called the London Declaration. What had previously been known as the British Commonwealth was no more.

The word 'British' was dropped, all member states were equal and they did not owe any loyalty to the King. They could be a republic with a president if they wished. The only prerequisite was to accept the sovereign as honorary 'head' of the club. If it was a downgrade for the monarch, George VI and his daughter were wise enough to see that it was simply the shape of things to come. Without the changes, the Commonwealth would have lost India, easily its largest member nation, and many other future members, too. Indeed, it might very well have imploded.

Step by step, the monarchy was having to adapt to a post-war world in which so many old certainties could no longer be taken for granted. On a personal level, that was clear enough at the beginning of 1950, as the Royal Family started to see intimate details of their private lives appearing in print.

Elizabeth II

Marion Crawford, the once-beloved and utterly trusted governess to the Princesses, had decided to sell her story to an American publisher. Her sensational tales of life inside the royal cocoon, from the nursery to the schoolroom, all through the war and right up to Lilibet's engagement, were almost all gushingly favourable. They were syndicated in magazines around the world and then, in greater detail, in a bestselling book called *The Little Princesses*. To the Princesses themselves, and also to their parents, it felt like rank betrayal. The stories might be sweet and syrupy, but the very fact that the world could read about Margaret's tantrums in the nursery, or Lilibet's yearnings for Philip, or Queen Elizabeth's frivolous approach to education, felt hurtful in the extreme. Much the same would be said and felt more than seventy years later when Prince Harry wrote his own memoir, *Spare*. It was not so much the content of his stories, most of them innocuous, which appalled Prince William in particular, but the fact that tender childhood memories had been casually sprayed across the public domain.

The background to Crawfie's memoir was a sorry tale of manipulation and naivety. Having devoted her life to the Princesses, the former governess was given a lifetime's tenancy of a cottage at Kensington Palace and made a CVO.* At the age of thirty-eight, she finally found love and married a Scottish ex-army officer-turned-bank manager called George Buthlay. He not only tried and failed to persuade the Royal Family to open accounts with his bank, but bullied Crawfie into believing that that she had not been adequately rewarded for her services. The biographer Hugo Vickers has revealed how she was cleverly lured into a contract with a US publisher who then

---

* Commander of the Royal Victorian Order, one rank below Knight or Dame.

rewrote many of her words. As Queen Elizabeth lamented to Lady Astor: 'We can only think that our late & completely trusted governess has gone off her head.'[16]

Crawfie would go on to write royal columns on major royal events for *Woman's Own* magazine, culminating in a rosy portrait of her former employers at the 1955 Birthday Parade. She had made it all up ahead of the event, which was then cancelled due to a train strike. By that time, however, the magazine had gone to print. Discredited as a writer, she retired to a house near Aberdeen, by the road to Balmoral, forever hoping that the Princesses might one day stop to say hello. They never did. After the death of Buthlay in 1977 and a rumoured suicide bid, she died at the age of seventy-eight in 1988. Crawfie was clearly an excellent governess, and her memoir leaves us with so many authoritative insights into the lives and characters of the Royal Family at a key moment in history. Though she wasn't the only courtier to write a memoir, since Mabell, Countess of Airlie also published her story (though with nothing like the same level of intimacy), the family never forgave their governess. 'Crawfie?' said Princess Margaret, when the subject surfaced one day. 'She snaked.'[17]

As the world was digesting the indiscretions of Crawfie, a pregnant Lilibet resumed life as a naval wife in Malta for four months in 1950. Once again, Prince Charles was left behind. The Princess returned to Britain during the summer and, on 15 August 1950, the fifth anniversary of the end of the Second World War, she gave birth to a girl, Anne Elizabeth Alice Louise, this time in her own home at Clarence House. The Duke of Edinburgh had been given a fortnight's leave to come home for the birth. It was also the first time in almost a year that he had seen his son. However, duty called back in Malta, where he had finally been given command of his own ship, the frigate HMS *Magpie*.

Elizabeth II

It is hardly surprising that Lilibet's maternal instincts have often been called into question. For fewer than four months after the birth of Anne, she left both children with the King and Queen and, yet again, flew back to Malta, thus missing Anne's first Christmas. For Charles, it was the second in a row without his parents. As noted earlier, it raised no adverse comment at a time when children from a Forces background might be separated from at least one parent for months on end. However, it shows that Princess Elizabeth's priority was to keep her husband happy and under her watchful eye, at the expense of her time with two very small children. For, while it was acceptable for naval wives to join their husbands on shore-based postings overseas, young children did not come too.

It is also possible, if not probable, that Lilibet was keen to maximize every last moment of relative freedom as a princess. The King's health was taking a further turn for the worse. This time, it was his lungs which were the problem, as he found himself weakened by what the Palace called 'catarrhal inflammation'.

George VI was already ensuring that his heir would have some basic training. In 1950, Princess Elizabeth had started to receive Cabinet documents, having seen her first state papers and having been made a Counsellor of State in her teens. Her father had despaired when he himself arrived on the throne wholly unprepared. 'I've never even seen a state paper,' he told his cousin, Lord Louis Mountbatten, on the first night of his reign. 'I'm only a Naval officer, it's the only thing I know about.'[18] He did not want Lilibet to end up in the same position.

By the spring of 1951, she was being called back from Malta to stand in for the King with greater regularity. He was starting to miss the sort of Forces parades he once loved, such as the presentation of a new colour to the RAF in May 1951. The next month, the Palace was reporting that the inflammation spotted

1947–52: Duchess Days

in his left lung was still there. It was left to Lilibet to host the upcoming state banquet for the King of Norway and to take her father's place at the Birthday Parade.

In between his naval duties, the Duke had also accompanied Lilibet on one or two important official visits, like her trips to meet the King of Greece and the Pope. He had been an invaluable confidence-booster and now she was going to need him more or less full-time. In July 1951, having only just worked the crew of *Magpie* up to the high standards he demanded, the Duke was told to hand on his command and come home. He told his crew that the previous eleven months had been 'the happiest of my sailor life'. At that point, he still had every intention of returning to it.

Though the Princess and the Duke were now based back in Britain, it did not mean they would have much more time to spend with their children. The couple were to take the place of the King and Queen on a big coast-to-coast tour of Canada and also the USA during the autumn. Lilibet would then stand in for the King at home when he finally embarked on that long-planned tour of Australia and New Zealand in the New Year. Just as the Edinburghs were about to set sail for Canada in September, however, doctors discovered a malignant tumour on the King's lung and decided to operate within days. The tour was postponed while the Buhl Room, formerly used as the Princess's maternity suite, was again reconfigured as an operating theatre for a three-hour procedure to remove his left lung. The King and the family were only told that this was necessary because of 'structural changes' to the organ. When Winston Churchill asked his own doctor, Lord Moran, why the doctors had used this terminology, he was told: 'Because they were anxious to avoid talking about cancer.'[19]

* * *

Elizabeth II

Once the King was stable, Lilibet and Philip finally set off for Canada, having received the King's permission to fly (still considered a relatively risky mode of transport) in order to make up for lost time. The royal baggage not only included mourning clothes, but also the requisite accession papers, should the worst occur. It was not an easy tour, with a 10,000-mile itinerary and mounting criticism that the Princess was not smiling enough, despite pleas from her new private secretary, Martin Charteris, to try. 'My face is aching with smiling,' she told him.[20] Nevertheless, Canadians warmed to a young, energetic couple pictured on a romantic sleigh ride, eating barbecued buffalo and enjoying an evening of square dancing with the Princess in a dirndl skirt and the Duke in jeans. Courtiers and politicians were quietly delighted to see a million loyal subjects in Quebec sing 'God Save the King' in French.

The Princess also had the first of what would be many visits to the White House as a guest of President Harry Truman. With Britain and the USA now fighting alongside each other in a new war in Korea, the tour was a vital piece of bilateral bridge-building. For many years afterwards, Prince Philip was fond of retelling the comic moment when the Princess was introduced to Truman's elderly and slightly confused mother-in-law, Madge. Back in Britain, Clement Attlee had just lost the 1951 general election to Winston Churchill. 'I'm so glad your father's been re-elected,' the eighty-nine-year-old told Lilibet.

Attlee had only called the election at that point out of respect for the King. He could have waited until 1952, but George VI was due to be in Australia and New Zealand. The monarch could hardly hurry back to appoint a new prime minister, so Attlee arranged the entire democratic process to suit the King's diary. In the event, the King's worsening health forced the cancellation of the tour down under anyway. However, he could not bear the idea of letting down his far-flung subjects once again, so it was agreed that the Edinburghs would go in his place. Just weeks after returning from North America, they were repacking. Though they had missed Prince Charles's third birthday while they were in Canada and the USA, they would at least spend Christmas with the children. Come the New Year, however, Charles and Anne were due to wave goodbye to both parents for the longest period thus far – an absence of more than six months.

On the eve of their departure, there was a farewell family dinner and a trip to the West End to see the musical *South Pacific*. The next day, the King went to Heathrow airport to wave goodbye to his daughter. Newsreel images of a gaunt, tired man gazing forlornly at his adored heir for the last time are often cited as proof that George VI knew this was a final farewell. The family believed otherwise. 'We thought that we had at least another year,' Elizabeth II told a senior courtier many years later. The courtier added: 'She certainly expected to see her father again.'[21]

The Edinburghs were full of excitement ahead of the trip, which would be a combination of travel by air and sea. The plan was to start in the British colony of Kenya, with a mix of official engagements and some private time, before boarding a converted liner, the *Gothic*, at Mombasa for the onward voyage to Ceylon and on to the Pacific. The Edinburghs could finally enjoy their wedding present from the Kenyan government – a lease on a handsome bungalow called Sagana Lodge. It was an ideal base from which to look for wildlife (they could even have started at home since, a few days before their arrival, a leopard managed to climb into a downstairs toilet).[22]

This leg of the trip was to include a night at Treetops, a famous three-bedroom lodge built into the branches of a giant

Elizabeth II

fig tree next to a watering hole in the Aberdare hills. It was not without its dangers. There was a 600-yard walk from the nearest vehicle track to the foot of the ladder leading up to the treehouse. Slats of wood had been nailed into trees along the path as an emergency escape route in the event of rampaging wildlife. An athletic young porter, Nahashan Mureithi, was also employed to run ahead as a decoy. Just half an hour before the royal arrival, forty-seven elephants had come charging through the same area. Mureithi recalled that this had not deterred the Princess one bit as she walked carefully but confidently to the Treetops base, with some of the elephants still in sight.[23] There was another unspoken danger. A new anti-colonial insurgency, the Mau Mau, was now starting to operate in the region. With this in mind, the Kenyan government had invited the celebrated big game hunter and tracker, Jim Corbett, to escort the party. He was to keep an eye out for predators on both four legs and two.*

The Princess was entranced by all that she saw, especially a duel to the death between two waterbuck. Corbett would later write a short book on his experience, in which he recalled how the Princess spoke so proudly of her father, of his medical recovery and of the fact that he had been shooting that very day. 'I have heard it said that when the Princess waved goodbye to His Majesty at the London airport,' Corbett wrote, 'she knew she would never see him again on earth. This I do not believe. I am convinced that the young Princess who spoke of her father that night with such great affection and pride and who expressed the fervent hope that she would find him quite

---

* Two years after the royal visit, a Mau Mau unit torched the treehouse and executed the staff, with the exception of Mureithi, who, though wounded, managed to run away.

1947–52: *Duchess Days*

recovered on her return, never had the least suspicion that she would not see him again.'[24]

The next morning, she was up at dawn 'with eyes sparkling and face as fresh as a flower' to see more wildlife, including a pair of squabbling rhino. Finally, after a breakfast of scrambled eggs, bacon, toast and marmalade, it was time for the drive back to Sagana Lodge and thence to Mombasa for the long voyage in the *Gothic*. The Princess, Corbett noted, was 'radiantly happy' as she came down the ladder from the giant fig tree. She had not the faintest idea that she had just become Queen of a substantial part of the planet.

At 7.30 a.m. in Norfolk, the King's valet, James MacDonald, had taken the monarch his morning cup of tea. He opened the bedroom curtains and started to run a bath. With no sign of movement, he gently shook his master's shoulder. One touch of the forehead confirmed his suspicions. 'I was sent a message that his servant couldn't wake him,' Queen Elizabeth recorded in a letter to Queen Mary. 'I flew to his room, & thought that he was in a deep sleep, he looked so peaceful – and then I realized what had happened.'[25] Doctors attributed his death to a sudden coronary thrombosis.

His private secretary, Tommy Lascelles, immediately contacted Buckingham Palace with the pre-arranged codeword for this moment: 'Hyde Park Corner'. His second-in-command, Edward Ford, was the duty man in London and was told to make haste to Downing Street. He found Winston Churchill working in bed as he announced he was the bearer of bad news. The prime minister was almost inconsolable. 'Bad news? The worst!' he exclaimed, hurling his papers to the floor: 'How unimportant these matters are.'[26] Ford's next task was to inform Queen Mary via her lady-in-waiting. Having lost the youngest

Elizabeth II

of her six children, Prince John, in childhood and the Duke of Kent in the war, George V's widow had now lost a third son. She seemed to be half-expecting it. 'Is it the King?' she asked when Lady Cynthia Colville came in with the news.[27]

The most important message was the one to Government House in Nairobi. However, the governor was already en route to Mombasa and the duty telegraphist assumed that 'Hyde Park Corner' was part of an address rather than a message. It was 10.45 a.m. in London and 1.45 p.m. in Kenya when the world was informed of the King's death via the radio, news agencies and emergency editions of the evening papers. Yet still, no word had reached Sagana Lodge.

Princess Elizabeth's private secretary, Martin Charteris, had gone for a spot of lunch at the Outspan Hotel when he was accosted by a journalist who had heard the news on the radio. Charteris instantly called the lodge to tell Mike Parker to find the Duke of Edinburgh. Parker later said that the Duke 'looked as if you'd dropped half the world on him'.

It was now an hour after the rest of the world already knew what Philip was about to impart. He took Lilibet out into the garden, where Parker observed them 'walk slowly up and down the lawn.'[28] Shortly afterwards, Martin Charteris arrived at Sagana Lodge to find Prince Philip lying on the sofa with *The Times* over his face and the new Queen at her desk, 'sitting erect, no tears, colour up a little, full accepting her destiny.'[29]

It fell to Charteris to put the time-honoured question asked of every new monarch. By which name would she reign?

'My own name,' she replied. 'Elizabeth, of course.'

Chapter Five

1952–55

A Reluctant Gloriana

The new Queen surprised everyone with her self-control during the long journey back to London. She had been almost apologetic to all the staff as she left Kenya, telling her lady-in-waiting, Pamela Mountbatten: 'I've ruined everybody's trip.'[1] According to the Duke's valet, John Dean, she did not cry openly on the flight home but left her seat now and then to do so privately in the aircraft toilet. 'She was completely calm, utterly composed,' her private secretary, Martin Charteris, later told Gyles Brandreth. 'For a long time she simply gazed out of the window.'[2]

One person who was having great difficulty containing his emotions all through those early days of the reign, however, was Winston Churchill. As he greeted his new monarch on her return from Kenya, he was red-eyed and, uncharacteristically, speechless. As his biographer, Andrew Roberts, records, the grand old statesman cried on hearing the news of the King's death, cried in front of staff while preparing his eulogy, cried en route to the airport to greet the Queen and was in floods at the late King's funeral.[3] Many of those at the Accession Council, the emergency meeting of the Privy Council to proclaim a new

Elizabeth II

monarch, would be similarly moved by the sight of a twenty-five-year-old young mother taking on the expectations of the nation and the headship of what, in the eyes of many, was still an empire. Harold Wilson called it 'the most moving ceremonial I can recall'.[4]

The first visitor to Clarence House, upon the new monarch's return, had been her grandmother, Queen Mary. Though grieving the death of a third child, the high priestess of royal standards had been determined to be the first member of the family to curtsey to the new sovereign. It was the sight of her elderly grandmother kneeling to kiss her hand, according to one observer, which 'absolutely horrified' Lilibet and finally brought home the enormity of the situation.[5]

The new reign already had a name. Even as some were still absorbing the shock of losing their wartime monarch, others were talking of a 'new Elizabethan age', with the prime minister leading the charge. 'Our thoughts are carried back nearly four hundred years to the magnificent figure who presided over and, in many ways, embodied and inspired the grandeur and genius of the Elizabethan age,' declared Winston Churchill in his broadcast to the nation on 7 February 1952. No one had ever called the late King's reign a 'new Georgian age'. However, the romantic imagery of Elizabeth I, heroic warrior queen of 'Gloriana' fame, transposed onto her young namesake was irresistible to the likes of Churchill. Journalists, cartoonists and artists loved the idea of a new incarnation (minus the red hair) rejuvenating her battered nation. Work began almost immediately on a 'Gloriana' opera by Benjamin Britten.

One person who was certainly not buying into the Tudor revivalist fantasy was the new 'Gloriana' herself. 'A great deal of nonsense was talked about it. It was a pity,' said Charteris, four decades later, by now having retired as Lord Charteris,

1952–55: A Reluctant Gloriana

during a long conversation with Peter Hennessy. 'It aroused expectations which were unattainable in the situation in which the country stood. And this led to some disappointment. Our situation was exactly the reverse.'[6] The Queen herself said as much in her Christmas broadcast the following year: 'Some people have expressed the hope that my reign may mark a new Elizabethan age. Frankly I do not myself feel at all like my great Tudor forbear, who was blessed with neither husband nor children, who ruled as a despot and was never able to leave her native shores.' She was talking from New Zealand at the time.

Here was a facet of the Queen's character – noted earlier – which contrasted, in particular, with that of Churchill and of her mother (and, in due course, that of her eldest son). It was one she shared with Prince Philip and which would serve her well all through her reign in times of trouble. At heart, she was a pragmatist, not a romantic. Elizabeth II's default position, when faced with making a decision, would be to consider precedent and practicality as well as what her father might have done. Her mother, an eternal sentimentalist, would always err on the side of tradition and emotion while abhorring all forms of change. She even took against her own newly minted title of Queen Mother – created to avoid the problem of having two Queen Elizabeths – which she called a 'horrible name'.[7] All through the early years of the new reign, there would be tensions between those nudging the young Queen towards modest reforms and the praetorian guard of the past, led by the Queen Mother deploying her customary putdown: 'I don't think the King would have done that . . .' Lilibet would always want to live up to the memory of her late father but, over time, her interpretation of his views could be at odds with her mother's.

Elizabeth II

Less than a fortnight after Elizabeth's accession, there was an early win for the old guard as Queen Mary triggered the first crisis of the reign. She had learned, via Prince Ernst August of Hanover, that the Duke of Edinburgh's uncle, Lord Mountbatten, had been boasting at a dinner party that 'the House of Mountbatten now reigned'.[8] Not content to let this be dealt with quietly within the family, she had summoned the prime minister's private secretary, Jock Colville (who had returned to his old boss in 1951), to register her alarm. He had reported the matter to Churchill, who had long shared her wariness of Mountbatten's intrigues. The prime minister also had his doubts about Philip, in keeping with the prevailing Establishment snobbery towards an impecunious princeling from a foreign monarchy, regardless of his distinguished war record.

Churchill raised the matter in Cabinet and decided that it was a matter on which he should give the Queen formal advice. Upon marriage, she had become Princess Elizabeth, Duchess of Edinburgh and her children had been styled 'of Edinburgh'. Now that she was the Queen, Charles had become Duke of Cornwall and a host of other titles while Anne was simply 'The Princess Anne'. In theory, the question of the family name need not become an issue for at least a couple of generations until untitled younger relatives were born further down the male line. However, Churchill wanted the Queen to resolve it right away and asked her, formally, to declare that the family name would remain 'Windsor'. This would put the House of Mountbatten firmly in its place. It would also force the Queen to make a public show of her husband's inferior status. As painful and awkward as this was for her personally, when the constitutional came up against the personal, there could be no contest (as members of the Royal Family, notably the Duke and Duchess of Sussex, would discover throughout the reign).

1952–55: A Reluctant Gloriana

The Duke of Edinburgh would famously reflect, privately, that he had been reduced to the status of 'an amoeba, a bloody amoeba.'[9] For such an 'alpha' man of action, who had already sacrificed a naval career at which he had excelled, it pained him deeply.

Mindful that Queen Victoria had set a precedent of renaming the Royal Family in her husband's name, Saxe-Coburg Gotha, Philip had tried to submit a memorandum to Churchill, via Colville, but to no avail. Churchill was sticking to the original edict of George V that the dynastic name should be the House of Windsor. It fell to the Queen's new private secretary, Tommy Lascelles, whom she had inherited from her father, to supervise the signing of the relevant papers. Now in the service of his fourth monarch, he later recalled standing over her like one of the 'barons at Runnymede', who had gathered around King John to prevent any backtracking on Magna Carta. Just weeks into the job, determined to reign in the image of the father she had idolized, the young Queen felt she was simply unable to overrule the late King's two most revered advisers. Years later, she told one minister – who told Valentine Low – that it had never occurred to her to quarrel with Lascelles. As she had put it: 'We just had to do what he said, the whole time.'[10] Yet it would have the effect of creating a hairline crack in the marriage, one of which Lilibet was acutely conscious and which would take several years to heal.

Churchill was happy to dictate to the couple on other matters, too, such as living arrangements. It soon became clear that both the Queen and the Duke of Edinburgh were keen to keep their young family at newly renovated Clarence House, while the Queen Mother was equally keen to stay put at Buckingham Palace. The prime minister enlisted Lascelles to affirm that monarchs 'belong' at royal headquarters and the Duke's back-channel protestations were ignored.

Elizabeth II

With heavy heart, plenty of tears and the same sinking feeling which accompanied her own 1937 childhood move after the abdication, Lilibet moved back in to Buckingham Palace with her young family. The Queen Mother came equally unhappily in the opposite direction. At least she would not be moving out of her home on the Windsor estate. The King had expressly wished that she should have Royal Lodge – 'the house we built & made for ourselves in Windsor Park'[11] – for the rest of her life. The Queen and the Duke would set up home at Windsor Castle, not least because Philip had a close connection to the place. Whenever a patronizing visitor made the mistake of asking how he was finding life in such a big castle, the inference being that it must be quite daunting for an incomer, he would reply: 'Well my mother was born here and my grandmother was born here so I know the place quite well.'

The Duke could be forgiven for thinking that there was no end to the petty slights of the Establishment when he arrived for the Queen's first State Opening of Parliament in November 1952. The consort's throne, which had been there for the wife of George VI, was no longer there for the husband of Elizabeth II. The parliamentary authorities had decided that a female consort outranked a male one (a groundless, arbitrary ruling which would not be reversed until 1967). It would be the same at the Coronation. Whereas George VI had been crowned alongside his consort at his 1937 Coronation, Elizabeth II would be crowned alone in 1953.

According to the Duke's old friend, Lord Brabourne, husband of his cousin, Patricia Mountbatten, Philip had endured downright hostility from the Queen's officials from the start: 'Lascelles was impossible. They were absolutely bloody to him. They patronized him. They treated him as an outsider. It wasn't much fun. He laughed it off but it must have

1952–55: A Reluctant Gloriana

hurt.'[12] Churchill even reprimanded the Duke, via his equerry, for travelling in a new-fangled aviation death-trap and thus, he claimed, endangering the entire future of the monarchy. The Duke had been using a helicopter to inspect the different locations of the vast array of Commonwealth forces encamped around the capital for the Queen's upcoming Coronation.

With little more than two months to go before the ceremony, Queen Mary performed what, to many, seemed like her final and grandest act of piety to the greater glory of the monarchy. Following a chilly February inspection of all the building work underway along the processional route of the Coronation parade, she returned to her home at Marlborough House and never ventured outside again. A month later, she was dead. It meant another grim funeral for Lilibet, resurrecting memories of the King's death a year before, and raising the awkward prospect of the brief return of the Duke of Windsor.

The famously acquisitive Queen Mary had dutifully left almost everything, including her jewels and treasures, to Lilibet, only reinforcing the mutual enmity of Princess Margaret whom she had always criticized for being 'too small'. Had Queen Mary been on her deathbed or in terminal decline at the time of the Coronation, the whole endeavour would have been in jeopardy. She had done her duty to the end. There would be murmurings of déjà vu half a century later when, in the run-up to Elizabeth II's Golden Jubilee, the Queen Mother did much the same, going peacefully to her maker two months short of the main national celebrations.

By the time of the Queen's Coronation on 2 June 1953, the nation could scarcely contain itself any further. The previous Coronation had been arranged with speed, in just five months, in order to heal the wounds of the abdication. The Coronation of Charles III would also be planned at pace, to maintain a sense of continuity and capitalize on the afterglow of the longest reign in history. There was no urgency in 1952. Much of London remained a bombsite, the nation was still on rations and Churchill wanted to present a revitalized Britain to the world. This was a Britain in which most people simply accepted that, having seen the nation successfully through two world wars, a monarchy was the natural order of things and a safer constitutional bet than a republic.

Once again, for the romantically inclined, here was an exuberant celebration of the age of chivalry. Ancient families invoked ancient rights to take ancient roles in the order of service. The Duke of Newcastle went to court to press his historic claim to present the Coronation Glove – and lost. The Earl of Shrewsbury had more luck in his quest to process with a white wand as Hereditary Lord High Steward of Ireland. The entire processional route was decorated with heraldic emblems. The best views in Westminster Abbey were reserved for the nobility in their robes and coronets. Some insisted on travelling in their own horse-drawn coaches (though Lord Shrewsbury's horses, borrowed from a brewery, were so spooked by the crowds that he ended up jumping out and hailing a taxi while the Duke of Devonshire's coachman got lost). The unrobed elected members of the Commons had to enter a ballot for a smaller ration of inferior seats.

While the Queen approached the religious elements of the service with the utmost gravity, she was as pragmatic as ever on the other arrangements. The government might have debated long and hard over the appropriate date for the event, juggling everything from local elections to the impact on the economy and the weather, but she was entirely relaxed about the date – with just one stipulation. Her love of horseracing had grown ever stronger since her first win with Monaveen – over the

1952–55: A Reluctant Gloriana

jumps – back in 1949. She had now firmly switched her attention to racing on the Flat (to such an extent that she would go on to become champion owner in both 1954 and 1957). The Earl Marshal (the hereditary master of ceremonies) and the government were informed that her Coronation could not clash with certain big race meetings at Newmarket, Epsom or Ascot.[13]

Many aspects of the Coronation have become part of the post-war narrative of British history, not least the advent of television as a mass medium. At the time of the Queen's accession in 1952, just 763,000 homes owned a television.[14] That had more than quadrupled to 3.2 million in time for Coronation Day, with an estimated 27 million viewers gathered round those early, grainy screens. In other words, a single royal occasion had accelerated a media revolution. This would give rise to another example of Coronation romanticism, though the actual story would turn out to be a myth. The ceremony was only televised, so it was said, because an enlightened and far-sighted monarch had insisted on sharing the day with her people. Indeed, according to this version of events, she had boldly fought against reactionary forces within both Church and state who were determined to preserve the ancient mystique of the service, safe in the knowledge that they had a ringside view themselves.

In fact, the archives show that the Queen herself was in the thick of the opposition to television cameras in Westminster Abbey. Speaking on her behalf at an early meeting of the Coronation Joint Committee in July 1952, Tommy Lascelles warned that television would expose the monarch to 'the great heat and blinding light' generated by lighting rigs. The Archbishop of Canterbury argued that it was 'unfair to expose The Queen and others to this searching method of photography'. The Dean of Westminster complained of the pressure 'if Her Majesty knew that she was being closely watched by so great a number of persons'.[15] All these views were relayed to the prime minister by Jock Colville in a report warning of the likely 'strain on The Queen (who does not herself want television)'.[16]

Colville also let slip the real reason for all this reluctance. It had nothing to do with lights and cameras, since there was no issue with the presence of film and newsreel units. What worried the Queen and her advisers was the prospect of live coverage capturing any blunders before they could be edited out. What they had not bargained for was a furious reaction from Parliament, the public and the press. The exclusion of the television cameras, and by extension the people, became a 'them and us'-style issue, with even staunchly conservative papers like *The Daily Telegraph* and *The Church of England Newspaper* joining the call for live broadcasting.[17] This led to a swift rethink by the Cabinet, the Church and the Royal Household. Fearful that their lofty opposition to the cameras might lead to direct criticism of the Queen herself, they were suddenly willing to seek a compromise with the BBC. A deal was struck whereby the whole service could be televised, provided that there was no filming of the anointing or of Holy Communion and that the cameras offered 'no more intimate view than that available to a spectator with one of the best seats in the abbey'.[18] This was all 'subject to The Queen's approval', and only then did she give her consent.

The effect of that decision was to cement 2 June 1953 in the national memory as one of the great days in twentieth-century history. Thrilled by the news that a British-led expedition had just made the first ascent of Mount Everest, the UK could enjoy – for a short while, at any rate – a sense of being on top of the world once more. The British Empire might now have come to an end, replaced by the fledgling Commonwealth of Nations, but here were all the trappings of an imperial power

1952–55: A Reluctant Gloriana

as 16,000 troops from every realm on every continent, of every creed and in uniforms of every colour, paraded through the capital on foot and on horseback in homage to a common sovereign. There were so many additional processions for Princes, Princesses, prime ministers and protectorates that the Royal Mews had to borrow another fleet of carriages from the film producer, Sir Alexander Korda.[19]

At the centre of it was the ethereally still, serene and youthful figure carried in her Gold State Coach to embrace her duty and destiny in a dumbstruck Westminster Abbey. She would look happy and elated afterwards but, during the short journey to the Abbey, onlookers observed an intense solemnity. Five and a half years on from the same journey to the same place for her wedding to Philip, she was now betrothed to the people. The crowning place of monarchs for the best part of a millennium, it had been transformed to four times its normal capacity for an event visible, for the first time, to the entire world. No matter that the Queen had pledged her life to her people six years earlier, on her twenty-first birthday, and had already reigned for more than a year. That moment when the Archbishop of Canterbury lowered St Edward's Crown onto her head – prompting an electric cry of 'God Save the Queen!' around the abbey, across the capital and far beyond – was deemed the consecration of that marriage between the monarch and her realms. It was one which would last longer than any other. The dismal weather had only seemed to add to the authentic Britishness of the occasion. It also made a star of another queen. Save for Elizabeth II herself, one of the most popular and fondly remembered participants that day would always be a beaming Queen Sālote of Tonga, defying the elements and steadfastly refusing to raise the roof on her carriage in solidarity with the rain-drenched crowds.

Elizabeth II

Tonga would not have to wait too long before the compliment was repaid. The Queen and her advisers were all too conscious that the Commonwealth needed to see its new monarch. She would always hate letting people down (hence those apologies in Kenya in the very first hours of her reign), and she was acutely conscious that her furthest realms had been deprived of a royal visit on multiple occasions. The Commonwealth had still been the British Empire when George VI had made his last journey overseas for his 1947 tour of South Africa. He had arranged visits to Canada, Australia and New Zealand but had to cancel due to illness. His daughter's subsequent attempt to reach the Pacific on his behalf had barely begun when his death had brought her straight home.

The much-postponed prospect of finally seeing a reigning monarch for the first time in history therefore meant that those parts of the globe were experiencing an even more virulent dose of Coronation fever as the Queen and the Duke of Edinburgh departed Britain in November 1953. It would be their longest absence yet from Prince Charles and Princess Anne, who would remain in the care of the Queen Mother and miss yet another Christmas with their parents. The monarch flew first to Bermuda and on to Jamaica before boarding the *Gothic* (the chartered liner that had been waiting for her in vain in Kenya the previous year). After sailing through the Panama Canal, they headed for Fiji and then on to Tonga. Even in her final years, the Queen would gleefully recall sitting cross-legged at Queen Sālote's banquet and being serenaded by nose flautists.[20]

The royal party arrived in New Zealand just in time for Christmas, where she delivered that broadcast about her 'Tudor forbear'. If the Kiwis were effusive in their welcome, Australia went further still when the Queen and Prince Philip arrived in

1952–55: A Reluctant Gloriana

January 1954. In the major cities like Melbourne, waiting crowds would exceed one million. As Dr Jane Connors chronicled in a fascinating doctoral thesis on the tour, entitled 'The Glittering Thread', small towns like Lithgow experienced the first and only traffic jam in history. It was officially estimated that 75 per cent of the Australian population travelled to see the Queen with their own eyes. Inevitably there were dramas, not least when the collapse of a grandstand in Cairns injured 500, and frantic social one-upmanship as civic worthies fought for royal introductions. The premier of Queensland, for one, inflicted a hand-numbing 260 introductions on the Queen in just forty-one minutes.

In every state, she was determined to meet and thank those who had fought for four generations of her family. For, in addition to rallies and receptions for veterans of both world wars, there were separate events for the old soldiers of another conflict: the Boer War. Inevitably, there were moments when it was all too much, one of which was caught on camera.

A three-man film crew waiting to capture the Queen's encounter with koalas, during a weekend break in Victoria, started rolling their camera as the door of the royal chalet opened. Out ran Prince Philip, followed by a flying tennis racket, flying shoes and a furious Queen ordering him back inside. The presence of a film crew meant that someone had blundered with the diary. Next to appear, verging on apoplexy, was the royal press secretary, Commander Richard Colville, who instantly retrieved the film from the gobsmacked cameraman. Not long afterwards, a tray of beer and sandwiches was offered in return before the Queen reappeared wearing her best smile. 'I'm sorry for that little interlude,' she explained to the trio, 'but, as you know, it happens in every marriage. Now, what would you like me to do?'

Elizabeth II

This incident, unearthed by Connors in a 1996 interview with the cameraman and first published by this author in 2011, is still fascinating on several levels. Not only does it show the balance of power between the Palace and the media in those early years, but it reminds us that, far from being a leisurely 'tour' in the customary sense, this six-month circumnavigation was the most ambitious and intensive royal expedition of all time. And, whatever the genesis of this epic royal bust-up, it also reveals that Elizabeth II's Herculean powers of composure and self-restraint were not limitless.

The royal couple were not reintroduced to their children until May 1954, by which time there had been a further addition to the family. The new royal yacht, HMY *Britannia*, had passed her sea trials and had made her maiden voyage out to the Eastern Mediterranean, bringing Prince Charles and Princess Anne. The children had a very happy private reunion with their parents in Libya at Tobruk (then still littered with the detritus of the siege and battle of 1941). From there, they all sailed home together as a family, with three-year-old Princess Anne having her first lesson in royal precedence. During their first Sunday morning service together in the Royal Dining Room, the captain (the Queen had rejected the idea of a ship's chaplain) recited the usual prayers for the Queen, the Duke, Prince Charles and 'all the Royal Family'. Whereupon a tiny voice piped up: 'He hasn't prayed for me, Mummy.'[21] Once back in the English Channel, *Britannia* picked up Winston Churchill for the final homeward leg. As the Queen would fondly recall, the prime minister was alongside her on deck as the yacht sailed up the Thames Estuary. Her observation that the Thames was looking rather muddy prompted an instant outburst of vintage Churchill at his romantic best: 'This, Ma'am,' he declared, 'is the silver thread that runs through British history . . .'[22]

Chapter Six

1955–60

Rifts

It was Churchill's twilight as prime minister. In 1953, shortly after the Coronation, he had suffered a stroke, but had insisted it be covered up while he soldiered on unsteadily. The Queen's long absence until the spring of 1954 had provided a perfect excuse for him to delay his retirement, and her return seemed to bolster him all the more. While others, including Churchill's own doctor, Lord Moran, had looked to the Queen as the one person who might be able to persuade him to retire, she felt in no position to advise the greatest statesman of the age to exit the stage. Moran had first suggested the idea in 1952 via her first private secretary, Tommy Lascelles, a staunch Churchill ally, who had rejected it.[1] Three years later, as 1955 dawned, the grand old statesman was tenaciously clinging to office, to the despair of his natural successor, foreign secretary Sir Anthony Eden. By now, Lascelles had been replaced by Michael Adeane, who had also worked for George VI but could see that it was time for Churchill to hand over. Churchill's family agreed. So, too, did his own private secretary, Jock Colville, who advised Eden not to argue with Churchill but to deploy 'amiability'.[2] That did the trick, although there were several false

Elizabeth II

starts as the prime minister aired an intention to go only to rescind it a few days later. When Churchill finally told the Queen, on 31 March, that he was going to step down, she immediately sealed the deal with a letter, via Adeane, saying that she 'recognised your wisdom in taking the decision'.[3] Whether this was the Queen's own shrewd move or Adeane's idea, it showed that Lilibet was now happy to assert herself with the most formidable political player of the age.

On 5 April 1955, dressed in a frock coat, Churchill went to the Palace for his formal resignation. The Queen and her officials were relieved when he declined her offer of a dukedom. Though the Palace had long held a policy of not creating new dukes, except royal ones, Churchill's closest allies felt that he should at least be offered the honour. The Queen agreed, having been assured by Jock Colville that the prime minister would say no, as indeed he did. She would dearly miss her audiences with the only prime minister she routinely referred to thereafter by his first name. Tommy Lascelles recorded in his diary that these occasions had been 'punctuated by peals of laughter' and frequently ended with Churchill 'wiping his eyes'.[4] One person delighted to see the back of the old man, however, was the Tory Party's long-serving heir apparent, Sir Anthony Eden.

His short premiership would be remembered for two episodes, both of which left the Queen in an uncomfortable position. On the day of her Coronation, while all eyes were on the Queen, a sharp-eyed journalist had noticed an intimacy between Princess Margaret and Group Captain Peter Townsend, the dashing, decorated wartime fighter who had been equerry to George VI. More pertinently, he was recently divorced from his wife, Rosemary. The mother of his two young sons had tired of him putting the Royal Family before his own and had sought love elsewhere.

* * *

1955–60: Rifts

Everything had changed after the King's death, when Townsend had been transferred to the Queen Mother's household at Clarence House, also home to Princess Margaret. Romance ensued and, in the run-up to the Coronation, the couple had confided in the Queen that they wished to marry. The last thing the Royal Household needed on the eve of the Queen's crowning was the spectre of a divorcé marrying into the family, less than two decades on from the abdication crisis. The Queen had, therefore, asked them to keep things entirely private and wait a year before making any further decision.

However, when Princess Margaret was observed picking a piece of fluff from Townsend's uniform outside Westminster Abbey, Fleet Street knew it was on to something. As the story was breaking, Tommy Lascelles and Winston Churchill had teamed up once again to direct the royal response on behalf of a worried Queen and a flabbergasted Queen Mother. Townsend was given an instant posting overseas, as air attaché to the British Embassy in Brussels, while the Princess was persuaded to let things lie for two years until she was twenty-five. This was the age at which a member of the Royal Family could wed without the monarch's consent, subject to the approval of Parliament.

It was inconceivable that the Queen would stand in the way of the beloved younger sister for whom she still felt so protective and sympathetic in the wake of the King's death; Elizabeth had the throne and a family, while Margaret, for all her privilege, had neither. It had always rankled that Lilibet, as heir to the throne, had received extra education, not least those history lessons at Eton with Sir Henry Marten, while this was not deemed a necessity for Margaret. It all left her harbouring the time-honoured resentment of 'the spare'. Though both Churchill and Lascelles had retired by the time she had to make up her mind, Margaret's romantic intentions had lost none of their constitutional and political significance. She was still third in line to the throne and destined to play an important part in public life – at public expense. How would the British people, the Church and the other Commonwealth realms react to her marrying a divorced man? Weighing up the options was now a task for Prime Minister Eden, a task made all the more awkward by his own status as a divorced man.

When the time came, Margaret and Townsend decided to go their separate ways. On 31 October 1955, the Princess issued her famous statement that she had reached her decision 'mindful of the Church's teaching'. Over the years, a popular narrative has taken root of a heartbroken Princess thwarted by an icy Establishment which threatened to snatch away her royal birthright, status and wealth if she followed the path of true love. Declassified Cabinet papers, however, have shown that the prime minister, and ultimately the Queen, had proposed a generous package. The Princess would have been able to marry Townsend and retain her title and royal lifestyle, the only concession being that she would have lost her place in the line of succession (as would any children of the marriage). Was that the stumbling block? Or had the Lascelles/Churchill strategy of keeping the couple apart for two years succeeded? There was a notable lack of urgency about their eventual reunion. Writing to Eden ahead of her twenty-fifth birthday in August 1955, the Princess told the prime minister she could only 'properly decide' about the future when they were eventually reunited – which would not be for another two months.[5]

The decision came as a huge relief within the palace. The Queen, never confrontational at the best of times, had done her best to avoid or subcontract family showdowns, as she would do for much of her life. When Margaret had tried to broach the subject at Balmoral during that summer, her elder sister had

1955–60: Rifts

made every attempt to avoid it.[6] Now, the first potential major crisis of the reign had been averted. The following year, Lilibet would face a very different political dilemma, one which would lead on to a painful and personal challenge.

The Suez affair is often likened to Britain's 2016 vote to leave the European Union in terms of the way it broke up families, friendships and international alliances. In July 1956, the Egyptian president, General Nasser, nationalized the Suez Canal, the great maritime link between the Mediterranean and the Indian Ocean, previously under British-French control. Eden, already sick with a form of sepsis, hatched a plot with France and Israel whereby Israel would invade the Sinai peninsula. This would kickstart a localized war, which would give Britain and France a pretext to recapture and 'protect' the canal. The operation had barely started – with the British public split down the middle – when concerted opposition from the USA and the Commonwealth brought it to a halt. Britain was forced into a humiliating retreat and Eden resigned soon afterwards.

Historians continue to debate how much Eden had told the Queen and whether she could or should have advised him against this shambolic adventure. More than half a century later, what remained etched in her mind was not the politics but her own sense of helplessness. It was a memory she would share with successive aides who worked closely with her. 'She always said it was one of her lowest points,' said one who knew her well in her later years. 'She told me she was four years into her reign, so still very young and inexperienced and being patronized by old men. Churchill had just gone, the new prime minister was ill and it was worse because Prince Philip was away.'[7] The Duke was, by now, on his way to open the Melbourne Olympics. 'I think the basic dishonesty of the whole thing was a trouble,' reflected Martin Charteris, her then deputy private

Elizabeth II

secretary, some years later.[8] Even more troubling, according to the Queen, was that her senior advisers were giving her conflicting advice about the wisdom of the Suez adventure.

All through her reign, there would be a trio of private secretaries. In 1956, the principal and most senior, Sir Michael Adeane (who had recently replaced Tommy Lascelles), had been in favour of the Suez operation, while the deputy, Charteris (who had been with her since Princess days), had been against. So, too, had been her number three, the assistant private secretary, Edward Ford. 'What the Queen learned from that was the importance of firm advice from her own team,' said her former aide. As the Queen told him: 'The worst thing was having three private secretaries arguing among themselves – and I couldn't get hold of Philip.'[9]

It is an intriguing and illuminating acknowledgement of the role of the Duke of Edinburgh in her decision-making, at a time when those 'old men' were doing their level best to keep him as far away from affairs of state as possible. Might she have been more combative – or at least confident with Eden – if the Duke had been there to embolden her? 'I don't think she welcomed his advice on anything constitutional,' said one former private secretary from her later years. 'In those days she just wanted his presence, his reassurance. But I suspect there were a few incidents early on when the Duke got his fingers burned, when things came to a head, and he said, "Don't expect me to get involved any more".'[10]

The slights and put-downs from the Palace old guard, noted earlier, were still ongoing. His response was to throw himself into a succession of innovative new schemes which continue to leave a lasting mark to this day. Two were created in the same year, 1956: the launch of the Duke of Edinburgh's Award, a confidence-building youth programme, and the first

1955–60: Rifts

Commonwealth Study Conference in Oxford, an attempt to find common cause between future captains of industry and future trade union leaders. Both ventures had plenty of critics. His award scheme was likened to the Hitler Youth and deemed a threat to the Scouting movement, while the study conference was attacked for radical socialist leanings (the main organizer, Peter Parker, had once been a Labour parliamentary candidate*). Yet more than 8 million young people worldwide can now claim a 'D of E' award, and past beneficiaries of the Duke's study conferences have included a prime minister (Australia's Bob Hawke) and Britain's former Labour home secretary, Alan Johnson, who later spoke of the programme as 'at that stage . . . the most important event of my life'.[11]

The Duke had no shortage of responsibilities. One of the Queen's first decisions after succeeding to the throne was to put him in charge of the royal estates and appoint him to succeed her father as Ranger of Windsor Great Park, a role he loved to his dying day. However, the constant carping of the Establishment old guard at home had left him restless and missing his days as a rising star of the Royal Navy. As previously discussed, the Queen's formal rejection of his family name in the first days of the reign had wounded him. Hence she had been happy to let him undertake his long trip in the new royal yacht, to open the Olympics in Melbourne on her behalf. From there, he was to set sail to some of the most remote parts of the Commonwealth and Antarctica. The television drama *The Crown* would later paint it as a riotous, debauched adventure through the South Seas, when it was actually a rather earnest scientific expedition through penguin territory. Indeed, the trip

---

* As Sir Peter Parker, he was chairman of British Rail under both Labour and Conservative governments.

was something of an epiphany. Not only did the Duke learn to paint, having invited the celebrated artist, Edward Seago, to join the party, but his study of the flora and fauna of the southern hemisphere would kindle a lifelong interest in bird-watching and nature. It was why, five years later, he was a co-founder of the World Wildlife Fund (WWF) and went on to become its hands-on international president for many years.

Around the world, the trip was attracting headlines for different reasons. The marriage of the Duke's equerry, Mike Parker, had mirrored that of Peter Townsend. While at sea, Parker's wife, Eileen, tired of coming second to the beck and call of royal service, had filed for divorce. The mere mention of the d-word so close to the Duke caused lurid international media speculation about the state of the royal marriage. Parker abandoned ship and, later, his royal role in a bid to quell the gossip.

By now, the world's press had been delving into every aspect of Parker's private life, including the Thursday Club, an all-male weekly lunch gathering above a London restaurant, where the equerry and his boss would escape the stuffiness of the Royal Household for a few hours each week. Though more boisterous and raffish than the average gentlemen's club, it had no show-girls or cabaret and simply involved good gossip and colourful jokes over oysters and wine. The Duke was hardly going to be getting up to any great mischief among a membership which included the editors of two national newspapers, several journalists, assorted actors – including Peter Ustinov and David Niven – and senior politicians. However, as the rumours swirled and grew, so did its new-found notoriety; if it was not quite painted as the Folies Bergère, then it was very much the sort of place where a member of the Royal Family should *not* be socializing in staid, late fifties London. The foreign press could

1955–60: Rifts

scarcely restrain itself, with the *Baltimore Sun*'s Joan Graham leading the charge under the headline 'London Rumors Of Rift In Royal Family Growing'.[12] The Queen's press secretary issued an extraordinary statement declaring that it was 'quite untrue that there is any rift between the Queen and the Duke.' Though it was humiliating for the Queen to have to acknowledge public doubts about her marriage, she must have approved the wording. However, it seems more likely that the response was driven by the Duke. As Mike Parker told Gyles Brandreth: 'The Duke was incandescent. He was very, very angry. And deeply hurt. There was no truth in the story whatsoever.'[13] Either way, it was an error of judgement by Commander Colville, as it meant that loyally deferential British papers, which had steadfastly ignored the story until now, had to report it, too. For millions of British royalists, it was the first time that they had even thought to question the strength of the Queen's marriage. The royal couple were finally reunited in Portugal, where their obvious, unfeigned happiness in each other's company laid the rumours to rest.

On their return, the Queen sought to draw a line under an episode that had caused her much distress and invoked memories of the Pat Kirkwood saga a decade before. She wanted to send a clear signal that she adored her husband as much as ever and asked Eden's successor as prime minister, Harold Macmillan, to endorse her plan to make Philip a Prince of the United Kingdom. Ten years on from relinquishing his Greek and Danish princely status in order to become a British citizen and marry Princess Elizabeth, he was princely once again. The idea had been floating around for a while, but now was the time for a public show of appreciation for her husband.

Feeling more appreciated and emboldened in his own home once again, Prince Philip started to help the Queen gently

Elizabeth II

modernize her Court. He also encouraged her to drop the annual ritual of debutantes being 'presented at Court'. An extra palace garden party for another 8,000 guests from across the social spectrum was subsequently added to the calendar, as was the Duke's suggestion of 'luncheons'. As far removed from the Thursday Club model as possible, these would include an eminent but random cross-section of national life. Every few months, a university academic, perhaps, plus an actress, a bishop, a headmistress and an army general would be among those pleasantly astonished to receive, out of the blue, an invitation to lunch at the palace.

An early champion of television, the Duke was also an enthusiastic supporter of proposals to switch the Christmas broadcast from radio to television. This would ruin Christmas lunch for the Queen, since, for the first two years, it would have to be transmitted live. Ever the pragmatist, she would always remember that inaugural live on-camera address in 1957 not for the added stress, but for the discomfort. 'I once talked to her about that first televised Christmas message and said it must have been a nightmare,' former prime minister David Cameron recalled. 'But it wasn't being live on TV which was the issue. She said the biggest problem was having to open all the windows at Sandringham to get all the cabling in. She said: "It's cold enough in that house as it is, but we had these massive cables going in and the whole place was freezing".'[14]

These were not random innovations. The Queen and Prince Philip had been reading the national mood. Any lingering Coronation-era uplift for the monarchy had now subsided while, post-Suez, Britain was unquestionably diminished, having been forced to desist from military action by the USA and others. In August 1957, a lesser-known magazine, *The National and English Review*, would acquire instant fame for carrying a surprisingly pointed attack on the Queen herself. The lengthy critique of a 'priggish schoolgirl' and her 'tweedy' Court earned the article's author, John Grigg, a public punch in the face from an aggrieved royalist. Soon afterwards, on the eve of the Queen's 1957 state visit to the USA, the journalist Malcolm Muggeridge wrote a similarly scathing piece for America's *Saturday Evening Post*, calling the Queen 'dowdy, frumpish and banal' and mocking the monarchy as 'a kind of ersatz religion'. Though both attacks were rooted in intellectual snobbery, with generous helpings of misogyny, it did not go unnoticed at the Palace that these were not being penned by radical republicans. Grigg was an Old Etonian Tory peer with the title of Lord Altrincham, Muggeridge a Cambridge-educated former deputy editor of *The Daily Telegraph*.

Five years in to her reign, the Queen had been toughened up by these early reverses. And, as she would find so often during her time as monarch, a good antidote to criticism at home was flying the flag abroad. Her 1957 state visit to France drew such large crowds that the police guard had to draw their ceremonial swords outside the opera. Later that same year, her state visit to the USA helped Britain move on from the Suez debacle in a way which no politician could achieve, culminating in a ticker-tape welcome from more than a million New Yorkers. She received a similarly delirious welcome from Chicago – and from Canada, too – in 1959 when she sailed the length of the newly opened St Lawrence Seaway in the Royal Yacht. It was not seasickness that took its toll during the voyage, however. As with that sensational visit to Paris in 1948, Lilibet was keeping a very happy secret.

Chapter Seven

1960–69

Mountbatten-Windsor

The arrival of Prince Andrew on 19 February 1960 has sometimes been likened to the start of the Queen's second family. Charles and Anne had been born to a princess married to a serving Royal Naval officer shortly before family life was turned upside down by events. Now, the Queen would dictate the rhythms of that family life; duties would fit in around the needs of Andrew, not the other way round.

The baby's name was another fillip for Philip, being that of his late father. So, too, was the Queen's plea to the government shortly before the birth, when she told the prime minister, Harold Macmillan, and later his acting deputy, R. A. 'Rab' Butler, that she wanted to change the family surname, for all those born in the future through her own line, to Mountbatten-Windsor.

Tellingly, both men would record how upset the Queen had been at this time. Butler later said it was the first time he had seen her in tears. The heavily pregnant monarch was clearly still wanting to ensure that Philip felt he was a valued master of his own home. As with the decision to make him a prince of the United Kingdom, so the change of surname was to atone

Elizabeth II

for the hurt felt by the Duke of Edinburgh back in 1952. In pursuing this, the Queen was egged on both by the Duke and by what the press magnate Lord Beaverbrook called 'overtures' from Lord Mountbatten, still as dynastically ambitious as ever.[1] It would surely not have happened under the Churchill/Lascelles axis, but the Queen was growing in confidence and stature with each passing year. In pushing this change, however, Lilibet would still have met ferocious resistance from the Queen Mother, in full 'I don't think the King would have . . .' mode. Loyal wife trumped loyal daughter, but it cannot have been easy. Hence the tears. No one could possibly have imagined that, decades later, the princely child who had been the catalyst for the new surname would be the first to be a plain 'Mr' Mountbatten-Windsor.

The Queen empowered the Duke of Edinburgh in other ways which would invoke the disapproval of the Queen Mother, notably the choice of education for Prince Charles. The Queen Mother was strongly in favour of sending him to Eton, but Prince Philip decided that his eldest son should follow his own path, first to prep school at Cheam in Berkshire and then on to Gordonstoun in the far north of Scotland. The Prince, famously, would come to loathe his schooldays in the Highlands.

The one time the Queen did take charge was during the Duke's solo trip to the southern hemisphere, hiring a friend to act as an avuncular companion to Charles and Anne. Michael Farebrother, an Old Etonian ex-Guards officer, had met Princess Elizabeth at Windsor during the war while stationed there with the Grenadier Guards. He had also been part of that select posse entrusted to chaperone Elizabeth and Margaret when they disappeared into the London night on VE Day. After leaving the army, he became the lifelong bachelor headmaster of a small Sussex prep school, leaving only to answer the summons to the royal nursery. As well as teaching Charles – 'a calm and thoughtful little boy with an artistic side' – and Anne, he would recall dancing to the wireless with the Queen Mother and Princess Margaret's fondness for rock 'n' roll.[2] Once Prince Philip had returned from his travels, however, all educational decisions had reverted to him.

At thirty-three, the Queen adored being a new mother all over again – but, within a year of Andrew's birth, she was throwing herself into global diplomacy once more. In June 1961, she welcomed President John F. Kennedy and his wife, Jacqueline, to Buckingham Palace in between two groundbreaking world tours. Just fourteen years on from the end of Empire, she made a state visit to India and Pakistan. Given the pain and mayhem of Partition in 1947 and the very mixed memories of imperial rule (her host, Prime Minister Jawaharlal Nehru, had been imprisoned by Britain nine times), there were obvious risks. Yet the welcomes were euphoric and the crowds in Delhi and Calcutta were perhaps the largest she would ever see in her life.

A similarly high-stakes mission was a tour of Africa. MPs at Westminster had called for one leg of the trip, her state visit to Ghana, to be cancelled due to an outbreak of bombings. However, the president of the newly independent republic, Kwame Nkrumah, was being wooed away from the Commonwealth by the Soviets and the Queen saw it as her task to woo him back. 'She loves her duty and means to be a Queen and not a puppet,' wrote prime minister Harold Macmillan.[3] Jubilant photos of her dancing with Nkrumah made headlines right round the world, with one exception. The new white supremacist regime in South Africa refused to publish images of a Black socialist firebrand dancing with the white Head of the Commonwealth,

Elizabeth II

the organization from which it had been ostracized following the introduction of apartheid.

Prince Andrew's birth had delayed another happy announcement, which was made a week later. Princess Margaret was engaged to society photographer Tony Armstrong-Jones. Though elements of the aristocratic old guard were appalled that the daughter of the late King Emperor should be marrying a photographer (some European royalty declined an invitation), there was a general sense of royal relief. Theirs would be the first televised royal wedding, followed by the first royal honeymoon in the royal yacht (paid for by the Queen to obviate complaints about public expense). At the threshold of the sixties, of course, no one had any inkling of the social revolution ahead, yet there was a clear sense of a rejuvenated monarchy moving with the times. It would soon have to move much faster, however, to keep up with the changing cultural and political landscape.

The Queen was growing wearily familiar with the internal problems of the Conservative Party, which had a habit of changing its leaders while running the country and leaving her to choose each replacement. When Churchill had resigned as prime minister, she merely had the straightforward task of appointing Eden, in the absence of a rival candidate. When he had resigned in January 1957 after Suez, she had been forced to choose between two clear candidates for the job, Rab Butler and Harold Macmillan. The party elders advised her that the latter commanded the greater support. The situation suddenly became very much more problematic in 1963 when Macmillan was suddenly hospitalized with prostate problems in the middle of his party's annual conference. He decided to resign while at least five of his colleagues were jostling for position.

1960–69: Mountbatten-Windsor

When the Queen came to his bedside to say farewell, he read out a prepared memorandum advising her that he had taken soundings from all sections of the party and that she should send for the foreign secretary, the Earl of Home, to replace him. Given that Macmillan had already resigned, he was not, constitutionally, in a position to advise her to do anything but she accepted his advice. Her decision attracted withering criticism from both Left and Right, although this was aimed not at her personally but at what ex-Tory minister and *Spectator* editor Iain Macleod called an elitist 'magic circle' of party grandees. However, the days of aristocratic prime ministers running the country from the House of Lords had ended with the retirement of Lord Salisbury in 1902. Lord Home would need to be an MP, so renounced his peerage, fought a hasty by-election and entered the Commons under his family name as Sir Alec Douglas-Home (he was already a Knight of the Thistle, hence the 'Sir').

The Queen could not have wished for a more congenial prime minister, one whom she knew socially and who spoke the language of grouse moor and country house. 'Of course, she loved Alec and Alec loved her,' her former private secretary, Lord Charteris, recalled years later.[4] 'I think she saw him very much as a fellow landowner of Scottish territory – almost a member of the family.' However cosy their rapport might be at a social level, it was politically toxic for both sides.

The appointment of a friendly Earl as prime minister came just weeks after a Conservative Party sex scandal which had touched the highest echelons of society. The Secretary of State for war, Jack Profumo, having had an affair with dancer Christine Keeler, the mistress of a Russian spy, then tried and failed to lie his way out of it and resigned. The tawdry episode had all unfolded at Cliveden, one of Britain's grandest stately

Elizabeth II

homes, where the Royal Family had been frequent guests. Among the public at large, there was a growing sense of a sleazy, out-of-touch, failing Establishment cadre which seemed to have much in common with the Royal Family. The risk of collateral damage to the monarchy was self-evident. In 1964, the Queen was booed in public for the first time (the boos had been aimed at her state visitor, King Paul of Greece, but it would have been unthinkable just a few years earlier). Satire and irreverence were on the airwaves and in print as a new wave of iconoclastic young media stars pushed back against old-school deference. Mods, rockers, pop and the Beatles were in the ascendant.

A discernible sense of mild disenchantment with the monarchy was not confined to Britain. In March 1963, the Queen returned to Australia and New Zealand for the first time since that triumphal post-Coronation tour to be greeted by respectable if unremarkable crowds. Nothing could ever replicate the hysteria of their first tour and, with the advent of television (which had not reached Australia until 1956), many people preferred to follow the royal couple on screen. Both the media and diplomats had also noted that the Queen looked tired and was showing, in the words of *The Guardian*, 'reservedly scant' appreciation for those crowds that did turn out. The 'smiling problem' would continue for many years to come.

The changing mood may help explain the Queen's acquiescence in one of the most bizarre Establishment cover-ups of her reign. In April 1964, British intelligence confirmed that the Surveyor of the Queen's Pictures, Sir Anthony Blunt, had been a Russian spy since the 1930s and through the Second World War, collaborating with some of the most notorious traitors of the Cold War era, including Guy Burgess and Donald Maclean. Rather than prosecute Blunt for treason, the home secretary decided he would be allowed to remain quietly in his post in exchange for a full confession and list of names. That would also spare various parts of the Establishment – notably MI5 and the Palace – from the taint of another humiliating scandal.

The Queen's private secretary, Sir Michael Adeane, was informed, but, officially, the Queen was not. Adeane and his colleagues must have been very happy to play along with the deceit. Blunt had been entrusted with several sensitive post-war errands on behalf of the monarchy, helping to retrieve Royal Family papers and treasures from German relatives before they could be looted by American and Russian occupying forces. It was later reported that Blunt was the mysterious intermediary who, in 1963, bought up a series of sketches of members of the Royal Family by Stephen Ward, a central figure in the Profumo scandal. Though the drawings themselves might not be controversial, the association certainly was. In other words, full exposure of Blunt could have been deeply embarrassing for the monarchy on multiple fronts, especially at a time when sleaze in high places was dragging down the ruling party.

So, what did the Queen really know? It seems inconceivable that a monarch who liked to be appraised of all matters great, small and trivial within the Royal Household, right down to misconduct by an errant footman, had no inkling that a senior courtier had confessed to treachery. Adeane may not have told her formally, in order to give her deniability whenever the truth was revealed (as it was by Margaret Thatcher in 1979), but she could not have failed to find out why, for the next eight years until his retirement, the man responsible for her art was somehow never in the same room as her.

The Palace can be as punctilious about *not* recording some things as it is about making formal records of others. In 2025, a declassified MI5 file revealed that she was officially informed

Elizabeth II

by Adeane's successor, Martin Charteris, in 1973. It was a year after Blunt's retirement from the palace, he was seriously ill and MI5 felt the Queen should be told before the truth emerged in an obituary (he would not actually die until 1983). The document reported her reaction: 'She took it all very calmly and without surprise: she remembered that [Blunt] had been under suspicion way back in the aftermath of the Burgess/Maclean case.'[5] As is shown elsewhere, the Queen was indeed unshockable. Another explanation for that lack of surprise, however, is that there was no surprise at all.

Six months after Blunt's confession, a thirteen-year run of four consecutive tweedy Tory prime ministers came to an end at the 1964 general election. After just a year in office, Sir Alec Douglas-Home was gone and Elizabeth II welcomed her first Labour government, just as she was also welcoming a playmate for Prince Andrew. 'Goodness, what fun it is to have a baby in the house again!' she exclaimed after the birth of Prince Edward on 10 March 1964. 'He is a great joy to us all.'[6]

The Queen soon settled into an easy rapport with Harold Wilson, the Yorkshire-born son of an industrial chemist. He realized that she enjoyed the human dimension of political gossip and was happy to share it. As Tony Blair would observe years later, the more traditional working-class Labour voters would always be the most pro-royal, and the Royal Family felt much the same way in return. It was the intellectuals and middle-class radicals from whom the Palace had more to fear. They hated rituals like kneeling and kissing hands in order to be sworn into the Privy Council. Few were more energetic than Wilson's Postmaster General, Anthony Wedgewood-Benn, who became obsessed with removing the Queen's head from the UK's postage stamps and even showed his plans to the Queen herself. Somewhat naively, he imagined that her polite interest equated to some sort of approval. Whatever thoughts she then passed on to Wilson at the subsequent weekly audience, the prime minister ensured that the plan went nowhere. 'Harold Wilson understood that the more radical you are, the more you need to keep the form of substance and tradition around you,' the writer Sir Antony Jay, veteran analyst of both royalty and government, told this author.[7]

In 1965, there was a further sense that the old order had moved on as the Queen led the world in mourning the death of Sir Winston Churchill. He had known her all her life and as far as she was concerned, it had been Churchill together with her adored father who had delivered Britain from annihilation. She had no qualms about abandoning protocol, allowing both the coffin of her greatest subject and the Churchill family to take precedence over the sovereign. By coincidence, it came as she was preparing for another landmark moment: her first state visit to Germany.

Though twenty years had passed since the end of the war, it was still fresh in so many minds. The Queen, personally, had been especially worried that adverse comment in the British press would sour the visit.[8] Equally, royal officials were certainly attuned to mutterings about the Royal Family being overly pro-German due to their own family roots and connections; it was not that long ago that the Duke of Edinburgh's German relations had been barred from his own wedding. The Queen had a cunning strategy of her own to get the tour off to a flying start. She had asked the designer Hardy Amies to create a dress to match the rococo décor of the venue on the opening night, the Schloss Augustusburg in Brühl. Her hosts and the German press were both astonished and flattered by the gesture. Before a word had been spoken, that turquoise silk satin dress had set the tone of a tour which, along with John F. Kennedy's 'Ich bin ein Berliner' visit two years before, is regarded as a key moment in West Germany's post-war rehabilitation. As she would show time and again through her reign, the Queen might have had a minimal interest in fashion, yet she fully understood its power as a diplomatic tool. And she also enjoyed using it.

As ever, the monarchy would be expected to lead the nation through triumph and disaster, never more so than in 1966. Three months on from handing the captain of the England football team the World Cup trophy at Wembley Stadium, she was in the Welsh mining village of Aberfan. In what remains one of the most shocking tragedies in post-war British history, a colliery slag heap collapsed, smothering the local school, leaving 146 dead, most of whom were children.

Years later, her decision not to visit the scene until eight days afterwards would lead to accusations of indecision or, worse, a lack of royal compassion. The official reason was that she did not want to hamper rescue efforts. The reality, according to those close to her, was that she was worried she would break down in public. It was just nineteen months since she had given birth to Prince Edward. There were profuse royal tears when she visited the home of one bereaved family, and she only just managed to maintain her composure when a little girl presented her with flowers and a card. It was signed: 'From the remaining children of Aberfan.'

Harold Wilson's government would be long-remembered for its social reform agenda. Laws on abortion, homosexuality and divorce were all relaxed, while capital punishment was abolished. The Queen was neither a 'hanger and flogger', nor an abolitionist. As her former private secretary, Lord Charteris, said years later, she had never been 'unduly perturbed' by the death penalty. However, she would ensure she was always readily available to the home secretary in case she was needed to sign a last-minute stay of execution, and rather enjoyed doing so. 'The bit that she did was always to let the chap off, you see,' Charteris explained. 'So she had the nice bit to do.'[9]

The Queen would soon find herself personally caught up in this incoming tide of what right-wing critics bemoaned as 'the permissive society'. In 1967, her cousin, the Earl of Harewood, a grandson of George V, sought a divorce from Marion, the mother of his three sons. He wanted to marry Patricia Tuckwell, the mother of another child, born out of wedlock, but, under the terms of the Royal Marriages Act, would need the Queen's permission.

Given the toxicity of anything to do with divorce in the royal orbit, after the Margaret/Townsend affair, the abdication and even the collapse of Mike Parker's marriage just ten years earlier, the Queen was troubled. She was very fond of Harewood, but fearful of any charges of hypocrisy from the formidable traditionalist wing of the Church of England. Just the year before, the Queen had attended the first multifaith service of thanksgiving for the Commonwealth in a London church, whereupon the Bishop of London had received complaints about 'heathen rites'. She turned, once again, to Harold Wilson for help.

A plan was hatched whereby she would formally seek the Cabinet's advice on whether to grant her consent to the remarriage. The Cabinet would unhesitatingly agree and she would be duty bound to follow their advice, while conveniently being absolved of any support for the dreaded d-word. It might be a classic royal fudge, but the royal pragmatist was extremely relieved to keep her conscience, her cousin and the traditionalists in her church at bay.

Elizabeth II

Incrementally but surely, the Queen found that her monarchy was modernizing at remarkable speed as the 1960s drew to a close. The time-honoured duty of the Lord Chamberlain's Office to approve every theatrical production was finally scrapped in 1968, and, much as traditionalists (and the Queen Mother) might see it as another salami-slicing of royal authority, Palace staff were secretly thrilled that they no longer had to censor the London stage. 'The Queen was very happy about it,' her former press secretary, Bill Heseltine, admitted years later.[10] Heseltine was himself an example of this modernization. A former high-flying young civil servant in his native Australia, he had been seconded to the Palace press office in 1965 as an assistant and quickly impressed (in due course, he would rise to the top job of principal private secretary). In 1968, he was appointed press secretary, replacing the famously media-wary Commander Richard Colville, the man Fleet Street knew as the 'Abominable No Man' for his reluctance to deal with the press.

There was another development in royal media coverage entirely beyond the Palace's control. As well as being the target of satirists and comedians, the Royal Family were now being pursued by a new breed of freelance photographer, led by a rebellious Yorkshire-born son of Italian immigrants called Ray Bellisario. He had worked as a regular magazine photographer until Richard Colville refused him accreditation for a royal tour. Enraged by the rejection, he soon discovered there could be more money in informal, undercover photography. With deference in steep decline as the 1960s progressed, there were now editors prepared to buy shots of Princess Margaret waterskiing or the Queen scowling at Prince Philip or Prince Andrew charging round Windsor Great Park on a Shetland pony. 'One of the things that started Belisario down the road to his deep antipathy to the organization,' Bill Heseltine told this author, 'was Richard's

1960–69: Mountbatten-Windsor

handling of him.'[11] The super-loyal Commander Colville had, inadvertently, contrived to create the 'royal paparazzi'.

Not long after that, the pace of change accelerated again, resulting in two royal milestones. In 1969, the Prince of Wales would turn twenty-one, and a special investiture service was planned for Caernarvon Castle, a Welsh coronation in all but name.* Unlike the investiture of the previous Prince of Wales in 1910, this would be the first royal ceremony designed for the small screen – and through the new medium of colour television, too. Bolder still was the Queen's consent for the first royal documentary.

Heseltine had argued that the time had come to explain the role which lay ahead for Prince Charles, and to show the monarchy in step with the times. 'The young ones had been kept far away from publicity while they were at school. And there was a feeling about them at the time that they were pretty dull,' Heseltine later recalled. 'At the same time, the Queen and Prince Philip, approaching middle age, were less newsworthy than they had been in the excitement of the early years of the reign.'[12]

The result was *Royal Family*, 110 minutes of fly-on-the-wall television, produced by the BBC, distributed by ITV and shown on both in June 1969. It proved so gripping that even more people watched it in Britain than another broadcasting milestone that summer: man landing on the moon. Millions sat glued to the Queen making salad dressing at a Balmoral barbecue, welcoming US president Richard Nixon to lunch, touring South America and taking Prince Edward to buy an ice cream. Respectful rather than deferential, the script, by Antony Jay, concluded on a reflective note: 'The strength of the

---

* Now known by its Welsh name, Caernarfon, the town was previously Caernarvon and, before that, Carnarvon – from which the Earldom derives.

Elizabeth II

monarchy does not lie in the power it gives the sovereign – but in the power it denies to anyone else.'

Two myths have taken hold. The first is that the film paved the way for the tabloid sensationalism which would bedevil the monarchy in years to come. The second is that the film was an embarrassing failure because it was withdrawn from circulation in the early seventies.

In fact, it was always going to have a finite shelf life, Heseltine told this author, because it was 'of its time' and 'not something which should be quarried for other programmes'.[13] Neither he nor his colleagues nor the family were in any doubt that the monarchy had to move with the times. 'In more cynical terms, the decision the Royal Family had to reach was whether they calmly sat back and let television devour them on its terms,' he explained, 'or whether they took a more active part in deciding how they might use TV.' And he laughed at any suggestion that the film was some sort of failure. Sold to 125 territories, it was repeated eleven times in Britain alone and was, at that time, the most successful television documentary in history. It also generated substantial royalties, which, under the terms of the contract, went to the Queen. She duly handed the lot to one of her charities, the British Academy of Film and Television Arts. It used the money to buy the grand Piccadilly headquarters in central London, where BAFTA continues to reside in style to this day.

Just a week after gorging on *Royal Family*, British viewers were enthralled once again as the cameras brought live coverage of the Prince of Wales's investiture at Caernarvon. Staged inside Edward I's ancient fortress, the ceremony had a Camelot-meets-*Star Trek* flavour, with plenty of sixties innovations, including a TV-friendly Perspex canopy over the stage and a princely coronet surmounted with a gold-plated ping-pong

1960–69: Mountbatten-Windsor

ball (the previous Prince of Wales, later Edward VIII, had walked off with all his regalia after his investiture).

However, official attempts to generate a carnival atmosphere in the small Welsh town could not conceal deep underlying tensions. The 'Troubles' in Northern Ireland would not commence for another six weeks, but a nascent Welsh terrorist organization was already responsible for bomb scares before, during and after the ceremony. Some bombs actually went off nearby (one within earshot), causing three deaths. These were turbulent times around the world, an era of assassinations and mounting civil disorder (even the president of France had briefly fled his own country the year before). The Queen knew the risks. She had been appalled by the shooting of President Kennedy in 1963, to the point that her doctors advised her against attending the memorial service in his honour at St Paul's Cathedral (she was five months pregnant with Prince Edward at the time). As noted earlier, she had been warned of extreme violence against herself in Ghana in 1961 and Canada in 1964. Now, though, terrorism was being focused directly at her family.

At the age of forty-three, the Queen suddenly did something she had never done before. She returned from Wales and went to bed for a week. The Palace let it be known that she was suffering from a 'feverish cold' and all engagements were cancelled. Years later, a senior official confirmed to this author that this was not down to a cold, after all, but to stress.[14] Whether it was the accumulated anxieties of seventeen years in charge, the unprecedented new levels of media exposure, the strain of a quasi-coronation against a backdrop of violence, or a combination of all of the above, we do not know. However, for the first and last time in her life, Queen Elizabeth II was having what amounted to a nervous breakdown.

Chapter Eight

1970–79

Walkabouts and Monsters

On 12 March 1970, the royal car pulled up at a civic engagement in Wellington, New Zealand, and out stepped the Queen and Prince Philip. At which point, they did not walk down the red carpet towards the official greeting line. Instead, they diverted to talk to the waiting crowds. 'How are you enjoying your day?' the Queen asked a group of women, who were so astonished that no reply was actually forthcoming.

The idea had simply been to add a little extra colour to the formulaic itinerary of royal tours Down Under. While the Queen's first visit to New Zealand and Australia in 1953–54 had been wildly successful, the next tour, in 1963, had been underwhelming if not an anti-climax. Her press secretary, Bill Heseltine, and his local colleagues came up with the idea of the royal couple meeting a few random ordinary people. The police were nervous, while old-school courtiers worried how the Queen was supposed to speak to someone without a formal introduction. When the idea was put to the Queen herself, however, she was all for giving it a go. It might not have kick-started much in the way of conversation, but that did not matter. 'The most important thing of all was that it got a name – "the

Elizabeth II

walkabout",' said Bill Heseltine.[1] That was thanks to a *Daily Mail* correspondent covering the tour, Vincent Mulchrone. 'The Queen went walkabout yesterday,' Mulchrone wrote, 'and the Monarchy is never going to be quite the same again.'[2]

He was not wrong. Wherever the Queen went thereafter, on that tour and subsequently at home, the crowds would come to expect these moments of public informality. Indeed, the walkabout would come to epitomize the gentle shift in the monarchy all through a decade which, while being a dismal period for a sclerotic Britain, would prove little short of triumphal for the Queen. Shortly after her return from the Pacific, the voters produced something of a surprise when they ejected Harold Wilson's Labour Party and returned Edward Heath and the Conservatives in the 1970 election. The night after his election win, Heath arrived late at a Windsor ball marking the seventieth birthdays of the Queen Mother, the Duke of Gloucester, Lord Mountbatten and the Duke of Beaufort. As he entered the Waterloo Chamber, there was an awkward moment as applause broke out from some of the less constitutionally correct guests.

However, anyone expecting that the new incumbent would make life easier for the Queen and the monarchy because he was a patrician Tory would soon learn the error of their ways. Heath had little small talk beyond his favourite subjects of classical music and sailing. He also had a deep disdain for one of the Queen's favourite institutions, the Commonwealth, regarding its growing membership as radical and anti-Western.

The organization of ex-British dominions and colonies was starting to create a stronger identity, too. It had already established a palatial headquarters in London thanks to the Queen, who had relinquished Queen Mary's old home, Marlborough House. Now, it was about to hold its first full summit, not in

1970–79: Walkabouts and Monsters

Britain but in Singapore, and the Queen was much looking forward to it. With just weeks to go, however, Heath formally advised her that she should not attend. He feared (rightly) that there would be anger from the African nations because Britain wished to sell helicopters to the pariah apartheid state of South Africa. She had no choice but to obey her prime minister, but, in private, she was dismayed. She would not let Heath pull a trick like that again. When the next summit was due to be held in Canada, in 1973, she and her staff ensured that her Canadian prime minister, Pierre Trudeau, invited her as Queen of Canada. She then accepted before Heath was even aware of it, leaving him unable to object. Pragmatism – but with a touch of mischief.

To this day, a favourite after-dinner game in political and media circles is to guess Elizabeth II's favourite prime minister (usually a contest between Churchill and Wilson). A secondary game is to guess her least favourite, with Ted Heath always in the mix. For his administration was also responsible for cajoling the Queen into one of the most brazenly political interventions of her reign: her vocal personal support for Britain's entry into the European Common Market.

Back in the 1950s, the UK, under Clement Attlee's Labour government, had turned down the option to join what would become the European Union, seeing it as a threat to British industry. All through the sixties, British prime ministers had tried to make amends, but had been thwarted by French president Charles de Gaulle, who had repeatedly vetoed the idea. By the seventies, de Gaulle had gone, and France, together with the other member states, was ready to welcome the UK. The issue was still dividing Britain, and still the subject of fierce parliamentary debate, when Heath decided that the Queen should pay a state visit to France regardless. Throughout her trip, his ministers handed her speeches extolling the joys of belonging to the Common Market. We can tell from the exchanges of draft texts between the Foreign Office and the Palace – and the repeated efforts of the latter to tone down the evangelical rhetoric of the former – that the Queen and her officials felt she was, at times, being pushed too far.[3] By the end of 1972, however, all had been agreed: Britain would become a new European partner on 1 January 1973.

The Queen and her family would even attend a special 'Fanfare for Europe' celebration concert at the Royal Opera House. Most extraordinary of all, however, was her Christmas broadcast six days earlier. This was – and still is – an occasion when the monarch speaks from the heart and not on 'ministerial advice'. In 1972, however, Heath's staff suggested that he should have sight of the Queen's address, as he might wish to offer some suggestions.

One private secretary from her later years remains astonished and indeed 'appalled' that her private secretary at the time, Martin Charteris, allowed the prime minister to put the following words into the Queen's mouth: 'I am speaking today to all the peoples of the Commonwealth. Britain is about to join her neighbours in the European Community and you may well ask how this will affect the Commonwealth. The new links with Europe will not replace those with the Commonwealth. Old friends will not be lost; Britain will take her Commonwealth links into Europe with her.' Some of the Queen's other realms, it should be remembered, were deeply unhappy about Britain turning away from her old Commonwealth 'kith and kin', having been loyal allies in times of trouble. It was no coincidence that the following year, Australia ditched 'God Save the Queen' as the national anthem.

The Queen had been reciting pure Conservative Party

1970–79: *Walkabouts and Monsters*

propaganda in her Christmas broadcast, but Cabinet papers show that there was no pushback from the Palace. 'The Queen was pleased to incorporate the amendments,' Charteris wrote to the Cabinet secretary.[4] Many years later, he said that his boss was not nearly as troubled by the European question as her eldest son. 'I cannot actually remember discussing it in detail with the Queen, though I did do with the Prince of Wales. And the Prince was certainly concerned about the future,' Charteris told Peter Hennessy. 'I'm sure it gave her concern. But there again, long training as a constitutional monarch means: "Que sera sera . . ."'[5]

Charteris's successors, who for the most part hold him in the highest regard, are bewildered by his acquiescence in Heath's plans. 'All I can say is I would never, never in a million years put something like that forward,' said one of her last private secretaries. 'I would never even have submitted it to her. It would never even have gone on paper. It was so obviously wrong constitutionally, regardless of the rights and wrongs.'[6] Charteris was unquestionably one of her favourite and longest-serving advisers. Yet both he and his boss were happy to allow a prime minister to commit what amounted to a gross overstepping of the mark.

In the Queen's defence, she could have been picking her battles carefully and perhaps had even weightier, more personal matters on her mind. Another unwelcome innovation of the Heath era was the most intrusive parliamentary investigation into the royal finances anyone could remember. This was not entirely down to Heath, however. In the last months of Harold Wilson's government, the Duke of Edinburgh had spoken a little too frankly in a television interview while visiting the USA.

'We go into the red, I think, next year,' he told NBC's *Meet the Press* in 1969, adding that he had already sold his racing

Elizabeth II

yacht and 'shall probably have to give up polo fairly soon.'[7] The logic was beyond dispute. Under ancient rules, an annual sum for the cost of the monarchy was fixed at the start of each reign – £475,000 in the case of Elizabeth II. Yet it took no account of inflation, which meant that the Palace was now running at a loss. As the Duke's son, Prince Andrew, would discover exactly fifty years later, following another television interview, language which might sound perfectly straightforward in royal circles could very easily come across as entitled whining to the general public.

Left-wing Labour MPs and trade unionists berated the Duke for his insensitivity while the press and public made merry with jokes about royal poverty. The following week, Harold Wilson had no choice but to say something in Parliament. He announced that whoever won the upcoming general election would establish a select committee to examine royal funding. That task duly fell to Heath. The longstanding convention that MPs could not discuss the Royal Family was temporarily set aside, and anti-royal voices like the Labour firebrand William 'Willie' Hamilton delighted in this rare opportunity to attack the Windsors, reserving his most acidic criticisms for Princess Margaret, whom he called a 'kept woman.'[8]

If it was an uncomfortable period for the Queen, it was worth the pain when, in 1971, Parliament agreed to more than double the Civil List to £980,000 a year. More worrying for her were calls from respected political figures for the Royal Household to be brought under public control as a government department, as happens in other European monarchies to this day. Heath rejected the idea of footmen and carriages being administered by a minister. He had also boosted the royal coffers. Little wonder, then, if the Queen was happy to accept some tinkering with her Christmas speech as a quid pro quo.

1970-79: Walkabouts and Monsters

That same year, she said farewell to her uncle, the Duke of Windsor, who died in self-imposed exile at his home outside Paris. She had seen him in person just a few days before his death, during her state visit to France. Both the French and British governments had been extremely worried that he might disrupt the state visit with an ill-timed death. Britain's ambassador, Sir Christopher Soames, even went as far as warning the Duke's doctor that his patient could perform one last service to the throne he had abandoned in 1936. 'The Ambassador came to the point,' Dr Jean Thin told biographer Michael Bloch, 'and told me bluntly that it was alright for the Duke to die before or after the visit but that it would be politically disastrous if he were to expire in the course of it. Was there anything I could do to reassure him about the timing of the Duke's end?'[9]

George V's doctor might have been prepared to administer euthanasia in order to ensure his patient's timely death, but Dr Thin was not. Though clearly close to death and attached to various tubes, the Duke had been determined to welcome his niece properly. He had moved from his deathbed to a chair and had changed into a loose-fitting blazer and shirt which could conceal his tubes. When the Queen arrived, to everyone's horror, he stood up to bow to her. They spoke alone for fifteen minutes. The Queen then emerged, red-eyed, for tea downstairs with the Duchess of Windsor, who was such a bundle of nerves that she dropped her cup. What had made the Queen so tearful, according to one of those in the entourage, was seeing such a powerful reminder of the father she had lost twenty years before.[10] Despite the seismic impact of the abdication, the Duke of Windsor's subsequent deceit about money and his dangerous flirtations with Nazism, even as Britain risked invasion, the Queen would always speak of him with fondness. 'She would often reminisce about him,' says one who knew her very well

Elizabeth II

in later life. 'She was never judgemental about him; never showed a side. She always referred to him just as "David". I sensed a real affection.'[11]

He had managed to perform that final duty to the Crown, waiting until a week after the Queen's state visit before dying. Her genuine fondness was reflected in her insistence on a full royal ceremonial funeral for her uncle at Windsor after three days of lying-in-state. The Welsh Guards carried his coffin on 5 June 1972 as all the Royal Family and the Establishment gathered to say farewell. Many noticed the Queen's tenderness towards the frail and plainly distracted Duchess, holding Wallis's hand and offering words of reassurance.

The family gathered together in very much happier circumstances the following year for the marriage of Princess Anne to British Olympic horseman Captain Mark Phillips. In sporting terms, it was a marriage of equals. Since leaving school in 1968, the Princess had pursued twin careers as a working member of the Royal Family and as an international competitor in the notoriously dangerous discipline of three-day eventing. In 1971, she had become European champion riding the Queen's horse, Doublet (in private, the Queen always loved to joke that she had bred both the horse and rider). She was also the most glamorous member of the family, appearing three times on the cover of *Vogue* and winning the 1971 BBC Sports Personality of the Year award (Manchester United's George Best came second). Hers was not only the first royal wedding televised in colour, but the first to allow camera close-ups of the key moments, creating the template for every royal wedding since. Yet the couple had only been married four months when they were subjected to one of the most terrifying ordeals faced by any member of the family in modern times.

On the night of 20 March 1974, they were returning from a

1970–79: Walkabouts and Monsters

charity film event and approaching Buckingham Palace when a Ford Escort overtook the royal vehicle, forcing it to a halt. Royal protection officer Inspector Jim Beaton jumped out, only to be shot by a lone gunman, Ian Ball, who was determined to kidnap the Princess. Beaton's attempt at returning fire was hampered by his wounded shoulder, whereupon his gun jammed. He was shot twice more while forcing his way between the gunman and the Princess, who was steadfastly refusing Ball's command to get out of the car. 'Bloody likely,' she told him when he shouted that he would be demanding a £1 million ransom (her words have often been misquoted as 'not bloody likely'). The royal chauffeur, a second policeman and a passing journalist were also shot before ex-boxer Ron Russell spotted trouble and intervened. He landed two blows on Ball, who then took flight, only to be floored by a third policeman. The Queen and Prince Philip were awoken in the midst of a state visit to Indonesia to receive the news, and soon found that their daughter had taken it all in her stride (as the Princess told this author years later: 'Strangely, I had thought about it before. One thing about horses and sport is that you have to prepare for the unexpected.').[12] However troubling the news might have been, the Queen continued with her state visit in Jakarta the following day as if nothing had happened.

By now, she was dealing with a prime minister who was both old and new. Harold Wilson was back in Downing Street. Despite agreeing not to call a general election while the Queen was visiting her Pacific realms in February 1974, Edward Heath had done just that (another blot on his royal copybook). Dismal industrial relations and energy shortages had brought Britain to such a low point that the prime minister felt impelled to seek a fresh mandate. The Queen had to abandon her tour of Australia, having only just arrived there, to fly home for the election result. It was not merely embarrassing, but also gave the lie to the cosy notion of all her realms being equal.

Back in Britain, the result was far from clear. Labour had won four seats more than the Conservatives, yet Heath insisted on seeking a deal with the third-placed Liberals, without success. The abiding convention, then and now, is that a prime minister remains in post until he resigns. But for how long could he do that? Would the Queen have to evict Heath? In the end, after four days of stalemate, Heath arrived at the palace to resign and the Queen sent for Wilson, who later wrote that their 'relaxed intimacy was immediately restored'.[13]

Senior officials, including former private secretaries, have attested to the Queen's fondness for Wilson. 'She liked him very much,' Bill Heseltine told this author.[14] Part of his appeal, said family friends, was that the Queen and Wilson both regarded royal heritage in much the same way, as a responsibility rather than a possession. 'The thing is that he wasn't at all chippy,' recalled Prue Penn, family friend and lady-in-waiting to the Queen Mother. 'I was talking to him one evening at the diplomatic reception and he looked at this Chinese vase and said: "Aren't we lucky to have all these treasures in this country". There was none of that "well, it's alright for some" attitude. The Queen was very fond of him.'[15]

It seems equally safe to say that few tears were shed on the eventual departure of Edward Heath. On his watch, she had been compelled to entertain two of the most objectionable visitors of her entire seventy-year reign.

First, in 1971, came the Ugandan despot Idi Amin, who had recently overthrown the country's president in a coup and was very eager to meet the Queen. Believing that Britain could do business with Amin, Heath arranged a lunch at the palace. It was not a success, although the Queen did manage to avert a

1970–79: Walkabouts and Monsters

war after Amin confided in her that he was planning to invade Tanzania to secure a land corridor to the Indian Ocean. Following lunch, she alerted her private secretary, who in turn informed the foreign secretary, who immediately quashed Amin's request for a new arms deal.[16]

Two years later, she was expected to lay on a full state visit for the monstrous Mobutu Sese Seko, dictator of Zaire, thanks to the Foreign Office's similarly naïve belief that Britain might secure some lucrative construction contracts. None ever materialized, of course. The Queen would always remember the visit, however, thanks to Mobutu's wife, Marie-Antoinette, who smuggled a small dog inside Buckingham Palace in her luggage. Having rashly asked the palace kitchens for some raw meat, Marie-Antoinette's subterfuge was revealed and Deputy Master of the Household Lord Plunket was summoned to be given the immortal instruction: 'Get that dog out of my house!' At a time of pan-European paranoia about the spread of rabies, this was an act of extraordinary rudeness and recklessness. Those close to the monarch say they could never recall seeing her in such a state. 'The Queen was very, very angry,' recalled her then press secretary, Ron Allison.[17] Martin Charteris would later reveal that she had been 'shaking' with rage. Patrick Plunket deftly relocated the royal corgis to Windsor, had the stowaway despatched into quarantine and ensured that one of the iciest state visits in history somehow continued to its futile conclusion.

How she would miss 'Patrick' after his death, from cancer, not long afterwards. A family friend since childhood, the urbane ex-Guards officer and art lover would even be described as the brother she'd never had. If Prince Philip was abroad, or even on the other side of the room at a big gathering, it would be Plunket, both consummate courtier and friend, who would be hovering alongside. His misleadingly anodyne title of

Elizabeth II

Deputy Master was shorthand for the Queen's fixer-in-chief, party-planner and confidant. That the Queen regarded the bachelor peer as family was clear enough after his death in May 1975. Not only did she attend both his funeral and memorial services, but she also erected a temple-style memorial to him in Windsor Great Park's Valley Gardens.

He would certainly have been a strong support during an especially unhappy period for the Queen. It had scarcely been a secret that the marriage of Princess Margaret and Tony Snowdon was falling apart, with both seeking companionship elsewhere. In 1976, the press revealed the Princess's relationship with Roddy Llewellyn, a good-looking landscape gardener fifteen years her junior. Lord Snowdon formally moved out, though he was, by now, already living with film producer Lucy Lindsay-Hogg. It was merely a question of deciding how and when to announce a separation which would have royal historians reaching back to George IV, if not Henry VIII, for similar marital discord so close to the throne. That it was not an even bigger media sensation was thanks to Harold Wilson.

On 16 March 1976, as the press were reporting that a split had been agreed (though not yet confirmed), Wilson announced his resignation. With his health and attention span starting to wane, he had told the Queen of his intention privately at Balmoral the previous autumn. He had done so knowing that he could trust her completely, but also so that he could later say that the decision had been his own and was not forced upon him. Why, then, did he choose that very day of that very week? Coincidence? Or a parting kindness to the Queen, knowing that even royal history of this magnitude would still be eclipsed by the resignation of the prime minister?

Two days later, having waited for their children to be home from boarding school, the Princess and Lord Snowdon formally

1970–79: *Walkabouts and Monsters*

announced their separation. The Queen would not take sides. She loved her sister unreservedly and would speak to her almost every day for the rest of her life. She also knew that Snowdon's record was hardly spotless. However, she recognized his devotion to the children, respected his discretion and acknowledged that life with the mercurial Margaret could be challenging in the extreme.

In particular, she was determined to make things as bearable as possible for her nephew, Viscount Linley, and niece, Lady Sarah Armstrong-Jones, then aged fourteen and eleven. 'The Queen loved David and Sarah. And she always had a really special bond with Sarah,' says a close family friend, pointing to a rare piece of royal film footage. 'We know the Queen wasn't touchy-feely, even with her own children, but there she is hugging Sarah close, just like a young mother. There's real tenderness. You can see the connection.'[18] The moment was captured during the filming of the 1969 documentary, *Royal Family*. The Queen is aboard *Britannia*, happily clutching a four-year-old Lady Sarah in her arms as they look out to sea, chatting animatedly together. Prince Edward is there, too, but he is being held by a member of the crew.

Now Lady Sarah Chatto (following her 1994 marriage to fellow artist Daniel Chatto), the Queen's niece gave a rare and touching interview for John Bridcut's BBC film *Elizabeth at 90*, praising the aunt who had always treated her and her brother as one of her own, making them 'part of her life really'. 'It's only cod psychology, I know, but Sarah is much more like her aunt than her mother,' said the family friend. 'Margaret was the great extrovert show-off. Elizabeth was the shy, conscientious, sensible one. I think the Queen saw a lot of her younger self in Sarah. She adored her. In fact, the whole Household adored her.'[19]

* * *

Elizabeth II

The late seventies was the nadir of twentieth-century post-war British fortunes. It was a period of strikes, rancour and such economic disarray that Britain had required a bail-out from the International Monetary Fund in order to stave off bankruptcy. At times, it seemed that it was only the monarchy – plus the new UK/French supersonic airliner Concorde and the occasional James Bond film – which gave Britain any cause to hold its head high. There was nothing new about the Queen's international pulling power, of course. Bill Heseltine remembered that her 1968 state visit to Brazil coincided with a moment of proper global importance: 'What really struck me was the day after we arrived, there was a presidential election in America. I opened the paper. The first seven pages were the Queen's arrival and on page eight there was a paragraph saying who had won!' By the second half of the decade, however, the UK was no longer seen merely as a mediocrity but, worse, as a failure.*

As the Foreign Office files reveal, it was only the prospect of staying with the Queen which lured French president Valery Giscard d'Estaing to London on a state visit in 1976. As the USA celebrated the 200th anniversary of revolution against George III, it was the Queen who was the guest of honour at independence celebrations up and down the Eastern seaboard. The centrepiece was President Gerald Ford's ball for her in Washington. After dinner, he invited her to join him for the first dance on the White House lawn. To the eternal embarrassment of White House staff – and the eternal amusement of the Queen – the bandmaster inexplicably chose that very moment to strike up 'That's Why the Lady Is a Tramp'. Over the

---

* In his gloomy 1977 farewell despatch from Washington, UK ambassador Sir Peter Ramsbotham summed up the prevailing US view of Britain as follows: 'An undisguised impatience with our lack of motivation.' (FCO 160/52/32.)

1970–79: Walkabouts and Monsters

border, as Queen of Canada, she took centre stage opening the 1976 Montreal Olympics, though she was also there as a very proud spectator. Princess Anne was a member of the luckless British equestrian team, valiantly remounting and riding on after a bad fall during the cross-country phase of the three-day eventing competition.

In short, the Queen, unlike the country, was on a roll. Her latest prime minister, Jim Callaghan, who had succeeded Wilson mid-term, was already looking ahead to an important landmark. There had not been a royal jubilee since George V's twenty-fifth anniversary as King in 1935. Now another Silver Jubilee loomed in 1977 and Callaghan wanted a national party. 'The Queen herself stressed to her prime minister that she wished spending on the celebrations to be kept to a minimum in this period of high inflation and wage restraint,' explained Bill Heseltine, by now her assistant private secretary.[20] However, as Churchill had discovered in the run-up to the Coronation, austerity does not lessen the public's appetite for a party. When Callaghan received a memo from the Home Office advising that there was not even enough money for floodlighting major London landmarks during the festivities, he replied: 'Bloody nonsense. I think this is pernickety bureaucracy. Let them light up for a bit.'[21] A wily old operator, of whom the Queen was fond (though not as fond as she was of Wilson), Callaghan was right.

The Silver Jubilee celebrations started on the other side of the world in the Queen's Pacific realms, amid some nervousness. It was only two years since the constitutional crisis in Australia when the Queen's governor-general, Sir John Kerr, had sacked the Labor prime minister, Gough Whitlam, following a stalemate over the public money supply. The Queen would always be grateful for the fact that Kerr had done it without asking her first. Yet, for years afterwards (even up to the present day), 'the dismissal' would remain a topic of passionate debate, giving fresh impetus to the campaign to replace the monarch with an Australian president. Yet apart from a few small protests, it had no impact on a jubilant jubilee tour.

Back in Britain, the festivities exceeded all expectations across the country. Most notably, an estimated one million people turned out for the main parade through London, and a similar number for her trip to both the Protestant and Catholic cathedrals in Liverpool. 'Liz Rules, Ok!' declared the graffiti artists – and the front page of the *Daily Mirror* on the morning after the main jubilee service of thanksgiving at St Paul's Cathedral. There was a long-remembered moment of controversy, too, during her address to Parliament, when she noted, somewhat tartly: 'I cannot forget that I was crowned Queen of the United Kingdom . . . Perhaps this jubilee is a time to remind ourselves of the benefits which union has conferred.' This was a clear riposte to the fledgling separatist movements in Scotland and Wales, which were just starting to demand some sort of national assembly.

Though Callaghan's government had approved the speech, Cabinet papers make clear that it had been written by the Queen and her private secretary, Martin Charteris.[22] It was perhaps the most political statement of her entire reign. But then it was the one political issue which worried her more than any other. As the most Scottish monarch since James I thanks to her mother, and twice descended from Robert the Bruce, she could not countenance the break-up of the union that she embodied.

Her dedication to the 'U' in UK meant that she was determined to visit Northern Ireland, even though this was the height of the Troubles and the home secretary, Merlyn Rees, was extremely wary of the idea. 'He'd have been very pleased

1970–79: Walkabouts and Monsters

if the Queen had called it off but she was determined to visit all parts of the United Kingdom in her jubilee year,' recalled her then assistant private secretary, Bill Heseltine.[23] It was deemed too dangerous for the Queen to stay in the province overnight, so she would be based on the royal yacht. Nor, said Rees, could she risk going anywhere by car due to the danger posed by hidden bombs. He stipulated that only one form of transport would do. As touched on earlier, the Queen was afraid of almost nothing – except helicopters. A dislike bordering on phobia had been reinforced by the death of her senior pilot* in a helicopter crash a decade earlier. 'She had never ventured into a helicopter before and, after that incident, was never very keen to do so,' said Heseltine. With no alternative, however, she completed two days of Northern Irish engagements by chopper. Rees had even tried to curtail the second day after an explosion at a university campus which was on the Queen's itinerary in Coleraine. She was having none of it. Having braved a helicopter two days in a row, she was not going to be troubled by a mere bomb.

She had found the Jubilee exhausting, exhilarating and hugely reassuring. Like her grandfather, George V, she had been touchingly surprised by the outpouring of popular affection for her. The end of the celebrations saw a fond parting of the ways. Martin Charteris, who had been with her from the start and had served as her principal private secretary for the past five years, had reached retirement. Very much on the modernizing wing of the Court, he had steered her through so many ups and downs and had been the chief architect of her jubilee. Impish, unstuffy, aristocratic without being grand,

---

* Air Commodore John Blount, Captain of the Queen's Flight and a kinsman of the singer James Blunt.

he would be fondly remembered for injecting humour into her speeches – and even the occasional fully fledged witticism. No one could be heard laughing more loudly when she delivered one, especially when he was the author. 'What fun he was. He did always laugh at his own jokes,' Prue Penn recalled. 'I remember the jubilee lunch in 1977 and every time there was a joke he'd written, he'd roar with laughter. Eric [her husband] nudged me and said, "Do look at Martin laughing at his own jokes." Eric used to say that after that generation, the jokes went.'[24]

At the age of fifty-one, Elizabeth II was now, imperceptibly but surely, edging from middle age towards a timeless, mother-of-the-nation space in her people's affections. It certainly felt that way on the morning of 15 November, when she arrived unusually late for an investiture at Buckingham Palace and, equally unusually, prefaced the ceremony with a few words: 'My daughter has just given birth to a son.' Princess Anne had made the monarch a grandmother following the arrival of Peter Phillips. It was also the first royal birth to take place in a hospital.

If Britain remained listless economically, it was not for a lack of government schemes involving that time-honoured carrot on the end of a diplomatic stick – the Queen. At no point in her entire reign (with the possible exception of the Mobutus) was she obliged to stoop as low as she did in June 1978, when she welcomed President Nicolae Ceaușescu of Romania and his wife, Elena, to Buckingham Palace.

The dictator's track record as a brutal autocrat was no secret. Jim Callaghan, however, had a very clear transactional strategy in mind when he asked the Queen to invite the Ceaușescus to stay. Romania was looking to establish an aviation industry and Britain wanted to ensure that this would involve the building of the British BAC 1-11 short-haul airliner. A state visit would seal the deal. The Queen made no complaint. This would be business, through gritted teeth, rather than pleasure. She had been called, in advance, by the French president, who forewarned her that on their recent visit to Paris, the Ceaușescu family had laid waste to their guest quarters, stealing loose objects and hacking holes in the walls to look for possible bugs. As Giscard's staff had told him: 'It was as if burglars had moved in for a whole summer.'[25]

In the event, the Ceaușescus were more respectful of the Queen and did not vandalize the Belgian Suite at Buckingham Palace. However, the couple and their entourage were so convinced that they were being bugged that they insisted on conversing outdoors in the palace garden. Equally fearful that the royal housekeepers would try to poison their clothing, they kept all the presidential baggage in sealed containers. Throughout her reign, the Queen would have to entertain objectionable people, including a former IRA commander (Martin McGuinness) who had tried to kill her and her family. Even so, the Ceaușescus took charmlessness to new levels. She would later reveal to the writer Sir Antony Jay how she did her best to keep contact to a minimum. 'She was telling me how she saw them in the garden when she was walking the dogs and managed to hide behind a bush to avoid them,' Jay told this author.[26]

'I would say without qualification that Ceaușescu was the most repellent guest she ever had to make do with,' said Bill Heseltine.[27] As with the Mobutus and Amin, the visit achieved nothing either diplomatically or commercially. Asked why he makes no mention of it at all in his extensive memoirs, the foreign secretary of the day, David (now Lord) Owen, was commendably frank: 'I try to pretend it never happened!'[28]

Owen and his prime minister would set her a more enjoyable and exotic task in the dying days of this Labour administration. British firms were, at least, enjoying considerable success in the Gulf states of the Middle East. While Britain was still enduring another long, cold round of industrial disputes, branded by the press as Callaghan's 'winter of discontent', the Queen, together with Prince Philip, embarked on the first royal tour of the Gulf states by a reigning British monarch and also by a female head of state.

The tour would also include the first – and last – attempt at a conventional interview with the Queen. As she reached Oman, the BBC's Keith Graves asked the Palace if he might seek her thoughts on this historic tour. The Palace declined but agreed that she could be filmed answering pre-arranged questions from the British ambassador, Jim Treadwell. It was not a great success. 'We've been very, very happy to see this for the first time. I think very impressive to see how the Gulf countries are using their oil revenues for such tremendous development,' the Queen noted, during some long and awkward pauses. 'Everybody's been very, very kind.' Afterwards a BBC spokesman admitted: 'We gave Mr Treadwell a briefing but he didn't quite get the hang of it. It isn't everything we hoped for but we still think it is a unique television occasion.'[29] It was not one that the Queen would care to repeat.

This was as groundbreaking as any journey of her reign so far. She enjoyed the sense of bolstering British trade but also of entering uncharted territory, especially for a woman. 'Let me say that I became very convinced of her liberal humanity on that trip,' observed the former Labour politician Alan Judd, the Foreign Office minister in attendance for much of the tour. By no means an ardent royalist, he came away fascinated by the Queen's acute political and social observations. 'She saw some of the underlying – what we would now call human rights – issues very clearly on her own account. And, in private, would give vent to her feelings.'[30]

The Duke and Duchess of York at the christening of their daughter, Princess Elizabeth Alexandra Mary, in 1926.

Below: Princess Elizabeth with her grandparents, King George V and Queen Mary, on the way back to Balmoral after a service at nearby Crathie Kirk. 5 September 1932.

Princess Elizabeth and her younger sister, Princess Margaret, in a miniature car, with their governess, Marion 'Crawfie' Crawford.

Princesses Elizabeth and Margaret at Balmoral with 'Uncle David', the Prince of Wales, in 1935.

Princess Elizabeth with two Pembroke Welsh Corgi dogs, Dookie and Jane, at 145 Piccadilly, London, July 1936. By the end of the year, her father would be King, and Elizabeth would be the heir to the throne.

Left: As she turned sixteen in April 1942, Princess Elizabeth started to undertake her first official engagements. Here, at Windsor, her father, King George VI, also introduced her to state papers. As she said years later: 'You can do a lot if you're properly trained.'

Below: Officer Cadet Prince Philip of Greece and Denmark was selected to entertain Princess Elizabeth and her sister during their parents' visit to Britannia Royal Naval College, Dartmouth, in 1939.

Princess Elizabeth's twenty-first birthday broadcast to her future subjects, on 21 April 1947, was one of her most famous speeches. Officially, it came from Cape Town, South Africa. Files in the Royal Archives show that it was pre-recorded at the Victoria Falls Hotel in what is now Zimbabwe.

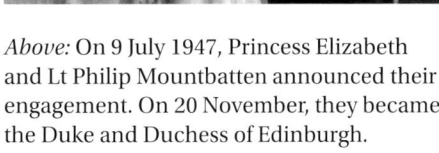

Above: On 9 July 1947, Princess Elizabeth and Lt Philip Mountbatten announced their engagement. On 20 November, they became the Duke and Duchess of Edinburgh.

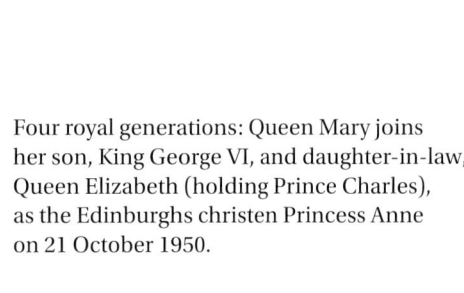

Four royal generations: Queen Mary joins her son, King George VI, and daughter-in-law, Queen Elizabeth (holding Prince Charles), as the Edinburghs christen Princess Anne on 21 October 1950.

Above left: Princess Elizabeth dancing with the Duke of Edinburgh in December 1950 at a Royal Navy ball in Malta. He was stationed there during the early years of their marriage, and it was where the future Queen could, briefly, lead a near-'normal' life. *Above right:* Elizabeth II lands on British soil for the first time as Queen, following the death of her father the day before. The Duke of Edinburgh holds back as the new monarch is greeted by Winston Churchill and Clement Attlee at London Airport. 7 February 1952.

Coronation Day, 2 June 1953. The crowning of Queen Elizabeth II is witnessed live by millions of people thanks to the advent of television (though they were seeing it in black and white).

Above left: The Queen and Duke of Edinburgh with Queen Sālote Tupou III in the grounds of the royal palace at Nuku'alofa, Tonga, in December 1953. The Pacific island was an early destination on the great round-the-world Commonwealth tour after the Coronation. *Above right:* The Queen dances with President Kwame Nkrumah of Ghana at the State House in Accra, 21 November 1961. Prince Philip takes to the floor with First Lady Fathia Nkrumah.

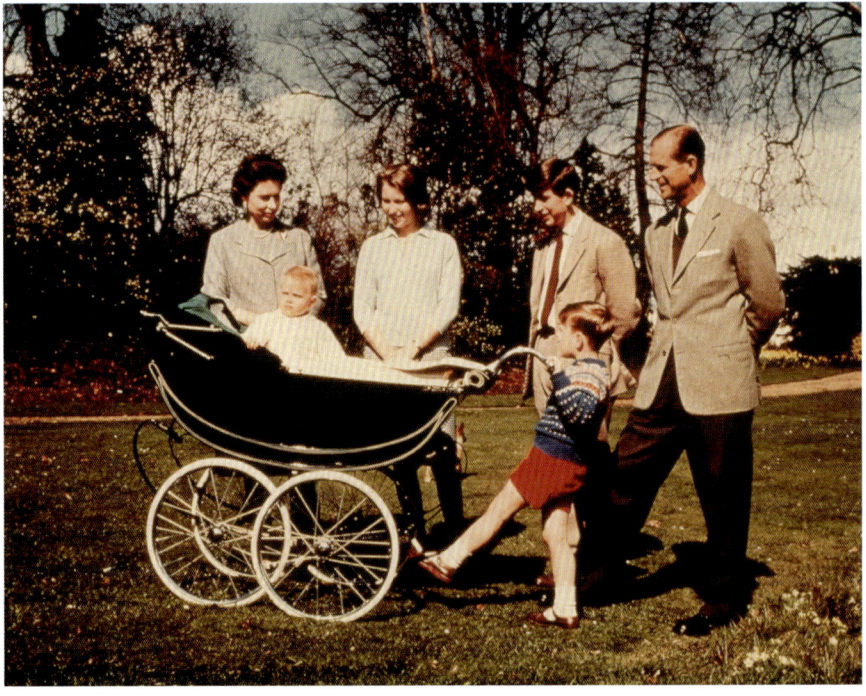

Prince Edward joins his parents and elder siblings at Frogmore House on the Queen's birthday, 21 April 1965. As she remarked: 'Goodness, what fun it is to have a baby in the house again!'

Following his investiture on 1 July 1969, the new Prince of Wales leaves Caernarvon Castle with the Queen. Behind the smiles, there is much nervous tension – with good reason.

All the family together at Buckingham Palace to mark the silver wedding anniversary of the Queen and Prince Philip on 20 November 1972.

A month after their engagement, the Prince of Wales and Lady Diana Spencer are photographed at Buckingham Palace with the Queen, 27 March 1981.

The Queen, riding Burmese, guides US president Ronald Reagan, on Centennial, around the grounds of Windsor Castle during his first European tour as president in June 1982.

Chapter Nine

1979–82

'Don't look back'

It was Jim Callaghan who made one of the most astute and oft-quoted observations on the Queen's relationships with all her prime ministers: 'What one gets is friendliness but not friendship. One gets a great deal of friendliness.'[1] And so it was an amiable farewell on 4 May 1979 when he came to offer his resignation to the Queen. Her relationship with his successor, however, preoccupies both historians and dramatists to this day.

The Queen's first female prime minister was also the closest to her in age, just six months her senior. Margaret Thatcher had won a safe working majority on a combative platform of curbing taxes, inflation and the power of the trade unions. It was clear that the consensus politics of the post-war era was coming to an end. For a monarch whose natural and constitutional instincts were to seek common ground and to avoid confrontation, there would clearly be testing times ahead. 'You might say that the Queen prefers a sort of consensus politics rather than a polarized one,' Martin Charteris acknowledged. 'If you are in the Queen's position . . . the less squabbling that goes on in the country, obviously, the more convenient and the more comfortable you feel.'[2]

Elizabeth II

Charteris also diagnosed a marked change in atmospherics. 'I suspect that [the Queen] found dealing with a lady prime minister not so easy as dealing with a gentleman prime minister for reasons which we can all understand. Men have a natural courtesy towards women. They perhaps love her a bit. It's so easy to get it going and get it nice. And I don't think it's necessarily as easy with a lady prime minister.'[3]

However, Mrs Thatcher's feelings for the Queen and the institution which she represented were self-evident whenever they met. 'She revered both the constitution and the monarch,' her press secretary, Sir Bernard Ingham, observed. 'That was manifest in the way she curtseyed. I've never seen anyone go so low and I wondered if she'd ever get up.'[4]

'I think, at the most basic level, the Queen just found it weird to be sitting opposite a female prime minister,' said a close (female) friend of the monarch. 'She liked big, strong, bombastic alpha males, not drippy ones. She just thought: "That's what men do and that's how they are." So she didn't always deal very well with strident or brilliant women. There would be huge mutual respect but it just wasn't her. And I think Mrs Thatcher fell into that category. But, privately, they were very similar, especially in the way they valued their husbands and the man's role within the family.'[5]

Kenneth Harris, who wrote acclaimed biographies of both women, observed some key commonalities: 'Neither of them is intellectual, introspective or philosophical; both are direct, matter-of-fact, down-to-earth, practical and perceptive. Neither of them is vain, narcissistic or pretentious.'[6]

Both women were, indeed, devoted to their husbands and had what would now be regarded as traditional views about male roles within the home. They had also both adored their fathers and, in many ways, tried to emulate them in their own

1979–82: 'Don't look back'

professional lives. The values of Alderman Alfred Roberts, Mrs Thatcher's shopkeeper father, were those that would shape her entire political life and premiership: hard graft, sound family finance, individual responsibility and civic pride. The Queen had watched how her father's dogged attention to constitutional duty had filled the void left by his glamorous, louche elder brother and how he had steered the country through the hardships of war and peacetime austerity.

The very different backgrounds of the two women would, inevitably, lead to certain tensions. Mrs Thatcher was alert to patrician snobbery, though not 'chippy' about it; her biographer, Charles Moore, noted that 'although . . . she certainly hated to be patronized by anyone, she was by nature deferential to social systems.' Her enemies, and the writers of *The Crown*, loved the idea of the suburban union-basher being tormented by royalty and snobs as she negotiated the social minefield of the annual prime ministerial visit to Balmoral. In fact, the Queen would have been appalled at the idea of anyone contriving to make one of her guests feel socially awkward. Even the famously anti-royal Australian prime minister Paul Keating spoke of his fond memories of being driven around the Balmoral estate by the Queen in 1993 while 'Phil was working the barbecue.'[7] When Harold Wilson was at Balmoral, he enjoyed playing golf with the Queen's then equerry, Jock Slater ('though his police protection officer was better at finding Wilson's balls than anyone else's,' Slater recalled).[8] With Mrs Thatcher, plainly, it was a classic case of town mouse versus country mouse. When the Queen was asked one day whether Mrs Thatcher would be joining a walking party up the hill, the monarch is said to have replied: 'I think you will find Mrs Thatcher only walks on the road.'[9]

In particular, Mrs Thatcher found it agonizing to be waited

Elizabeth II

on by the Royal Family during the traditional family barbecue, and even more so to watch the Queen doing the washing up. On the first such occasion, she could not restrain herself from trying to assist. This prompted the Queen (according to one of those present) to mutter in a stage whisper: 'Would someone tell that woman to sit down.'[10] Mrs Thatcher famously enclosed a pair of washing-up gloves with her thank-you letter.

Her friends and allies have talked of her being up and about first thing on the day of her Balmoral departure in order to make a prompt getaway, yet she was always equally punctilious about getting there on time. As Palace staff were only too aware, she could arrive well in advance of her weekly audience of the Queen, whereupon a nervous equerry would have to make polite if agonized conversation with the prime minister in an anteroom until the allotted time.

'The Queen was full of respect for the way that Mrs Thatcher had fought her way to the top. She was fascinated by it,' says one veteran of that era. 'But that didn't mean she couldn't also see her amusing side.'[11]

One senior Cabinet minister, who worked at close quarters with both women, observed that the Queen could be 'slightly quizzical' about Mrs Thatcher. 'I think she basically thought that Margaret Thatcher was a slightly comic character,' they said, adding that they never detected any frostiness. 'Margaret Thatcher could get herself slightly worked up over things and the Queen found that all just ever so slightly strange and funny. But I think that's all there is to it. I don't think there's any more than that. Just a certain amusement.'[12] Lord Luce, another former Tory minister who later worked for the Queen as Lord Chamberlain, noticed something similar, pointing to a lunch he attended with both women long after Mrs Thatcher's retirement. 'Margaret . . . was expressing some strong views and the Queen was rather amused,' said Luce. 'And then Margaret said: "If I was defence secretary, I would invade this and I would do that." At which point, the Queen looked at her watch and, with a twinkle in her eye, she said, "I think it's time to go now!"'[13]

What everyone would like to know most of all, of course, is what happened in those audiences. One common perception, widely believed, is that Mrs Thatcher did all the talking, based on a fondly exasperated remark often attributed to the Queen: 'Mrs Thatcher never listens to a word I say.' Bill Heseltine once asked the Queen whether Thatcher was like William Gladstone, of whom Queen Victoria complained: 'He speaks to me as if I were a public meeting.' The Queen told Heseltine that it was certainly not that sort of encounter, but added tellingly: 'I wasn't given much encouragement to comment on what was said.'[14]

Another of the Queen's most senior advisers, however, provides an intriguing counter-theory pointing to that lack of ego mentioned earlier. 'I would often hear the Queen say to someone that "so-and-so wouldn't let me get a word in edgeways",' says the former aide. 'Except I knew that she very often *had* got a word in edgeways. So it would be a shame if people are left imagining that she was easily cowed or hectored, because she was not. This was just a very clever deflection. If someone said, "Why didn't you tell Mrs Thatcher to do x?", it would be much easier to say, "I can never get a word in". But it was really just the Queen's way of gently saying: "Back off". Anyone with a greater ego would find that impossible but the Queen had a very low ego. It was the same when a family member asked her a difficult question and she might say: "Oh, my private secretary never tells me anything" or "You'll have to take it up with so-and-so because they tell me to do these things". It was such a brilliant tactic. She was so much cannier than she let on.'[15]

Elizabeth II

On one issue, the Queen and Mrs Thatcher were certainly in robust disagreement. Just like Edward Heath before her, the prime minister was no fan of the Queen's beloved Commonwealth. There were early stresses in their relationship just weeks into Mrs Thatcher's first term in Downing Street ahead of the upcoming Commonwealth summit in the Zambian capital, Lusaka. As mentioned earlier, there had been credible reports that communist guerilla forces over the border in war-torn Rhodesia, just 70 miles away, were planning to hit the Queen's plane with a rocket. This had already happened to other civilian aircraft in the region. Mrs Thatcher was also expecting a furious row with the other member states over the Commonwealth's increasingly hard-line stance against the minority white government ruling Rhodesia. The new prime minister would much rather the Queen stayed away. On 2 July 1979, just days before the summit, Mrs Thatcher pointedly told reporters that she had yet to give the Queen 'firm advice' on whether she could attend the summit. Just hours later, Buckingham Palace issued a tart response, with a spokesman confirming it was the Queen's 'firm intention' to attend.[16] New to the job, the Commonwealth and the Queen, Mrs Thatcher backed down. Here we have another telling glimpse of the way in which the Queen would gradually assert her authority over her British prime ministers when it came to Commonwealth matters. Back in the sixties, when the organization had appointed its first secretary-general, Canada's Arnold Smith, at its new headquarters in London, Harold Wilson's government had treated him like a clerk and ranked him below the lowliest ambassador in the order of diplomatic precedence. The Queen promptly intervened to ensure he was ranked above all other diplomats at the Court of St James's.[17] As noted, when Edward Heath kept her away from one Commonwealth summit, she worked around

1979–82: 'Don't look back'

him to ensure she did not miss the next one. Mrs Thatcher was now the latest to learn that the Head of the Commonwealth saw the role as more than a titular one.

As it turned out, however, the Queen would do Mrs Thatcher a great favour. The summit host, Kenneth Kaunda, had been planning to deliver a vicious speech denouncing Mrs Thatcher on the eve of the conference. The Queen made a very firm, personal plea to him while travelling in the back of the presidential limousine and persuaded him to do no such thing (her intervention is actually logged in the Foreign Office file on the visit).[18] This undoubtedly prevented the collapse of a summit which went on to be an astounding success, laying the framework for the Lancaster House talks in London and, in due course, the transformation of white Rhodesia into majority-rule Zimbabwe. The Queen had faced down her prime minister, braved a potential rocket attack, rescued the Commonwealth from a fresh schism and turned an important summit into an historic one. Mrs Thatcher had even ended up dancing with Kenneth Kaunda at the end. After a sticky start, the monarch and her new prime minister appeared to be something of a winning combination. It would not be long, though, before another formidable woman entered the Queen's life.

Since he had left the Royal Navy in 1976, Prince Charles's every public appearance had been accompanied by the same murmured question from the press and public: was there anyone *special* in his life? There had been a respectable succession of girlfriends, including a pretty, charismatic peer's granddaughter called Camilla Shand, with whom the Prince had been besotted. However, he had missed his chance when he was at sea and she had married cavalry officer Andrew Parker Bowles. In his early twenties, the Prince had said he wanted to be married by thirty. That birthday had been and gone with no change to his bachelor status when his life was thrown into bitter turmoil by an act of savagery.

On the sunny morning of 27 August 1979, his great-uncle and much-loved mentor, Lord Mountbatten, had been murdered by an IRA bomb during a family boating trip in Ireland. Three others, including Nicholas Knatchbull, Mountbatten's fourteen-year-old grandson, were killed. The Prince, already prone to bouts of gloomy introspection, was bereft, as were all the family. The Queen loved 'Dickie', for all his meddling, appreciating his avuncular devotion to both Philip and to his great-nephew, Charles. Her instant response after the murder was to invite Nicholas's twin brother, Tim, and sister, Amanda, to stay at Balmoral while their parents recovered in hospital. Tim Knatchbull would always remember the Queen's tenderness as they reached the castle – 'like a mother duck gathering in some young'.[19] (She would be doing exactly the same there eighteen years later for her own grandsons.) The following summer, Prince Charles was at a casual post-polo barbecue in Sussex when a pretty fellow guest struck up conversation and told him that she had felt very sorry for him, watching him at Mountbatten's funeral.

He had met Lady Diana Spencer before only in passing, during a brief period when he had dated her elder sister, Lady Sarah. Now, he was charmed by the sensitive, upbeat kindergarten teacher. Diana was no stranger to royalty herself. Her father, Earl Spencer, had been equerry to the Queen in the early days of the reign – as Viscount Althorp – and had leased Park House on the Sandringham estate, prior to inheriting the family seat of Althorp in Northamptonshire.

Park House had previously been leased from George V by the family of Johnny Spencer's wife, Frances. Her mother, Lady

1979–82: 'Don't look back'

Fermoy, was a lady-in-waiting to the Queen Mother. Diana, in other words, was from pedigree courtier stock on both sides. Along with her younger brother, Charles, she had grown up mixing with Princes Andrew and Edward during the school holidays. So, she was excited but not overawed when the Prince of Wales started calling with invitations to dinner and the theatre. Next came the ultimate test: a trip to Balmoral. Though Diana was never wildly keen on country sports, she had been marinated in the rhythms and rituals of the country houseparty since childhood. She understood the need to be out in all weathers by day, to dress for dinner, to be a good sport and muck in with whatever after-dinner game might unfold. Though she was, as she told Andrew Morton, 'shitting bricks . . . terrified, because I had never stayed at Balmoral and I wanted to get it right', she passed the Balmoral challenge with aplomb.[20] The Queen, it is said, was suitably impressed – though, given that her son was now thirty-one and had brought a number of girlfriends to stay over the years, she was not going to rush to judgement. According to biographer and *Majesty* magazine editor Ingrid Seward, her initial verdict was that Diana would be a more suitable match for Prince Andrew.[21] Soon afterwards, the press had worked out that they might have unearthed the future Queen, and every aspect of Diana's life was subjected to forensic scrutiny.

The public learned that her parents had been through an acrimonious divorce when she was young; that the children had continued to live with their father, who had remarried, to Raine, former Countess of Dartmouth; that her mother had also wed again to Peter Shand-Kydd; that her two older sisters had families of their own while her younger brother was still at Eton. Her flatmates in London's Earl's Court became minor celebrities, as did her Mini Metro. Crucially, for a large section of British society, and certainly for the Royal Household, there was one thing about Diana that the press had failed to unearth: a 'past'.

After nearly three decades on the throne, the Queen was still – just – the star of the royal show as far as the media were concerned. Soon after Diana's visit to Balmoral, the monarch was back on the world stage and making headlines for two very different reasons. An historic meeting with the Pope was followed by a Mediterranean tour culminating in perhaps the most spectacularly chaotic state visit of her entire reign. Her host, King Hassan II of Morocco, was paranoid about being assassinated or poisoned and rearranged every event at the last minute, to the dismay of royal officials and the Foreign Office minister in attendance, Douglas Hurd. It was bad enough when the Queen had to wait in her car outside the state banquet for the best part of an hour, but then a royal lunch and equestrian display in the desert turned into an embarrassing shambles.

'The King was busy in the kitchen sacking cooks, destroying the menu, and all the hours passed because he simply wasn't happy with the arrangements. Eventually lunch happened but not until five o clock,' Hurd recalled. 'She always enjoyed telling the story that, as she was sitting there with no lunch, and the world's press watching, a footman suddenly crawled up on all fours, said "Cognac, Majeste?" and thrust a glass of cognac into her hands.'[22]

Sensational media reports of an epic 'royal snub' the following day enraged the King even more.[23] He 'hissed' at Hurd that it was all the fault of the British ambassador and that he wanted him sacked. 'I was completely new. It was my first trip of this kind,' Hurd recalled. 'So I consulted Prince Philip, who burst into laughter and said "You do absolutely nothing".'

The next day, the Queen was preparing her return banquet

1979–82: 'Don't look back'

on board the royal yacht when she received the King's message asking her to delay the event by an hour. As Hurd recalled: 'Most people would have been thrown into a terrible tizz but the Queen just said: "We can't do that. We've asked people for a certain time. Please explain I will perfectly understand if His Majesty is late".'[24] In the end, he was not merely late, but also turned up with several uninvited guests and his own food. Whereupon, as Hurd recalled, the ranting started all over again: 'He was hissing at me in French.' The King added that he was cancelling an upcoming meeting with an important British trade delegation.[25]

The trip would be a good example of that 'steel in her spine' which Lord Charteris described. 'The King's dealings with the Queen were entirely different,' Hurd explained. 'He was scared of the Queen, and she was in scary mode.' That was certainly the case when the King tried to blame all these problems on her assistant private secretary. 'I'll thank you not to talk about my staff like that,' the Queen shot back.[26] As one member of the British entourage recalled admiringly: 'He took it on the chin from her!'[27] The courtier in question was Robert Fellowes, the brother-in-law of Lady Diana Spencer.

In February 1981, the feverish speculation was over. The Palace announced the engagement of Charles and Diana. The Queen immediately invited her future daughter-in-law to move in to Buckingham Palace to prepare for the wedding and offer her some respite from the press camped out on the doorstep of her London flat. The monarch was naturally delighted by the engagement but determined not to be an interfering mother-in-law. She had also assumed, naively perhaps, that a girl who knew her way around Sandringham and Balmoral could simply slot in to Court life. The Duke of Edinburgh, who had been pressing his son to make a decision either way out of consideration for

Elizabeth II

Diana and her reputation, could feel vindicated. While Prince Charles stuck to a long-planned series of engagements all over the world, Diana was left in the hands of a few well-meaning but much older and mainly male members of the Royal Household to find her way around.

As the wedding drew nearer, the bride already had her doubts – and she was not the only one. Diana had found the constant attention and burden of expectation oppressive. She had bouts of bulimia and suffered a near-breakdown at the back of the royal box during Ascot's Royal Meeting and had to be taken home. The Prince was worried too, and sought the advice of his grandmother rather than his parents. One cousin on the Queen Mother's side of the family later revealed that he had asked her how he would know if he was doing the right thing. 'Would you mind if Diana married somebody else?' she answered. When the Prince said that he would, the Queen Mother replied: 'You obviously do love her.'[28] Friends of the Prince were starting to worry. 'He would ask married friends what they did when their wives suddenly locked themselves in a room,' said one, 'and they wouldn't know quite what to say.'[29] These wobbles did not go unnoticed by the Queen. Even her old equerry, Earl Spencer, the father of the bride, shared his own doubts with the monarch.[30] In her view, these were understandable pre-wedding nerves and both Charles and Diana had made their choices. Not known for being solicitous of those showing signs of frailty – 'Oh look, she's keeled over again,' she observed when Mrs Thatcher fainted at a diplomatic reception – the monarch was unsympathetic.[31] 'The Queen was incredibly kind in so many ways but she was also a member of the "pull yourself together" generation,' noted one who worked with her for many years.[32]

A prime example of that occurred just a month before the

1979–82: 'Don't look back'

wedding, as she was riding down the Mall on the Birthday Parade and shots rang out from the crowd. The gunman, Marcus Sarjeant, a troubled seventeen-year-old, was instantly jumped on by one of the Guardsmen lining the route. His replica Colt pistol contained blanks, but no one knew that at the time. The Queen simply calmed her long-serving mare, Burmese, and rode on. With the benefit of hindsight, the incident tends to be downplayed and has been largely forgotten. However, a close aide has now revealed her real thoughts at the time: 'She had no idea they were blanks. And when she saw the police running past, she feared the worst. She said to me: "I saw all the attention heading behind me and I thought that someone had shot my husband." It was unusual for her to say "husband", which is why I remember it so well. And she explained that she just kept staring ahead and going forwards because that is what you do. She said to herself, "Don't look back," because she was afraid she might see the Duke's body. It was her way of dealing with it.'[33] Grainy film footage shows the moment after she has turned the corner on to Horse Guards and realizes that the parade appears to be continuing. It is only then that she allows herself a quick glance over her left shoulder. The look on her face after seeing that the Duke is trotting along behind is one of unabashed joy. Indeed, it was possibly the smiliest that Elizabeth II had ever been on a parade ground. 'Funnily enough, it's one of those things you often think about riding down the Mall: who might at any minute do something crazy?' Prince Charles reflected years later. 'You must continue as Mama did. You can't rush off in panic.'[34]

Both Charles and Diana applied the same philosophy on the morning of 29 July 1981. In her confessional revelations to Andrew Morton years later, Diana would talk of her severe bulimia on the eve of the wedding and her elation the next

Elizabeth II

morning as she opened Prince Charles's gift of a signet ring and his message: 'I'm so proud of you and when you come up I'll be there at the altar for you tomorrow. Just look 'em in the eye and knock 'em dead.'[35]

To the world, the scenes at St Paul's Cathedral seemed like a fairy tale come true, even before the Archbishop of Canterbury, Robert Runcie, said as much in his address. This was the greatest on-screen royal moment since the Coronation. There was a global intake of breath as the billowing ivory silk creation of David and Elizabeth Emanuel, with its 25-foot train, finally emerged from the Glass Coach with Lady Diana on the arm of her smiling if unsteady father (he was still recovering from a stroke). The Queen, typically, had been focusing on the practicalities and had already spotted one errant horse in the procession. She informed the commanding officer of the Household Cavalry, Andrew Parker Bowles, who immediately removed the offender from the return journey.

Britain had not been a happy nation in recent months, after some of the worst rioting of the twentieth century, notably in Brixton and Toxteth. Margaret Thatcher's economic reforms had some way to go before gain followed pain. Yet, as the Prince and the new Princess of Wales had their first kiss on the balcony of royal headquarters, cheered to the sunny summer skies by the largest Buckingham Palace crowd in a generation, the monarchy had, once again, shown its unique ability to lift the mood and the global standing of the United Kingdom. Was this the post-Coronation high point of the reign of Elizabeth II?

Only eleven monarchs in English and British history had reached thirty years on the throne. When Elizabeth II did so in 1982, there were no celebrations whatsoever. She had refused to countenance the idea, believing that her Silver Jubilee had

1979–82: 'Don't look back'

been quite enough. Yet in the space of just six weeks, she would experience some of the proudest, happiest, saddest and downright nastiest moments of her long life.

She was already looking forward to two great landmarks: historic first visits to Britain by the Pope and by the new president of the USA, Ronald Reagan. By the time these two events occurred, Britain was not only unexpectedly at war in the South Atlantic, but her own son was in the thick of the action.

Following the invasion of the Falkland Islands (British sovereign territory since 1833) by Argentina, Mrs Thatcher had despatched a 'task force' to liberate them. It was a huge military and political gamble led by the Royal Navy's two operational aircraft carriers. Prince Andrew was a helicopter pilot in one of them, HMS *Invincible*. Mrs Thatcher had given serious thought to preventing the Prince from going, on the basis that he would be a prestige target and thus draw down enemy fire on those around him. The Prince and his parents were adamant, however, that he should do his duty. 'It would have destroyed any credibility as a professional that I had,' the Prince told this author.[36] The Queen was aware that shielding her son could even call into question her own position as head of the armed forces. Mrs Thatcher had plenty of other battles to fight and relented.

Britain needed all the allies it could muster and none mattered more than the USA. The presidential visit, in June 1982, is remembered for the historic image of the Queen riding with Reagan through the grounds of Windsor Castle. Much more than just a photo opportunity, it was about shoring up unequivocal American backing at a time when some voices in Washington viewed Argentina as a bulwark against communism in South America. The Foreign Office files reveal just how excited Reagan was about staying at Windsor Castle and, especially, the prospect of joining the Queen on horseback.[37]

Elizabeth II

She was determined to make the president as welcome as possible (even securing a star of the Reagans' favourite television drama, *Brideshead Revisited*, for the banquet*). And it worked. As well as likening Britain's Falklands conflict to the Second World War, the president also offered the Queen something she had always wanted: an invitation to Hollywood. Had he asked her to make a state visit, it would automatically have meant going back to Washington. So, he formally invited her to pay an 'official' visit to California, where he had previously been governor. She was elated.

The following year, amid atrocious weather, she was feted at the studios of 20th Century Fox, dined at Trader Vics in San Francisco and was the first world leader invited to a Tex-Mex barbecue at the Reagan ranch. The rain was so bad that she nearly didn't make it. When Nancy Reagan apologized for the downpour, the Queen was having none of it. 'No, no, this is an adventure!' she told her.[38] It was a reminder of her lifelong excitement when doing something a little differently, especially if there was a risk it might go wrong.

During the Reagans' three-day Windsor visit in early June 1982, they had noticed one guest who looked miserable at their first dinner and who was not there at all for the second. Two weeks later, on 21 June, the Princess of Wales gave birth to a boy. The Queen was as thrilled as anyone and insisted on a prompt visit to the hospital where she declared: 'Thank goodness he hasn't got ears like his father.'[39] She was already on a high following national rejoicing seven days earlier. The Argentinian forces had finally surrendered in the Falklands after the most audacious and successful military operation since the Second World War. The Queen and the country could

---

* Anthony Andrews.

1979–82: 'Don't look back'

now look forward to some deliriously happy homecomings, including that of her own son.

There was, however, one shocking, indirect result of that Reagan visit. With the Queen entertaining the president down at Windsor, the staff at Buckingham Palace had been slacking. When a housemaid alerted security to say she was sure she had seen a strange man prowling around, she was told she must be mistaken. She was not. Michael Fagan, an unemployed thirty-two-year-old with drug and mental health problems, had managed to climb inside the Palace gardens, up a drainpipe and in through an open window. To his amazement, he was able to wander round the state apartments and sit on one of the thrones. He even helped himself to a bottle of wine before quietly leaving the way he had arrived. He had found it all so exciting that he decided to come back a month later.

He returned via the same route, triggering several alarms. The policeman on duty assumed there was some sort of fault and switched them off again. Fagan would later recall 'following the pictures' into the private apartments, breaking a glass ashtray along the way and cutting his hand. At around 7.15 a.m. on 9 July 1982, the Queen awoke to find a barefoot man by her bed, dripping blood and holding a piece of broken glass. As Fagan told police later, he had suddenly had the idea of slitting his wrist in front of her. It was the intruder's good fortune that Prince Philip, facing a dawn start for an early engagement, was sleeping in another room. While some might have screamed or fainted or simply frozen, the Queen had the presence of mind to stay calm and encourage him to talk. All the while, she was pressing the alarm button by her bed – in vain, as it turned out, as the duty policeman had finished his shift at 6 a.m. Eventually, a maid appeared and, so it is said, shouted: 'Bloody 'ell, Ma'am, what's he doing here?'[40] Help was summoned and

Elizabeth II

Fagan was arrested. After three months in a psychiatric hospital, he was released.

So many aspects of this story still seem incredible. Perhaps the most extraordinary of them all was what happened next. The Queen was, understandably, furious with the ineptitude of the police and might well have wanted instant answers. However, she was also due to hold an investiture at eleven o'clock that same morning. More than a hundred people and their families would already be on their way to the Palace for arguably the proudest day of their lives. Despite her horrific start to the day, the Queen was not going to let them down. She arrived precisely on time, spoke to each recipient one by one in the time-honoured way and presented them with their honours. Until they opened a newspaper the following day, none of them had the faintest idea that she had just endured the stuff of horror films. Not for the first or last time, however, she was faintly surprised that anyone should be surprised. As she told someone, who told Douglas Hurd: 'You seem to forget that I spend most of my time conversing with complete strangers.'[41]

What upset her far more was the news she received less than a fortnight later. On 20 July 1982, the IRA planted two devices in London. One killed seven members of the Band of the Royal Green Jackets as they performed a lunchtime concert in Regent's Park. Another was a nail bomb which killed four soldiers and five horses of the Blues and Royals as they were processing through Hyde Park en route to the Changing of the Guard. Shortly afterwards, the same commanding officer who had led the same regiment on that triumphal royal wedding procession the year before received a call from the Queen herself. 'I'm so terribly sorry,' she told Lieutenant Colonel Andrew Parker Bowles. 'It's the most ghastly day of my life.'[42]

Chapter Ten

1983–91
'Let's have him'

To the wider world, mid-eighties Britain seemed resurgent and reinvigorated under a female triumvirate of the Queen, the Princess of Wales and Margaret Thatcher – now in her second term of office following a thumping post-Falklands election win. Four months after the vote, the monarch and prime minister would be drawn closer together through the uncharacteristically discourteous action of their mutual friend, Ronald Reagan. On 25 October 1983, Mrs Thatcher had the awkward task of informing the Queen that one of her realms had been invaded by the USA. President Reagan had sent troops into the Caribbean island of Grenada following a Marxist coup. He had done so without first consulting, or even warning, its head of state – Elizabeth II. According to Household veterans of that time, Mrs Thatcher was actually more upset about this than the monarch herself. The Queen, said one former private secretary, was no more than 'peeved'.[1] After all, her own vice-regal representative, the governor-general, had been in favour of the US invasion and, besides, Marxist coups were not to be encouraged.

Order restored, the Americans soon withdrew and transatlantic bonhomie swiftly resumed. A year later, the Queen was actually back in the USA, this time on a rare foreign holiday, when the two women were, once again, drawn together in the face of a crisis. On 12 October 1984, the IRA exploded a bomb inside Margaret Thatcher's Brighton hotel during the Conservative Party conference, killing five people. The Queen received the news at a ranch in Kentucky, where she was inspecting horses, and immediately started making plans to return home, uncertain if she still had a prime minister. Mrs Thatcher was having none of it when monarch and prime minister finally made contact on the telephone a few hours after the explosion. Charles Anson, then with the royal party as a diplomat, recalled Mrs Thatcher's attempt to sound upbeat as she began: 'I hope you're having a nice time.'[2]

As noted earlier, however, one growing point of tension between Downing Street and Buckingham Palace was the Commonwealth. By the mid-1980s, all the member states were in favour of imposing sanctions on the racist apartheid regime in South Africa. All, that is, except one – Britain. Margaret Thatcher believed that sanctions were hardest on the poorest in South Africa and also bad for British business. Matters came to a head at the 1985 Commonwealth summit in the Bahamas, at which the UK refused to budge, leaving Elizabeth II in a very awkward position. She was Queen of several countries that backed sanctions, she was Queen of the arch-opponent to the plan and she was the head – the figure of unity – of an organization that might implode over the issue. To make matters worse, many member states announced they would boycott the upcoming Edinburgh Commonwealth Games due to be held on her very own Scottish doorstep.

The Queen was powerless to do anything about any of the above except to be seen as a calming, uniting influence.

1983–91: 'Let's have him'

Whereupon she was appalled, all of a sudden, to find herself portrayed as a politically partisan activist scheming against an equally appalled Mrs Thatcher. The front page of *The Sunday Times* of 20 July 1986 was uncompromising. 'Queen dismayed by "uncaring" Thatcher,' ran the main headline, above a story based on 'sources close to the Queen'. Those sources reported that the monarch found her prime minister to be 'uncaring, confrontational and socially divisive'. Further lengthy coverage inside claimed that the monarch was not just worried about Mrs Thatcher's position on the Commonwealth, but on her forceful handling of the recent miners' strike and even her decision to allow US bombers to attack Libya from British soil. The Queen, said the newspaper, was fearful of 'long-term damage to the country's social fabric'. When Sir William Heseltine, by now knighted and her principal private secretary, first got wind of what was coming, he urged the Queen to contact Mrs Thatcher to reassure her that that there was no question of her 'being aware of anything being said which could lead to this kind of conclusion.'[3]

However, the paper's editor, Andrew Neil, was adamant that his story was very properly sourced and Mrs Thatcher's team knew *The Sunday Times* well enough to realize that this was not mere gossip. According to the prime minister's private secretary, Robin Butler, the whole thing hurt her deeply. 'Personally, she was in awe of the Queen and would be deeply hurt if she felt the Queen was not approving of what she was doing,' he told this author.[4] Denis Thatcher confided in one of the Queen's ladies-in-waiting that his wife was extremely distressed. So, too, for that matter, was the Queen. The idea that, after more than three decades of impeccable constitutional impartiality, she would suddenly undergo a character transplant and recklessly seek to undermine a prime minister with a substantial democratic mandate was both

Elizabeth II

bewildering and upsetting. That question, though, was now being addressed across the media. As Princess Margaret told a friend: 'That was the only time I've ever seen her cry.'[5]

Eventually, the truth emerged. The story had indeed come from a source 'close to the Queen', namely her press secretary Michael Shea. It turned out he had spoken to two *Sunday Times* journalists and had been airily ruminating on the monarch's likely world view through the prism of his own centrist opinions. He then spent two weeks insisting it was not him, before conceding that it was. 'He certainly thought that he had been very clever in getting an important piece of journalism slanted to give a picture of the Queen's views which he thought the public would find sympathetic,' said one of his senior colleagues, 'but panicked when he realized what he had done.'[6] Rather than sack him on the spot, his bosses (and his ultimate boss) waited a few months and then he was quietly moved on to a press role at Hanson PLC, allowing him to pretend it was of his own volition. Sir William Heseltine later acknowledged that Shea had not had any choice. Downing Street had also played its part in his removal.[7] It would help clear the air. Both sides had gone out of their way to appear untroubled by the episode. Shortly after Shea's admission, the prime minister had been a guest at Holyroodhouse, where the Queen pointedly seated Mrs Thatcher as close to her as possible. In between them, she seated Michael Shea, who apologized to the prime minister. Nonetheless, both women would feel bruised by the affair for some time.

There was one very happy distraction for the Queen in the midst of all this. In the very same week, she was celebrating the marriage of her second son, Prince Andrew, to Sarah Ferguson. The bride had been introduced to Prince Andrew at the suggestion of the Princess of Wales.

1983–91: 'Let's have him'

Diana actually had a lot in common with Sarah, whom the press and public instantly came to know as 'Fergie'. Once again, here was a girl who had grown up on the fringes of the Royal Family (in Sarah's case, because her ex-Cavalry officer father, Major Ron Ferguson, was polo manager to the Prince of Wales). Both had experienced the trauma of divorce as young children. In both cases, they had remained with their fathers while their mothers had moved abroad.

Unlike Diana, however, Sarah had previously been in a long-term relationship, living for several years with former racing driver Paddy McNally, two decades her senior. Just five years on from the Waleses' wedding, attitudes towards pre-marital cohabitation were changing fast. Besides, Prince Andrew was sliding quickly down the line of succession following the arrival of the Waleses' second son, Harry, in 1984, so there was no serious prospect of 'Fergie' being Queen.

Moreover, Andrew was enjoying one of the upsides of being 'the Spare', as Prince Harry would later describe his status as a second son. For the public had always been less censorious when it came to his behaviour. Andrew's image was that of a boisterous, laddish warrior Prince rejoicing in his media soubriquet of 'Randy Andy' (a nickname first acquired at school). He'd had a well-documented string of girlfriends, including an American actress, Koo Stark, of whom the family were very fond, before he met Sarah at a Windsor lunch during Royal Ascot. Seated next to each other, they bonded over a profiterole-eating game. As the wedding approached, no article was complete without a reference to the hearty, flame-haired, joke-loving, face-pulling party girl as 'a breath of fresh air'. The Queen was delighted. Sarah exhibited none of the inner turmoil she had spotted in Diana; as events would reveal soon enough, the bride was seldom consumed with self-doubt. And the

Elizabeth II

Queen was thrilled for Andrew, giving him the same precious pre-abdication title held by her father – Duke of York – on the morning of his wedding at Westminster Abbey.

It has long since become received media and public wisdom that Andrew was the Queen's 'favourite son'. One family friend put it slightly differently: 'He'd been this wonderful baby after the ten-year gap with her older children. He wasn't sensitive like Charles but, rather, all things that her husband had been – a straightforward, handsome naval officer. On the other hand, he was a seven-year-old who never grew up.' Some of these childlike tendencies could be almost endearing, like his collection of teddy bears. Others suggested more deep-rooted issues. 'He never drank alcohol and always stuck to room-temperature water,' the friend continued. 'Fair enough, but I once asked him why and he answered like a child: "I tasted it once when I was a teenager and I didn't like it." That's why the Queen would always worry about him.'[8]

Outwardly, the Royal Family appeared to be in full bloom with another young glamour couple at the monarchy's disposal. The Duke of York would continue his career in the Royal Navy while the Duchess built a portfolio of charities. Like Lilibet and Margaret six decades earlier, there would soon be a new pair of York Princesses: Beatrice, born in 1988, and Eugenie, born in 1990. All the while, the Prince and Princess of Wales remained the most in-demand couple on the planet. They had enjoyed a dazzlingly successful tour of Australia and New Zealand in 1983, taking Prince William with them. Following the birth of Prince Harry in 1984, the Prince and Princess were back on the world stage together a year later with city-stopping visits to Italy and the USA. 'Dianamania' reached a new peak at the Reagan White House after the Princess was swept onto the dance floor by John Travolta. However, the Queen was not to be entirely eclipsed.

1983–91: 'Let's have him'

The public was reminded of her standing as a global stateswoman as she became the first reigning monarch to land in China. In Shanghai alone, she was greeted by two million people on a single drive through the city. These were the largest crowds since her tour of India twenty-five years before, while Foreign Office files show substantial diplomatic and commercial breakthroughs as the tour progressed.[9]

In Britain, it would always be remembered for Prince Philip's chance remark to a group of Edinburgh University exchange students: 'If you stay here much longer you'll all be slitty-eyed.' One of them repeated it to a British journalist, and the UK press would write of little else for days afterwards. The story went on to enter royal folklore, forever after resurrected in any list of ducal 'gaffes'. Sir William Heseltine would always remember delivering the news headlines to the royal couple. 'I had worse moments,' he recalled, 'but not too many.'[10]

Thankfully for the Palace and the Foreign Office, the story made no impact in China whatsoever, as the Chinese media simply ignored it. There was, correspondingly, almost no media interest in a remarkable royal event the following year: the Queen's one and only abdication. Following a military coup in Fiji, where she was head of state, there was no restoration of democracy as there had been in Grenada. She could not expect her governor-general – her Fijian self – to give official recognition to an armed insurrection, nor to risk his life rejecting it. So she told him to resign, thus terminating her position and her Fijian throne. Margaret Thatcher was appalled and tried in vain to object, until it was pointed out that the Queen of Fiji was under no obligation to listen to the prime minister of Britain. The *Sunday Times* brouhaha inadvertently concocted by Michael Shea the year before might have grossly overstated Palace/Downing Street splits. However, they still existed, and here was another one.

Elizabeth II

That same year, 1987, the prime minister won her third consecutive election. Britain was flourishing economically on the back of a surging financial services sector, albeit with much of its old industrial base in terminal decline. Margaret Thatcher appeared in command of all that she surveyed, though cracks were starting to appear if anyone looked closely. The same could be said for the monarchy.

The first rumours were beginning to circulate that the Waleses were drifting apart (as the Prince's biographer, Jonathan Dimbleby, would later reveal they were). The Queen had been well aware of trouble in the marriage for years. As Diana later revealed: 'She indicated to me that the reason why our marriage had gone downhill was because Prince Charles was having such a difficult time with my bulimia.'[11] Nevertheless, the royal expectation was that everyone should just soldier on and the press continued to fill the papers with largely positive reports of the younger members of the family. There was, however, an increasing sense that the Duchess of York's main aim in life was to be on holiday (one newspaper noted that she went on nine holidays, comprising ninety-nine days of vacation, in the first nine months of 1987).[12]

A sense of the family just starting to lose touch was epitomized by Prince Edward's disastrous if well-intentioned idea of cajoling some of them into a game show. Having recently graduated from Cambridge, he had boldly thrown himself into the notoriously tough basic training programme for the Royal Marines. He then went the way of most candidates and dropped out, receiving much more in the way of unkind media criticism than any due respect for having given it a go in the first place. The Queen, like Prince Philip, had a great deal of sympathy, which explains why they subsequently agreed to support Edward's first venture in a new quest to forge a career in

1983–91: 'Let's have him'

television. The Prince had drawn up plans for a revival of the old knockabout, gladiatorial game show *It's a Knockout*, except this would involve royalty and celebrities larking around in a pantomime medieval castle.

The cast included proper A-list talent, including actors Sir John Mills and Christopher Reeve, singers Dame Kiri Te Kanawa and Tom Jones, and sport's Gary Lineker and Nigel Mansell. Prince Edward had also recruited the Yorks, who were in their guffawing, thigh-slapping element, and a notably less enthusiastic Princess Royal. The result was an hour and a half of slapstick buffoonery and custard-pie capers. The press had been left to watch the event remotely in a marquee. They were underwhelmed, all the more so when the Prince stormed out of the subsequent press conference, smarting at their lack of enthusiasm.

The show would draw a bumper primetime BBC audience and raise more than a million pounds for charity, but at a price to the monarchy. 'The thing that appalled me was that we were kept in total ignorance of it until the last moment when it had all been set up,' the Queen's senior private secretary at the time, Sir William Heseltine, told this author. 'I think Edward had the feeling he had to justify himself because he'd just left the Marines. That was a case where the Private Secretary's advice was not required. He knew what the advice would be and he didn't want to hear it. I think the Queen thought: "The poor boy is suffering from the criticism of leaving the Marines; let him get on and do this." But I don't think anyone expected it to be quite as awful as it was.'[13]

What was supposed to make the Royal Family look relatable and fun had, instead, looked undignified, out of touch and cringeworthy. Who could now blame critics of the monarchy if they were going to attack it as a soap opera? There was no

Elizabeth II

sense of impending crisis, no darkening clouds overhead. Yet there was a feeling of complacency and disconnection, such as when a Pan-Am 747 was blown up above the Scottish town of Lockerbie just before Christmas 1988. This was not an Aberfan-type situation in which the Queen was waiting for the right moment to attend. Aside from one appearance from Prince Andrew, who made some inept remarks about such a disaster being 'statistically' probable, the Royal Family did not appear in Lockerbie. Soon afterwards, the Queen admitted to her staff that this had been a mistake.

Wisely, she had not assumed the years of sunshine and plenty would go on for ever. In 1984, she had made one of the shrewdest managerial decisions of her life when she appointed a new Lord Chamberlain. Often likened to the non-executive chairman of a company board, the Lord Chamberlain is the man (there has yet to be a female office holder) who ensures that all the different departments of the Royal Household do their jobs. In appointing the 13th Earl of Airlie, however, the Queen was kickstarting the reform of her entire monarchy. That would require both authority and brains, and David Airlie had both.

Descended from a long line of courtiers, his family castle, Cortachy, was near that of the Queen Mother's family at Glamis. A direct contemporary of the Queen, he had grown up with her, so much so that she would sometimes refer to him as 'my twin'. His study would always contain the earliest photograph of the Queen at the wheel of a car. It was the pedal car he had received on his fourth birthday and he was the cross-looking little boy in the photo who had clearly been ordered to allow Princess Elizabeth to have a go in it.

After military service in the Scots Guards, he had run his family's Scottish estate before pursuing a very successful career

1983–91: 'Let's have him'

in the City of London, rising to be chairman of a major bank, Schroders. Throughout it all, he had remained a trusted royal friend and ally. Indeed, his American-born wife, Virginia (née Ryan), became a long-serving and very popular lady-in-waiting to the Queen. As David Airlie began to think about life beyond the City, the Queen had a request. She had not forgotten the toxic debates about the royal finances in the early seventies. She knew that the institution was living beyond its means under the watchful eye of a prime minister with a fanatical loathing of sloppy finances, even royal ones. The Royal Household needed serious reform if it was to avoid the nightmare of being answerable to some faceless government agency. Would her 'twin' take charge at the Palace?

After conducting his own reconnaissance, Lord Airlie brought in a small team of accountants led by Michael Peat, whose family firm, Peat Marwick, had ties to the Royal Household. Airlie commissioned him to undertake a forensic analysis of every aspect of the royal machine. Within six months, Peat had drawn up a 1,383-page report containing 188 proposals, and the two men took it to the Queen. Though she knew it would cause great pain, and would certainly upset her mother, the pragmatist Queen gave Lord Airlie the brisk instruction: 'Get on with it.'[14]

From streamlining staff dining or the feeding of the horses right down to the proverbial changing of the light bulbs, the reforms started to bring down the costs. Crucially, it meant that the Lord Chamberlain could prove to the government that the best people to set budgets and targets for the Royal Household were the Household staff themselves. In her final months as prime minister, Margaret Thatcher and the Leader of the Opposition, Neil Kinnock, jointly agreed a new funding arrangement for the monarchy. Instead of coming on bended

Elizabeth II

knee with a bill each year, the Palace would get a fixed annual sum for ten years and make long-term plans accordingly. The next issue was fixing that sum at a sensible level, given that runaway inflation could eat it all up and ruin the monarchy. Airlie and his team negotiated an annual £7.9 million. As it turned out, inflation remained stable and the Airlie plan would not just last for the next ten years, but would remain unchanged for twenty. The Queen and her 'twin' were not to know it, but this new arrangement would prove a godsend when things started to go wrong. And they would soon go very wrong indeed.

In late 1990, a Tory leadership challenge against Mrs Thatcher left her authority damaged beyond repair, and she went to the Queen to resign. Barely able to speak through her tears on the way in, she emerged somewhat brighter with the Queen's parting gift.[15] The monarch had appointed her to the Order of Merit, limited to just twenty-four of the most eminent people of their times. Other honours would follow, but this one was entirely in the personal gift of the monarch, ranking the tearful ex-PM alongside Winston Churchill, Mother Theresa and Florence Nightingale.

The Queen had never known anyone like Mrs Thatcher, and would always be fascinated by her. 'Do you think Mrs Thatcher will ever change?' she would often ask her colleagues (to which Lord Carrington was once reputed to have replied: 'No, Ma'am. She wouldn't be Mrs Thatcher if she did.').

After another leadership battle, the task of following the 'Iron Lady' fell to her chancellor, John Major. In one royal regard, he was definitely an improvement on Margaret Thatcher. Since spending an earlier part of his career in Nigeria, Major was a firm fan of the Commonwealth.

1983–91: 'Let's have him'

Having said farewell to one of the political titans of her age, the Queen was about to be introduced to another. At the next Commonwealth summit, in Zimbabwe, she was checking the final table arrangements ahead of her banquet for all the leaders, whereupon she was informed that an extra space was needed. No one was entirely sure who had invited the last-minute addition. Out of prison for less than a year, Nelson Mandela was not (yet) a leader or even a minister, but he was a fan of the Commonwealth – and the feeling was mutual. 'Let's have him,' the Queen replied instantly. 'Lay another place.'[16] South Africa had been such a key part of her life. It was where she had first set foot on foreign soil; she had been Queen of South Africa until its white minority government imposed the apartheid system of racial segregation, left the Commonwealth and ejected the Crown in 1961. Having fought the system and spent twenty-seven years in prison for his principles, Mandela had become a global symbol of democratic resistance, and now free elections loomed thanks in no small part to years of pressure from the Commonwealth. These might be early days, but he was already a statesman in the making, and this experienced stateswoman wanted to make him as welcome as possible. The Queen told her new private secretary, Robert Fellowes, that she wanted Mandela seated where she could catch his eye – Fellowes sat next to him for good measure – and, later on, ensured that they had their first chat over the after-dinner coffee.[17] 'You're looking well, taking into account your tight schedule,' Mandela told her. 'I may not look so good tomorrow,' the Queen replied chattily, adding: 'Someone asked me if I'd been to Africa before – which was nice of them . . .'[18] Theirs would be one of the most enduring and unconventional friendships of her later years, lasting through a period of dramatic upheaval, for the Queen on a personal level and for the world.

Elizabeth II

The fall of the Berlin Wall in 1989 and the subsequent collapse of the Soviet empire (not to mention the summary execution of the Queen's erstwhile house guests Nicolae and Elena Ceaușescu) felt like the start of a new world order. In a matter of months, that old alliance of the USA and the UK was back on the battlefield, along with a coalition of forty nations, following the invasion of Kuwait by the Iraqi despot, Saddam Hussein. As British troops prepared to go into battle to liberate the small Gulf kingdom, the Queen broadcast a 'special message' expressing her pride in her armed forces and the nation's hopes for 'a just and lasting peace'. It was highly unusual. Indeed, it was the first emergency televised address by a monarch, echoing the wireless broadcasts by her father at key moments in the Second World War. She had not done this during the Korean War or the Falklands conflict. And it had been her idea, not that of the government. So why now?

One former aide suggested that, with the departure of Mrs Thatcher, she may have felt a little more confident about emphasizing her role as head of the armed forces.[19] It may have also been motivated, in part, by her reading of the national mood towards her family.

Three months earlier, as the build-up of troops and weapons was intensifying, there was another broadside against the monarchy from *The Sunday Times*. Though ostensibly a Conservative paper, its Australian-turned-American owner, Rupert Murdoch, was no fan of the Royal Family, nor was his dynamic young editor, Andrew Neil. The paper launched a withering attack on the 'young royals', contrasting the Windsors' enthusiasm for shooting parties, ski trips and winter sunshine with all those ordinary servicemen and women preparing to risk their lives in the Gulf. 'This country is at war, though you would never believe it from the shenanigans of some members

1983–91: 'Let's have him'

of Her Majesty's clan,' the paper announced in an editorial that went on to denounce 'a mixture of upper-class decadence and insensitivity which demeans the monarchy'.[20] The paper had touched a nerve and the unusual broadcast suggested that the head of the armed forces had taken note. It was also a reminder that, however much the 'young royals' might hog the headlines, good and bad, the public should remember who was really running the show.

In the event, the allies would achieve an overwhelming victory with a bare minimum of casualties. The Queen would soon be on her way to the USA for a celebratory state visit hosted by President George Bush. Her tour would be best remembered for the welcome podium, which obscured everything except her hat, and her opening line to a joint session of Congress two days later: 'I do hope you can see me today.' They were on their feet from the start. 'That speaks to her character. You know, rather than be insulted, she saw the humour in it,' President George W. Bush, who would host the Queen himself sixteen years later, told this author. 'That's the woman I got to see.'[21]

The Gulf War had lasted a matter of weeks and had left the Western alliance unrivalled on the world stage. For the Queen and her monarchy, however, the worst crisis in modern royal history was about to begin.

Chapter Eleven

1992–95

'Horribilis'

It would become one of the most famous phrases she ever uttered. Yet she nearly never said it. Other great lines from the reign of Elizabeth II – such as 'recollections may vary' or 'grief is the price we pay for love' – were only ever delivered in written form. 'Annus horribilis', however, came from the Queen's mouth. But only just.

On the morning of 24 November 1992, the Queen was about to leave for the Guildhall in the City of London for a long-planned lunch to celebrate forty years on the throne. Ahead of that year, she had consented to very little in honour of what was emphatically *not* to be called her Ruby Jubilee. However, she had agreed to attend this lunch and to make a speech afterwards. Now that the day had dawned, there were a number of reasons for cancelling. Not only did she have a bad cold which had left her croaking with a sore throat but, four days earlier, her family home had been ablaze and she had breathed in a lot of smoke while retrieving personal items from her private apartments.

The fire was but the latest in a series of personal calamities – including collapsing royal marriages and a chorus of media

Elizabeth II

and political complaints about the family finances – which, by her own admission, had tested her sanity. She had also spent the previous forty-eight hours in crisis talks with her senior advisers ahead of two closely guarded, historic decisions which would be announced in the days ahead. Her stress levels were even higher than that week when she had disappeared with nervous exhaustion in the summer of 1969.

'I can't make a speech today. I haven't got a voice,' she told her private secretary, Robert Fellowes. 'Prince Philip will have to do it.' Gently but firmly, the wise old courtier persisted. 'If there's one speech that no one else can do, it's this,' he told her. 'It's the one speech you have to make if it's going to be made at all.'[1] Reluctantly, but pragmatic and stoical as ever, she had a compromise solution. 'Alright,' she told Fellowes. 'I'll do it at the beginning of lunch when I've got something of a voice.' If it achieved nothing else, the speech would set a precedent which she would observe for the rest of her reign. Whenever possible, she would speak before a meal rather than at the end.

The assembled politicians and City luminaries sat in total silence, without so much as a clink of a glass, as the small, reedy voice reverberated through the sound system. 'Nineteen ninety-two is not a year on which I shall look back with undiluted pleasure,' she declared. 'In the words of one of my more sympathetic correspondents, it has turned out to be an "annus horribilis".' The phrase – Latin for a 'terrible year' (or 'One's Bum Year' in the words of *The Sun*) – had been coined by her retired assistant private secretary, Sir Edward Ford. However, the point of the speech was not to dwell on her misfortune, but to call for a sense of perspective. 'I sometimes wonder how future generations will judge the events of this tumultuous year. I dare say that history will take a slightly more moderate view

1992–95: 'Horribilis'

than that of some contemporary commentators,' she continued. 'No institution – City, monarchy, whatever – should expect to be free from the scrutiny of those who give it their loyalty and support, not to mention those who don't.' And then came a direct plea to the media: 'We are all part of the same fabric of our national society, and that scrutiny, by one part of another, can be just as effective if it is made with a touch of gentleness, good humour and understanding.'

Even a political veteran like Douglas Hurd, then foreign secretary, was astonished: 'I sat up sharpish in my seat because it was quite different from anything she'd said before.'[2] 'It was portrayed as a cry for help, and the fact that she had this terrible throat made it all the more powerful,' said one senior member of her staff later. 'But it was really her saying: "You're not just dealing with me and my family. You're dealing with an institution and you really are knocking it about a bit." And I think she felt her children were getting a very hard time at the hands of the press. She would almost sooner it was all directed at her. As Robert Fellowes put it: "It was about asking for a little bit of common sense and a little less hysteria".'[3]

To call 1992 a 'tumultuous' year was an understatement. It had opened on a high note, with the release of one of the most memorable royal documentaries ever made, *Elizabeth R*, directed by the BBC's Eddie Mirzoeff. The production had enjoyed intimate access after Mirzoeff had quickly discovered the secret to filming a happy and relaxed Queen: familiar faces. So, he hired the same cameraman, Philip Bonham Carter, and sound recordist, Peter Edwards, who had not only worked on that groundbreaking film, *Royal Family*, twenty-three years earlier, but had also filmed her Christmas broadcasts for many years with the BBC's David Attenborough. 'She was extremely comfortable with them,' recalls one of her staff.[4]

Elizabeth II

Once again, the writer would be Antony Jay, whose accompanying book would go on to change the way the monarchy viewed itself. Back in 1969, the original project had been supervised by a new young press secretary, Bill Heseltine. He was now about to retire from the top job of principal private secretary and would give the new film his blessing. It even featured commentary from the Queen herself as she reflected on the rhythms of royal life over shots of her entertaining presidents on her yacht or walking with grandchildren and ponies at Balmoral. Along with the Guildhall lunch, it was one of just a handful of the projects she had approved for her fortieth year on the throne. As Mirzoeff explained, the Palace had started to feel that the Queen – now reaching retirement age – was being eclipsed. 'There was a feeling that attention had been drifting away towards the younger members of the family – especially after *It's a Knockout* – and I think, at that point, they wanted to put the focus more on what the Queen does,' said Mirzoeff. 'There was a sense of: how do we justify all this if the Queen is out of sight? She was doing tours and yet no one was reporting it. The younger royals were all over the papers. It was partly a question of: how do we pull this back?'[5] Even if the Queen was not naturally vain or competitive with the rest of the family (who could often be competitive with each other), she was always very conscious of her position. Like many women who, for years, had successfully juggled a family and a career in a predominantly male workplace, why should she be expected to stand by and see others feted for less? 'The Queen didn't care much about her image but she did care about the way the job was perceived,' said a senior courtier of the period. 'So, no, she didn't need much persuading to do this. The Duke of Edinburgh didn't want anything to do with it, though. He'd been very involved with *Royal Family*, almost running the show.

1992–95: 'Horribilis'

But times had changed. If he wasn't part of it, he didn't want to know.'[6]

The documentary was a great hit when it aired in January 1992. For a few days, the public would be left with the impression of a kindly, energetic matriarch at the helm of a contented, united family working to keep Britain on the world map. And then everything started to unravel. In that same month, a newspaper obtained a batch of photographs of the Duchess of York holidaying with an American oil executive, Steve Wyatt, who was clearly more than just a good friend. The Duke and Duchess started consulting divorce lawyers. The following month, the Prince and Princess of Wales were on an official tour of India when the Princess pointedly posed alone in front of that global symbol of love, the Taj Mahal. The Prince had been undertaking a series of dry official engagements in Delhi at the same time. No amount of royal spin-doctoring could explain away the forlorn subtext of that image of the Princess, which dominated front pages around the globe the next morning. In March, news leaked that the Yorks were formally separating. It was not only personally painful for the Queen, but constitutionally embarrassing too, as the story bumped the forthcoming general election off the front pages. By convention, the Royal Family are supposed to lie low during elections. The Queen ensured private messages went to the chief combatants, especially Neil Kinnock's Labour Party, which, having just secured its first lead in the opinion polls, wanted to be leading the news. 'It was not exactly a formal apology but it was incredibly awkward,' said a senior courtier of the time.[7] One month further on, it was announced that the Princess Royal and Captain Mark Phillips were finally divorced after a long separation. The Princess had, by now, settled into a new relationship with the Queen's former equerry, Commander Timothy Laurence.

Elizabeth II

To the surprise of the opinion polls and the commentariat, the general election was won by John Major. His government were keen to deploy the diplomatic clout of the Queen right away, to show his European Union counterparts that he was more pro-EU than his predecessor. He sent her to Strasbourg to deliver what the European Parliament, to this day, calls an 'explicitly pro-European speech' and, just weeks later, she went back to France on a state visit. The British press, however, barely noticed. The papers were completely dominated by extracts – in where else but *The Sunday Times* – from a shocking new book, *Diana: Her True Story*.

Among its astonishing claims was that the Princess had been suffering from serious eating disorders, while her loveless marriage had even driven her to contemplate suicide. Reassured by the Queen's private secretary (and Diana's brother-in-law), Robert Fellowes, that the Princess had not colluded with author Andrew Morton, senior Establishment figures lined up to denounce the book. When it emerged soon afterwards that Diana had, indeed, communicated everything to Morton via an intermediary, Fellowes was dumbstruck and offered his resignation to the Queen. Through it all, both the press and the politicians were asking an entirely different question. It might be a non-sequitur but it simply would not go away: the marriages of the Queen's children were falling apart, so why did she not pay tax? Nor was it just the usual suspects from the far left making these noises. Conservative commentators and MPs were starting to ask the same question.

There was no respite for the Queen during her summer break at Balmoral. On the morning of 20 August, the royal party – including both the newly separated Yorks – came down to breakfast to find that the *Daily Mirror* had nine pages of photographs of a topless Duchess and her 'financial adviser'

1992–95: 'Horribilis'

John Bryan, by the swimming pool of a villa in the South of France. The images showed various intimate moments, such as Bryan kissing her toes and the Duchess applying sun cream to his bald patch. A French paparazzo had been able to take the images at leisure despite the presence of two police officers protecting the Duchess's daughters, Beatrice, four, and Eugenie, two.

By now, even *The Independent*, a newspaper famous for its non-coverage of royal news, joined the calls for the Queen to pay tax. While the *Mirror* recorded one of the highest sales in its history, *The Sun* was not to be outdone and published the transcript of a bugged telephone conversation (more than two years old) between a miserable Princess of Wales and an old friend, James Gilbey, who called her 'Squidgey'. Diana's description of the agony of a Sandringham Christmas with her frosty in-laws was not only splashed over the paper but replayed on a premium phone line for thirty-six pence per minute. A Balmoral guest over those days had never seen the Queen seem sadder and later told author Graham Turner that she had looked 'ashen' and on the brink of tears after the latest revelations appeared.[8] As ever, she also had a formidable ability to rise above these personal setbacks, usually with the help of animals. The following day, the same guest was amazed to see the Queen 'absolutely transformed' and smiling broadly as she and Prince Philip joined an estate gamekeeper to go ferreting for rabbits.[9]

By now, lawyers for the Prince and Princess of Wales had been examining options for a separation, though the Queen urged them not to do so before an important, long-planned autumn tour of Korea on behalf of the government. The couple put on a united front, promoting British exports and bilateral goodwill, but their personal unhappiness was palpable. On their return, they had a bitter argument about putting on another show of unity for their sons, who were coming home from school for the weekend. The Prince had arranged a house party with old friends and children of the same age. The Princess announced that she would be taking the boys elsewhere. It was the final straw. Both resolved that the time had come to announce a parting of the ways the following week. At that very moment, fire engines from across the South East of England were racing to Windsor Castle.

On 20 November 1992, the staff at Windsor had stopped for their customary 11 a.m. tea break (back then, a tradition as sacred as the Changing of the Guard). Minutes later, an unattended builders' lamp set fire to a drape erected during restoration in the state apartments in the north-east corner of the castle. By the time the alarm had been sounded, the fire was already spreading through ceiling voids and heading in two directions: through the semi-state apartments and south towards the Queen's private apartments, but also west through the mighty St George's Hall and on towards the priceless treasures of the Royal Library.

The only member of the family in residence was a newly single Duke of York, revising for some naval exams. He helped organize human chains of staff and volunteers in a frantic operation to evacuate paintings and furniture out into the Quadrangle. The Queen rushed straight to Windsor, with an urgent rescue plan of her own. 'She went into her own apartments to take a few precious things to safety, because only she knew what they were and where they were,' her press secretary Charles Anson recalled.[10] Though not in danger, she was exposed to the smoke now billowing its way from the public to the private parts of the castle. She then joined the Duke of York and the Lord Chamberlain, Lord Airlie, to monitor the rescue operation.

1992–95: 'Horribilis'

'Awful, awful, awful,' was how Airlie remembered that 'dark, miserable drizzly November day'.[11] The only modest consolation was that it was not actually raining as priceless treasures were stacked all over the grass. To add to the sense of doom and gloom, it was also the Queen's forty-fifth wedding anniversary, but Prince Philip was undertaking charity engagements in South America. The Queen returned to Buckingham Palace alone. Alerted to her imminent arrival, Anson was part of an impromptu group who felt that the least they could do was turn out to welcome her back. As they all prepared to offer some sort of condolence, they were surprised to find the Queen gamely clinging to whatever slender positives she could draw from her dreadful day. Anson would never forget it: 'She just shrugged her shoulders and said, "It was ghastly, but at least we managed to save the pictures." Her spirit was not broken in any way at all.'[12]

Privately, though, it had pushed her to the limit. After retreating to the Queen Mother's home at Royal Lodge for the weekend, her thank-you letter was candid: 'It made all the difference to my sanity after that terrible day.'[13] Nor was she under any illusions about what was coming next. As Lord Airlie later concluded: 'That fire lit other fires.' One of those was already sparking even as the fire brigade were still dousing the wreckage of Windsor.

Surveying the damage, the Heritage Minister, Peter Brooke, confidently announced that the government would rebuild the castle back to its original condition. He had assumed that this would play well with a public united in sympathy for the Queen. He quickly discovered that he had seriously misjudged the national mood.

Even traditional allies of the monarchy were unmoved, arguing that the old Establishment was deluded and the Royal

Elizabeth II

Family should foot the bill. The prime minister of the day was aghast. 'I thought the media reaction to the Windsor fire was mean in the extreme, and I was quite shocked,' John Major told this author. 'Windsor Castle is a national asset. To claim that it isn't seems to be mealy-mouthed in the extreme.'[14] However, Janet Daley, writing in *The Times*, was among this new wave of pro-royal critics. 'The terrible fire raises questions about the royal family that can no longer be fudged,' she warned the House of Windsor. 'While the castle stands, it is theirs, but when it burns down, it is ours.' And Daley's chief complaint was that same old festering sore of an issue: tax. 'The suspicion that the royals are having it both ways does not help the cause of those who would support them. For the Queen to pay no taxes on her private wealth implies that she is not an ordinary citizen.'

On the very morning that this was published, 24 November 1992, the Queen was about to stand up to deliver that 'annus horribilis' speech. Her words dominated the evening news and next day's newspapers, but it was not her only landmark ('bombshell' in tabloid parlance) announcement that week.

Over that shattering weekend at Royal Lodge, the Queen had convened an emergency meeting of her top advisers, including Lord Airlie. Just two days on from the speech, John Major stood up in Parliament to announce that the Queen would now, indeed, voluntarily pay tax like everyone else. The tax exemption had been a 1937 deal quietly fixed between the Queen's father, George VI, and prime minister Neville Chamberlain, as the new King faced ruin paying off his elder brother after the abdication. The former Edward VIII had lied about his wealth and had demanded a high price for the royal estates. Successive governments had maintained the arrangement.

Sir William Heseltine, when private secretary, had tried to

1992–95: 'Horribilis'

raise the tax issue with the Queen in the eighties but had been pushed back. Papa had drummed into her that his deal with Chamberlain was sacrosanct. 'This was a very important concession and was not to be challenged,' said Heseltine.[15] John Major was adamant that the Queen did not need to pay tax and told her so.[16] The Queen Mother was so implacable that the Queen could not face telling her. Despite her innate courage and tungsten resolve in so many other ways, here was a classic example of Elizabeth II subcontracting intra-family confrontation. Fellowes was sent to break the news. He would recall a long pause, after which the Queen Mother responded: 'I think we'll have a drink.'[17]

The tax change remains one of the watershed decisions of the Queen's reign. It was a moment when her intuition and survival instinct outweighed filial loyalty and family pressure, not to mention prime ministerial advice, all of which were urging her to maintain the status quo. For all that, she could see the way in which one set of problems, namely family marital woes, could be conflated with entirely unrelated financial issues to create the gravest reputational crisis for the monarchy since the abdication. It greatly irritated her and her staff when the press painted her tax announcement as a panic-stricken royal response to the latest run of bad headlines and, thus, a victory for the media. Major had made it clear to the Commons that the Queen had been proactive, not reactive. He stressed that it had been the Queen herself who had asked him to start exploring royal tax arrangements back in the summer. However, there was no denying that the announcement had been rushed forwards. It was not just the fire that had focused her mind. So had the fact that yet another royal 'bombshell' was heading her way – fast.

Just two weeks later, John Major was on his feet in the

Commons once again to announce that the Prince and Princess of Wales were to separate. He added that this would not, in due course, prevent the Princess from becoming Queen. Those who worked with the Queen later remain baffled by the decision to declare this on the floor of the House of Commons. 'It could have been announced very simply in a statement from the Palace,' one of her most senior advisers told this author. 'It was an extraordinary move by the Queen and John Major and Robert Fellowes to announce it in Parliament. Instead of treating it as a sad, personal issue, it was now a legitimate mainstream debate. It was dreadfully awkward. I simply couldn't envisage that happening in her later years. Maybe they were just punch drunk by the pace of events.'[18] For the rest of his life, up to his death in 2024, Sir Robert (later Lord) Fellowes would reassure his successors during periodic royal storms: 'However bad it gets, it will never be as bad as that.'[19]

There was still more to come. Just days later, the text of the Queen's Christmas message was leaked to *The Sun*. In the scheme of things, this was not remotely damaging to the monarchy and the broadcast was hardly sensational. 'As some of you may have heard me observe, it has, indeed, been a sombre year,' she reflected. 'But Christmas is surely the right moment to try to put it behind us.' The fact that the paper had splashed her words in advance, however, felt almost spiteful, rather like telling someone what was in a Christmas present before they had unwrapped it.

The year did, finally, give the Queen one cause for celebration when her daughter was remarried – to her former equerry. The Princess and Commander Tim Laurence did not want a civil wedding, and the Church of England did not conduct weddings for divorcees with a living ex-spouse. The Church of Scotland had no such qualms, however, and so the couple

1992-95: 'Horribilis'

chose Crathie Kirk next to Balmoral. Not that long ago, the family and the Royal Household had been dismayed by the prospect of an equerry marrying in to the family. 'You must be either mad or bad or both,' Tommy Lascelles had told Peter Townsend when the latter revealed his love for Princess Margaret in 1953.[20] By now, the Queen was just grateful for some authentic family happiness. Tim Laurence had long gone from the Palace back to the Royal Navy, where a promising career (including a decoration for combatting IRA gun smugglers) would continue to the highest levels. And, besides, who was going to quarrel with Princess Anne? Theirs was the smallest and cheapest royal wedding in history. The press and public were kept well away from the church, restricted to a local car park. Relations between the media and the Palace had reached such a low point that even a mobile snack van selling tea and food to the press was ordered to leave. Since Balmoral Castle had been closed up for the winter, just one room was opened for a short reception of soup and sandwiches before the family headed back to Aberdeen Airport. The honeymoon consisted of a weekend in an estate lodge. Even the monarchy's harshest critics would have struggled to find fault with Princess Anne's bargain budget wedding.

Despite the Queen's best efforts to look to a better year ahead, it seemed as if 1993 might turn out to be a match for the one before. For it opened with another tabloid transcript of a bugged phone call, this time a deeply intimate and excruciating six-minute telephone conversation between the Prince of Wales and Camilla Parker Bowles. Even critics of the monarchy regarded it as an appalling intrusion. The royal debate moved back to more familiar ground as the Palace announced details of the new plans for the monarch to bring royal taxation in line with arrangements. The media response was grudging.

Elizabeth II

There was particular criticism for the news that there would be no death duties on monarch-to-monarch transfers of wealth. The argument for this was that monarchs, unlike everyone else, cannot use conventional retirement planning and tax allowances because they never retire. *The Mirror* published a cartoon depicting a money-grabbing Elizabeth II under the headline 'HM Tax Dodger'.[21] Insiders say that it reduced her to tears.[22] Having defied her parents and modernized the royal finances, while being assured by her government that she did not have to do so – and having listened to the popular mood – she had been vilified for her troubles. And it hurt. However, those around her report that she never felt defeated by the events of this period.

Looking back, her press secretary over those years, Charles Anson, was always struck by her outward calmness – 'never irritable; completely steady' – and her stoicism: 'The issue was sometimes embarrassing, but she got on with it. It is immensely reassuring in those situations to work for someone who isn't knocked back.'[23] Mindful that the whole situation would have been a lot worse if Lord Airlie had not made his reforms to the Royal Household during those years of sunshine and plenty in the eighties, she was also ready to use this crisis to make changes.

The previous in-house upheavals had involved the way in which the monarchy was managed and funded. Now it needed to think deeper and ask itself a more fundamental question: what is the monarchy for and what should it be doing? Antony Jay's book *Elizabeth R* had prompted some fresh ideas. Instead of waiting to be asked to do things, often by the same old arch-royalists, it should identify areas of national life that had been overlooked. Developing these ideas was an innovative young deputy private secretary, Robin Janvrin. Ex-Royal Navy

1992–95: 'Horribilis'

and Foreign Office, he had arrived via the Palace press office, like Bill Heseltine before him. A new office was created inside the Palace called the Co-Ordination and Research Unit, with a young, analytical staff. In time, there would be meetings of senior members of the family plus senior staff to seek an agreed position on broad issues, from the future of the royal train to the number of family members on the balcony at major moments. It would become known as the Way Ahead Group. There was no vote. The Queen was the boss, though a reluctant one. 'She was not good at committee meetings,' a senior official conceded.[24] 'The problem was that it should really have been just the Queen, Prince Philip and Prince Charles, but the others all wanted to be there too and it got too big.' Staff would recall Prince Andrew holding forth at length on matters such as royal transport. One of the officials involved remembered a general consensus forming on the need to reduce the number of more distant family members on the balcony at major moments. Even then, the official recalled, there was no decision: 'The Queen wasn't prepared to accept that, so it didn't happen.'[25] Ultimately, the Prince of Wales gave up coming and the group fizzled out. Monarchy by committee was abandoned.

One of the ironies of all these problems at home was that the mid-1990s would also be the period when the Queen was at the height of her powers as an international stateswoman. The collapse of communism in Eastern Europe had opened up a great swathe of the world which, previously, she could never have visited, but which was now crying out for a state visit. Places like Hungary, Poland and the Czech Republic were bowled over to receive a world leader who had represented stability and freedom all through the years of totalitarianism. There were three stand-out adventures which reminded her

Elizabeth II

and the British public that the monarchy was not, as the commentariat routinely described it, a soap opera, but a very significant diplomatic tool and something to be proud of. They were also moments of blessed relief for the Queen herself.

In the summer of 1994, the leaders of all the wartime Allied nations gathered in Britain in the run-up to the fiftieth anniversary of D-Day. The assault on the Normandy beaches on 6 June 1944 was instrumental to the liberation of France, which in turn led to the liberation of Europe. Three nations had been in the vanguard – the UK, the USA and Canada – and the Queen's father had been head of state of two of them. She would host the first stage of the commemorations in Portsmouth, starting with a state banquet at the Guildhall in Portsmouth. The prime minister, John Major, later recalled that it had been the Queen herself who had overruled government officials to avert an awkward seating drama, as noted earlier. 'The Queen had been placed next to two European royals, and [US] President Clinton and [French] President Mitterrand had been placed well below the salt at the other end of the table,' he recalled. 'The fairly frosty response from an official was that elected presidents were lower in protocol than monarchs! The Queen's reply, broadly, was: "Of course, people will expect President Clinton and President Mitterrand to sit beside me and, in any event, I see my cousins all the time." So the two presidents did indeed end up flanking the Queen.'[26]

The next day, the Royal Family and world leaders (plus this author) boarded the royal yacht for the commemorative re-invasion of France. Escorted by Allied warships, Britannia led a fleet of cruise ships carrying thousands of veterans and their families back to the beaches and the *bocage* where history was made half a century before. Obvious, if unspoken, was the

1992–95: 'Horribilis'

Queen's unique connection with the wartime generation, the only world leader present who had served in uniform during the Second World War (and who had known and worked with Winston Churchill). That link would become even more apparent at the sixtieth, seventieth and seventy-fifth anniversaries in the years ahead.

The most powerful scene of the fiftieth anniversary commemorations was the final big event: the parade of veterans past the Queen on the sands at Arromanches. There had been another problem for the protocol people as the old servicemen lined up on the beach. There was still no sign of the French president, and the tide was starting to come in. If President Mitterrand did not turn up soon, some of the veterans would be paddling, if not swimming. What to do? The issue was instantly resolved after the intervention of an exasperated Prince Philip, once again coming to the rescue with brisk, unanswerable plainspeak. 'Who does he bloody think he is?' he exclaimed. 'King Canute?' Whereupon the command was given and off they marched.[27]

Four months later, the Queen became the first British monarch to pay a state visit to Russia. 'You and I have spent most of our lives believing that this evening could never happen,' she told President Boris Yeltsin at the state banquet in the Kremlin. 'I hope that you are as delighted as I am to be proved wrong.' He certainly was, so much so that he broke with longstanding Kremlin protocol to travel from Moscow to St Petersburg, the old imperial capital and the second stage of the state visit, where the Queen would host a return banquet in the royal yacht. Russian leaders, by tradition, did not attend return banquets and certainly not outside Moscow. Similarly, British monarchs, by tradition, did not make speeches at return banquets, but the Queen made an exception at this one. After dinner, she summoned a gavel and made a short, impromptu

Elizabeth II

address saluting Russia and its president. She sat down and the dinner continued, whereupon there was a huge crashing sound which one guest likened to 'a bomb'. President Yeltsin thumped the table, stood up and paid his own tribute. Famously fond of a drink, Yeltsin was certainly well-refreshed. The British foreign secretary, Douglas Hurd, had noticed during dinner that the president had not liked the white wine but had guzzled his glass of claret almost immediately, so Hurd 'summoned a footman' to keep him topped up. But Yeltsin had been charmed by the Queen, and the feeling was mutual. 'The Queen took a real shine to Yeltsin. She admired him,' said Sir Robert Woodard, the captain of *Britannia*. 'I think she thought that a man who can control a country this size has to be very special.'[28]

The royal yacht was also a central element of the third of these consecutive milestone trips. In the spring of 1995, the Queen sailed into Cape Town to be greeted by newly elected President Nelson Mandela on the quayside. The symbolism was personal and poignant. This was how she had arrived in South Africa on her very first overseas trip with her parents in 1947, ahead of her twenty-first birthday speech. She had steadfastly refused to visit the country all through the years of apartheid. Now, full democracy had resulted in the election to the presidency of that man she had met in Zimbabwe four years before. One of Nelson Mandela's first executive acts was to reattach South Africa to the Commonwealth, in recognition of the organization's fight against apartheid. As Head of the Commonwealth, this was a source of enormous pride and pleasure for the Queen, and she was keen to visit as soon as possible.

Here was another important insight into the Queen's pragmatic world view, since there was a striking similarity between this visit and her groundbreaking trip to Russia (quite apart

1992–95: 'Horribilis'

from the starring role played by *Britannia*). In both cases, the Foreign Office had shown a great deal of nervousness about sending the Queen to two volatile countries which were only just emerging from decades of oppression. Both were places where violence was endemic. The British ambassador to Russia, Sir Brian Fall, remembered the prevailing resistance to any state visit to Moscow. 'There were plenty of people in the Foreign Office saying that we should wait until they had a "proper" democracy,' he said. 'But that would have been too late.'[29] The Queen had agreed with him.

Sir Robert Woodard recalled exactly the same official faint-heartedness when it was suggested the Queen should visit South Africa. Nervous diplomats fretted that there had been a lot of civil unrest and that Britain was not universally popular thanks to Margaret Thatcher. 'The foreign secretary was worried and the Queen overruled him,' said Woodard, who was present during one discussion about the putative visit. 'She said: "Mr Mandela is getting advice from lots of people but no one's actually giving him any help. He needs physical assistance and he needs a show". She was going to give him one.'[30]

And that she did, during a wildly popular tour all the way from South Africa's Atlantic coast to the Indian Ocean, one which only reinforced her firm friendship with Nelson Mandela. He would not only make a triumphal reciprocal state visit to Britain the following year, but they would remain in close contact long after he left office. He was probably the only non-royal world leader who would routinely call her 'Elizabeth', and certainly the only one who would once greet her with the words: 'Oh, Elizabeth, you've lost weight!'[31] Nor were there many statesmen to whom the Queen would refer openly, as she did on Mandela's state visit to London, as 'this wonderful man.'[32]

The Queen would look back on that trio of overseas missions

Elizabeth II

as among the greatest high points of her life. What makes them more remarkable is that they took place over a period of just ten months at one of the lowest points of her whole reign. They were not only testimony to Elizabeth II's power of endurance, but possibly helped to explain it, too. With so much unhappiness at home, she found it positively rejuvenating and even relaxing to swap Britain for the world stage.

All of these very successful adventures, however, left a bittersweet afterthought which the Queen, for now, would push to the back of her mind. For, at the very moment the royal yacht was playing its majestic part in such spectacular international state occasions, *Britannia*'s days were numbered. Just a fortnight after that great voyage to Normandy, the government announced that the yacht was going to be decommissioned when it came to the end of its current phase of operations. All ships need periodic refits to keep them seaworthy, and it had been decided that the cost of equipping *Britannia* for the twenty-first century would be too much. Ministers would retain an open (if not very enthusiastic) view on a possible replacement.

The yacht had been so much more than a comfortable floating embassy. The Queen could take on almost any challenge if she woke up in her narrow starboard cabin with its original set of G-Plan furniture. She said as much to Robert Woodard when he was appointed captain. 'People who know us at all know that Buckingham Palace is the office, Windsor Castle is for weekends and the occasional state thing and Sandringham and Balmoral are for holidays but they aren't what I would call holidays,' the Queen told him. 'For example, there are ninety people coming to stay with us at Balmoral this summer. The only holiday I get every year is from Portsmouth the long way round to Aberdeen, when I can get up when I like and wear what I like and be completely free.'[33]

1992–95: 'Horribilis'

Meandering through the Hebrides with the family, making last-minute plans on where to drop anchor for a picnic or a walk was her idea of Heaven. It was where the children had been happiest when young. Above all, it had been the one home she had been able to shape and design herself. The castles and palaces had been inherited ready-baked. Even when she and Prince Philip had renovated Clarence House, which they had loved, there was only so much they could do. *Britannia* was different.

Together with the Duke of Edinburgh, she had taken the keenest interest in the project codenamed 'Ship 691'. It had been her choice to dispense with the original design, modelled on the first-class state rooms of an ocean liner. She wanted greater simplicity and cleaner lines and asked the designer, Hugh Casson, to make it less 'lavish'. She had chosen the fixtures, fittings and carpet, while the Duke had made some important suggestions for the exterior. The blueprint for the yacht was an existing design for a North Sea ferry, but the Duke tweaked it to produce a more elegant bow and a colour scheme of dark blue with bands of red and gold. Because the Royal Yacht Service only had one ship, unlike the warships of the 'grey' navy, the crew never changed. As a result, the Queen and her family got to know them by name – in some cases even coming up with the names. Falklands veteran William French arrived as Royal Steward in the mid-eighties and forever after proudly rejoiced in Prince Philip's nickname for him – 'Froggy'.[34]

John Major would always remain adamant that spending millions on refitting the yacht during those dark years would have backfired on the monarchy. Within the Royal Family, the Duke of Edinburgh, the Prince of Wales and the Princess Royal were, privately, keen on the idea of a replacement. The Queen probably was too, though she could also see the pitfalls. Years previously, during painful cuts to the Royal Navy in the sixties, she had told Harold Wilson that she was content to let *Britannia* go to save money. He had declined the offer. Both Major and his successor, Tony Blair, say that the Queen never queried the decision to lose *Britannia*. Nonetheless, she would certainly mourn the moment.

There was a more immediate and even more personal loss for the Queen during this period. On 22 September 1993, she received the news that her lifelong assistant, dresser and confidante, Bobo MacDonald, had died. The forthright daughter of a Scottish railway worker, Margaret MacDonald had been with her mistress since the nursery, where the tiny Princess had given her the name 'Bobo' and never called her anything else thereafter. She was the only person outside the family who was allowed to touch the Queen and also to call her 'Lilibet'. Correspondingly, no one outside the family would address Bobo as anything other than 'Miss MacDonald'.

All through the trials of the Second World War and on through Princess Elizabeth's courtship with Prince Philip, Bobo was the keeper of the secrets. Once the Princess reached adulthood, Bobo became her dresser. Like Susan the corgi, she even went on the royal honeymoon. As a dying George VI stood on the runway waving off his eldest child for the last time on that freezing January day in 1952, his parting words were: 'Look after the Princess for me, Bobo.' And so she would, an indefatigable gatekeeper and dispenser of home truths whatever the situation. It was said that Bobo was the only person, other than Prince Philip, who could reduce the Queen to tears. Palace newcomers would be warned: 'Do not upset Miss MacDonald or you'll ruin the Queen's day.'

On board *Britannia*, where she was known as 'QE3', Bobo had her own cabin, which could never be used by anyone else

1992–95: 'Horribilis'

if she was not on board. 'She was pretty scary because she had the ear of the Queen night and day,' Sir William Heseltine recalled. 'I always felt we got on very well. She paid an exaggerated deference to members of the Household but you knew jolly well where the power lay.'[35] Theirs was a unique relationship familiar to courts down the ages. All through his years as Prince of Wales and into his time as King, Charles III would remain devoted to his childhood nanny, Mabel Anderson (another daughter of Scotland's north-east). Former private secretary Lord Fellowes would fondly recall that when Elizabeth II's most senior officials had difficulty persuading the Queen to do or wear something, the best conduit might often be Bobo. The fiery former nursemaid would reply: 'Och, my wee small girl's getting spoiled.'[36] The problem would then be sorted. Devoted to the Queen, Bobo never married and retired to a palace apartment immediately above the monarch so that Lilibet could drop by to reminisce. There was a delightful tradition that, on Bobo's birthday, roles would be reversed and it would be the monarch who brought her dresser and lifelong companion a cup of tea in bed. The Queen led the mourners at her funeral.

Chapter Twelve

1996–97
'These are for you'

Fleet Street's royal correspondents had never been busier. As well as covering the rounds of regular Royal Family events, there was the intriguing question of the future, post-separation modus vivendi of the Princess of Wales. Wherever she went, a huge media circus would follow, as happened right from the start of her new international solo career, which began with a humanitarian tour of Nepal in early 1993.

The Himalayan kingdom, run by the autocratic King Birendra, was not sure how to treat a separated semi-detached Princess. Late one evening, Crown Prince Dipendra (who, eight years later, would go on to kill most of his own family and then himself) shut down central Kathmandu to take the Princess joyriding in his sports car. This was certainly not something that would ever happen on an official royal tour. On the other hand, Diana had arrived with the British overseas aid minister, Baroness Chalker, and the pair made a formidable diplomatic duo, to the delight of the Foreign Office. Similar trips would take Diana to Zimbabwe, Moscow and Argentina.

At home, her every move was tracked by hordes of paparazzi, whether she was undertaking charity engagements or just

Elizabeth II

going to the gym. She had remained at her London marital home, Kensington Palace, while Prince Charles divided his time between his country house, Highgrove (which the Princess had never liked), and a new flat in St James's Palace. Although it was clear that Diana was not happy in her quasi-royal existence, there was no obvious alternative. Above all, the press were preoccupied with the possibility of any new man in her life, particularly former Life Guards officer James Hewitt. The Prince had resumed his friendship with Camilla Parker Bowles, who would divorce her husband in 1995.

The Queen was content to let the situation drift rather than to confront it. After all, single life for the Prince was a relatively straightforward continuation of his longstanding work on behalf of his charities and the Queen. Since establishing the Prince's Trust with the contents of his Royal Navy pension in 1976, he had watched it grow into the UK's largest youth opportunity charity. Without the glamour of the Diana years, his tours at home and overseas took on a more earnest tone and attracted less press interest, although his 1994 trip to Australia suddenly made global headlines. While the Prince was presenting prizes in a Sydney park, a man came charging at the stage firing a gun. As with the attack on the Queen in 1981, the attacker was a troubled youth and the gun contained blanks, but no one knew that at the time. The Prince's calmness, bordering on nonchalance, won him much praise, even from hardened Australian republicans. His mother watched the television news with a mix of relief and gnawing déjà vu. She had been following the tour carefully for very different reasons and had been closely involved in what was supposed to be the Prince's main engagement of the day.

The central purpose of the trip had been to convey the Royal Family's equanimity in the face of growing calls for Australia

1996–97: 'These are for you'

to swap the monarch for a home-grown president. This was the dream of the country's new Labor prime minister, Paul Keating. He had already been to Balmoral to lay out his plans to the Queen (who is said to have emerged from that meeting echoing her mother's response to the news of royal taxation: 'I really do need a very large drink.'[1]). The centrepiece of the Prince's trip Down Under was supposed to be his landmark speech assuring Australia that the monarchy was only there to serve and that there would be 'no hard feelings'. In the event, the shooting stole the show.

The Prince's senior advisers had decided that the time had come to show him and his work in a new light. Journalist Jonathan Dimbleby was invited in to produce an ITV television documentary and an authorized biography. The programme was a wide-ranging portrait of a thoughtful heir to the throne, passionate about his country and his causes. However, it would be best remembered for a single remark in which the Prince stated that he had been faithful to his wife until the marriage had 'irretrievably broken down'.

If the Queen was unhappy about the on-screen confession, she was much more upset about the book. Not only was it serialized in *The Sunday Times*, the paper which had led the charge on royal taxation, but the extracts appeared on the eve of her state visit to Moscow, thus upstaging one of the great moments of post-war royal diplomacy. The Queen was cross personally as well as professionally. For what really pained both her and the Duke of Edinburgh was the book's accusation that they had failed as parents. In particular, it criticized the Duke for 'habitual' rebukes and an 'inexplicably harsh' attitude towards his eldest son. On the eve of the royal departure for Moscow, the Duke told this author: 'I've never discussed private matters and I don't think the Queen has either. Very

Elizabeth II

few members of the family have. I don't know why it has happened or how it has happened. I'd rather not get involved in it.'[2] The Queen, said a friend, was 'extremely upset' but found some solace in the fact that she was far away, with her yacht, making history in a country where the last royal family had been through something very much worse.[3]

The Dimbleby project had another, entirely unforeseen effect. If the Prince could have his say, then presumably the Princess could speak out, too. It enabled an unscrupulous BBC reporter called Martin Bashir to mount a campaign of deception to lure the Princess into responding with a television interview of her own on the BBC's *Panorama*. His duplicity, and the extraordinary internal conspiracy to bury it, would not be uncovered until nearly a quarter of a century later.

On the night of 20 November 1995 (the Queen's wedding anniversary), he pulled off one of the broadcasting sensations of modern times as the Princess lifted the lid on her 'crowded' marriage and, worst of all, voiced her doubts that Prince Charles would be capable of 'the top job'. Charles's documentary had studiously avoided criticism of Diana and, indeed, barely mentioned her. In return, however, she had aimed the lowest blow. She was careful not to criticize the Queen and insisted that she 'admired' her mother-in-law. However, Diana added that she saw herself as a 'queen of people's hearts'. The Queen was not at home to watch it, but at London's Dominion Theatre with Prince Philip. For once in her life, she must have been thrilled to be on duty at the Royal Variety Performance, on this occasion watching Cliff Richard and comedy duo Cannon and Ball. She watched a recording of *Panorama* on her return. It was enough to snap her immediately out of her three-year state of self-denial and wishful thinking. There could be no middle way, let alone a rapprochement. The status quo

1996–97: 'These are for you'

was no longer tenable. All the Queen's achievements of recent years, and there had been plenty, increasingly seemed little more than footnotes to the Charles and Diana show.

The summer of 1995, for example, saw great commemorations of the fiftieth anniversaries of VE Day and VJ Day, with the Queen, the Queen Mother and Princess Margaret at the centre of it all. One of the Queen's closest advisers during this time talked of the way her confidence had drained away ahead of these events. 'She actually thought no one would turn up,' the adviser added, even though the Mall ended up full to bursting. Nonetheless, the chart-busting ratings for *Panorama* and the debates which followed across the media had left the Queen as low as anyone could remember her, with Prince Philip now playing a key role. The damage caused by the interview had profound constitutional implications. Yet, the Queen's senior adviser, her principal private secretary, Sir Robert Fellowes, was unavoidably compromised, since he was Diana's brother-in-law. 'Robert was doing his best but in an impossible position,' recalled a senior official of that time. 'So Prince Philip was very involved.'[4] Distraught she might be, but the Queen was also now emboldened. Whatever the long-term implications for the monarchy's relationship with the Church of England, that was for another day. The imperative was that the Prince and Princess of Wales should end their marriage and start afresh. The Queen demanded that they seek a divorce.

In the summer of 1996, Diana, Princess of Wales embarked on a new life without the style of 'Her Royal Highness'. In removing it, the Queen was not being vindictive, but logical, since someone now not married to the Royal Family could no longer be royal. Her aides pointed out that it also, helpfully, meant there could be no opposition to stripping the Duchess of York of her 'HRH' too. Both divorces came through within weeks of each other. The Princess had employed a combative firm of legal streetfighters who had secured her a settlement worth around £17 million from the Prince. The Duchess, however, had used a more traditional firm of solicitors and had ended up with little more than the standard payout for a naval wife. Given her more expensive tastes and boundless extravagance, that modest settlement would sow the seeds of her increasingly desperate money-making in later life. It would become an obsession with disastrous consequences for the House of York.

Though no longer royal, Diana still had her apartment at Kensington Palace as part of her agreement. She was still the mother of the future King and there was no acrimony when it came to sharing equal custody of William and Harry. Diana would now take bolder steps towards a new existence. She had developed such an interest in health and medicine that she had started attending hospital operations, even embarking on a new romance with a Pakistan-born heart surgeon, Hasnat Khan. Stripping back her portfolio of charities to a core handful, she also became not merely an advocate but an activist in the campaign to ban landmines. Her trips to war zones in Angola and Bosnia brought home the horrific cost to civilians in a way that no politician could.

Given that the British government's position was not to demand a ban until everyone else did, this took her close to party politics and, thus, the constitutional edge. But what were the rules for an ex-royal Princess? Did royal rules and conventions still apply? The Queen certainly thought they did. She had long spoken of Diana using a relatively fond expression of exasperation – 'quite mad' – but was privately furious when Diana's first major post-divorce global mission clashed with her own state visit to Thailand. One minute the regular royal correspondents were dutifully following the Queen round

1996–97: 'These are for you'

Bangkok with the King of Thailand. The next, they had vanished to Sydney to watch the Princess attending a glitzy fundraiser for an Australian charity. Here was a cruel illustration of where royal soft power lay in the final few years of the twentieth century.

The underlying tension highlighted the sense that the monarchy's problems had not gone away. Even before it began, 1997 was going to be a challenging year for the Queen. A general election was due, and seemed almost certain to return a radical new Labour government with plans for constitutional reform high on its list. After years of negotiation, Britain was also scheduled to hand over its most prestigious overseas territory, Hong Kong, to China.

The year began with a much-publicized two-hour national television debate on the Royal Family organized by ITV and called *Monarchy: The Nation Decides*. Held in an arena inside Birmingham's National Exhibition Centre, it rapidly became a bearpit as a toxic, ill-tempered shouting match unfolded. Though the monarchy secured two thirds of the closing vote of more than 2.5 million people, the heat and fury generated by the programme was a source of grave concern inside the Palace. At the heart of the debate was the same question that Diana had raised in her *Panorama* interview: could the monarchy survive under King Charles?

That might depend on what Diana was planning to do with her new-found, post-royal independence. It had certainly left her less inhibited in her private life. She was well aware of official suspicions about the owner of Harrods, Mohammed Fayed, a coarse bully who had been denied British citizenship and had been embroiled in accusations of bribing MPs (his record as a rapacious sexual predator would only emerge after his death). Yet Fayed had the yachts, jets, helicopters and villas to entertain Diana in a royal style, which the British monarchy would certainly no longer be proffering. Her romance with Hasnat Khan had also cooled, largely at his behest. By the summer of 1997, Fayed had also engineered a tepid summer romance of sorts between Diana and his son, Dodi. One friend remains adamant that, for Diana, this was a mere summer 'fling' in order to encourage some sort of renewed interest from Hasnat Khan. As Diana and Dodi returned to Britain from a Mediterranean cruise, the Fayed jet stopped over in Paris. Dodi, his strings being pulled as ever by his puppet-master father, had promised Diana a romantic dinner in the City of Light.

Up at Balmoral, Diana's sons were preparing to be reunited with their mother. They had spent August in the Highlands with their father, the Queen and the rest of the Royal Family. The boys adored their summers in Scotland with their grandmother, as did all the Queen's grandchildren. 'To me Balmoral was always simply Paradise. A cross between Disney World and some sacred Druid grove,' Prince Harry wrote in his book, *Spare*. 'I was happy there. In fact, it's possible that I was never happier than that one golden summer day at Balmoral: August 30, 1997.'[5] The Queen felt much the same. She was never happier than when the family were filling the castle in summer, and Balmoral's restorative powers were more welcome than ever that year. She was just starting to get used to her first Labour government in eighteen years. John Major's Conservatives had now been soundly beaten by Tony Blair's 'New Labour' modernizers, whose agenda was clearly going to require some deft navigation by the Queen. Blair was planning to remove the hereditary element from the House of Lords, with obvious implications for a hereditary head of state, and he would be heading up to Balmoral fairly soon for the usual prime ministerial weekend. He had plans for Scottish and Welsh legislatures,

1996–97: 'These are for you'

too, invoking memories of the Queen's vinegary remarks about devolution back at the time of her Silver Jubilee. On a more personal note, Labour had campaigned noisily against the plan for a new royal yacht, a last-minute addition to the Conservatives' election offering.

It had been careless and clumsy of Major to turn the yacht into a political issue, given that any big royal-related measure should always have cross-party support first (as had been the case when the Labour government of Clement Attlee had commissioned *Britannia* in 1951). The Tories had thus dragged the Queen into the election. Now they had lost and, by implication, so had she. Just weeks before her escape to Balmoral, there had also been that handover of Hong Kong to communist China, with the Prince of Wales lowering the flag. Once again, *Britannia* had played a key role, carrying the Prince away from the handover ceremony with elegance and grandeur. The royal yacht had always known how to make an entrance. Now that she had made a spectacular imperial exit, she would head for home and an emotional goodbye ceremony later in the year. All in all, therefore, it had been a badly needed Balmoral escape for the Queen as August came to an end and thoughts turned to autumn.

In the very early hours of Sunday 31 August, the telephone woke up Robin Janvrin at Connachat, a small, two-bedroom cottage three miles west of Balmoral. With the castle full of family, the Queen had given her duty private secretary this quiet berth on the estate, next to the Woods of Garmaddie. Janvrin picked up the phone to hear the familiar voice of Sandy Henney, press secretary to the Prince of Wales. She was acting as duty press officer for the Royal Family over the Bank Holiday weekend and had just heard, via a journalist, about a serious car crash in Paris involving Diana, Princess of Wales. Janvrin immediately got dressed and contacted the duty

Elizabeth II

equerry to let the castle know he was on his way with important news for the Queen. Soon afterwards, the monarch, the Prince of Wales, Prince Philip and Janvrin were gathered in the library and following the course of events through the early hours of the morning. At first, it was clear that Dodi Fayed was dead and that Diana was fighting for life in hospital. At 4 a.m., she lost that fight. The Prince of Wales took the agonizing decision to let his sons sleep. He would break the news to them in the morning.

One version of post-war British history has painted the death of Diana as the gravest existential threat to the monarchy since the abdication. It is safe to say that the Queen did not regard it as such, because her first response was to treat it as a family tragedy and handle it as a grandmother. It was not until eight hours after the first news broke of the accident that she had her first conversation with the prime minister, as he prepared to head for church near his constituency home. 'She was philosophical, anxious for the boys, but also professional and practical,' Blair wrote years later. 'She grasped the enormity of the event, but in her own way. She was not going to be pushed around by it. She could be very queenly in that sense.'[6] She, too, was preparing to head for church with William and Harry in the royal party. Her overarching priority was to keep things as normal, as familiar, as comforting as she possibly could for their benefit. It seemed to be working. Later that day, the Queen Mother called her friend and lady-in-waiting Prue Penn, telling her: 'The extraordinary thing is those boys haven't cried.'[7] She seemed unsure whether this was a good or bad thing.

The days that followed have been analysed in forensic detail, chronicled in political diaries and dramatized on both big and small screens. The Queen's innate pragmatism would serve her well at certain times. However, her instinctive caution against

1996–97: 'These are for you'

gestures and stunts would not. On that first day after Diana's death, rapid decisions needed to be made for the repatriation of the body. They were largely taken in-house and without debate. Though there were existing plans for bringing home a deceased member of the Royal Family, these had not involved doing so inside a day. Nor had they been framed around someone who was no longer, technically, royal. As would be the case all week, this would be a matter of thinking afresh. Led by her officials, the Queen grasped that point instantly. In those early hours of Sunday morning, it was already decided that an RAF aircraft from 32 (Royal) Squadron would collect Diana's sisters and the Prince of Wales, fly to Paris and bring her back to RAF Northolt in London.

Among the many narratives that has since gained currency is that the Spencer family fought to give Diana a private funeral. From the outset, the Queen was opposed. 'It wouldn't work,' she said firmly in those early hours. A key figure in these discussions was her private secretary, Sir Robert Fellowes, husband of Diana's sister Jane. As the news started to break, he was at his home in Norfolk with Jane, liaising between Janvrin, alongside the Queen at Balmoral and the Cabinet secretary, Sir Robin Butler, in London. Fellowes was also part of the Spencer family discussions over the telephone in those early hours. It had been Diana's elder sister, Sarah, who initially made the point that Diana would have preferred a private family funeral. Fellowes gently pointed out that the nation would not wear that and there was no disagreement. The idea was quietly dropped. As he later recalled to a colleague: 'It was a matter for discussion very, very early on. But it was not realistic. The family took no persuasion that it just couldn't be a family thing.'[8]

Another story which has become received wisdom is that, from the very outset, the Royal Family were paralysed with indecision; that the Blair government had to rescue them from a baying mob and steer them safely to Diana's funeral. That has evolved, in part, because key political figures like Tony Blair and his communications secretary, Alastair Campbell, have published their own accounts, while former government advisers have shared their versions of events with scriptwriters and the media. The instinctive response of the Queen's team over the years, however, was to say nothing. Inevitably, that has created an impression of sure-footed political dynamos helping the poor old plodders from the Palace. The chronology, however, shows a somewhat different story.

By the time that Downing Street officials joined the first main planning meeting at Buckingham Palace on the Monday morning, a great deal had already happened on the Sunday. The Lord Chamberlain, Lord Airlie, had taken charge in London, alongside the unflappable comptroller (master of ceremonial), Lieutenant Colonel Malcolm Ross. Airlie gave Ross one instruction, as he told this author: 'I said, "The one thing is this – don't look at a file. This has to be *de novo*." In other words, this had to be done quite differently.'[9]

That same day, Airlie drew up a list of policy points which would form a strategy for the week. The funeral, for example, should lean in favour of public sentiment rather than officialdom. It should be about 'balancing dignity with informality'. He specifically warned against using long-established protocol for drawing up guest lists and wanted a generous mix of Diana's charities. He wanted the procession to 'break with tradition and be somewhat radical'. The next morning, he sent all this in a memo to the Queen at Balmoral and recalled the prompt response: 'The answer came back, saying: "Go ahead".'[10] Blair's head of communications, Alastair Campbell, who was present at the first Palace meeting, would later acknowledge that Airlie had been in the driving seat and was working towards a 'healing event'.[11]

At this point, the mob was not baying anyway. That would come later in the week, as grief followed its customary course from shock to anger. Diana's death had been caused by a car chase with photographers, so the press, unsurprisingly, received much abuse in the first day or two. There then evolved a nebulous sense that the Royal Family did not share the public's pain, epitomized by their decision to remain locked away at Balmoral. Suddenly, the absence of a flag at half-mast above Buckingham Palace took on totemic importance, led by the red-top tabloids for whom any deflected anger was welcome.

Here, the Queen was not prepared to budge. Her pragmatic instincts, which would normally lead her to the least worst solution to any given problem, were trumped by her reflex opposition to hollow gesture politics or what Prince Charles would sometimes call 'clever Dick modernism'. By longstanding convention, the Palace would only fly the Royal Standard when the sovereign was in residence. It did not fly the Union flag because that was only flown over a royal fortress like the Tower of London or Windsor Castle and the palace was not a fortress. Several former advisers believe that if she had not been cocooned inside Balmoral, she would have listened to those, like Robin Janvrin, who were advising a change of flag policy. It did not go down well with the Queen. One colleague referred to Janvrin being 'scarred'.[12]

As the flowers piled up outside Buckingham and Kensington Palaces – an estimated 60 million would be laid that week – so the pressure mounted for the Queen to make some sort of show of compassion. She knew that these demands were being driven by the media and by the most vocal onlookers the news crews could find in the crowds. As a grandmother, she was sure that the majority of people would understand a grandparent attending to her grieving grandsons. Nonetheless, her closest allies and friends were reporting back on the strange and disturbing tone of a different section of the crowd. 'What was sinister was the total silence,' Lord Airlie recalled. 'I went out myself into the crowd incognito to try to understand the mood, and, frankly, I failed to do so. But, as I went back into my office at Buckingham Palace, I said to myself, "Just pay attention." And that is what we did.'[13]

The prime minister wrote in his memoirs that, by midweek, he had spoken to the Prince of Wales. Both men were of the same mind. 'The Queen had to speak; the royal family had to be visible. However tough it was for him personally, for all the obvious reasons, he and the boys couldn't hide away,' wrote Blair. 'They had to come to London to respond to the public outpouring.'[14]

By the next day, Thursday, as the front pages screamed 'Where Is Our Queen?' (*The Sun*) and 'Show Us You Care' (the *Express*), Blair was ready to push. Yet he found that the door was open anyway. The Queen was already planning another trip to church and an address to the nation – a live one. 'She didn't need to be persuaded to do a broadcast or to do it live,' said one of those in the thick of the planning that week. 'She said: "Don't forget I used to do my Christmas broadcasts live in the early days". She was fully focused.'[15] The main thing was that she was returning to London. The way she handled it remains one of the bolder judgement calls of her life.

After flying back down from Scotland, the Queen and Prince Philip were driven to Buckingham Palace, where they pointedly stopped the car outside the gates. A vast crowd looked on in that 'sinister' silence which Lord Airlie had noted earlier in the week. This was a situation quite unlike any which the Queen had experienced in her reign. There had been protests, of course, over the years and even the odd flying egg just five years earlier during a visit to Dresden in former East Germany. But she had never had a vast, brooding mass of people standing solemnly on her own doorstep. It would only have needed a couple of hysterical shouters to scupper the moment and, possibly, lead to ugly confrontations. But there was still no sound. The Queen and the Duke inspected some of the messages on the floral mountain by the railings and then walked over to move gingerly along the public lines. Suddenly, she was handed a bunch of five red roses by eleven-year-old Kathryn Jones. 'Would you like me to place them for you?' asked the monarch. 'No,' the girl replied. 'These are for you.'[16] At which point, as the Queen's team still recall vividly, there was finally a noise: rippling, growing applause.

As day was about to give way to night, the Queen appeared on television at last. She was framed by the windows of the palace's Chinese Drawing Room, with the flower-bearing crowds moving hazily in the background. Clearly in authority and in control, she conceded that the country had felt 'incomprehension' and 'anger'. 'No one who knew Diana will ever forget her,' she went on, adding that 'millions of others who never met her, but felt they knew her, will remember her.' Without acknowledging her critics, she added that 'we have all been trying to help William and Harry come to terms with their devastating loss.' Tony Blair later called it 'near perfect'.[17]

The next day's papers, though not quite so generous, were of like mind. *The Times* called it a 'triumph of regal humility' which had 'softened' the hardest republican hearts. 'All this week, Britain has lurched between pandemonium and paradise,' the paper declared in an editorial. 'Today, perhaps, as

Elizabeth II

Diana, Princess of Wales, is laid to rest, the nation may recover its equilibrium.'[18]

It might have recovered, but it certainly struggled with its composure. The sight of the Princes marching behind their mother's coffin, crowned with a wreath and a card saying 'Mummy', tested the flintiest viewers among a global audience of 2.5 billion. The boys had agreed to walk to Westminster Abbey at the suggestion of Prince Philip, who joined them, along with their father and Diana's brother, Earl Spencer. 'I remember feeling numb. I remember clenching my fists. I remember keeping a fraction of Willy always in the corner of my vision and drawing loads of strength from that,' Harry wrote many years later.[19] Moments earlier, the world had witnessed an equally powerful sight. As the coffin passed Buckingham Palace from Kensington Palace, en route to be joined by Diana's sons, the Queen stood waiting to salute her former daughter-in-law. The monarch who bowed to no one bowed to Diana.

Inside the abbey, the service was every bit as 'somewhat radical' and Diana-ish as the Queen's team had hoped, though not for the reasons they had anticipated. Certainly, the presence of hundreds of charity volunteers and Sir Elton John singing a Diana tribute was not normal at a royal funeral. But the real surprise came as Earl Spencer climbed to the lectern to deliver his address.

His contempt for the press was to be expected, but he also took a swipe at the monarchy. His sister, he proclaimed, 'needed no royal title to continue to generate her particular brand of magic.' He also made a promise to Diana that her 'blood family' would protect her sons 'so that their souls are not simply immersed by duty and tradition, but can sing openly.' Because it was a hot day, the Great West Door of the abbey had been left open, allowing the charity representatives at the opposite

1996–97: 'These are for you'

end from the VIPs to hear the applause breaking out in the streets outside. So they clapped too. Slowly moving through the abbey like a Mexican wave, but with a sound like raindrops on metal, the noise made its way up the Nave, into the Quire and finally up to the South Transept where the Royal Family were sitting. They did not, however, regard the Earl's words as any sort of criticism of themselves. 'It seemed pretty clear that Spencer was having a go at the press, not us, and that is how everyone saw it – at least until later on,' a member of the Royal Household recalled. 'Then the press, predictably, started painting it as an attack on the royals.'[20] Prince Harry, in his book, wrote that it was an attack on both, noting: 'Truth hurts.'[21]

With the BBC cameras dutifully pointing elsewhere at this point, as pre-agreed, the viewers missed the sight of the two young Princes, dry-eyed but visibly distracted, half-clapping. However, a small group of invited press, including this author, were on a gantry opposite the family and saw it all. The Prince of Wales, who was visibly more emotional than his sons, patted his knee. The Queen sat immobile. She had moved a long way in that dreadful and tumultuous week, but the Supreme Governor of the Church of England had never clapped in church in her life. She was not about to start now.

Chapter Thirteen

1998–2002

'We must speak of change'

As the mourners filed out of Westminster Abbey, still trying to take in the enormity and drama of Diana's farewell, a wise old veteran of world affairs recognized a small group of senior Royal Household figures about to head back to the Palace. 'I've never forgotten it,' said one of them. 'It was Sir David Frost, whom I knew quite well. He told us: "You may think this is a very, very dark moment. But the monarchy is going to emerge much stronger because of this." And it did. It allowed us to move the whole thing forward, managing progress by disaster.'[1]

The Royal Family would adapt carefully but surely to the post-Diana landscape. The media were on constant alert for signs that the monarchy had been forced to make changes, whereas the Queen would hold firm to her mantra of 'evolution' rather than token gestures. She was not suddenly converted to the idea of 'stunts' or anything else that felt inauthentic. Instead, incremental change continued steadily.

'After Diana's death, we perhaps included what you might call more human interest and fun in the Queen's official programmes. It was more of a touch on the tiller, really,'[2] said

Elizabeth II

Mary Francis, the Queen's assistant private secretary and the first woman to be part of the trio of senior advisers (the team of principal, deputy and assistant private secretaries, one of whom had to be on duty day and night). Francis herself was an example of new thinking, an ex-Downing Street mandarin with no military, diplomatic or family connections who had been hired for her track record of delivering results in the Civil Service. As with the arrival of Mrs Thatcher in 1979, many had wondered how the Queen would deal with a female senior adviser when Francis was recruited in 1996; this was still a time, as noted, when female members of the Royal Household were politely reminded that trousers were not acceptable office wear. The Queen had always had ladies-in-waiting, of course, usually friends of a similar age serving as honorary companions. It was very different to having a female executive in the private office. However, the Queen was soon grateful for extra female support during some challenging moments. As she prepared for a harrowing visit to the scene of the 1996 massacre of sixteen children and a teacher at a primary school in Dunblane, she knew that she was going to struggle with her emotions. She chose her team accordingly. As well as Princess Anne, she asked Mary Francis to be her duty private secretary, telling her office: 'I want a woman with me because they understand.' Sure enough, away from the cameras, say her closest staff, she wept copiously that day.[3]

Francis would also play an important role in a very sensitive constitutional moment. The opening of the Scottish Parliament in 1999, the first national legislature north of the border in nearly 300 years, would require deft handling by the Palace. Too much pomp and the Queen would be diminishing the sovereignty of Parliament at Westminster. Too casual, and she would be accused of rudeness, as she had been on her

1998–2002: 'We must speak of change'

post-Coronation visit to Scotland in 1953. Back then, many had expected her in her Coronation robes and were upset when she arrived in a day dress. Mary Francis went to great lengths to source the right Scottish designer to create an appropriately stately dress in shades of thistle and heather.

The Queen was feeling this sense of gently shifting tectonic plates in many ways. Two of her greatest allies – both invaluable stalwarts and consiglieri during recent troubles – were doing something she could never do. Her childhood friend and Lord Chamberlain, David Airlie, along with her principal private secretary, Robert Fellowes, were retiring. She would dearly miss them. Airlie had been that 'twin' from the neighbouring Scottish castle, while the Queen had known Fellowes since he was a baby. His father had run the Sandringham estate and Princess Elizabeth had even attended his christening. It led to one of her finest and funniest lines as she stepped forward to speak at his leaving party: 'Robert is the only one of my private secretaries I have held in my arms!' It is one of the strangenesses of being royal that the lives of others always move to a different beat. However trusted and indispensable great stalwarts have become, most will, eventually, stop working, perhaps move home and, inevitably, slow down. The monarch always has to go on regardless with new people. However, because there would always be three private secretaries working together, it would be a straightforward case of moving Robin Janvrin, up from second-place deputy to the top spot of principal private secretary.

He had long advocated trying out new marketing and research tools, including opinion polls, and found that there was now a greater appetite for this sort of 'evolution' (the Queen loathed the word 'modernization' as much as she disliked 'corporate'). He had an ally in Prince Philip, who also liked to canvass discreet opinions from trusted opinion-formers. 'Prince Philip had this "Whither the Royal Family?" group. I went to one,' recalled Douglas Hurd, who left politics at the 1997 election and went on to become High Steward of Westminster Abbey. 'He was in charge, no doubt about that. We focused a lot on whether there were too many royals and I think the feeling was that there were.'[4] The family was about to expand, however.

On 19 June 1999, Prince Edward married Sophie Rhys-Jones, a public relations consultant. Theirs had been a different sort of royal romance. They had been a couple for five years before announcing their engagement, the bride's parents were happily married and Sophie had not grown up on the outskirts of royal life but in rural Kent. Nor did the couple – or the Queen – want a repeat of the big set-piece state occasion London weddings of the eighties. Rather, they would marry in the relatively smaller setting of St George's Chapel, Windsor, unwittingly setting a new trend for royal weddings for the next two decades.

The Queen had always found Edward the most easy-going of her three sons, not as introspective as Charles, nor as bombastic as Andrew. After the matrimonial turmoil of 1992, the monarch was very happy to allow Edward to bide his time. She liked Sophie's maturity, her willingness to learn the royal ropes and the fact that she did not see herself as 'a breath of fresh air'. On the wedding day, the Queen gave Edward the newly minted title of Earl of Wessex, explaining that it was a stop-gap. He would become a duke in due course, but both his parents wanted him to become Duke of Edinburgh, ensuring that his father's title lived on into the next generation. The Queen had adored her four and a half years as Duchess of Edinburgh. Edward had also become increasingly involved in the running of the Duke of Edinburgh's Award,

1998–2002: 'We must speak of change'

one of his father's proudest achievements. Rather than simply let the dukedom pass to the eldest son in the usual way, and then vanish into the mix when Prince Charles became King, it would live on if it was recreated for Edward. It might be breaking with tradition, but there had been a fair bit of that going on already since the 'annus horribilis'.

The century and the millennium would draw to a close with what would turn out to be a spectacularly joyless party. The government was at the height of its modernizing mania, dubbed 'Cool Britannia' by the press. This would be embodied in a bold new temple of ideas called the Millennium Dome, originally dreamed up by the Major government and then embraced by Blair's 'New Labour' neophiles. A latter-day watered-down homage to Prince Albert's Great Exhibition, it had been built at Greenwich, the fixed point from which the whole world calibrates its time zones and time itself. The Dome would be opened on Millennium Eve amid great fanfare. It was inconceivable that the Queen should not be there, even if she had spent every New Year's Eve for as long as anyone could recall at Sandringham.

As the costs of the Dome edged upwards towards the billion-pound mark, no one could agree on what it should contain – or what, indeed, it was for. Come the night, the Queen and Prince Philip looked underwhelmed as they took their seats next to the Blairs for an unmemorable opening show of song, dance and acrobatics. The evening did not improve. As Britain finally entered the twenty-first century and the Third Millennium at midnight, there was the customary hand-holding to the singing of 'Auld Lang Syne'. Conspicuously not crossing her arms in the traditional way, the Queen reached for Tony Blair with her left hand, Prince Philip with her right and went through the motions of joining in. Her granite face, however, said it all. This was not the way she had envisaged welcoming in the twenty-first century. At a conference of senior Blairite advisers and spin doctors ahead of the millennium, her then private secretary, Robert Fellowes, had been asked how the Queen might wish to mark the occasion. 'I think she'll want to go to church,' he replied. At which point the room had fallen silent.[5]

The Queen and her monarchy had proved more durable than the critics had imagined. During the troughs of the '90s, it had become received wisdom among republican-minded intellectuals that the House of Windsor was in terminal decline. In 2000, the left-wing weekly *New Statesman* collated the prevailing views of some eminent contributors. 'It's a sign of the tragic immaturity of Britain as a nation that we should be obsessed in the year 2000 with a reactionary old woman who has never done anything except act as a parasite on the body politic,' wrote historian Piers Brendon.[6] 'Elizabeth the Last,' proclaimed Professor Stephen Haseler.[7] The one inconvenient stumbling block, as those middle-class republicans in Harold Wilson's Labour ranks had found a generation earlier, was exactly that 'tragic immaturity' of the public and not just in Britain.

Just ten weeks into the twenty-first century, the Queen was on an unexpectedly jolly trip to Australia. The previous November, the country had held a referendum on whether to dispense with her services. The political and media establishments had been firmly in favour of abandoning Elizabeth II in favour of an Australian president on the eve of the new millennium. With Sydney preparing to host the 2000 Olympics, what better way to highlight a strong and confident nation looking to the future, not the past? Ahead of the vote on 9 November, all but one of Australia's daily newspapers said so, too. And then, inexplicably, the electorate had voted to keep her by a clear overall majority (55 versus 45 per cent). The Queen, say

1998–2002: 'We must speak of change'

those close to her, was pleasantly surprised by the result. 'She was rather touched but also wise enough to realize that multiple factors were involved and it was not just a ringing personal endorsement for her,' said one.[8]

There had been two miscalculations by the overwhelmingly middle-class, white, urban, university-educated professionals who were running the republican campaign. First, they had underestimated the extent to which the public trusted a monarch more than a politician. Second, they had assumed that the growing numbers of 'new' Australian citizens – those with no Anglo-Saxon heritage – would feel less loyal to the Queen. In fact, as republican campaigners like future prime minister Julia Gillard later acknowledged,[9] it was often those who had fled warzones, poverty and tyranny who particularly welcomed the sense of stability which Elizabeth II represented.

There was no triumphalism in her walkabouts or speeches as she and Prince Philip toured Australia in March 2000, but rather a sense of healing after a long and often ill-tempered debate. The Royal Family's personal woes had provided much ammunition for anti-royalists, and they had used it. She, herself, employed the main speech of an upbeat tour to promise that she would 'continue faithfully to serve as Queen of Australia', adding: 'That is my duty. It is also my privilege and pleasure.'

She arrived back in Britain to a reminder that there could be no complacency. Plans were well underway for a big pageant and parade to mark the Queen Mother's one hundredth birthday in the summer. This was originally due to be shown live on the BBC, but then the management had a change of heart. It would not be televised after all, ostensibly because it would mean shifting the popular daily soap, *Neighbours*, from its regular slot. Obvious but unspoken was the fact that a party for a one-hundred-year-old wartime Queen did not appeal to

Elizabeth II

the modernizers now driving the 'Cool Britannia' agenda inside the political and media establishments. The Conservatives immediately criticized the BBC for its disrespect, noting that the BBC director-general, Greg Dyke, had close links to the Labour Party.

What caused alarm within the Palace, however, was not the implicit snub to the Queen Mother, but a deeper point. The Queen and her family were always acutely aware that the greatest threat to the monarchy was not the pitchforks of the mob, but irrelevance. If the public no longer wanted to share in a major royal landmark moment like the Queen Mother's one hundredth, then reserves of relevance were running worryingly low. As it turned out, ITV stepped in to save the day. The network went on to enjoy its best early evening ratings for seven years. The Queen Mother's delightfully chaotic parade (which had been disrupted by an IRA bomb scare) was watched by more than three times the audience for *Neighbours*. Once again, the public's affection for the Queen and her monarchy ran much deeper than either their critics or the new Establishment cared to admit. The Palace made no comment, but the Queen's view seemed clear enough. She did not wait for the next honours list, but conferred a knighthood on the pageant producer, Major Michael Parker, two weeks later.

Every time the Queen's confidence crept back, another blow like the BBC's cancellation of the pageant would corrode morale once again. It was going to take time, but step by step, royal self-esteem was improving. During the Queen's 2000 state visit to Italy, her itinerary included a grand reception with the fashion industry in Milan. Over the years, she had grown hardened to sneering remarks about her fashion sense, the most regular criticism usually being that she looked 'frumpy'. It did not help that the Queen had no great interest in clothes.

1998–2002: 'We must speak of change'

'I have never known a woman less vain or less interested in fashion and design,' said a senior former (female) staffer.[10] Another senior aide recalled: 'I once showed her a shortlist of portraits of herself for a new stamp. She just took one look and said: "I look like Queen Sālote [the statuesque former monarch of Tonga]! I don't care. Can you just choose one?" She just wasn't bothered.'[11] A former designer for the Queen countered that she was not entirely uninterested: 'She did care about fashion, but she was just more concerned that people focused on her words rather than her wardrobe.'[12] Her broad philosophy about clothes was that they should be practical and enable people to see her in a crowd. As she once told a milliner: 'I can't wear beige because people won't know who I am.'[13] Yet, the assembled high priests of global fashion left the Milan reception singing her praises that day in 2000. 'She is, simply, one of the most elegant women in the world,' declared Miuccia Prada,[14] while Mariuccia Krizia noted: 'The Queen is above fashion.' No one had called her a 'fashion icon' for a long time. Even the assiduously non-fashion-conscious Queen was cheered by the next day's headlines. This was not entirely by chance, however.

Following the loss of her lifelong dresser and confidante, Bobo MacDonald, the Queen had come to rely on another straight-talking custodienne of her wardrobe, jewellery and private thoughts. She had first met Liverpool-born Angela Kelly during a state visit to Germany, where the divorced mother-of-three was working as a housekeeper at the British Embassy residence. Kelly's no-nonsense cheerfulness had caught the royal eye and she was offered a job at the palace in 1994. By 1998, she held the title of 'personal adviser and curator' and was not only choosing the Queen's wardrobe, as Bobo had done (with mixed results, hence the 'frumpy' barbs). Kelly's fine eye for material and detail meant that she also started designing some royal clothes herself. This did not always endear her to established royal dressmakers. One day, when asked for her opinion on a new dress, Kelly had been typically forthright, creating a 'frosty' atmosphere in the room until a passing Duke of Edinburgh made a similar observation as he asked: 'Is that the new material for the sofa?'[15]

As commentators and members of the public became increasingly complimentary about the Queen's appearance and her style, so, inevitably, did her confidence grow – along with her faith in 'Angela' – or 'AK47' as she was known among royal staff. 'AK' herself was amused to be likened to a Russian assault rifle. The nickname was rooted in both affection and respect. As staff had learned with Bobo, one should never patronize a woman who had the monarch's ear morning, noon and night, not to mention her shoe size, too. On her tour of inspection before the palace garden party season, the Queen would always warn the First Aid team (entirely correctly) that the same problem occurred every year: people being crippled by the brand-new footwear they had bought especially for the occasion. She never had to worry on that count. Whenever she herself had a pair of new shoes, they would always be properly worn in – by Angela Kelly.

By now, staff were starting to notice that suggestions which would have been rejected out of hand just a few years earlier were receiving a cautious welcome. In 2000, for example, the Queen agreed to several sittings for the famous – and famously unforgiving – artist, Lucian Freud. One fellow head of state who was astonished by this was George W. Bush, himself an artist after leaving politics. 'This amazed me. It requires somebody with a lot of confidence to say to Lucian Freud: "Of course you can paint me",' Bush told this author. 'Lucian Freud was an incredibly

1998–2002: 'We must speak of change'

talented artist, but he painted some pretty ribald subjects. He's got a painting style which I would not call traditional. If Her Majesty granted permission, that speaks to a lot of confidence.'[16]

The regal self-confidence started to wobble again, however, as the Queen prepared for her most significant personal milestone yet. Her Silver Jubilee celebrations in 1977 to mark twenty-five years on the throne had been a happy consolidation of her comfortable and assured position at the apex of the nation. Britain certainly had its problems, people would say, but at least it had the Queen. It had manifested a personal popularity that had never been in doubt. Her Golden Jubilee, on the other hand, would be a test and a challenge. This time, it was the House of Windsor, rather than Britain, which was having the problems. Could the Queen use the celebration to reset and reboot her monarchy? If not, it would be hard to dispute that, after fifty years on the throne, the reign of Queen Elizabeth II had been, if not a failure, then a disappointment.

The countdown to her jubilee had been overshadowed by global shock and personal sadness. As the Queen sat aghast watching the United States paralysed by terror attacks on 11 September 2001, she received news that one of her oldest friends, 'Porchie' Carnarvon, had died that same day. Henry Herbert, otherwise known as Lord Porchester (hence the nickname) before becoming the 7th Earl of Carnarvon in 1987, was the owner of Highclere Castle (of *Downton Abbey* fame). He had been a close friend of the Queen since she was a teenage Princess and he was a young Guards officer stationed at Windsor during the war. Though usually included on any list of potential suitors for the Princess (his regular invitations to royal parties showed that the King and Queen clearly approved), the Princess already had her heart set on Prince Philip at that point. Gossip columnists would occasionally try to infer that she burned a lingering flame for 'Porchie', but no one would ever take the stories seriously and the Queen was also a great friend of his wife, Jean. 'Porchie' and the Queen shared a passion for racing and, from 1969 until his death, he was the Queen's racing manager (a role continued by his son-in-law, John Warren, now racing manager to the King). Their greatest moment together came in 1974 when the Queen won two 'Classics', the 1000 Guineas at Newmarket and the Prix de Diane at Longchamps in Paris with Highclere, the Queen's bay mare named after Porchie's family seat. His death would be the first of three grave personal blows in just six months.

The horrors of what would forever be known by its American designation, '9/11', would change everything. The Queen led the nation in mourning for the suffering of the UK's pre-eminent ally. Just one small gesture, her decision to play the US national anthem at the Changing of the Guard, resonated deeply across the USA, as did one line of her message to the American people: 'grief is the price we pay for love'. She held a memorial service at St Paul's Cathedral and cancelled her autumn tour of Australia, along with the biannual Commonwealth summit. However, the global uncertainty only added to the all-pervading sense of nervousness about 2002. At the start of the year, *The Times* revealed that the number of jubilee events planned was just a tiny fraction of those held in 1977. Though it was partly down to extra bureaucracy, the paper was predicting a humiliation. 'Palace fears jubilee flop over red tape', it declared.[17] If the Queen had not feared a 'flop' until that point, she certainly did now. 'There's no doubt she was not confident about it,' said one of the Queen's most senior aides.[18]

On 6 February, she quietly marked the fiftieth anniversary of her accession. The jubilee was now, formally, underway. And yet, just three days later, the Queen suffered the heaviest

1998–2002: 'We must speak of change'

blow to befall her since her father's sudden death in 1952. Princess Margaret was dead. Her sister, soulmate, confidante and daily tonic-cum-tormentor had never fully recovered from a stroke in 1998, and had then suffered serious burns from scalding bath water a year later. She had been bedridden all through Christmas and, following another stroke, had been taken to King Edward VII Hospital, where she died in her sleep.

Lilibet had always loved Margaret dearly, however exasperating she could be at times, and the pair would speak almost every day. 'She was fiercely loyal to the Queen,' said Prue Penn, godmother to Princess Margaret's daughter, Sarah. 'I remember one day she told me: "I had the most terrible dream that the Queen was dead so when I woke up I just had to call her. I just needed to hear her voice. I got through to the palace and said it was very important."' Eventually, the Princess managed to get through to her sister. 'I just wanted to hear your voice!' she exclaimed. 'It's a little difficult right now,' the Queen replied, 'because I am with the prime minister.'[19] 'Margot', as she was known in the family, was a law unto herself. The younger ones were terrified of her. 'She could kill a houseplant with one scowl,' her fellow 'spare', Prince Harry, noted.[20] Diana, Princess of Wales, however, had 'adored' her – 'she was wonderful to me from day one.'[21] When he was the Queen's private secretary, Robert Fellowes would sometimes meet Margaret to discuss family matters in the Palace swimming pool. 'You swim in your lane alongside me in mine and we'll talk,' she would instruct him, 'but no splashing!'[22]

Princess Margaret's funeral took place in the same location, St George's Chapel, Windsor, on exactly the same day as that of George VI fifty years earlier. Their father's death had hit Margaret even harder than it had hit Lilibet. Some would say that, for all her privilege, Margaret's unsettled,

Elizabeth II

unsatisfied, melancholy life thereafter showed that she had never quite recovered.

Margaret had rejected a grave in the Frogmore burial plot for 'minor' royals, insisting on spending eternity in the crypt of the tiny George VI Chapel. Since it only had room for the coffins of her parents and, in due course, Elizabeth and Philip, there would be space for ashes alone. She had, therefore, requested a cremation.

As her coffin, covered in her standard, was carried out to the hearse which would take it to the municipal crematorium in Slough, there was a desperately poignant moment. The Queen Mother, herself recovering from a bad fall at Sandringham, had insisted on flying down to Windsor for the funeral. Now, aged 101, she was insisting on rising to her feet in tribute to her daughter.

The guests then adjourned to the castle for a final wake, where Lady Glenconner, one of the Maids of Honour at the Coronation, was told that the Queen would like a private word. Formerly Lady Anne Coke and now best known as the author Anne Glenconner, she had been a long-suffering lady-in-waiting to Margaret and was the friend who had originally invited Roddy Llewellyn to meet the Princess. Their relationship was later revealed by a paparazzo during a tryst in Mustique. 'Thank you for introducing her to Roddy,' the Queen told Lady Glenconner. It was a touching and telling remark. Margaret's affair with the garden designer seventeen years her junior ended amicably after seven years, and Llewellyn went on to have a wife and three children. However much the Queen must have disapproved of the Princess's scandalous Caribbean romance with a toyboy, this showed that, as a sister, her greatest wish had been for Margaret to find some sort of happiness, as she evidently had.

1998–2002: 'We must speak of change'

Despite losing Margaret, the Queen refused to change any of her Golden Jubilee programme. She pressed on with anniversary tours of Jamaica, New Zealand and Australia, plus that rearranged Commonwealth summit. All the while, her greatest worry was the Queen Mother, who, as ever, found great solace in familiar routine. At the age of 101, she continued to welcome the Eton College Beagles on their annual visit to Royal Lodge. 'She used to lay out these trestle tables covered in food,' her lady-in-waiting, Prue Penn, recalled. 'There would be a huge basket of Mars Bars and you'd see these boys stuffing their pockets!'[23] The Queen Mother was also still planning her annual houseparty for a favourite race meeting, the Grand Military at nearby Sandown Park, and would even have a winner (her last, as it transpired). By Easter, however, she was fading.

On Easter Saturday, the Queen was riding in Windsor Home Park when she received an urgent message to head for Royal Lodge. Margaret's children, David and Sarah, were already there, watching their grandmother drifting in and out of consciousness. The Queen made it just in time. As William Shawcross records in his official biography: 'Queen Elizabeth was able to say goodbye to her daughter.'[24] Moments later, the royal chaplain, Canon John Ovenden, recited the prayer: 'Now lettest thou thy servant depart in peace.' And she did.

Her farewell was the nearest thing to a state funeral without actually being designated as one. Over three days and nights, more than a quarter of a million people queued to pay their respects in Westminster Hall. The previous lying-in-state there had been that of Winston Churchill, and before that, George VI. Here was the last of that great triumvirate of wartime national figureheads. The queues grew so long that the opening hours were extended and then extended again until they went through the night.

Elizabeth II

On the evening before the funeral, the Queen appeared on television, saluting a mother 'full of courage and service, as well as fun and laughter.' Seven queens and seven kings plus representatives from 162 countries were among the mourners at Westminster Abbey the next day. An estimated one million people lined the route down to Windsor, applauding the coffin all the way. There had been constant applause for the Queen, too, wherever she went. In years gone by, there would only have been respectful silence. This might have been a modern – perhaps even a post-Diana – way of mourning, but the monarch told the family that she had found it immensely moving and reassuring. The Queen Mother's timing had been fortuitous, if not immaculate. Close friends privately wondered whether she had subconsciously wanted to absent herself before the jubilee began in earnest, just as Queen Mary had done weeks before the Coronation in 1953.

There was almost no time for Court mourning. The Queen had again decided that no Golden Jubilee engagement would be shelved. Days later, the great anniversary tour of the United Kingdom was due to begin at Cornwall's National Maritime Museum in Falmouth. The Queen and Prince Philip arrived to find a sparse crowd, barely one-deep. Even the most cynical, republican-minded commentators waiting to record this landmark moment felt sorry for her. 'I'll never forget that – the terrible feeling of coming out into an empty street,' recalled one of the royal entourage, still wincing at the memory.[25] And then the tour moved on to the centre of Falmouth. At which point all was explained. The entire population was waiting there. The same thing happened as the Queen and Prince Philip moved on to the cathedral city of Truro and thence across the border into Devon. Exeter was rammed. Thus began a pattern that would be replicated over the weeks ahead as the couple

1998–2002: 'We must speak of change'

traversed the entire United Kingdom. Millions turned out. It was starting to feel like 1977 and that long summer of bunting and street parties all over again.

Along the way, the Queen made a speech to both Houses of Parliament in Westminster Hall, where her mother had been lying in state just a month earlier. 'If a jubilee becomes a moment to define an age, then for me we must speak of change. The way we embrace it defines our future,' she said. One way of embracing it would be to turn Buckingham Palace into a stadium over the central jubilee weekend in June. A giant classical music event was followed two nights later by Party at the Palace, a riotous pop concert which would earn the Queen a golden disc from the music industry for CD sales.

For one very senior royal aide at the heart of all these events, there is one scene which encapsulates the moment Elizabeth II was back on top. 'Brian May up on the roof!' he said without hesitation, recalling the sight and sound of the great rock guitarist from the band Queen perched on top of the palace.[26] As May's soaring, solo electric national anthem rang out above a packed audience on the lawn and an estimated one million people filling the surrounding streets and parks, the real Queen could finally bury any residual fears of that dreaded 'flop'.

Ten years on, she had finally moved on from the fire and fury. Nonetheless, it had taken its toll. 'I know the Latin is not quite right,' said one very senior former adviser looking back on her life, 'but it wasn't just an annus. It was a decadus horribilis.'[27]

Chapter Fourteen

2003–11

The Winners' Enclosure

At long, long last, the Queen's lifelong 'smiling problem' seemed to be lifting. She had always acknowledged it herself. 'Oh, I must snap out of this and look smiley,' she told a lady-in-waiting at a wedding back in the sixties. Friends would loyally point out that she would develop a twitch if she had to radiate all the time and, besides, she loathed artifice and pretending. As Elizabeth II entered the sixth decade of her reign, however, the resting glum face simply started to cheer up.

At first, she seemed to be smiling more, and then most of the time. There was a new serenity about her. She was freer now, partly because she no longer worried about her increasingly frail mother and sister, and partly because she had ceased to be the serious, sensible schoolmistress caught between the glamour of youth and reverence for her late mother. 'Of course she misses her mother every day because they talked every day,' said a senior member of her Household. 'They were a tremendous double act but it wasn't a comfortable role for the Queen, always to be told how marvellous her mother was.'[1] The Queen Mother had continued to lead her quasi-Edwardian way of life with an impish, girlish glee, lauded to the end without

Elizabeth II

a single Red Box or ministerial audience to interrupt the fun. Now, as it fell to the Queen to enjoy a little more of the mantle of 'the nation's favourite granny', there was simply more of a twinkle in the eye. 'At about the time the Queen Mother died, the Queen effectively became the "Mother of the Nation",' explained Sir John Major.[2]

Abroad, there was less to smile about, however. The Queen would soon be waving British troops off to war again. It would all feel rather familiar. Tony Blair, now in his second term as prime minister, had joined the alliance led by US President George W. Bush to invade Iraq. Britain, under Margaret Thatcher and then John Major, had supported Bush's father, President George H. Bush, in the first Gulf War to liberate Kuwait from Iraq's Saddam Hussein. Now, Bush Junior would seek to topple Hussein altogether.

The UK's involvement was deeply divisive among the public, with millions taking to the streets in protest. Blair pressed ahead and, for good measure, asked the Queen to invite George and Laura Bush on a state visit in 2003. She had met them both during her last state visit to Washington as a guest of Bush Senior. Now she was repaying the compliment to Bush Junior. 'I'm fond of her. And, the more I've learned about her, the fonder I've become,' Bush told this author years later. 'We stayed in the Belgian Suite, which is very historic, and we weren't over-scheduled. Laura and I could relax.'[3] The Bushes were very much more congenial guests than the previous occupant of the Belgian Suite. Just five months earlier, Russian President Vladimir Putin and his then wife, Lyudmila, had been to stay. Such was the topsy-turvy geopolitical landscape at this point of the reign. The Queen, as ever, would roll with it uncomplainingly. Besides, the Putins were undemanding and nothing like those previous Eastern bloc visitors, the dreadful Ceaușescus.

2003-11: The Winners' Enclosure

'They knew how to behave,' a senior household figure recalls (they had also met the Queen before; Putin was the taciturn ex-KGB deputy mayor of St Petersburg who had made all the arrangements for the royal yacht during the 1994 state visit).[4] One member of the family who was especially keen to meet the Russian delegation was the Duke of York, now enjoying a new career as a trade envoy for British exporters following his departure from the Royal Navy in 2001. 'We did press the Navy very hard to keep him on but they couldn't find a suitable role,' a senior royal aide now admits.[5] The Duke would go on to make several trade missions across the former Soviet empire, and became so friendly with the oil-rich republic of Kazakhstan that, in 2007, the president's son-in-law agreed to buy the Duke's former marital home, Sunninghill Park, for £3 million more than the asking price.

If regular criticism of the Royal Family, such a feature of life in the 1990s, had started to fade, it was still proving hard to generate much excitement in the monarchy's regular activities. Post-jubilee, post-Diana and with William and Harry yet to take on public roles, the monarchy had dropped back down the news schedules. 'The thing that really surprised me in the early noughties wasn't that people were negative. The surprising thing was just how hard it was to get any press interest in anything the Queen was doing at all,' said one senior official of that time. 'I remember her state visit to Malta in 2005 and she opened the CHOGM [Commonwealth Heads of Government Meeting] there as well. It was just so depressing. Apart from a few lines in a few papers at the start, there was nothing. It may as well not have happened.'[6]

There was one last piece of unfinished business for the monarchy, a vital epilogue to the sadness of the '90s. As was now beyond doubt, the future happiness of the Prince of Wales was dependent on his relationship with the former Camilla Shand. They had been boyfriend and girlfriend back in the early seventies, until the Prince went to sea with the Royal Navy and Camilla had married cavalry officer Andrew Parker Bowles. Andrew's family had long been friends of the Queen Mother and the newlyweds would always move in royal circles, so much so that the Queen would later give Andrew and Camilla a corgi called Flame. The couple were regular royal house guests. Prince Charles was a godfather to their son, Tom.

Andrew even saved the Prince from injury, if not something worse, when the Prince was despatched to confer independence on newly democratic Zimbabwe in 1980. As military aide to the governor, acting Lieutenant-Colonel Parker Bowles was ordered to check the Prince's itinerary in advance. It included a visit to an agricultural college where the royal VIP was due to ride a 'domesticated' African buffalo. As a cavalry officer, Parker Bowles decided that he should test the animal first, only to be thrown off and badly gored. As he went on to command the Household Cavalry, he would see more of the Royal Family professionally as well as socially. Yet the Parker Bowleses were growing apart, and not just because of Camilla's friendship with the Prince. Andrew had no shortage of female company. The couple would divorce in 1994, with Andrew going on to remarry in 1996, while Camilla resumed her relationship with Prince Charles as his own marriage to Diana unravelled.

After Diana's death, as it became even more clear that Camilla was, in the words of the Prince's staff, 'non-negotiable', the Queen found herself in a difficult position. Whatever her feelings as a mother and as a friend of the Parker Bowles family, her position at the top of the Church of England left her conflicted. She was not a prude. As she had remarked in 1992, as the marriages of three of her children collapsed: 'I've decided

2003-11: The Winners' Enclosure

I'm not old-fashioned enough to be Queen.'[7] But she was of her generation and wary of endorsing the Prince's relationship with the ex-wife of a brother officer. 'You have to remember that her views were a generational thing,' said a close member of her circle at the time. 'She'd never forgotten the shock of the abdication and what could happen when it was love versus duty. And never underestimate the way she would follow the public mood. She would insist on seeing a cross-section of the Palace post every day and she was getting a lot of angry letters about Charles and Camilla.'[8]

Her senior advisers had been split on the issue too, an echo of her dilemma during Suez. In the latter half of the '90s, her principal private secretary, Sir Robert Fellowes, had been against the Queen being formally introduced to Camilla, while the two deputies, Robin Janvrin and Mary Francis, had been in favour. 'I was very sympathetic about Camilla,' Francis recalled. 'Robin and I were probably on the more progressive wing, in that respect, but you don't expect the Royal Family to be ultra-progressive.'[9] Acutely sensitive to the memory of Diana and the feelings of his sons, the Prince knew that things would have to move gradually but, by 1999, he had made his first public appearance with Camilla. Other family members – especially, it is said, Lady Sarah Chatto – urged the Queen to accept that this was the future. In 2000, she was re-introduced to Camilla at a Highgrove birthday party that the Prince was holding for ex-King Constantine of Greece. It was a brief and friendly introduction, with a low curtsey from Camilla, and a bridge had clearly been crossed. However, the couple's relationship still had to move forward at a ponderously slow pace, out of respect not just for public opinion but for the Queen herself.

Many remain baffled that the Queen should have had a

Elizabeth II

longstanding personal fondness for Camilla on the one hand yet a steadfast reluctance to embrace a marriage to her son on the other. 'It was her opposition which made it last so long. There was considerable reluctance because of her fears for the institution,' said a senior official, pointing to the age-old inner clash between Elizabeth, wife and mother, and Elizabeth II, constitutional monarch and Supreme Governor of the established Church. The Duke of Edinburgh, who had helped to bolster the Queen's resolve when it came to pushing Charles and Diana towards a divorce, also liked Camilla personally but remained on the sidelines now. 'He was not going to get involved,' said the official.[10] However, Elizabeth the pragmatist could also see that Prince Charles and Camilla were an enduring love match. Having made clear her own position on what she would and would not do at the wedding, she gave the union her blessing and, on 10 February 2005, the couple announced their engagement with a spring wedding scheduled for Windsor Castle. Their path to the altar was far from straightforward. They could not marry in church, so there would need to be a civil wedding first and then a blessing at St George's Chapel. Plans to hold the civil wedding in the castle ran into licensing problems (the ceremony would happen in the town hall), and there were even questions over the legality of such a wedding for royalty. To cap it all, the death of the Pope shunted the whole thing back by a day so that the Prince could fly to Rome to represent the Queen at the funeral.

It could not be denied that, for all the privileges of his position, the Prince of Wales and Mrs Parker Bowles had faced some unique obstacles – and had surmounted them all with determination and dignity. The Queen said as much in her speech on the afternoon of 9 April 2005. She had made it clear from the start that she would miss the civil wedding ceremony, another moment where Supreme Governor had trumped

2003-11: The Winners' Enclosure

mother. However, she attended the service of blessing at St George's Chapel and hosted the reception. Here, she could be the proud mother wanting every happiness for her son and showed it by breaking convention. Instead of the usual speech from the father of the bride, guests would hear from the mother of the groom. 'Many of the guests were not expecting it at all. Someone just tapped a glass and there was the Queen talking,' said one of the Household involved. 'It was her idea. She'd decided she could not go to the civil wedding but, having navigated all the official problems, this was her informal way of showing approval and marking the occasion. And then she came out with every racing metaphor in the book.'[11] It was Grand National day, after all. Recognizing the hurdles which had confronted Charles and Camilla in their quest to be together, while also listing many of the National's most infamous fences, she proclaimed that Charles and Camilla had now 'reached the winners' enclosure.'

A decade on from the end of their first marriages, the couple would still have many hurdles to come, not least the question of titles. Though she was now Princess of Wales, Camilla had absolutely no wish to encroach on sacred space and was very happy being Duchess of Cornwall. To calm things further (for there were still some loudly proclaiming that they would never accept a crowned Camilla), the Palace let it be known that, in due course, she would be known as 'Princess Consort' rather than Queen. The Queen herself thought that this was a 'brilliant' solution, according to a former private secretary.[12] That these conversations could now even take place was a Rubicon moment for the Royal Family.

Elizabeth II had never been terribly enthusiastic about birthdays, regarding them as a perfectly decent excuse for a cake (or, in her case, a parade), but no measure of anything except

Elizabeth II

stamina. In 2006, she accepted that others would be more excited about her eightieth than she would herself, and marked the occasion with a modest Windsor walkabout and a set of stamps (an improvement on her seventieth, when she had ruled out any stamps).

On her official birthday in June, the Household Division had decided to mark her eightieth with a rifle salute known as a feu de joie, a cascade of shots fired in rapid succession like a machine gun. The Coldstream and Welsh Guards duly performed their rat-a-tat salute expertly beneath the palace balcony. The Queen did not like it, however, telling one officer that it 'felt like a firing squad'. It would not be repeated.

She was much more interested in anniversaries which, in her view, required a degree of hard graft and effort, like jubilees and wedding anniversaries. Ahead of their own Diamond Wedding celebrations in 2007, the Queen and the Duke arranged their journey to the upcoming Commonwealth summit in Uganda with a stopover in Malta, happily spending their anniversary in the island where they had lived blissfully as a young naval couple.

Though both in their ninth decade, their appetite for travel was undimmed. In the year of her eightieth, the Queen and Duke made back-to-back state visits to three Baltic republics, whereupon the Duke then bolted on a quick solo trip to Iraq where one of his regiments, the Queen's Royal Hussars, were on active service in the Maysan desert. Six months later, the couple were making a state visit to the USA, including a trip to Jamestown, Virginia to mark the 400th anniversary of England's first American colony. They were almost the only people present who had also attended the 350th.

Family, friends and officials were noticing that this new happier, more confident monarch was starting to show to outsiders what others had always seen in private: a new directness, a willingness to risk a pithy remark when she might previously have kept her counsel. Senior ministers had long noticed her reticence to go off-script. 'If there is a downside, it is that the Queen is not keen on making off-the-cuff speeches,' former Tory foreign secretary, Douglas Hurd, told this author around this time. 'She thinks it's dangerous, which it obviously is.'[13]

Now, though, she was a little less buttoned-up. At a media reception during her Golden Jubilee, she had been noticeably more relaxed with her opinions. Meeting a group of journalists from France, including Marc Roche of *Le Monde*, she talked about the imminent presidential showdown between Jacques Chirac and the far-right Jean-Marie Le Pen. Roche was startled by the candour of her reply: 'I hope France votes well!'[14] No one was in any doubt about what she meant.

When Chirac was at her banquet for the G8 summit in Scotland in 2005, she enjoyed gently putting him on the spot about a recent blunder in which he had been caught by a boom microphone making very rude remarks about British and Finnish food. 'She asked – with a certain amount of mischief – for an explanation of why Finland had been so upset with France,' Tony Blair recalled with much amusement.[15] During a visit to the London School of Economics in the November just after the 2008 crash, she went to the nub of the issue, crisply asking the finest financial brains in the land, 'Why did nobody see it coming?' At around the same time, Home Secretary Alan Johnson was attending a Privy Council meeting and lunch at Windsor Castle where he was surprised to be seated next to the Queen. He was even more surprised when she launched, unprompted, into the main news story of the day: the ongoing inquest into the death of Diana. 'I thought we'd better keep off the subject,' Johnson recalled. 'But the Queen talked about it

Elizabeth II

in the most frank way, about how the thing had run and run and run.'[16]

This new confidence manifested itself in other ways. Although she had been monarch longer than anyone since Queen Victoria, it was not until now, in her sixth decade on the throne, that she decided to do something which her great-great-grandmother and others had done at a much earlier age. She created a decoration in her own name. Nor could anyone possibly accuse her of a vanity project. For, unlike other medals and orders, the Elizabeth Cross remains one that no one would ever want to receive – gifted to the next of kin of servicemen and women who die on operations. As one of those close to her explained, she had given it a great deal of thought and it was just 'very her'.

The Queen was also becoming more confident politically. In June 2003, Tony Blair's government had announced surprise plans to abolish one of the grandest and oldest offices in the land, that of Lord Chancellor. As well as being the nation's senior law officer, the Lord Chancellor had always had close ties with the sovereign, including a key role in the appointment of any regent. Now Blair and his modernizers had decided to split the duties and jettison the title and the office.

The Queen was, privately, very angry. It was not just the casual attitude to history and tradition which upset her, but the fact that Blair had not sought her views on something in which she clearly had both a personal and constitutional stake. Had this happened in the early days of the Blairites, when royal morale was at rock bottom and a radical new government was in its prime, then perhaps she would have been too meek to put up a fight. On this occasion, say those close to her, she was willing to assert her regal authority. The Lord Chancellor was swiftly unabolished. No one knows exactly what was said to

2003-11: The Winners' Enclosure

whom, but it is highly likely that the Queen deployed her usual negative tactic: 'Are you sure?', followed by more questions.

The same happened when Blair's Ministry of Defence was denying a British visa and medical aid to a Gurkha veteran who had won the Victoria Cross in the Second World War. Civil servants had decided that Tul Bahadur Pun, eighty-four, had not demonstrated sufficiently strong ties to Britain. We have some idea of what happened next, as a BBC camera crew filming a documentary which I wrote, *Monarchy*, happened to capture the moment the Queen was holding her daily 11 a.m. meeting with her private secretary, Robin Janvrin. 'I have had quite a lot of letters about the Gurkha VC,' said the Queen. 'It's obviously worried people enormously, hasn't it?' 'Shall I get more on that?' asked Janvrin. 'I think it would be useful,' the Queen replied. 'I've only read about it in the paper.'[17] Very shortly afterwards, Pun magically received his visa. Again, we do not know the exact sequence of events but it is more than likely that Tony Blair or one of his colleagues had heard a firm, familiar voice asking, once more: 'Are you sure?'

The political revolving doors were turning again soon enough. After winning a third election, Blair had finally made way for his right-hand man and Chancellor of the Exchequer, Gordon Brown, who was appointed by the Queen just in time for the market crash of 2008. Neither Brown nor Labour really recovered as the 2010 election loomed. All the polls suggested that Britain was heading for a hung parliament which, as ever, was the outcome least wanted by the Queen and her officials. Again, it is a moment that reveals a new steeliness which would have been unlikely in the early part of the reign and equally improbable during the 'horribilis' era. For the Queen made it clear that she would be leaving London when polling day came around and would not be coming back until the politicians

Elizabeth II

had produced a person for her to appoint as prime minister. There would be no re-run of that nervous weekend in 1974 when Ted Heath had not won, had not lost and was not moving.

She had also appointed a new private secretary, following the retirement of Sir Robin Janvrin (as he had become). In came Christopher Geidt, an ex-intelligence officer whose outwardly rosy demeanour concealed a beady eye for future problems which should be eliminated before they started. He had worked closely with the Cabinet secretary, Sir Gus O'Donnell, and senior constitutional experts like Peter Hennessy to draw up some basic guidelines ahead of the election. These had been published in a document called the Cabinet Manual. As the Queen herself had remarked to Hennessy during a visit to his students at Queen Mary and Westfield College in 1992, 'The British Constitution has always been puzzling and always will be.' The manual was supposed to be a way of making it less so, even if there was a risk that some people might start to treat it as Britain's first written constitution.

Right at the start, it made two points very clear. First, after an election, a prime minister remained in post until he or she resigned. Second, that it was for the politicians at Westminster to 'determine and communicate' who was 'best placed' to form a government. In other words: leave the Queen out of it until you have a name. Just to underline this, however, she would be playing a performative constitutional role by disappearing to Windsor, pending a decision. Here was another sign of renewed confidence, an unspoken reminder that she was not going to sit around twiddling her thumbs while the politicians argued.

Sure enough, the 2010 election did produce a hung parliament, followed by a long weekend of constitutional horse-trading. Out of it emerged the Queen's first coalition government. It would be led by the Conservatives' David Cameron in partnership with the Liberal Democrats' Nick Clegg. The Queen's first prime minister had served in the army of Queen Victoria. Now, she was appointing a man who had been at prep school (Heatherdown) with her youngest son.

After Heath, Thatcher and Major, Cameron was something of a Tory throwback, a tennis-loving Oxford-educated Old Etonian. Although he was the grandson of a baronet (and his wife, Samantha, was the daughter of one), he was a young, non-'tweedy', non-military ex-public relations executive (what his friend and adviser Steve Hilton would describe as 'lower upper class'). He was even distantly related to the Queen as a descendant of William IV, via the Sailor King's affair with the actress Mrs Jordan. Crucially, his would be the most consequential government for the Royal Family since Stanley Baldwin had presided over the abdication of Edward VIII.

On Cameron's watch, the government would legislate on a vast range of fundamental royal issues: money, succession, marriages, faith and the dissolution of Parliament. It would all happen during a third golden phase of the reign. The first had the euphoria of the Coronation period, while the second had stretched from the Silver Jubilee to the wedding bells of the eighties. Now those bells were about to ring again.

The Queen was delighted by the prospect of her first coalition government. 'I think this coalition is going to be rather good for the country,' she told her neighbour at a lunch just weeks after the election. 'Since we live in a time of unprecedented change, let's try to make the most of it.'[18] 'I think if you're the Royal Family, it's quite nice to have a coalition because you have to work with all politicians,' Cameron told this author. 'It suited the mood of the times. And I think it quite suited the way the Royal Family were thinking about things.'[19]

Elizabeth II

The early signs were not so promising, however, as Nick Clegg pushed through one of his party's preconditions to forming a coalition. A new Fixed Term Parliaments Act would make elections occur automatically every five years, thereby stopping a prime minister picking a date for electoral advantage. The Queen and the sharp-eyed Christopher Geidt disliked it for two reasons. First, it effectively erased her constitutional right to dissolve Parliament. Second, it was very unclear what happened if a prime minister lost the confidence of the House of Commons mid-term, spelling potential trouble for the monarch of the day. One senior Palace aide now looks back on it as 'a total dog's dinner'.[20] Peter Hennessy recalled royal alarm about 'the howling void' in the detail.[21] It would be repealed within a decade, much to the Queen's relief.

The new government was still just settling in when a rare but very welcome royal news event cleared the front pages of everything else: a wedding engagement. Since leaving Eton, Prince William had spent four years at St Andrews University in Scotland before embarking on a career in the armed forces. While at university, he had met and fallen in love with a fellow student, Catherine Middleton. Despite a subsequent break in the relationship, true love had prevailed and, on 16 November 2010, they announced their engagement.

The pair had actually been living together for some time without any objection from the Queen, but, then, her church seemed fairly relaxed on the matter too. As the Archbishop of York, John Sentamu, noted memorably just before the marriage, many modern couples 'want to test the milk before they buy the cow'.[22] This story had echoes of Prince Edward and Sophie Rhys-Jones.

Catherine had not grown up on the periphery of royal life, nor in a mud-splattered world of dogs, horses, guns and country sports like so many of William's friends. She came from a very happy, secure entrepreneurial family in semi-rural Berkshire, and William came to love the unstuffy, affectionate stability he found chez Middleton. While a few snobbier matriarchs quietly grumbled that the future King should have found his bride on a ducal grouse moor or the hunting field (in other words, he should have picked one of their own), the public were universally thrilled with William's choice.

All through the relationship, the Middletons had endured intensive scrutiny from a media which had insisted on rebranding Catherine as 'Kate'. Privately educated at Marlborough (like William's cousin, Eugenie), she was pretty, athletic, good-humoured, breezily self-confident but not extrovert. She had a family tree spanning the full strata of British life, including squires, miners and a grandfather in the Royal Air Force – in which Prince William was now serving as a search-and-rescue pilot.

The Royal Family – and, most importantly, Prince Harry – embraced her from the start. Ever since the death of Diana, the overarching rule, set by Prince Charles and by the Queen, was that the two Princes should be allowed to make their own decisions and life choices, as long as they had good advice. Their father had equipped them with their own small but independent household, led by a canny former Irish Guards and Special Forces officer, Jamie Lowther-Pinkerton. Catherine's arrival would not involve any change to the arrangements. Harry, by now happily ensconced in an army career, was certainly not to be moved aside. The first-floor study which the brothers shared at St James's Palace would simply become a study for three. Their first port of call for advice – and money – would obviously be their father. The Queen, however, had also asked Sir David Manning, the ambassador to Washington

Elizabeth II

during her 2007 state visit, to be an unofficial adviser and sounding board for this fledgling royal unit. She had assessed him over a private dinner during the state visit – 'he had no idea he was being interviewed,' a royal aide revealed – and he was then invited to take on the honorary role on his retirement from the Foreign Office.[23] The Queen had been inspired by her own experience as a trainee monarch. 'She told me that she had been very grateful when her father had given her General "Boy" Browning as a wise old hand when she was starting out in the forties,' the aide told this author.[24] Her grandsons were always welcome to contact her, but she was well aware that it could be daunting for trainee royalty to navigate the ways of the Royal Household. The Queen had previously done something similar after Diana's death when she had asked former prime minister Sir John Major to be the boys' 'special guardian' with regard to their inheritance from Diana. She did not want to be accused of interfering. She did not want to be accused of not caring either.

When it came to William's choice of bride, he had neither needed nor received any advice from anyone. But as the wedding drew nearer, he realized he would need some help. The commissars of protocol within both the Palace and government had a rather different vision for the occasion than the happy day which he and Catherine envisaged. This time, his adviser would be the Queen herself.

'I came into the first meeting for the wedding, post-engagement. And I [was given] this official list of seven hundred and seventy-seven names – dignitaries, governors, all sorts of people – and not one person I knew,' William told this author. 'I looked at it in absolute horror.' So, he turned to the Queen and asked if this was compulsory. 'She said: "No. Start with your friends first and then go from there." And she told me to bin the list.'[25]

2003–11: The Winners' Enclosure

William had come to appreciate her advice more and more by this stage. The Queen, in turn, was starting to send him on important missions on her behalf. A few weeks before the wedding, for example, she asked him to convey her condolences to the people of New Zealand after a terrible earthquake hit the city of Christchurch. 'There's no question you can ask and no point you can raise that she won't already know about,' the Prince said afterwards. 'Being the young bloke coming through; being able to talk to my grandmother and ask her questions and know that there's sound advice coming back is very reassuring.'[26] Theirs was a much easier relationship than the one which the Queen had enjoyed with Prince Charles when he was the same age. As his official biography observed, 'in those days, the Queen rarely found occasion to confide in her son,'[27] while the Duke of Edinburgh would communicate with Prince Charles mainly via memo. Prince Charles would turn, instead, to Lord Mountbatten for advice.

On 29 April 2011, London enjoyed an experience it had not known for twenty-five years, as the centre of the capital ground to a halt for a royal wedding. There was no public holiday; both the Queen and the government were alert to charges of royal overreach. Critics – and there were already complaints about the estimated £20 million security bill – might start to dredge up memories of the Prince's parents' wedding day. Nonetheless, an estimated one million lined the streets along the route from Buckingham Palace to Westminster Abbey for a day of giddy, uncomplicated royalist euphoria.

On the morning of the wedding, the Queen had invested William as Duke of Cambridge, while she had lent Catherine her 'Halo' tiara. The Queen's father had commissioned it for her mother and it was a piece of great personal importance to her. She had done her best to let the couple make it a personal day on their own terms, but had made one forceful intervention. When Prince William had let slip to his grandmother that he was planning to wear his RAF uniform, the sartorial portcullis came crashing down. 'I was given a categorical: "No, you'll wear this"!' She was adamant that, having only just appointed him as Colonel of the Irish Guards, she wanted him marrying in Guards scarlet rather than RAF grey-blue. 'You don't always get what you want, put it that way,' the Prince added. 'But I knew perfectly well that it was for the best.'[28]

The Queen did, indeed, have good reason to see William marrying in his Irish Guards uniform – and not just because she wanted a splash of colour at the altar. At the time, she had all things Irish on her mind, for she herself was in the midst of organizing one of the personal high points of her reign: the first state visit by a British monarch to the Republic of Ireland. If Elizabeth II had drawn up the proverbial 'bucket list' at this stage of her life, then Ireland would have been close to the top of it. Here was the UK's nearest neighbour – the only nation with which it shared a land border – and one with arguably the most horse-mad population on the planet. And yet, this pioneering Queen, who had been the first monarch to visit so many parts of the world, had never set foot in the place. She would often talk wistfully of seeing the hills of Ireland from her yacht or from over the border from Northern Ireland. She was acutely conscious that when her grandfather, George V, had been the last monarch to visit, in 1911, Ireland had still been part of the United Kingdom. Civil war, historic resentments and, latterly, 'the Troubles' within Northern Ireland had always made a state visit too problematic.

When the politicians on both sides finally agreed that the time had come for a visit in 2011, precisely one hundred years on from George V, the Queen was so thrilled that she did something very unusual. She asked her staff to cram it with more engagements, not fewer. 'The Irish just expected her to go in and out in a day or two,' said a former private secretary. 'So they were amazed when we said we wanted four days and then when we named all the places she wanted to visit. That was all her idea.'[29] When the Irish tentatively suggested that she might pay her respects at a place sacred to Irish nationalism, the Croke Park stadium where British forces massacred innocent civilians in 1920, the Queen instantly agreed. This would not just be a week of warm words, horses and happy photographs alongside a pint of Guinness.

The genesis of the visit was the new-found era of relative peace in Northern Ireland following the 1998 Good Friday Agreement and the decommissioning of terrorist weapons. However, renegade anti-British units had never gone away. The greatest security operation ever mounted in the Republic was a reminder of the ongoing terrorist threat. The vast majority of Irish people were delighted to welcome the Queen via their televisions, but there could be no walkabouts. Nonetheless, two moments would stand out in a tour with significant consequences for more harmonious relations across the religious divide in Northern Ireland. One came as the Queen laid a wreath at Dublin's monument to the martyrs of Irish independence, whereupon she performed a pronounced bow. The other came at the state banquet, when she prefaced her speech with words of Gaelic. Wearing a dress embroidered with 2,091 crystal shamrocks, she acknowledged the 'heartache, turbulence and loss' felt by both nations during the past century. Even Irish republican diehards like Gerry Adams acknowledged that her words had been 'genuine'.

She loved every aspect of that tour, gladly maintaining contact for years afterwards with a chatty fishmonger she met

Elizabeth II

in the old rebel city of Cork. Pat O'Connell would send her letters, she would reply and, on one occasion, she invited him to a reception and private audience at Buckingham Palace. 'Oh, my fishmonger's come over!' she exclaimed as she walked in. The visit led on to even greater diplomatic breakthroughs. A year later, the Queen would be shaking the hand of a former IRA commander, Martin McGuinness, who had once conspired to kill her and her family. Two years on from that, McGuiness would be in white tie as her guest at Windsor Castle for the state visit of the new Irish president, Michael D. Higgins. This would be, without question, the high water mark in the history of UK–Irish relations (which then rapidly went downhill after Britain's exit from the European Union). It was pure statecraft – and it was down to Elizabeth II more than any politician.

The Queen's sun-kissed spring of 2011 was not over yet. Soon after her return from Ireland, she was welcoming Barack and Michelle Obama on a state visit to Buckingham Palace. Once again, it was a case of the Queen creating the diplomatic momentum, not simply being carried along by it.

There had been much acrimony between the Obama White House and 10 Downing Street, both under Gordon Brown and David Cameron. However, the Obamas had hit it off with the Queen at their first meeting in 2009 when in London for a G20 summit. The monarch and first lady had bonded over a very jolly discussion about the agony of shoes, and media reports that Michelle Obama had committed some sort of faux-pas by putting an arm around the Queen were entirely wrong. The two women had been comparing heel sizes. The first lady called her 'a living symbol . . . as human as the rest of us'.[30]

So, the Obamas were delighted to accept a state visit invitation to the palace for 2011 and enjoyed themselves so much that the Queen had to bring the party to a close. She nudged the chancellor, George Osborne, who was unsure what to do. So she turned to her Lord Chamberlain, Earl Peel. 'The Queen said to me: "Could you tell the president I'm about to retire?",' Peel recalled. 'He was in a corner with Tom Hanks and various other star-studded individuals. So I said: "Mr President, just to let you know the Queen's about to retire."' Obama cheerfully took the hint. 'He was very amusing,' Peel added. 'And his wife was very impressive, too. I'd sat next to her at lunch earlier. As we walked across the room, he looked at me and said: "How did you get on with the first lady at lunch? How was her etiquette? Did she know which knife and fork to use?"' 'Disappointing at first,' Lord Peel joked, 'but she got there by the end.'[31]

The whole visit continued in a similar spirit of good humour. Obama's top aide, Ben Rhodes, recalled the scene back in the Belgian Suite as Obama sat up with his speechwriting team reflecting on how much fun he was having and how much he 'loved the Queen', who reminded him of his grandmother, Toot.[32] The Secretary of State, Hillary Clinton, was thoroughly enjoying the royal hospitality, too. Lord Peel recalls her asking if she could pull back a net curtain for a better view of a guard of honour. He told her to go ahead, at which point the American ambassador suddenly scolded her for breaching security. 'Oh, piss off!' Clinton shot back. The visit left US/UK relations in a much-improved state. David Cameron went on to have an enhanced and enduring rapport with Obama for the rest of his time in office. As he recalled: 'The Queen certainly made life easier for me.'[33]

Chapter Fifteen

2012–16

Diamond Days

As prime minister, David Cameron would have a lot to do with the Queen and her family. It was not all happy news. There was an awkward moment when he had to sack the Duke of York from his role as an ambassador for British trade. By this point, *The Mail on Sunday* had revealed that the Duke had not only maintained his friendship with a convicted American sex offender called Jeffrey Epstein, but had stayed at the financier's New York home since Epstein's release from prison. A photograph then emerged of the Prince with an arm around a teenage girl who had been abused by Epstein. Thus began Andrew's slow fourteen-year descent to ex-royal pariah status.

'I think I was responsible for gently saying to Her Majesty that he had to stand down as a trade envoy,' Cameron recalled. 'It was all pretty much fixed. But I was just to reference it for the official log. The Queen was worried about him but she could see the logic.' It was not just the Duke's Epstein connection which was the problem. 'It had been getting embarrassing,' Cameron recalled. 'Andrew kept turning up to things and making terrible remarks. I'd seen it myself at

Elizabeth II

Davos* where he was going to his receptions and was just a bit crass. He had his way of doing things and it wasn't what you wanted. He was very good with all the tyrants but he started being opinionated saying we were too squeamish about dealing with these people. His speeches would always just have three or four inappropriate things. Unlike the rest of the royals, who were very good at knowing where to stray and where not to stray, he was straying all over the place.'[1]

Andrew was at the peak of his oafishness at this point, exemplified by his behaviour just weeks before his demotion. An eminent public servant was arriving with his family and several hundred other guests on their way to an investiture at Buckingham Palace. 'We were walking across the Quadrangle and suddenly this blue Bentley appeared and did a handbrake turn, throwing up gravel over other people's cars,' a family member recalled. 'Someone said "I bet that's Andrew." And sure enough it was. And everyone was talking about it as we went in because it had just spoiled things. He lived at Buckingham Palace whereas we were just the little people going in there for our big day. And he just had to make it all about him.'[2] There had been a similar episode at Windsor a few years earlier, when grooms from the Royal Mews had been riding some of the Queen's horses on the estate. One had waved a firm hand at an approaching car which was revving its engine aggressively. It pulled alongside and, through the window, the Duke of York bellowed at her: 'Who the f*** do you think you are?' He then demanded her name. 'What's more, he even took it up with the Queen – in person,' a former member of the Household recalled.[3] Nothing was done.

At home and abroad, similar stories would do the rounds (and continue to emerge). One British diplomat in Moscow

---

* Swiss home of the annual World Economic Forum.

would remember a trade-related visit by the Duke during which his top priority seemed to be the acquisition of a fur hat: 'He had a selection of them delivered to his hotel late in the evening – come to think of it, by some very pretty shop assistants.'[4] 'We had him for a day and he insisted he had to come by helicopter. The royal ones were booked so they rented one from Harrods,' a former lord-lieutenant from this period recalled. 'At one point, it blew over some hoardings and he gave the pilot a roasting in front of everyone even though it didn't matter. Then he started shouting at the two women who were with him because they didn't know where his raincoat was. Whenever lord-lieutenants got together, we would swap notes on what a nightmare he was. No one wanted him.'[5] No one wanted to relay these stories to the monarch, however. And despite her keen interest in the smallest goings-on within her household, she did not want to be informed. Out of loyalty to her, the Andrew problem had been allowed to fester.

One former Cabinet minister remembered that, through this period, the Queen was touchingly concerned for her ex-daughter-in-law, who had continued to live – on and off – with the Duke ever since their divorce. 'She was obviously fond of Andrew but strangely fond of Fergie. She said: "Oh, I just worry that they don't have any money." It was rather sweet.'[6]

Royal money was certainly on the minds of those in the new coalition government, which took office just in time for some tricky discussions between the Palace and the Treasury. For 250 years, the monarch had received a government grant, called the Civil List, to cover the running costs of being head of state (while non-state costs were funded via the Duchy of Lancaster and private investments). In return, successive monarchs had given the government all the revenues (a very much larger sum) from that vast landholding, the Crown Estate.

Elizabeth II

The problem with the Civil List was that it needed regular renegotiation in Parliament. This not only made long-term planning difficult, but risked a political row with headlines like 'Queen demands a pay rise'. David Airlie had managed to change the system so that haggling only occurred every ten years, not annually as before. The Royal Household had then been so rigorous with its finances that it had managed to stay on the same budget for two decades in a row.

As Cameron and his team arrived in 2010, however, it was all up for review again and would need a substantial increase due to inflation and rising costs. Cameron's chancellor, George Osborne, decided to tear up the whole thing and create a new funding formula. In essence, the monarch would receive a fixed percentage of the Crown Estate revenues. The Queen's staff and the Treasury agreed a figure of 15 per cent, which would translate to the minimum required to meet the monarchy's costs. Osborne thought that he had actually driven a hard bargain at a time of economic austerity. Then Crown Estate profits soon began to rise. 'What happened subsequently is that Britain recovered quite quickly,' Osborne acknowledged. 'The Crown Estate was well run, so they [the monarchy] had more money than anyone expected.'[7] Over time, the rate was so generous it would need to be cut, while the Sovereign Grant would also fund the restoration of Buckingham Palace. After 250 years of the Civil List, here was one piece of modernization which the Queen would welcome with open arms. No wonder she was fond of this coalition.

Osborne and his team also modernized another royal income stream. Since medieval times, the Duchy of Cornwall had funded the heir to the throne – but only if the heir was male. The Queen had been a victim of this fourteenth-century sexism. As noted earlier, during her days as a Princess, she never saw a penny of the duchy revenues, which reverted to the Treasury simply because she was a girl. It would now be a unisex arrangement. Of all the royal reforms ushered in by the coalition, the most significant and historic were those involving gender and marriage. It had always been the case in the royal line of succession that boys trumped girls, a system known as male primogeniture. No matter that any public poll of the top five monarchs in history would automatically include three queens (in no particular order: Elizabeth I, Victoria and Elizabeth II), the story of the Crown was predominantly a male one.

Now that Prince William was married, however, there would almost certainly be children. And what would it say to women in a twenty-first-century Britain if a first-born girl was then leap-frogged by a younger brother? The sagacious Christopher Geidt had seen this problem looming and discussed it with the Queen and Cameron. This was law and not down to the Queen herself; it was a matter for her ministers, but it would clearly need more than her signature. It required her tacit support. Many politicians had previously tried to tinker with the laws of succession but had dumped the idea as being too arcane and complex, not least because it would need the agreement of all the other fifteen nations or 'realms' of which the Queen was head of state. Geidt had spotted an opportunity, however. All those realms would be at the upcoming summit of the fifty-four nations of the Commonwealth in Perth, Western Australia. So Cameron and the host, Australian prime minister Julia Gillard, agreed to convene a mini-summit within the summit for the leaders of all the Queen's realms, from mighty Canada to tiny Tuvalu.

As it turned out, they all rather enjoyed playing a walk-on part in royal history and happily agreed to pass legislation ending male primogeniture for monarchs. What's more, they agreed to repeal the Royal Marriages Act, which compelled all lineal descendants of George II to seek the monarch's permission before marrying. In future, only the first six in line to the throne would need approval. They also lifted the rule which ejected members of the Royal Family from the line of succession if they married Roman Catholics. So, in the space of an hour, one gathering in a Perth meeting room had torn up a bundle of ancient laws which, over many centuries, had inspired murder, rebellion, revolution, war and assorted plots by William Shakespeare. Though she was not in the room and technically had no choice, the Queen accepted it all, though without any great enthusiasm. 'It was one of those things where she would have said: "Well it's inevitable",' says a very senior long-serving courtier. 'It didn't necessarily mean that she advocated it. She just got on with it.'[8] The traditionalist in her would always be innately cautious about tearing up centuries of precedent and established practice, whereas the pragmatist in her knew and accepted the rationale.

There was a sad footnote to that summit. The Queen had privately taken a decision to cease all long-haul travel, not on doctors' orders but for a more poignant reason. 'Prince Philip had just turned ninety, he was going to stop travelling and she was worried about being separated from him for long in case something happened,' said a senior aide of the period. 'So when she said goodbye to Australia, she knew she was never coming back.'[9] Nor would there be any further trips across the Atlantic. Her 2010 tour of Canada, followed by a stopover in New York to address the United Nations and visit the memorial to 9/11, had been her last to North America. Nonetheless, there was also now a clear sense within the Palace that the good times really were back. 'These were moments to be savoured. She had earned them and they might not last,' said one of her most senior aides. 'So she was going to enjoy them.'[10]

It meant that Elizabeth II entered her Diamond Jubilee year with nothing to prove, finally confident that she had

2012–16: Diamond Days

future-proofed the monarchy for at least a couple of generations. The Prince of Wales and his sons, together with the Princess Royal and the Wessexes, would take on the international side of her sixtieth anniversary celebrations. As with previous jubilees, however, she would tour the United Kingdom. It all started off on Accession Day with a short visit to a Norfolk primary school, near Sandringham, where teachers had been explaining the monarchy to the pupils using Nicholas Allan's bestselling picture book *The Queen's Knickers*. She arrived to find a washing line decorated with elaborate craftwork replicas of what small children imagined her underwear might look like. She was delighted, although one or two members of her entourage were a little surprised that the Queen should have to inspect depictions of her own pants on such an auspicious day. It was, at least, a vivid illustration of the seismic societal and cultural change during her long reign.

The centrepiece of the jubilee was a long weekend which would become unexpectedly dramatic. The Tory peer, the Marquess of Salisbury, who had been the architect of the great VE Day party in 1995, had agreed to organize a gloriously ambitious pageant on the Thames, inspired by Canaletto's paintings of great eighteenth-century river processions. The idea was for the Queen to sail down the river surrounded by a flotilla of a thousand boats reflecting every strand of British and Commonwealth history, from a Māori war canoe to a fleet of the Dunkirk 'little ships' and a floating belfry. It would receive no public money (at the Queen's insistence) and rely on sponsorship and affection for the monarch.

Delightfully chaotic, it started under grey skies and was then pummelled by horizontal rain driven by a perishing easterly wind blowing straight into the face of the seven-mile procession. Several people were hospitalized with hypothermia. Declining the option of two theatrical thrones on the deck of their river cruiser, *The Spirit of Chartwell*, let alone invitations to go inside, the Queen and the Duke insisted on standing throughout, waving to the million-plus crowd lining the banks. David Cameron recalls being on the jetty at the finish to welcome the Queen back on to dry land. As other members of the Royal Family stepped ashore, wet and shivering, the Duchess of Cornwall joked to him: 'She'll have us all killed. She can cope with this stuff. The rest of us are freezing to death!'[11]

No one had enjoyed the maritime mayhem more than the Duke of Edinburgh, though the exertions and the weather had taken its toll. He had not drunk enough fluids. Knowing he would be on public display for hours, he had not wanted to have to disappear to the loo. That same evening, he was hospitalized with a bladder infection. Though the Duke would be home again soon enough – the Queen told David Cameron that he had spent his hospital stay happily watching cookery programmes by Jamie Oliver and Rick Stein – his absence lent a sombre note to the grand finale of the jubilee weekend as the Royal Family appeared on the palace balcony two days later. The Queen and Prince Charles had decided that this would be an important moment to point to the future of the monarchy. Rather than pack the balcony with the wider family, as in years gone by, the Queen and Prince Philip would be joined only by the central players – Charles and Camilla, plus William, Catherine and Harry.

Here again was a sign of Elizabeth the pragmatist going against Elizabeth the traditionalist. As noted earlier, the Queen had previously rejected all suggestions that she should trim balcony appearances because the optics suggested a costly and bloated monarchy. Now she was doing just that. It was certainly a snub to the rest of the family. The Princess Royal and Prince Edward took it well enough, while the Duke of York was incan-

2012–16: Diamond Days

descent at yet another demotion. Now, with no Prince Philip present, the line-up looked even leaner. From then on, a new phrase would enter regular media use, one frequently attributed to Prince Charles: the idea of a 'slimmed-down monarchy'.

The jubilee was merely Act One of one of the liveliest and happiest summers of the Queen's reign. Less than two months later, the eyes of the world were on London again for the 2012 Olympics. No city had ever staged the mighty sporting circus three times, nor could any world leader boast quite such a close connection as Elizabeth II. Her great-grandfather Edward VII had opened the 1908 London Games and her father had done the same in 1948. As Queen of Australia, she had sent Prince Philip to open the 1956 Melbourne Games. As Queen of Canada, she herself had opened the 1976 Montreal Games, at which her own daughter was competing. Princess Anne, as president of the British Olympic Association, had been part of the bid to bring the 2012 Games to London, helped by the Queen, who had thrown a sumptuous banquet to flatter the International Olympic Committee. What's more, footage of the Queen's Golden Jubilee celebrations had played a key role in the final pitch video shown to the IOC on voting day. Few families on Earth could boast an Olympic pedigree quite like the Windsors. So, when the organizers of London 2012 had a bold idea for some extra royal participation, the Queen was ready to listen.

As head of state, she would obviously be expected to declare the Games open. But what about doing something unexpected, too? The producer of the opening ceremony, award-winning Hollywood director Danny Boyle, had been planning ways to make the London Games as far removed from the previous Olympics – in China – as possible.

'They started off thinking how could we be different and better than Beijing,' recalled David Cameron, whose government would foot the bill. Some of Boyle's proposals, Cameron said, were 'ridiculous Leftie stuff', like getting two old enemies from the Northern Ireland 'Troubles', David Trimble and Gerry Adams, to parade through the stadium jointly holding a flag of peace. 'Then Danny said: "We've got this great idea",' Cameron told this author. 'I remember the hair standing on the back of my neck thinking: "Oh my God, that's just the best." We were sitting in the study in Number 10, him on the sofa and I was in the chair.'[12] Boyle had worked out that, globally, the two most popular and recognizable British names were James Bond and the Queen. Why not get them to appear in a video together? Bond actor Daniel Craig would arrive at the palace to meet the Queen, who would have one line: 'Good evening, James.' The pair would then jump into a helicopter together, fly across London and parachute into the stadium – the Queen leading the way – whereupon live-action cameras would switch to the royal box as Elizabeth II appeared for the formal opening.

Cameron readily agreed to raise it with the Queen at his next audience, without even running it past his officials. 'I didn't say to anyone that I was going to mention it. When you went to see her, you've got your hour and you've got, say, four topics. But I would also try to say something that was interesting because you're trying to have a chat that's not too formulaic. I remember saying: "Look, some people are going to come and talk to you about this. I've seen the treatment by Danny Boyle. Two of the best things about Britain are James Bond and you and, you've got to say yes." It was a bit gushing. And I remember thinking I sounded like a sort of excited teenager. I then shut up because I knew I shouldn't bang on but I was very glad I said it because I really wanted it to register.' He also remembered the Queen's cryptic reply. 'She said "we'll see" – with a smile.'[13]

The smile might have been because she had already been

approached via another route, according to a senior Palace insider. Boyle had also raised the idea with the main organizer of the Games, former gold medallist Lord [Sebastian] Coe, who had run it by the Princess Royal. Her advice was simple: 'Ask her.' Coe knew her deputy private secretary, Edward Young, who took the plan to the Queen. 'Funnily enough, it was one of those decisions that was actually taken quite quickly,' Young recalled.[14] The only people at the Palace entrusted with the secret were Young, the Queen's page Paul Whybrew (who would appear in the film, along with her corgis) and her dresser. Angela Kelly would need to make two versions of the opening ceremony dress – one for the Queen and one for the stunt double jumping out of the helicopter. Kelly opted for impeccably neutral peach on the basis that it was the one colour which is not in any nation's flag.[15] The Queen's only request was for a tweak to her one-line script. It would be more authentic for her to say 'Good evening, Mr Bond' rather than 'James'. Boyle agreed.

The gasps of happy shock on the night of 27 July 2012 echoed around the world, around the stadium and right up to the royal box. Lord Coe remembered sitting in the royal box behind Princes William and Harry, both astonished and thrilled to see the Queen apparently floating down into the stadium and both yelling: 'Go, Granny!' The following day, the Queen's cameo role was global front-page news. Within the Palace there was a recognition that this was not a 'new' Queen, nor that she was taking her role any less seriously. 'The Bond film worked because it was just bringing out another side of her which, for decades, she had kept very well hidden,' explained one of her closest aides.[16]

The Queen also understood the importance and value of scarcity. Having made such an indelible mark on the 2012 Olympics, she was then happy to withdraw and let others shine.

Elizabeth II

The Olympic Charter is clear that each Games should be formally closed as well as opened by the head of state, but the Queen was happy to amend the rule. As the closing ceremony approached a fortnight later, she was up at Balmoral for her holiday and was not going to leave. Logic dictated that this should be a job for the Prince of Wales or else Prince William, but the Queen had another idea. The stand-in head of state would actually be Prince Harry. What she and he knew, but the world did not, was that the twenty-seven-year-old Prince would shortly be deployed back to Afghanistan on active service. All the family were, understandably, very worried about him, but also very proud. So the Queen decided that all those senior to him in the line of succession should absent themselves and let Harry take centre stage in front of the world. Later on, he would often talk (and write) about his 'special relationship' with his grandmother. Moments like this would underline it.

David Cameron looked back on this period of wedding rings, Olympic rings and the jubilee as a fresh turning point. 'You really felt that after the Diana years and so on, the royals were back on peak form,' he said. 'The Queen was very confident about everything she was doing. The machine was sort of ticking over nicely. She was at the height of her powers. You never thought she missed a beat. She was physically strong and mentally at one hundred per cent.'[17] One private secretary of the period remembered receiving calls from one or two prophets of doom. 'It had all gone so well in 2011 and 2012 and I remember these wise old colleagues, long in the tooth, saying: "Ah yes, but brace yourself. You'll be back at the start again in 2013." But we weren't.'[18] This royal 'ring cycle' had another six years – and two royal weddings – still to come.

The following year, the birth of Prince George made Elizabeth the first monarch since Victoria to be able to look three reigns

2012–16: Diamond Days

ahead (and the birth of George would be followed by Princess Charlotte, born in 2015, and Prince Louis in 2018). At which point, the Queen could very easily have said: 'My work is done now.' Others were certainly having that idea. Indeed, there was now a serious epidemic of abdications across the royal world. Over a matter of months between 2013 and 2014, Queen Beatrix of Holland, King Albert of the Belgians, King Juan Carlos of Spain and the Emir of Qatar all announced that they were passing the baton to a younger generation. So, too, did another de facto monarch, Pope Benedict.

Elizabeth II had restored her monarchy to levels of respect and popularity similar to those she had enjoyed in her early days, all the more impressive given the changing demographics as a monocultural, church-going society morphed into a multicultural, secular, devolved and increasingly dis-United Kingdom. There was, however, never the slightest suggestion that the Queen might hand over. On hearing the news of Queen Beatrix's abdication, the third resignation of a Queen of the Netherlands in her lifetime, Elizabeth II is said to have shrugged and replied: 'Typical Dutch.' 'She didn't mention abdication. She might talk about a regency in a relaxed, jolly way, saying she would rely on us to do the right thing and not defend her corner if she had some dreadful stroke and couldn't speak,' said a senior official. 'So we just kept an eye on the Regency Act and any Cabinet reshuffles.'[19] (The list of those eligible to appoint a Regent under the Regency Act includes the Lord Chancellor and the Speaker of the Commons.)

In the space of eight months, she said goodbye to two contemporary giants of her reign and lifetime. Her presence at the funeral of Margaret Thatcher on 17 April 2013 made it emphatically clear that she had regarded her as an exceptional leader. The Queen had not attended the funeral of another prime minister since that of Winston Churchill. Her staff had assisted with the arrangements, making it close to a state funeral in all but name. Her comptroller, Sir Malcom Ross, had even suggested giving it a royal designation by calling it 'Operation Iron Bridge', until the idea was vetoed by a pedantic police chief who told him: 'Only royals get bridges.'[20] As she had done at Churchill's farewell, the Queen stood back at the end to allow the Thatcher family to take precedence. As Christmas approached, she received news of the death of Nelson Mandela. He was, unquestionably, among the world leaders she had most admired of the hundreds she had known. She could not attend his funeral on 15 December 2013, having made clear to all that she had now given up long-haul travel. The Prince of Wales would be there, however.

The same policy meant that she could not join Commonwealth leaders for their 2013 summit in Sri Lanka, her first no-show at a Commonwealth summit since that unhappy absence enforced by Edward Heath in 1971. Again, she would send the Prince of Wales, whose careful but good-humoured handling of a fractious summit would stand him in good stead when the time came to choose the next Head of the Commonwealth.

By now, the Queen's horizons may have been more limited, but her appetite for trying new things was not. She devised a new form of stripped-down state visit to suit her advancing years. In April 2014, for the first time, she made a day trip to Rome to see President Giorgio Napolitano of Italy. He was the same age, had led his nation through much recent turmoil and had been very sad when the Queen had cancelled a state visit at short notice the year before due to a stomach bug. She always hated letting people down, so, when he reissued the invitation, she was keen to do her best. 'When Napoletano asked her again, she said: "Maybe we could do it in a day. Let's try!",' said one of her senior staff. 'She just loved the concept of doing something she'd never done before. Then she said: "We've got this new Pope, I suppose we've got to see him. But if I'm going for the day, I can't do that whole black mantilla thing. Go and talk to them and sort it out".'[21] It was agreed with the cardinals that the Queen could meet Pope Francis privately in his hostel and, thus, get round the usual onerous dress code.

Clearly enjoying tearing up the rulebook, the Queen made some further changes to the usual state visit template. 'She said: "No equerries. No ladies-in-waiting. Philip and I will just go with the girls." She just wanted a skeleton team.' The only other members of the entourage would be her assistant private secretary, Samantha Cohen, and her dresser, Angela Kelly, both of whom were Roman Catholics. As Cohen would later recall to a colleague, the Queen loved the simplicity of it, declaring on take-off: 'This is so much fun!'[22] She had also greatly enjoyed working out what sort of gift to give a Pope who had forsaken all forms of luxury. Her solution was a hamper of products from the royal estates, including palace honey, Sandringham cider and Balmoral whisky. The most Vatican-friendly Supreme Governor of the Church of England since the Stuarts, Elizabeth II had now met five Popes. Only two of her predecessors, Edward VII and George V, had met even one.

The Queen so enjoyed her slimmed-down state visit that she applied the same principle a year later when she was invited by President François Hollande of France. She would bolt a day of state visiting onto her trip to Normandy for the seventieth anniversary of D-Day. 'We did say to her that she might want a translator, as she hadn't been to France for ten years, hadn't been to Canada for four and had no French in her life,' recalls a former private secretary. 'And she was rather surprised. She said: "No. Why would I want a translator?" And she was absolutely fine. It was Hollande who didn't speak very good English who was insecure about it. She had this truly amazing memory.'[23]

Her travels would come to an end the following year with a state visit to Germany, fifty years on from her epic debut there in 1965, and, finally, a trip to the 2015 summit of all the Commonwealth nations in dear old Malta. The last engagement there for the Queen and Prince Philip was a boat trip around the harbour of Valetta. This was the island where they had enjoyed those carefree years as the Duke and Duchess of Edinburgh, with picnics on the beach, afternoons at the polo, romantic strolls around the gardens of the Villa Guardamangia and evenings spent dancing away at the Phoenicia Hotel. Now, sixty-five years later, they were even reunited with Freddie Mizzi, the clarinettist in the band which used to strike up 'People Will Say We're In Love' as soon as Lilibet and Philip swept in to the Phoenicia's ballroom. It was a sweet, nostalgic note on which to call time on the adventures of the most widely travelled monarch in history.

At home, however, there was no sense of winding down. David Cameron remembered her as unfailingly interested in the ebb and flow of politics. 'She would often kick off an audience by saying: "Oh, I've just watched the news, and the House looked rather heated today". So you'd start off with that. She loved a bit of gossip about what was going on in Whitehall. So I'd say something like: "Oh, Vince Cable's being a nightmare."* And she loved all that. She was very relatable. She had a great sense of mischief and a winning smile. She liked to laugh.'[24]

---

* Liberal Democrat MP and Secretary of State for Business under the coalition.

2012-16: Diamond Days

Cameron recalled that she was amused by his description of *The Audience*, Peter Morgan's stage play about the Queen and her prime ministers, which included a scene in which the David Cameron character appears walking in a rather strange way. 'I did say to my wife: "I don't walk like that, do I?" and she said I did,' Cameron recalled. 'So I told the Queen that and she was amused. I also told her that, in the play, I sent her to sleep talking about Europe. I asked her: "That's not true, is it?" She found all that very funny.'[25]

The true political situation was becoming anything but funny. Indeed, just as the second decade of the twenty-first century would usher in great royal highs, it would also be marked by the gravest internal political divisions for several generations. In 2014, a public vote was causing the Queen perhaps more anxiety than any in her lifetime. She had always viewed general elections, like party politics, as something for others to ponder. Historians are fond of quoting the wise old clerk of the Privy Council, Sir Godfrey Agnew: 'The Queen doesn't make fine distinctions between politicians of different parties. They all roughly belong to the same social category in her view.'[26] If that made her sound rather superior, a very senior Conservative Cabinet minister of the period thought otherwise: 'She had very good instincts.' Though the Queen was 'obviously very posh', she had 'very rooted views about what the country is thinking ... It's not Conservative and it's not Labour; it's very in the middle. I thought the other members of the family were quite aristocratic. But, with the Queen, it wasn't like talking to a very grand duke at all.'[27]

In 2014, however, none of that applied as the people of Scotland voted on whether to secede from Great Britain. The Queen was in an impossible position. Her private views were clear enough. She could not unwrite that speech in her Silver

Jubilee year when she had pledged herself to the Union. She could claim direct descent from Scotland's greatest hero, Robert the Bruce, through two lines. She also felt viscerally Scottish, especially when striding around the Highlands in her family tartan. Cameron recalled how, each summer, his weekly audiences would turn into a 'countdown to Scotland' as she ticked off the days until she was back at Balmoral.[28] Yet, the separatist Scottish National Party wanted to disunite her kingdom and it now commanded a majority in the Scottish Parliament which she herself had opened. That is why Scotland was being given a vote on the issue.

As an opinion poll showed the independence campaign edging into the lead, with just days to go, Cameron suggested that the Queen should make the gentlest of interventions – what he later called 'a raising of the eyebrow'.[29] Leaving church at Crathie, she remarked to onlookers that she hoped Scots would think 'very carefully' before casting their vote. It was an impeccably neutral sentiment. It could hardly be said to have had any great impact on a result which went 55–45 per cent in favour of the Union, but that was not the point. Had the unthinkable occurred, the Queen would not have wanted to go down in history as the last monarch of the United Kingdom without having said something.

That had been a Scotland-only vote. It would be followed two years later by an even more ill-tempered debate involving the whole country. Having won a second election in 2015, without the need for a coalition, David Cameron had promised a referendum on whether to leave or remain in the European Union. The narrow vote to leave, on 23 June 2016, would cost him his job and would have seismic, long-term political, diplomatic and economic repercussions. The Queen, who had been so enthusiastic during the journey in to the Common Market –

even endorsing British membership in that 1972 Christmas broadcast – was assiduously impartial as Britain hovered at the exit. Here was a schismatic, binary issue on which she was determined not to have a view.

Hence the Palace's dismay in the run-up to the vote, when *The Sun* placed her in the Brexit camp under the sensational headline 'Queen Backs Brexit'. It reported that, over a lunch, she had apparently said: 'I don't see why we just can't get out.' It then turned out that the lunch had happened five years earlier, long before any referendum had even been mooted. Her officials were in a quandary. How angry should they be without inadvertently suggesting the story was right or wrong? In the end, the press adjudicator, IPSO, ruled that the headline was misleading while the story – her asking what was stopping Britain from leaving – was not.

Many 'remain' voters, including constitutional experts like Peter Hennessy, pointed out that they had voiced similar thoughts over the years. 'You always sensed that, like most of her subjects, she thought that European cooperation was necessary and important, but the institutions of the EU sometimes can be infuriating,' was David Cameron's verdict years later.[30] A senior Cabinet minister of the period was (and remains) convinced that she did not want to leave: 'From the conversations I had with her about the referendum, at the time of it, I would say she was for staying in the EU. I wouldn't say she was a massive enthusiast for the European Union, but she didn't think we should leave.'[31] Yet a senior courtier, with many years of working with and for the Queen, was confident in his assessment after her death: 'I think she was anti [EU].'[32] 'Some people say she was pro-Brexit, some people said she was against it. I think that tells you more about them than it does about the Queen,' said the former Brexiteer and Tory minister

Elizabeth II

Sir Jacob Rees-Mogg, who saw the Queen regularly as Lord President of the Privy Council. 'People reflected their own views onto her.'[33] The fact that so many eminent voices could authoritatively place her on both sides would suggest she had maintained a faultless neutrality. The argument overlooked one other basic point: she had no vote anyway.

The Queen received the Brexit result early on 24 June via her duty private secretary, Edward Young. Cameron's private secretary, Chris Martin, had called Young at 1 a.m. to say that the result was going to be for 'leave' and that he should tell the Queen. Young decided not to wake her at that point but arrived at the palace early, wrote a detailed narrative of events, including the 4.40 a.m. official result, and asked a housekeeper to deliver it to the Queen's bedroom at 6.30 a.m. She needed to be ready for the prime minister's imminent resignation, since Cameron had told his team that, having fought to remain, his position would be untenable if he lost. 'The memo added that a call had been fixed with Cameron so he could call her before he called [senior Brexiteer] Michael Gove,' said one insider. The memo was later returned with a handwritten note from the Queen. 'Make sure this goes to the Archives,' she wrote. 'It's an important document.' She wanted historians to be absolutely clear about the precise timeline of events of one of the most momentous nights in post-war history.

One year on from the vote, the pro-European camp made a belated attempt to claim the Queen as one of their own when she opened Parliament wearing a blue hat with yellow stars. At one angle, it looked very much like the EU flag. A coded message? Her dresser, Angela Kelly, later insisted that it had been a coincidence, adding that the speculation had 'certainly made us smile.'[34]

Chapter Sixteen

2016–18

'My sincere wish'

The Queen had now entered her tenth decade, marking her ninetieth birthday with a private family dinner. The following day she had two very special visitors to Windsor Castle. Barack and Michelle Obama had wanted to be the first non-family members to convey their congratulations. The outgoing US president was on a valedictory world tour as he approached the end of his second term in office and had timed his itinerary around the Queen. His ambassador to Britain, Matthew Barzun, later revealed to this author that he had been under orders from the Obama White House to try to lure the Queen on one last visit to the USA.

He had made his pitch when he was invited to a 'dine and sleep' dinner party at Windsor Castle in April 2015, along with actress Maggie Smith and the governor of the Bank of England. 'I was seated next to the Queen and I had a little bit of business I was trying to do,' he recalled. 'The president really wanted her to come to Washington one more time and we were trying to figure out a way.' Barzun did his best to suggest some options – 'I didn't want it to turn into a business meeting' – but the Queen gently pushed back. She was not budging from her ruling on long-haul travel. However, as Barzun recalled, she had another idea: 'She said: "Why doesn't he come here?" You could just tell that she was going to make it happen one way or the other.'[1]

And she did. On 22 April 2016, Marine One thundered over Windsor Castle and descended on the Home Park. There had been some delicious jostling between the Queen's staff, the White House and the US Secret Service after the Queen let it be known that she and Prince Philip would drive out to collect the Obamas in their Land Rover. The Secret Service were insistent that the president could only be driven by them in their vehicle. The Palace politely but firmly pointed out that the Queen was the host. The dispute finally worked its way up to the Oval Office, where President Obama had to make the final call – and sided with the Queen. The result was a very congenial lunch.

Obama's senior aide, Ben Rhodes, remembered the post-prandial mood when he greeted the Obamas back to the US Embassy residence in London afterwards. 'I was at Winfield House when the helicopter returned and what was powerful is it was as if they had just come back from lunch with some friends. They were joking that they had a couple of beers at lunch and they'd talked about Brexit and [the president] was surprised at how candid she was in assessing the situation.'[2]

The Queen had thoroughly enjoyed the lunch. She was equally happy later, on that very same evening, when the Obamas went round to dinner at Kensington Palace with the Duke and Duchess of Cambridge and Prince Harry. Prince George had been allowed to stay up, in pyjamas and dressing gown, to greet the guests. It meant that four generations of the family were now actively engaged in soft power diplomacy at the very highest level. 'He [Obama] was impressed that William, Harry and Kate went out of their way to make that about as

2016–18: 'My sincere wish'

casual as something like that can be,' Rhodes recalled. 'It can't be truly casual but I think the Obamas were struck by this younger crowd. The royals wanted it to feel like just a few people coming over for dinner. And I think they succeeded at that.'[3]

The previous year, the Obamas had welcomed the Prince of Wales and Duchess of Cornwall to Washington. Weeks after their informal supper at Kensington Palace, Michelle Obama would join Prince Harry for the opening of his Invictus Games in Florida. Looking back over Obama's two terms in office, Ben Rhodes pointed out that no other non-US family had enjoyed as much presidential facetime as the Windsors. Ultimately, though, it was all down to the Queen. 'He [Obama] saw how much the Queen went out of her way to make a black American president feel as welcome as possible. That was very powerful. She and Prince Philip – people who, generationally and racially, couldn't be more distinct from the Obamas – were really trying to strike up a genuine friendship,' Rhodes observed. 'Obama felt a great deal of loyalty and an affinity for her because of how nicely he had been treated and he was going to treat her family with the same warmth and openness.'[4]

His admiration was explicit. Towards the end of his second term, Obama delivered a speech at the funeral of Israel's Shimon Peres. In it, he spoke of 'giants of the twentieth century' whom he had been privileged to meet; 'leaders who have seen so much, whose lives span such momentous epochs, that they find no need to posture or traffic in what's popular in the moment'. They were Nelson Mandela and Elizabeth II.

Large parts of the world were now coming afresh to the story, if not the legend of Elizabeth II. In 2016, a lavishly produced new series called *The Crown* launched on Netflix. It was created by Peter Morgan, who, as well as writing *The Audience* for the stage, had written *The Queen*, the Oscar-winning film about the royal response to Diana's death. Now he would dramatize the Queen's entire life in epic style over six series with ten episodes in each. Some plotlines would take great liberties with the facts, and there would be plenty of bizarre errors. A number of those close to the family felt that it was bad enough to make up a drama about someone who was still alive, worse still while she was still doing her job. Neither the Queen nor the Duke of Edinburgh watched it. Some institutions close to the monarchy loyally refused to be involved, including Eton College. Arch-rivals Winchester College had no such qualms about taking the Netflix shilling, so *The Crown*'s Eton scenes were filmed at Winchester. The Foreign Office was similarly happy to rent out Lancaster House, which would appear on screen as Buckingham Palace. As the series progressed, it expanded to include the woes of the younger royal generations. Though garlanded with awards early on, the producers' decision to press on through and beyond the death of Diana would prove to be a hubristic one. Despite acclaimed performances by Dominic West (Charles) and Elizabeth Debicki (Diana), the show lost its way, its charm and a lot of its original viewers. Nonetheless, its early success and impact was a reminder of the unique star power, as well as that soft power, of Elizabeth II. And the real-life drama was about to prove rather more compelling.

The third and final golden phase of the Queen's reign still had some way to run, though she would now be operating without the greatest ally and supporter of them all, her 'strength and stay'. In 2017, the Duke of Edinburgh announced that he would be stepping back from public life. In trademark style, it would not be a slow, half-hearted withdrawal but a clean break, concluding with a final march-past by the Royal Marines, of whom he had been Captain General for sixty-three years, longer than anyone in history.

2016–18: 'My sincere wish'

The Queen had been growing increasingly concerned about him. She would frequently curtail a late morning meeting with a private secretary, saying: 'Now I must go and give Philip his lunch.'[5] All through the marriage, she had been keen to ensure that he had felt like the master of his own home, putting him in charge of the family estates, appointing him Ranger of Windsor Great Park, entrusting him with the children's education and so on. 'She was very aware of the need to let him be the man, to let him be the head of the household,' noted one senior aide of the time. 'She was assiduous in those rituals that allowed that to happen, right down to all those family barbecues. But, now, as he became more frail, she was doing more of the other side of all that. She was enjoying being more of the housewife in the relationship.'[6]

Not unreasonably for a man in his mid-nineties, the Duke could be increasingly irascible. One former member of staff during that period recalled being accosted by him on the royal train as he was studying the day's itinerary on an Ordnance Survey map. 'He was saying: "Why the bloody hell haven't you done it this way?" And his logic was completely accurate because it was not the most direct route between events but you had to do them in an order and they would not always be in a straight line.'[7] Another senior official remembers attempting some upbeat small talk with the Duke shortly before his departure for the summer at Balmoral: 'I said: "What is the grouse news this year, Sir?" And he said: "I don't know, and I don't give a f***."'[8] Members of the Royal Household learned to tread warily if they were sitting near the Duke at lunch. 'One day, he could be charming and you'd have a fascinating conversation about whatever he was reading. But I remember another day, I just said the word "organic" and he exploded. It was like dealing with an Alsatian because you never knew if you would have this purring lovely, cuddly animal or if you would fear for your life.'[9] However, he still stood ramrod-straight, the Queen still adored him and he was definitely not about to become a little old man. 'I remember meeting the Duke around that time, not long after I'd met Roger Moore and he was a few years younger than him,' recalled the wife of a senior politician. 'All I can say is that the Duke was so much more handsome.'[10]

One upside was that, as the Duke grew older, the press and public became more forgiving. For years, the media would feign deep shock after the Duke's latest risqué remark and add it to the endlessly repeated anthology of so-called 'gaffes', be it joking to a woman with a guide dog about training 'eating dogs for the anorexic' or his reply on being introduced to a young fashion designer: 'Well, you didn't design your beard very well.' As he himself once said ruefully: 'I am only trying to break the ice but, sometimes, when you break the ice, you go through it.' More often than not, his efforts were appreciated. Kenneth Rose was at a Welsh Guards dinner where the Duke was expected to read out the Queen's formal response to the regiment's formal loyal greetings. He started off reciting the same message he had delivered so many times before – 'Her Majesty has the honour to tell Her Colonel . . .' – before dropping his speech. 'I can't go on with this rubbish!' he concluded. 'We all found it frightfully funny – except for a few old stuffed shirts,' Rose recalled.[11]

By the Duke's tenth decade, however, the press had decided that it simply no longer seemed fair to feign shock at his occasional gaffes. Rather, it was time to celebrate them.

In June 2015, while attending a seventy-fifth anniversary lunch with the last surviving pilots of the Battle of Britain, the attempt at an official photograph had goaded him beyond endurance. 'Just take the f****** picture!' he shouted on live

2016–18: 'My sincere wish'

television. The following day, there was no outcry in the press, merely amusement. If a royal war hero having lunch with a bunch of war heroes happened to drop a profanity, it was hardly a story any more. On the day his retirement was announced, the Duke showed he had lost none of his flair for a pithy response when the mathematician Sir Michael Atiyah said he was sorry to hear he was standing down. Quick as a flash came the Duke's retort: 'Well, I can't stand up much longer!'

His retirement would, inadvertently, trigger another departure from the Queen's inner circle. On the day it was announced, her principal private secretary, Sir Christopher Geidt, convened an urgent meeting of the households of all the members of the Royal Family to demand that everyone now had to rally round the Queen. As in any Court, there were plenty of simmering jealousies of the man at the top, and Geidt had his rivals. Some of those felt that he was now straying outside his own lane by telling the other households what to do. His speech had not gone down well in the Prince of Wales's office. This was the trigger for those rivals to coalesce and put pressure on Geidt to move on. He had incurred the wrath of the Duke of York, who was said to hold him responsible for the loss of his trade envoy role and for excluding his family from the plans for a 'slimmed-down' monarchy. Across Whitehall and Westminster there was bewilderment that such a shrewd and successful operator should be edged out after chaperoning the monarchy through so much change with so little turbulence. In years gone by, the Duke of Edinburgh might have emboldened the Queen to push back against the putsch, but the Duke had made it clear he wanted nothing more to do with Palace politics. Loyal to the end, Geidt did not wish to put the Queen in an awkward position. He moved quietly to the House of Lords and a portfolio of directorships elsewhere. He would be replaced by his deputy, Edward Young, another shrewd lateral thinker who had not come to the Palace via the usual military/diplomatic route but through Westminster and corporate communications. After thirteen years at the Palace and as the mastermind of events like the Queen's Olympic appearance and her state visit to Ireland, Young was seen as a calm consigliere, with an open mind to judicious innovation.

As autumn arrived, there was another small but significant indicator of change. For the first time, the Queen would not lead the nation in saluting the 'Glorious Dead' at the Cenotaph on Remembrance Sunday. The chance of a mistake – or, worse, a fall – was too great. Walking up and reversing down a step unaided in direct sunlight (depending on the weather) might be straightforward enough, but not for a ninety-one-year-old on live television.

A somewhat downbeat year would suddenly spring a great burst of positivity at the end. On 27 November 2017, the Prince of Wales was 'delighted to announce the engagement of Prince Harry to Ms Meghan Markle'. The 'Ms' was noteworthy. The Queen had never much liked the term, and women being presented to her at garden parties were only asked if they wished to be introduced as 'Miss' or 'Mrs'. However, times moved on and Harry's fiancée, a divorced American actress, wanted to be 'Ms'.

By now, Harry had left the army for regular royal duties and a number of charity ventures. Chief among these was his newly created Invictus Games, an international sports tournament for wounded veterans. It had rapidly become an outstanding success, greatly boosted by the support of the Obama White House (for which, as noted earlier, Harry had the Queen to thank). In the summer of 2017, the Games were taking place in

2016–18: 'My sincere wish'

Toronto, where Meghan filmed her legal drama, *Suits*. It was there that the couple finally stepped out together in front of the cameras. The Royal Family had met Meghan long before that, however. Harry had first introduced her to the Queen the previous October on the Windsor estate. It had been an impromptu Sunday lunchtime encounter at Royal Lodge, home of the Duke of York. Casually dressed, the young couple were on their way to see Princess Eugenie when they learned that the Queen had already dropped in on her way back from church. Meghan had a quick crash-course in curtseying from Sarah, Duchess of York in the garden, before going inside and bobbing down before the Queen (she was later heavily criticized for her irreverent reprise of the moment in a Netflix documentary). The twenty-minute chat was deemed a great success on all sides, with the Queen happy to learn that Meghan was living and working in a Commonwealth country. The next major test was tea with Prince Charles and the Duchess of Cornwall. According to Harry, they instantly warmed to Meghan's story of adopting a rescue dog, and Harry left feeling 'exultant'.[12]

On the same day as the engagement announcement, Harry and Meghan appeared for the formal engagement photographs in the garden of Kensington Palace, followed by the customary television interview. There were already a few signs that this was not going to be a re-run of the previous royal wedding. When William and Catherine announced their engagement, they also met the royal press corps over a cup of tea in St James's Palace. Harry and Meghan had put the media on the far side of a pond in the garden on a grey afternoon and there would be no interaction. Harry had previously complained about 'racial overtones' in some of the early reporting on Meghan, whose mother, Doria, was of African American heritage. In their interview, the couple had also emphasized a 'passion' for 'change'. The Queen would be more encouraged by the fact that they also talked excitedly about the Commonwealth. Overall, it felt like a very modern romance. The Prince had met the first biracial royal bride on a blind date. Meghan, who 'didn't know much about him', had only asked one question beforehand: 'Is he nice?' A transatlantic courtship had followed and Harry had proposed over a roast chicken. St George's Chapel, Windsor was booked for 19 May 2018.

As the date grew nearer, a series of private and public dramas ensured that it would be quite unlike any previous royal wedding. The couple had asked Princess Charlotte to be a bridesmaid, but tensions between Meghan and the Duchess of Cambridge over the bridesmaid dresses would reduce both women to tears. Another pre-wedding row, which would continue to create headlines years after the wedding, concerned Meghan's choice of tiara. The Queen much enjoyed offering a piece from her own tiara collection to a royal bride, when required. She had not done so for Diana, who had wanted to wear the Spencer family tiara. Nor had she done so for Sarah Ferguson before her wedding to Prince Andrew, since the Queen herself commissioned a brand new piece, known as the 'York' tiara, for the future Duchess of York (who continued to retain it after her divorce). However, other brides would be invited to borrow one. 'Her Majesty would pick out a small selection which she thought would suit that bride and ask her round to try them on and choose one,' said a former staffer. 'It was her lovely way of bonding with the bride. She did it with Sophie [Rhys-Jones] and with Catherine [Middleton]. But there wasn't that bonding with Meghan because she turned up with Prince Harry.'[13] No one was entirely sure why the Prince had to come, too. His memoir suggests that it was a joint invitation; insiders say otherwise.

2016–18: 'My sincere wish'

As Harry later wrote himself, it was a magical experience and Meghan had a clear favourite – Queen Mary's diamond bandeau. However, the mood turned sour nearer the wedding when the couple rang the Palace to ask the Queen's dresser and curator, Angela Kelly, to send over the tiara. Meghan wished to practise putting it on. According to *Spare*, Prince Harry's memoir, and also *Finding Freedom*, the sympathetic account of the couple's royal woes by Omid Scobie and Carolyn Durand, Kelly was proving to be aloof. 'To my mind, Angela was a troublemaker,' the Prince wrote, suggesting that the Queen's dresser had taken a personal dislike to his bride and was being obstructive.[14]

Matters came to a head when Meghan flew in her hairdresser (from Paris, according to Harry;[15] from New York, according to Scobie/Durand[16]) for a 'hair trial'. 'People were frustrated – and confused. Why was it so hard to set up a time for Meghan to try the tiara with her hairdresser?' wrote Scobie and Durand, adding that Harry was forced to go directly to the Queen as a result. The Prince, in his account, said that he did not. 'I considered going to Granny, but that would probably mean sparking an all-out confrontation,' he wrote, 'and I wasn't quite sure with whom Granny would side.'

Insiders have now revealed that word did, indeed, reach the Queen, who took the side of her dresser. She was not pleased that the Prince had been calling around the Royal Household demanding that the tiara be dispatched forthwith. As the monarch told one of them: 'It's not a toy'.[17] She even recalled that, ahead of the 2011 royal wedding, Catherine Middleton's hairdresser had practised using a plastic tiara from the accessory chain, Claire's. Why could Meghan and her hairdresser not do the same? She told Kelly to ignore the phone calls.

Elizabeth II

There were also two reasons, said the insiders, why the tiara was not simply produced at the click of a finger to suit a visiting hairdresser (quite apart from the less-than-straightforward protocols for transporting royal gems). First, it was Easter Court, with the Queen and her staff based at Windsor and also preoccupied with guests for the Royal Windsor Horse Show. Second, and of greater importance, was the question of provenance. The diamond bandeau tiara had very little known history, beyond the fact that Queen Mary had commissioned it in 1932, using a diamond brooch – a wedding present from the county of Lincolnshire – as its centrepiece. It had seldom been seen in public since. Angela Kelly and her team had been trying to verify that it had no awkward backstory – like the Timur ruby (alleged imperial loot) or the Cambridge emeralds (reclaimed at vast expense from Queen Mary's dead brother's mistress). Every centrepiece of a royal wedding is subject to forensic global scrutiny. Even if the tiara had only a few offcuts from South Africa's mighty Cullinan diamond, that could be enough to generate furious headlines about colonial theft. 'Can you imagine how that would have gone down on the wedding day?' asked one member of staff.[18] It had taken a great deal of research. Once due diligence had been done, there was great relief around the Palace. 'Harry had been on to everyone about this. We thought Angela was like the fairy godmother who had delivered,' said a source. 'But when she called Kensington Palace, she was put through to Prince Harry who just said: "Get it here now."' And that was the end of the conversation.'[19] Harry later wrote that 'Angela appeared out of thin air' and asked him to sign a release for the tiara. He said that he thanked her but also added that 'it would've made our lives so much easier to have had it sooner.' Whereupon, according to his memoir: 'Her eyes were fire. She started having a go at me.' He had replied, 'Angela, you really want to do this

2016–18: 'My sincere wish'

now? Really? Now?' He added that she gave him a look which made him 'shiver.'[20]

As would be the case with much of the Harry and Meghan story, recollections would vary. As one staffer recalled: 'There was already an atmosphere before Angela arrived. Meghan was nowhere to be seen. Harry poked the box and said "Is that it?" Then he stood over Angela and said he did not like her whining to his grandmother. Angela gave it straight back. She said that she did not like him getting all these people to push her when she was just doing her job. She tried to tell him about the history and how it was for their own sake, but he walked out. She decided to put it down to pre-wedding nerves.'[21] Kelly left royal service after the death of the Queen and refused to discuss the matter further. 'All Angela did,' said a former colleague, 'was to try to protect them.'

Kensington Palace neighbours remember seeing clusters of nervous wedding planners waiting outside at first light. An early riser with one eye on the clock in her native Los Angeles, Meghan had introduced a can-do Californian snappiness that chafed with some of those within the royal machine used to a slower pace. All royal weddings have had their glitches, but never one like the dramas with the bride's father.

Meghan would have no family present at the ceremony except her mother and her divorced father, Thomas Markle, a retired television lighting director, now living in Mexico. He was under orders from the couple to say nothing to the press, but was increasingly upset at media depictions of him as an oddball recluse. So he hatched a secret deal whereby a news agency would take flattering pictures of him preparing for the big day and then syndicate the images. No sooner was the plan exposed than he was hospitalized with a heart attack and suddenly he wasn't coming. The bride's family was down to one, so who would walk her up the aisle? Harry's father asked Meghan if he might have the honour of accompanying her to the altar. According to Harry, the offer 'very much helped' Meghan get over the pain of her father's no-show.[22] According to a friend, the Prince of Wales was somewhat surprised by Meghan's reply: 'Can we meet half way?'[23] She wanted to make her grand entrance to the chapel alone. The Prince would then wait at the entrance to the Quire for the last few yards to the altar.

Hundreds of thousands packed Windsor's Long Walk on a cloudless May morning for a first glimpse of the bride arriving at the castle (they would not see much; she arrived late from her Cliveden House hotel suite and had told the chauffeur to put his foot down). Inside the castle, the guests had all arrived in good time via a fleet of courtesy buses. Here was a collection of Harry's friends from school, the military and his Gloucestershire childhood mixing with Meghan's showbusiness cohorts. One royal friend remembers spotting actor George Clooney and US talk-show host Oprah Winfrey wandering around St George's Chapel looking at engravings and royal tombs. 'I happened to be standing with Oprah and I said "Hi, there". I just thought I'd better make conversation. I think people like this couldn't believe that they were in this old English church just wandering around. No one was giving them food or drink but no one was bothering them either, no one was taking photos, everyone was ignoring them. So it's just me and Oprah. It was bizarre. I think they liked this weird Englishness.'[24]

On the morning of the wedding, the Queen had made Harry the Duke of Sussex, a title last created for one of the wayward sons of King George III (it had died with him in 1843). Like the entire country, she was thrilled to see one of the monarchy's

2016–18: 'My sincere wish'

greatest assets finally find the happiness and the family unit he had craved. For much of the world over a certain age, the abiding image of Harry was that shellshocked little boy walking behind his mother's coffin in 1997. He had been with his brother then. Now the warrior prince was there at the altar, blinking hard, with his brother beside him again.

Whatever the hour, much of the world was glued to live coverage of a ceremony with all the much-loved trappings of a royal wedding – state trumpeters, a full royal turnout, a carriage procession for the happy couple – plus some joyful innovations, including an impassioned address from the head of America's Episcopal Church and a gospel choir. There was a generous celebrity quotient, too, even if some people were puzzled by Oprah Winfrey's top-tier placement opposite the Royal Family, when she barely knew the bride and groom. That would be explained in due course. The bride had also devised a special tribute to the Queen. Her veil included beautiful embroidered details of the flowers of every country of the Commonwealth.

In glorious sunshine, the wedding had been a brief but badly needed healing moment for a very grumpy nation. Nor was it – quite – the last landmark in this third golden period of the Queen's reign. On 12 October 2018, St George's Windsor held another wedding for another grandchild. Princess Eugenie, younger daughter of the Duke of York, was marrying drinks executive Jack Brooksbank. Status-conscious as ever, Prince Andrew and his ex-wife, Sarah, had been determined that Eugenie should have a comparable wedding to Harry, with live television coverage, a carriage procession, celebrity guests and so on, albeit in front of a smaller audience. The Queen happily agreed to Andrew's demands.

After all, Eugenie and Jack had been patient. After a

Elizabeth II

seven-year romance, they had been thinking of marrying sooner but had been content to let Harry and Meghan go first, in line with the royal pecking order (the hierarchy did not always work against Harry and Meghan, despite some of their subsequent complaints). Even before Meghan had selected Queen Mary's diamond bandeau, Eugenie had already been round to see the Queen to choose her tiara – the seldom-seen Greville emerald kokoshnik. She had gone alone, without her fiancé. Though some had expected her to wear the York tiara which had been made for her mother, it was not entirely surprising that she did not.

It had been a very satisfactory year for Elizabeth II. Besides seeing two grandchildren find happiness, she had also resolved an issue which had been a source of growing royal anxiety for many years. Indeed, it was one at the very top of the Queen's list of 'must-do' challenges in the final years of her life, but it required considerable nerve on her part.

Just a few weeks before Harry's wedding, the leaders of the Commonwealth had all met in London. This had enabled the non-travelling Queen to join the member states for one last time (the biannual summit would not be held again in Britain for many years to come). This would, therefore, be her last chance to make a frank request.

As everyone was well aware, the role of Head of the Commonwealth was not a hereditary one. In her case, it had simply been a fait accompli after the Indian prime minister, Jawaharlal Nehru, had sent a telegram welcoming her to the role after the death of her father in 1952. However, it was far from clear what would happen next time. The last thing a new King Charles III would want or need was a Commonwealth leadership contest at the start of his reign. In her welcome speech to the fifty-four member states at Buckingham Palace,

2016–18: 'My sincere wish'

the Queen took a carefully calculated gamble. She stated that it was 'my sincere wish' that 'one day' her son should 'carry on the important work started by my father'. The leaders took the hint. In their communique at the end of the summit, the message was unanimous: 'The next Head of the Commonwealth shall be His Royal Highness The Prince of Wales'. The Queen was both delighted and relieved. 'That was a nervous moment,' one of her senior aides later admitted. 'The Prince of Wales had done an enormous amount of work over the previous ten years. Even so, it was brave of the Queen to stand up in the Ballroom and say: "You're going to have this free and fair discussion about who may be the next head. But, just to be clear, as you go and enjoy my hospitality: that's the guy. And it's my sincere wish." She knew she was taking a risk. But you have to be brave.'[25]

The Queen wanted to strengthen family ties between the Commonwealth and the next generation, too. With that in mind, she had already appointed Harry as her Commonwealth Youth Ambassador. The monarch had also asked one of her most trusted aides to help the couple establish their own household within Kensington Palace. For many years, Samantha Cohen had been her assistant private secretary, alongside Sir Christopher Geidt, and had been dismayed by his departure. After Geidt was pushed out of the Royal Household, she decided to go, too. The Queen had the highest regard for the unflappable Cohen, the most senior woman in her private office (the monarch had attended her Palace leaving party), and persuaded her to return to help the Sussexes. Australian by birth, like Sir William Heseltine before her, Cohen had a deep understanding and affection for the Commonwealth and its ways. The Queen was also keen to help Meghan learn the royal ropes. In *Finding Freedom*, Scobie and Durand claimed that she had received little training in what to expect. 'She had hoped to take etiquette lessons,' the book reported, 'but curiously they were never on offer.'[26]

That is not how Palace staff remember those days, as the Queen invited the newly-wed Duchess to leave Harry behind and join her, one-on-one, for an overnight trip to Cheshire in the royal train. 'The Queen was really wanting to give it a go,' an insider recalled. 'She was so sweet, she had brought Meghan a present and tried so hard. The train always left at eleven o'clock at night and the Queen was on the platform to welcome her. They had breakfast together in the morning and she was always trying to do small things, to show her the ropes and bring her in.'[27]

The Sussexes' first official overseas trip together would, predictably enough, be a Commonwealth tour, an extensive journey across the Pacific, including two of the Queen's most important realms, Australia and New Zealand. It began with a happy surprise. The Duchess was expecting a baby. She made it clear that the tour would proceed as planned. And so it did.

Back at home, work was underway to help Meghan build a portfolio of patronages with meaning. The Queen was keen on two in particular. After forty-five years as patron of the National Theatre, she was keen to hand it on to Meghan, given her acting credentials. It was even suggested that the Duchess might have the occasional walk-on part in stage productions (a sweet idea, though one possibly unlikely to appeal to a former television star). Another important gift from the Queen was the Association of Commonwealth Universities. 'It would allow Meghan a platform to give speeches with substance around the world. She could talk about, say, women's rights in Africa but without being political,' explained a Palace aide. 'The Queen knew it was time to hand these on and was really excited for Meghan. The Sussexes were in a good place.'[28]

Chapter Seventeen

2019

'One hell of a lady'

A dormant memory began to stir, sending the first shivers through the Royal Household. Might the upward graph line of royal good fortune now finally be due for a downturn? Some Palace veterans would later point to the end of 2018, when the Queen's innocuous Christmas message triggered a blistering social media assault. It had been another tempestuous political year. Cameron's replacement as prime minister, Theresa May, was clinging on to office with her party still split down the middle over Brexit, much like the country itself. In her annual broadcast, the Queen had simply called on people to set aside 'deeply held differences' and be more generous to one another. Class warriors instantly attacked her for being 'out of touch' because she was speaking with a 'gold' piano behind her (the gold-painted instrument had once belonged to Queen Victoria but was now owned by the Royal Collection Trust).

There was further trouble a month later, at the start of 2019, when Prince Philip caused a car crash while driving alone on the A149 near Sandringham. He had pulled out into the path of a car carrying two women and a baby. Though there were

Elizabeth II

no serious injuries, it could have been very much worse. At ninety-seven, the Duke accepted that his driving days were over. 'He was an appalling driver. When he had that accident I wasn't at all surprised,' admitted one Sandringham regular. 'He was always chatting away if there was a person in the passenger seat, usually a gamekeeper. And the Queen's driving was terrible too. She would insist on driving one of the Land Rovers to a shooting lunch. Fortunately, someone else usually drove back.'[1]

Within Kensington Palace, relations were already starting to cool between the Cambridges and the Sussexes. Despite wildly over-optimistic talk of a new royal 'dream team' or, even more fancifully, a 'Fab Four', resentments were growing. The Sussexes, like any exciting new prospect, were attracting the bulk of the media attention and invitations at this stage. Yet, they had a smaller staff, a smaller budget and a very much smaller house.

In March 2019, it was announced that the brothers would be splitting their offices. The Cambridges would keep their headquarters at 'KP', while Harry and Meghan would move their home to Frogmore Cottage on the Windsor estate and look for a new office at Buckingham Palace. There was a sound long-term business case for doing so. Once there was a change of monarch, William would become Prince of Wales and inherit the Duchy of Cornwall. Harry, who would still be dependent on his father, would then have to swap cost centres and become part of the King's operation. Hence the need to move the Sussexes to royal HQ at some point. Why not now, while the palace was undergoing major restoration work?

The problem, say insiders, was the way it was handled. The Royal Household naturally deferred to the elder, senior brother. 'They were dealing with two brothers but they treated it like a corporate split, with Harry being farmed off to a new sales division,' was the impression of one Palace veteran.[2] When Harry went looking for space at Buckingham Palace, he was offered a gloomy back office. Sections of the press had started to pick up stories about unhappy staff leaving the Sussexes and tears over bridesmaids' dresses. A 'Duchess Difficult' narrative, once underway, was difficult to stop.[3]

The couple and their fans would later put this down to evidence of latent racism within the media and even at the Palace. The reality pointed to culture clashes and staff exasperation when well-meaning attempts to save the couple from pitfalls – like 'Tiaragate' – would lead to accusations of disloyalty or even xenophobia. As the authors of *Finding Freedom* noted, Meghan had arrived from a world in which 'free clothes' and 'discounts' were an accepted trade-off for celebrity endorsement. 'It had to be explained that, aside from official gifts, which were registered, anything else had to be paid with a proper bill to show the Keeper of the Privy Purse,' one staff member recalled. 'The Palace can't take freebies. Let's just say that did not go down well.'[4] Harry's book recorded gravely that one member of staff had been fired for trying 'to get freebies'[5] but then went on to praise Meghan because 'she shared all the freebies she received.'[6] One staffer was dismayed after working for weeks on a major news event for one of the Duchess of Cornwall's charities only to be told to shelve it because it would clash with a big announcement for Prince Harry's Invictus Games. Those Palace rules and hierarchies, which the couple professed to find so irksome, could work both ways.

The couple's dislike and distrust of the media was such that when the Duchess gave birth to a healthy baby boy, both were back home even as the media received a bulletin saying that she had gone into hospital. The Palace was then accused of lying, and not only by the press. The Metropolitan Police had gone to considerable trouble to create a strategy for crowd control around the hospital. 'People from the Met were calling up the Palace and asking why we had lied – which we hadn't,' said one royal staffer caught in the middle. 'The Sussexes just hadn't told anyone. I think it was one area where no one could tell Meghan what to do. It was a case of "I'm going to show you who's boss".'[7]

The press would not complain for long. Normally, they would not see an image of the Queen with a new family arrival until the christening. Two days after this birth, however, a photograph was released of the Queen and Prince Philip with their new grandson, named Archie, alongside the proud parents and Meghan's mother, Doria. The image of the beaming Queen and the African American yoga instructor, the great-grandmother and grandmother of a shared baby boy, was as historic as it was delightful.

America was much on the Queen's mind as she prepared for the state visit of the president of the USA. Donald Trump had been invited two years earlier by prime minister Theresa May soon after his election. It had been decided that the state visit should be bolted on to the seventy-fifth anniversary of D-Day in June 2019. Demonized by the left (and quite a few on the British right, too), Trump attracted noisy protests wherever he went. He was also a fervent Anglophile, an ardent royalist and he wanted to bring his whole family to the palace. His friendship with the Queen had started the previous year when he dropped into Windsor after an official visit to meet Mrs May. Indeed, the British foreign secretary, Jeremy Hunt, later admitted that it was only the promise of tea with the Queen that had clinched that earlier trip: 'We were told by the Americans, "If you want him to come and it involves tea with the Queen, he'll come".'[8]

Before tea, there was the usual inspection of the Guard of

2019: 'One hell of a lady'

Honour. Trump's media critics made much of his alleged 'rudeness' walking down the ranks of the Coldstream Guards in front of the Queen, when, in fact, he had done exactly the right thing: the guest should always go first. They formed an immediate rapport, said one of those present, over the fact that they both had Scottish mothers and Scottish land (Balmoral in her case, golf courses in his). 'The first time I met her, we were only supposed to have fifteen minutes, and it just went on because she liked me and I liked her,' the president told this author. 'She was so clever and we talked a lot.' He smiled as he recalled trying to persuade her to name her favourite occupant of the White House. 'I kept asking her: "Who was your favourite president? Was it Reagan? Or Eisenhower?" and she just said: "They were all very nice." That sort of thing.'[9]

Mr Trump decided to switch tack. He explained that he then began to ask her about Downing Street. 'So then I tried her on: "Who's your favourite prime minister? Must have been Churchill, right?" And she said again: "No, they were all very nice."' At which point, President Trump twigged. 'So I realized: that's why she lasted seventy-five years without a complaint – because she was so good at it. The rest of us would have said: "Oh, I liked so-and-so." But she was so clever. And I know she liked me because we talked a lot.'[10]

A meeting scheduled for fifteen minutes lasted for the best part of an hour. Afterwards, Mr Trump gladly posed for individual photos with the Queen's staff at the bottom of the stairs. 'No one's too proud not to have a selfie with me!' he said, beckoning a very senior (if bashful) courtier across for a shot.

The tea party was just a trial run for the full state visit the following June, when the president and first lady, Melania Trump, arrived with Mr Trump's four adult children (Donald Junior, Ivanka, Eric and Tiffany), plus two spouses (Jared

Kushner, husband of Ivanka, and Lara, wife of Eric). It was unusual to have such an extended clan gathering for a state visit, but the Queen was perfectly happy if Britain's most powerful ally wanted to bring them. The only two notable absentees from the home team were Prince Philip, whose clean-break retirement was holding firm, and the Duchess of Sussex. She was said to be busy looking after Archie, although her well-publicized criticisms of Mr Trump in her pre-royal acting days might have had something to do with it.

The two heads of state renewed their easy rapport. The next day, they sat next to each other at the D-Day commemorations on Southsea Common as the Queen told the veterans: 'It is with humility and pleasure on behalf of the entire country – indeed the whole free world – that I say to you all: thank you.' A senior insider admitted that there had been a few Palace worries about that line. 'You have to think twice before claiming to speak for the planet in front of the US president,' the insider explained. 'The Queen was the only person who could possibly stand up in front of Donald Trump and say, "I am speaking on behalf of the whole free world", and she enjoyed that.'[11] So, evidently, did the president. After the ceremony, the Lord Chamberlain, Earl Peel, had the formal duty of accompanying the Trumps to Southampton Airport for their onward flight to Normandy. As he bid farewell on behalf of the Queen by the aircraft steps, Trump put his hand on Peel's arm and declared: 'So far as the Queen's concerned, I've only got one thing to say. She's one hell of a lady!'[12]

For the monarch, foreign politicians were a piece of cake compared to the domestic variety. The unresolved ramifications of the Brexit vote were still dragging on after more than three years. Despite the majority view expressed in the referendum, it was not the majority view in Parliament, where MPs and peers

The Queen and Prince Philip at Kunming on her historic trip to China –
the first by a British monarch. October 1986.

Though the first extracts are emerging from Andrew Morton's explosive biography of the
Princess of Wales, the Royal Family put on a united front at Trooping the Colour. It is
the midpoint of what the Queen would call her 'annus horribilis' – 1992.

The Queen and Prince Philip return to Buckingham Palace on 5 September 1997, the eve of the funeral of Diana, Princess of Wales. The initial solemn silence of the crowd is finally broken – by the sound of applause.

Farewell, *Britannia*. The Queen does her best to contain her emotions as the Royal Yacht is finally decommissioned in December 1997, after more than forty years and a million miles at sea.

The Golden Jubilee of 2002 was a turning point for the monarchy. Despite previous warnings of a 'flop', the final parade down the Mall on 4 June – with the Queen and Prince Philip in an open vehicle – saw such euphoric scenes that they were later used in the winning bid to stage the 2012 Olympics.

The Prince of Wales and the new Duchess of Cornwall leave St George's Chapel, Windsor, following the Service of Prayer and Dedication after their marriage on 9 April 2005.

The Queen's historic state visit to Ireland in 2011 led to an even greater diplomatic breakthrough in Belfast, June 2012, when she shook the hand of former IRA commander Martin McGuinness, then Deputy First Minister of Northern Ireland.

On the balcony after her official ninetieth Birthday Parade in June 2016, the Queen is joined by the Duke and Duchess of Cambridge and their children, George and Charlotte, plus Prince Harry and Prince Edward, then Earl of Wessex.

June 2018. The Queen is joined by Prince Harry and the former Meghan Markle – now Duke and Duchess of Sussex, following their wedding in May – as she presents the Queen's Young Leaders Awards for outstanding young people across the Commonwealth.

The Queen and US president Donald Trump raise a toast at the state banquet at Buckingham Palace on 3 June 2019. Due to the Covid pandemic that followed, President Trump would be the last state visitor of her reign.

Queen Elizabeth II and Prince Philip were together at Windsor during the Covid pandemic. Here they look at a homemade card, from their great-grandchildren Prince George, Princess Charlotte and Prince Louis, marking their seventy-third wedding anniversary in 2020.

Just weeks after the death of Prince Philip, the widowed Queen is joined by Prince Charles and the Duchess of Cornwall, plus the Duke and Duchess of Cambridge, at the monarch's reception for G7 leaders at Cornwall's Eden Project, 11 June 2021.

Dressed in 'Edinburgh Green' on 29 March 2022, the Queen attended the memorial service for Prince Philip at Westminster Abbey, accompanied – at the last minute – by the disgraced Duke of York. He had taken the place of the lady-in-waiting who had been supposed to escort her, which was widely seen as a gesture of support from the Queen rather than the other way round.

The Queen commenced her Platinum Jubilee celebrations in June 2022 with her annual Birthday Parade and a balcony appearance. As was not unusual by this stage, she used a stick.

On 6 September 2022, Elizabeth II prepared to appoint her last prime minister. Her smile conceals the very great effort she has made to be on parade for her most important constitutional duty. Two days later, the whole world was in mourning.

Above: The new Prince of Wales, King Charles III, the Duke of Gloucester, the Princess Royal and the Duke of Sussex walk behind the coffin of Queen Elizabeth II in the procession to her Lying-in-State in London on 14 September 2022.

Left and above: Elizabeth II had sittings for more than 200 portraits during her lifetime. The last was for Basia Hamilton, who gave a copy of the finished painting to the Queen's last state visitor, President Donald Trump. It now hangs in pride of place in his Mar-a-Lago home.

sought to undo the damage or confound the will of the people, depending on one's point of view. The Queen had become increasingly worried about the toxic mood at Westminster. She said as much in a thinly veiled speech to the Sandringham Women's Institute earlier in the year, saying she wanted to see people 'coming together to seek out the common ground'. Such was the febrile mood that one *Times* columnist even attacked these sentiments for being overtly political. 'The Queen is wrong,' declared Matthew Parris. 'This is, of course, all about Brexit. It was inappropriate for the monarch to intervene.'[13] Whatever the Queen's indecipherable view on the Brexit vote, it can be stated with much greater certainty that she had strong views on the delivery of Brexit. 'MPs should not vote against their constituents' wishes,' she told a lunch guest at this time.[14]

She was also doing her bit to heal Britain's multiple rifts with the rest of Europe. Every member state of the European Union would receive a royal visit over this period, or else, in the case of the Kings of Spain and the Netherlands, be invited to pay a state visit to Buckingham Palace. In particular, the Queen was even prepared to make one important exception to her 'no overseas travel' edict which came in following that last trip to Malta in 2015. She had secretly agreed to a return to the Republic of Ireland. It was hardly 'abroad' given that it was part of the British Isles, and it was particularly impacted by Brexit due to its land border with the United Kingdom. Edward Young, the private secretary who had coordinated the great state visit there in 2011, had been working on a return trip with a theme of 'celebrating normality'. It would not be a state visit, thus avoiding Dublin and politics, but an 'official' visit with a shamelessly equestrian angle, including a return visit to the Coolmore stud which she'd seen and loved in 2011. 'The Irish had basically said "name your date and do what you like" and she would have loved it,' said a member of her team. 'But then the Duke was getting frailer and frailer and wouldn't be coming with her. So she kept saying "Let's see how Philip is." She was so worried about him. It would have been the icing on the cake even if it hadn't achieved anything.'[15] It was not to be. Given the hugely beneficial impact of her 2011 visit on improving relations across the Irish Sea, and their subsequent collapse after Brexit, it is intriguing to imagine what the Queen might have achieved with another trip.

By July, she was appointing a new prime minister after Theresa May had failed to get her Brexit deal through Parliament. The ruling Conservative Party had chosen Boris Johnson, who went straight to the Queen to 'kiss hands'. He was her fourteenth British prime minister and her opening words, so he told his staff immediately afterwards, had been: 'I don't know why anyone would want the job'. Some commentators professed outrage that he had leaked the contents of a private chat, but the Queen was pretty used to that after nearly seven decades of politicians and political memoirs. 'She knew humans don't change and politicians don't change. She learned in her twenties that most conversations would get retold in due course,' said one of her most senior advisers. 'She had found there was usually a twenty-five per cent exaggeration with most stories. Funnily enough, it didn't put her off. She was always very careful and just reduced by twenty-five per cent whatever she might say, knowing that it would get exaggerated in the retelling.'[16] It remains an intriguing insight into her dealings with politicians. And she was in for a lively time with Boris Johnson.

In the midst of that year's summer holiday at Balmoral, she was contacted by the new prime minister to be told that he wanted her to prorogue Parliament. A trio of Privy Counsellors, led by Lord President of the Council, Jacob Rees-Mogg, would be heading to Balmoral to convene the necessary meeting to ratify the decision. If Parliament was going to block Johnson's Brexit strategy, so the prime minister argued, then he would shut down Parliament for five weeks. In the prevailing political climate, it was an incendiary move. The Queen, according to insiders, deployed her 'Are you sure?' tactic several times. Her officials immediately sought private 'soundings' – unwritten legal advice – and were assured that the prime minister was entirely within his rights. A story has taken root that the Queen was somehow ambushed and angered by this sudden decision, a claim rejected by Rees-Mogg. 'The people who didn't like Brexit and didn't like Boris have said this was all very difficult and it's absolute nonsense,' he said.[17] The Queen's officials had been briefed the week before, but the Cabinet were not told until the day of the meeting to avoid any leaks – whereupon the news leaked immediately. Besides, few could miss the instantly recognizable sight of a besuited Rees-Mogg striding through Heathrow to catch a plane to Aberdeen. 'I'd only just gone through security when the security man asked for a selfie,' he recalled. At Aberdeen Airport, the three counsellors were picked up by an estate minibus, along with the Queen's long-serving hairdresser, Ian Carmichael, who was also heading for the castle. If the politicians were worried, Carmichael assured them that he had been so nervous the first time he cut the Queen's hair that he would hold his breath during each snip for fear of breathing on her. The party were further entertained by the fact that, for the entire journey to Balmoral, they were following a television van from Sky News which was racing to be there in time to film the very people sitting in the vehicle behind. 'Sadly, they went straight up to the main gate while we peeled off to the back entrance,' Rees-Mogg recalled.[18]

The politicians were made 'very welcome' and given coffee

Elizabeth II

and cake by staff until the allotted appointment in the library. As with every Privy Council meeting, Rees-Mogg went in first for an audience with the Queen and found her in excellent form as she shooed an elderly corgi – 'which seemed to be both deaf and blind' – out of the room. 'I don't want to claim a familiarity that I really didn't have. But my impression was that the Queen was very, very happy doing her job,' he recalled. 'And if the Privy Council turned up, she didn't think this was a terrible imposition. She thought: "Here I am, I'm in my nineties. I am still doing my job and I'm doing it properly and nobody else can do it." To say it excited her was overstating it because she'd done it all her life. But she was not a non-entity. Having her holiday interrupted was part of the fun of being monarch.'[19] The actual council business was fairly brief, and then the Queen had an informal chat with all three counsellors about their holidays. Before sending them off for sandwiches and a drink, she urged Rees-Mogg and his colleagues to leave by the main exit: 'You must go out that way because Alastair needs his pictures and you mustn't let him down.' The Queen knew that Sky News was at the end of the drive and that the channel's distinguished ceremonial commentator, Alastair Bruce, was covering this sensational political development live on air. Bruce also happened to be a Major-General, a herald at the College of Arms, Governor of Edinburgh Castle and, above all, a friend of the Royal Family. It is another endearing example of how the Queen, in the midst of high political drama, was thinking of how she might help a family friend. 'I'm sorry to say that we left as we arrived, through the back,' Rees-Mogg admitted. 'But a camera did catch us back at the airport.'[20]

By now, Johnson's opponents were already accusing him – and by extension the Queen – of 'a coup'. Subsequent legal action in the High Court came down in Johnson's favour, but

2019: 'One hell of a lady'

the senior Supreme Court then went on to rule that the decision had been unlawful – an excruciating position for the Queen. To this day, Palace insiders believe she had no option. Insiders say that she was phlegmatic rather than furious. 'She had seen politicians in action for seventy years and nothing much could surprise her any more,' said one. 'But it was certainly embarrassing.'[21]

'I really don't think Johnson properly saw where that was going,' said another former royal aide. 'But, ultimately, the sovereign acts on the advice of the prime minister and there are only so many ways the sovereign can say "Are you sure?" You are on very dangerous constitutional ground if you then say no.'[22]

Johnson would eventually break the Brexit deadlock by calling an election for December 2019. Mid-campaign, it would be shunted off the front pages and news bulletins by an extraordinary royal implosion, one which would cause the Queen great pain: the ejection of her second son from public life.

Since being sacked as a trade envoy eight years earlier, the Duke of York had continued pursuing questionable business dealings with questionable regimes. However, he had also developed a successful programme for business start-ups called Pitch at the Palace which had gone some way to rehabilitating his tarnished image. Then, early in 2019, the spectre of Jeffrey Epstein loomed once more when the Duke was named in another court action. In July, the paedophile was behind bars again facing new charges of sex trafficking. In August, he committed suicide, though there would be plenty of theories that he had been murdered. The BBC's *Panorama* was now working on an investigation which would include an interview with Virginia Guiffre (née Roberts), an Epstein victim who claimed she had been forced to have sex with the Duke when

Elizabeth II

she was seventeen. Rather than respond to *Panorama*'s request for comment, the Duke decided it would be better to tell his own story to the BBC's *Newsnight* programme – and interviewer Emily Maitlis.

Over the course of forty-five minutes, he insisted that he had 'no recollection' of meeting Roberts and produced a bizarre series of alibis and excuses to debunk her story. He could not have met her on the night in question, as he was taking his daughter to a Pizza Express in Woking at the time. He could not have been the sweaty man Roberts remembered on the dancefloor of Tramp nightclub, because he was incapable of sweating. Quite apart from the technicalities, it was the lack of self-awareness which made it such gripping television. He did not, on balance, regret meeting Epstein, because of the financial contacts. He only remembered being in Woking because it was so manifestly beneath his royal position to be in such a town. The Duke had only been with Epstein in New York after the sex offender's release from prison because he was 'too honourable' to sever the friendship remotely. Whatever the legalities, the court of public opinion rapidly reached its verdict. Here was a man who, despite his active service in the Falklands, was guilty of letting down his country and his Queen.

Bordering on tragic was the fact that he thought it had all gone rather well, and called the Queen to tell her so. Within the family and the Royal Household, there was cold fury that he had gone against all internal advice and had somehow obtained the Queen's consent to bring BBC cameras into the palace. 'Everyone in his office had been told that this should not happen,' said a senior official of that period.[23] 'The Duke had an overriding belief that he was better than the rest of us,' said the Lord Chamberlain, Earl Peel. 'His self-confidence and entitlement was off the scale.'[24]

2019: 'One hell of a lady'

The Duke's charities, some of which had very long royal connections, were now disowning him. He had also broken the cast-iron royal rule that the family should keep a low profile during general elections. The collapse of the Duke's marriage had eclipsed the 1992 election campaign at a critical phase for the Opposition, forcing the Queen's private secretary to apologize to the politicians. Now, twenty-seven years later, his tawdry friendship with a paedophile was pushing politics to the margins again. When he even surfaced as a question in a televised debate featuring party leaders, the Queen knew that she had no option. In tandem with the Prince of Wales, she could see no alternative to Andrew's removal from public life. After all, public duties only work when the public wants to see someone, as they manifestly did not in this case. The only concession would be that he could frame it as his own magnanimous decision, which he did.

Preparing Andrew's letter of resignation, said one of those involved, was 'the worst' moment they could recall for the Queen. 'She was very, very down. She was very stoical. She understood the need. But it was very, very painful.'[25] The Prince of Wales knew how difficult it would be for her, and how the Duke might try to reverse the decision later. His usual tactic after receiving disagreeable tidings would be to drop in for tea with the Queen when her officials were not around and persuade her that he should be allowed to do whatever it was he wanted to do after all. Not this time. With the Prince of Wales on tour in New Zealand, he did try a rearguard action to resurrect a planned visit to Bahrain on behalf of Pitch at the Palace. It seemed that the old tea-with-the-Queen strategy had worked once again, until the moment the Prince awoke in New Zealand – whereupon Andrew's exclusion order from public life was reinforced.

Elizabeth II

Around the palace, memories were still fresh of a recent physical altercation after the Duke demanded that the Master of the Household, Vice Admiral Tony Johnstone-Burt, accommodate an event for his Pitch at the Palace. 'It was a routine household matter. The Duke wanted to have a reception and there wasn't any room. It was as simple as that,' recalled a senior member of staff. 'Tony said he'd have to wait his turn like anybody else and the Duke went for him.'[26] It was not just an outburst of expletives and a jab of a finger but what one member of staff described as a 'kinetic' blow.[27] Even by Andrew's standards, it caused astonishment.

Johnstone-Burt had been a helicopter pilot during the Falklands war, like Andrew. He had then gone on to a very distinguished Royal Naval career, rising to captain of the carrier HMS *Ocean* and commanding Joint Helicopter Command before becoming a popular, long-serving Master of the Household. His department included more royal employees than any other and had established protocols for workplace incidents. Johnstone-Burt reported the matter to his boss, the Lord Chamberlain, Lord Peel, who raised it with the Prince of Wales, who in turn raised it with the Duke. The Lord Chamberlain then received a call from Andrew, who was unapologetic. 'I gather you've been calling people and causing problems,' he said. So Lord Peel went to see the Duke in person and made it very clear: 'I've been told you've been treating members of the household in a wholly inappropriate way. It's got to stop.'[28]

The incident with the Master of the Household was not formally raised with the Queen, since it had been raised with almost everyone else. The Duke's behaviour was so alarming that it stirred Prince Philip from his retirement to write a letter of apology to Johnstone-Burt. Andrew was prevailed upon to write one himself (described by one member of staff as a 'sorry

2019: 'One hell of a lady'

not sorry' letter). When the matter did reach the Queen and a senior member of staff tried to downplay it to spare her blushes, she was unfazed. 'Oh, I'm sure he did it,' she replied. 'That's the sort of thing he does.'[29] It would certainly not deflect Johnstone-Burt from his duties. He would receive a knighthood the following year and remains in post as one of the longest-serving Masters of all time. There would be no further manhandling of staff. The episode would also explain why, as Andrew found himself ostracized from public life, he was so bereft of Palace allies (and also why royal staff still talk about the 2013 BBC comedy drama *Ambassadors*, featuring a boorish minor royal trade envoy called 'Prince Mark').

This had been precisely the sort of disagreeable family issue – so often involving Andrew – which the Queen would gladly leave to others. In private, however, he still had her ear. 'She was always worried about him. She saw him as vulnerable and felt he had been manipulated by bad people and she took him at his word,' said one long-serving member of the Royal Household. 'He was like his father in that he could be rude to people but he was just not as intelligent. He'd be at a telecoms event and he'd ask "What's Orange?" and everyone would go: "What did he just say?" He created a character that allowed him to survive in the circles he mixed in which was this rude blustering boring man. But I'll also say that it's so incongruous, this idea of him chasing young girls. Because he did have girlfriends but they were all age appropriate. He sometimes went to nightclubs but he did not drink, he did not take drugs. There was nothing predatory about him.'[30]

One friend of both Andrew and his nemesis during the Epstein years recalled that the Prince was particularly fond of a friend of Epstein who was certainly not under-age. Indeed, Andrew was only four years older than CNN business reporter

Felicia Taylor (the daughter of actor Rod Taylor, who died in 2023 aged just fifty-nine). 'Felicia came to stay at Royal Lodge when Fergie and the girls were away,' said this source, adding that Epstein would mock the Prince behind his back while simultaneously using him to open doors: 'Jeffrey used to make fun of Andrew and say how "dumb" he was. He told me he was taking Andrew on the planes to meet these dictators and do business deals. Andrew would mean they would get into receptions and meet people and Jeffrey would do a deal and he said he gave Andrew a cut.'³¹

The same friend remembered meeting Andrew at Royal Lodge during his annual New Year 'retreat', when he would have the house to himself while his ex-wife and daughters were on one of their winter holidays. He was undergoing various rejuvenating and cleansing therapies in the basement. Andrew told the friend that this was 'what [Princess] Diana had told him to do so that he could then go back to his partying.' Or, as Andrew put it in an email to Epstein: 'This week is all about me; for one week of the year it's great, time to put something back into me before the rest of the world starts sucking it out in all their greed and demands.'³²

The same source also remembered – as would others – Andrew's almost childlike pride in his royal trappings. 'He had all these uniforms in a wardrobe and then he took out each one to show me and explain it. Then he drove me round the estate. I remember him pointing out Elton John's house and I said, "Let's drop in." He said, "I'm a Prince. I can't just turn up unannounced." He was really very charming.' As the former royal staffer put it: 'He can talk about golf and helicopters but he can't talk about anything else. He doesn't read. He doesn't have many friends and he never grew up. He was a sitting duck for someone like Epstein.'³³

Chapter Eighteen

2020–21

Recollections

There would be further pain for the Queen as the Sussexes' royal modus operandi started to unravel as quickly as it had started. Following Archie's birth in May 2019, an autumn tour of southern Africa had begun with great promise, especially as the couple took Archie with them. Harry made a poignant trip back to the minefields of Angola where his late mother had done so much to change world opinion about landmines. The fact that Angola had aspirations to join the Commonwealth was an added bonus. But then, mid-tour, all the carefully calibrated diplomatic work was upended by the couple's decision to talk about themselves. Details were suddenly released of legal action by the Duchess against *The Mail on Sunday* for publishing a private letter she had sent to her father. It was accompanied by a statement from the Duke attacking 'relentless propaganda' against the couple. The Duchess gave an interview to ITV's Tom Bradby in which she started to cry on being asked if she was 'okay'. Soon after their return, they left for a quiet Christmas in Canada, away from the Royal Family.

The couple returned to Britain early in the New Year, minus Archie, who had remained in Canada. They then suddenly

Elizabeth II

issued an unprecedented statement after the end of the working day on 8 January, as the news media were just clocking off. It proclaimed that Harry and Meghan were effectively resigning from royal life. They would now be undertaking a 'transition' and seeking a 'progressive new role', 'stepping back' from royal duties and working towards being 'financially independent'. Yet they would still be supporting the Queen on both sides of the Atlantic.

The Royal Family had only been given a few minutes' notice in order to prevent leaks and any pre-emptive royal spin. Harry later wrote that the couple had been proposing a move abroad and a dual role for some weeks, that the Queen had been in favour in principle, that he had sent his father a proposal and that nothing had happened. Now back in Britain, the couple wanted to press ahead and desperately wanted a meeting with the Queen, even contemplating a surprise appearance at Sandringham. Naively, Harry believed that if he could just talk her through their plans, all would be well. He had called her before he left Canada and she had been ready to chat. He had then been fobbed off by officials once he landed. As one of them later told Valentine Low: 'There was a danger that a private conversation could be interpreted very differently by two people.'[1] There could be no cosy, Andrew-style tea-with-the-Queen unwritten deals on something as fundamental as being part-time royalty. It is one of those moments where the rest of us might wonder why a grandmother could not just talk it through with a grandson. However much the Queen might love Harry, this was not a matter for Granny, but for the Queen, as custodian of the institution. And that meant officials. Besides, as noted, she disliked direct confrontation, especially on an issue with long-term implications for other members of the family. The Prince of Wales and Prince William would need to have a say. The Sussexes might think it was all about them, but it was not.

As the Palace had been obfuscating, the Sussexes had therefore gone on the offensive, laying down the way things were going to be from now on. If they imagined that it was a cunning first move in a game of royal chess, they had been very poorly advised while they were plotting their strategy in their borrowed Canadian bolthole. They were certainly not expecting the Palace to move as swiftly and firmly as it did. To the surprise of both the media and the Sussexes themselves, there was an almost immediate response from 'Royal Communications'. It stated baldly that these were 'complicated issues' and would 'take time to work through'. In fact, they would not take much time at all.

The Queen's principal private secretary, Sir Edward Young, and the Prince of Wales's private secretary, Clive Alderton, had been working more closely over the past two years since the retirement of Prince Philip. Prince William's private secretary, Simon Case, a high-flying civil servant on secondment from Whitehall, was also in this loop. Young was at Sandringham with the Queen when the Sussexes' demand dropped and she was clear on one thing from the start: now that this issue had blown up in public, it could not be allowed to fester.

What the press instantly branded as 'Megxit' had a different name within the Palace. The family talked about 'UDI', a reference to the Rhodesian crisis of the mid-sixties when the minority white government there issued its 'unilateral declaration of independence' from Britain. That had not ended well. The Queen and the Prince of Wales were as one on the need for speed: the longer the absence of clarity, they agreed, the greater the scope for misunderstanding. Their officials would draw up various options for initial consideration but, ultimately, the

Elizabeth II

Queen was adamant that there could be no halfway house. She had imposed the same rule on the previous generation in 2002, when the Earl and Countess of Wessex had found that they could not run private companies in parallel with royal duties without a conflict of interest. They had opted to stay in.

Meghan had already returned to Canada when the Queen invited Harry to Sandringham for a family meeting a few days later. There would be no conference-call dial-in from Canada either. No one could be sure who else might be listening in, or recording, at the other end. In his book, *Spare*, Prince Harry painted a vivid picture of being ambushed by officials and weak-willed family members as he attempted to negotiate a middle way, with the Queen at the head of a long table being non-committal. She had hated those Way Ahead Group family committee meetings back in the nineties. This one must have been even more disagreeable. Those on the Palace side still had some sympathy. One said: 'The options for Harry and Meghan were either/or and there was no way that the couple could just come back to royal duties as it would mean admitting that all the things they had said were wrong. That so-called "Sandringham Summit" was quite brutal. But the Queen was absolutely solid from the start: no half-in, half-out.'[2] Grudgingly, the couple chose out.

The subsequent statements made it clear how each side regarded the result. 'I am pleased that together we have found a constructive and supportive way forward for my grandson and his family,' said an upbeat statement from the Queen, adding that she had also insisted on a twelve-month review process to allow the Sussexes to return to the fold if they wanted. She was not holding out much hope, however. When a friend asked if she thought the couple might ever return, she was blunt. 'Of course not,' she replied. 'They took the dogs.'[3] In a downcast speech to a charity, before leaving Britain, Harry concluded: 'Our hope was to continue serving the Queen, the Commonwealth and my military associations, but without public funding. Unfortunately, that wasn't possible.'

The mood soured further when it transpired that the couple had been secretly working on a 'sussexroyal.com' brand during their Canadian retreat. Like their original declaration of independence, it smacked of poor advice, since British company law imposed various rules on trading as 'royal' and the Sussexes had not secured any approvals. A curt statement later confirmed they would drop the name. They returned to Britain for one last round of valedictory official duties – on Commonwealth Day, appropriately enough. Joining the Queen for the annual service at Westminster Abbey on 9 March 2020, they sat near (but not next to) William and Catherine without being seen to exchange a word. By nightfall, Meghan would be on her way back to North America. Harry would soon follow.

For all the harsh words spoken, and all the petulance and delusions they had shown in their dealings with an institution that has never pretended to be anything other than hierarchical, they could have been treated more sensitively by the royal machine. They would certainly be a grave loss to a shrinking monarchy. Meghan had been 'royal' for just 660 days, but was now a private citizen once more. Harry was turning his back on his birthright and thirty-five years at the heart of the Royal Family. Under the circumstances, it seemed rather unfair for the headline writers to describe this whole sad, sorry episode as 'Megxit'.

The royal pragmatist had stood her ground, at great cost. As a mother and grandmother, the previous six months had been as trying as any since the loss of her own mother and sister nearly two decades earlier. However, the end of that seven-year 'ring cycle' of good fortune – running from William's wedding right through to Eugenie's – did bring one positive outcome. 'It felt awful, really awful. Prince Philip had his crash, then we had the prorogation business, Epstein, *Newsnight* and UDI – it was like London buses all coming along at once,' recalled one of those in the thick of it. 'Short term, there was a lot of pain. But it did catalyse the long-term strategy very effectively. Because it really brought the "big three" much closer together.'[4]

The Queen, the Prince of Wales and the Duke of Cambridge and their senior staff were now liaising on all sorts of issues beyond whatever the latest family crisis might be. 'The principals were all talking together more and so were their staff. That was the first time that had happened like that in a long time,' the insider continued. 'It's easy enough when you're dealing with happy stuff but it really matters when there are difficult things. I remember the Queen being very touched when William just rang her up out of the blue about something minor to ask her: "What do I do?" He hadn't done that for a long time. All three were in lockstep and it carried on like that for the rest of her life.'[5]

This new-found unity would soon be put to a fresh test. Within a fortnight of the Sussexes' final bow at the abbey, the country and most of the world was suddenly under a form of house arrest. The emergence of a potentially lethal flu-like coronavirus saw panic in the shops and in the markets as shares crashed and the economy shrank by 25 per cent. Britain had not seen such a dramatic impact on daily life since the Second World War. For an institution that thrives on visibility and human interaction – 'I have to be seen to be believed,' as the Queen was forever quoted as saying (though no one could ever quite pin down when and where) – this was a fundamental challenge.

2020-21: Recollections

Given that old people were particularly vulnerable to the virus, the Queen and Prince Philip would need to be very careful, too. At the outset, she was not. On Wednesday 18 March 2020, she had been due to meet the prime minister for their weekly audience. Boris Johnson's staff noticed that he had a cough and it fell to his chief adviser, Dominic Cummings, to tell him he simply could not go breathing all over the Queen in case he was shedding the virus. Johnson protested that it was his constitutional duty and he would jolly well go. Cummings's reply is variously recorded as 'that's completely insane' or 'you will kill the f****** Queen. Are you f****** mad?'[6]

In fact, Johnson was not being entirely mad. For the Queen was of a similar mind. She had come to the fatalistic view that when one's number was up, so be it. 'The prime minister considered it his duty to be there to do it face to face,' her private secretary, Edward Young, later revealed. 'And the Queen considered it her duty too – in a sort of Blitz spirit, "Well, I've got to die sometime" attitude. But it really was not the moment for taking unnecessary risks.'[7] As one of her senior staff later put it: 'She certainly wasn't a germaphobe.'[8]

What happened next has echoes of the struggle between King George VI and Winston Churchill over who should be allowed to accompany the Allied fleet on the invasion of Normandy in June 1944. Both monarch and PM had wanted to be there. In the end, it was wise officials who managed to stop them setting sail. Like the wily Tommy Lascelles back in 1944, Edward Young had a plan. He would tell the Queen that Downing Street had 'cold feet' about the audience. Johnson's private secretary, Martin Reynolds, would tell the prime minister that the Palace wanted to cancel and that the conversation should be on the phone. 'Which was very lucky,' Young added, 'because, by the end of the telephone call, the prime minister had started coughing.'[9]

Elizabeth II

The Queen retreated with Prince Philip to Windsor. The Master of the Household, Vice Admiral Tony Johnstone-Burt, drew up a rigorous regime whereby a skeleton staff would operate in isolation around the royal couple. He also knew that the best way to sell it to his bosses was to make it sound both upbeat and naval, so he called it 'Operation HMS Bubble'. It would be no different to the crew of a ship being away from home for weeks at a time. The royal couple settled in to their new way of life very easily. Indeed, it meant that they saw a good deal more of one another. Up until then, the Duke had been spending much of his retirement at Wood Farm on the Sandringham estate, his favourite retreat, while the Queen spent her working weeks at Buckingham Palace. It was not a separation, but simply how he liked to spend what he viewed as his final days. 'What people hadn't quite appreciated was just how much he was retiring from everything when he announced his retirement,' said a senior official, explaining why the Duke had wanted nothing to do with the issues of Andrew or Harry, let alone challenges like prorogation. 'He was, sadly, a man waiting to die really, by that stage, almost wishing death would get a move on. It made things very much lonelier for the Queen.'[10] Now, they would be closer than they had been for the past three years. 'HMS Bubble' certainly fared better than its sister ship at Birkhall, where the Prince of Wales went down with the virus days later.

As the politicians struggled with the enormity of the task ahead, following the declaration of a national lockdown on 26 March, the Royal Family was under pressure to show leadership. *The Times* criticized the Queen for saying nothing. However, she was biding her time, waiting for the right moment. That came on 5 April, when she delivered a special address to the nation. She had wanted it done properly, like her Christmas

2020–21: Recollections

broadcast. This was to be family-gathering television on an early Sunday evening, albeit in wholly different circumstances from her regular 25 December slot. It could not be a grainy Zoom or Teams video message of the sort which the whole country was now using to communicate.

A well-scrubbed BBC unit was summoned to set up in the White Drawing Room of Windsor Castle, leaving behind a single hermetically sealed cameraman to switch on. 'Together we are tackling this disease,' the Queen said calmly, 'and I want to reassure you that if we remain united and resolute, then we will overcome it.' What gave it such added emotional heft was her reminder that it had been in this same castle, exactly eighty years earlier, that a fourteen-year-old Princess Elizabeth had stood before a microphone at the height of the Blitz. Alongside her little sister – 'Come along, Margaret' – she had reassured millions of worried children that 'all will be well'. Here she was doing exactly the same, this time as a great-grandmother. 'Future generations will say the Britons of this generation were as strong as any,' she said, before an ending which had been the subject of a great deal of internal debate. As noted throughout this book, the Queen was steadfastly unsentimental. Successive private secretaries and ministers had struggled to insert jokes, puns or superlatives into a text without finding a red pencil mark through their handiwork. Martin Charteris, who had more success than most, would recall a speech in which the line 'I am very glad to be back in Birmingham' was returned with the word 'very' crossed out.[11] She meant no offence to Birmingham but felt it smacked of insincerity. On this occasion, Sir Edward Young had proposed a conclusion with a line from the most popular song of the Second World War. According to one of his team, the daily Red Box had included several drafts which had repeatedly come back crossed out on the grounds that the line was 'too whimsical'.[12] Eventually, he pressed the point in person and the Queen finally agreed. So it was that she ended her address with echoes of Vera Lynn's great wartime refrain: 'Better days will return; we will be with our friends again; we will meet again.'

The longest-serving broadcaster in history had just delivered an address as powerful as any in her eighty years on the airwaves. 'I thought that was the classiest thing she did,' former prime minister David Cameron reflected, 'because she didn't often do things like that and she was so confident in doing it.'[13] As for the timing, it could not have come at a more appropriate point. At the very moment the Queen's words were being transmitted, the prime minister was on his way into intensive care. That cough had turned critical. 'We later heard that one reason he was so ill was that he had been waiting to hear the Queen's speech before going to hospital,' said one Palace official.[14] Quick-witted officials now had to address previously unthinkable constitutional questions. Edward Young would later tell colleagues of the urgent conversation with his opposite number in Downing Street as he sat in a London bus shelter on that Sunday evening taking the call about Johnson. The two private secretaries had no precedents for what might happen next. How could the Queen appoint a new prime minister if the existing one was alive but in a coma and therefore un-resigned? From whom should she take advice in that scenario? What if both the monarch and prime minister died at the same time? There would be no issue about the royal succession, but the sense of national crisis might be overwhelming. As Young would later tell Boris Johnson himself, it would have been much simpler if the prime minister were dead rather than incapacitated.[15]

In the event, Johnson pulled through and the Queen established new expertise in meeting people via Zoom. Edward

2020–21: Recollections

Young and his colleagues soon learned that Covid had driven some very useful changes. First of all, the public could see and hear more of the Queen's interactions with ordinary people. Previously, these would go entirely unrecorded during a normal walkabout or a reception, but her happy chats with nurses or soldiers or teachers could be heard loud and clear. They also helped to establish an important precedent, and monarchs and their royal private secretaries do love precedents.

For some years before Covid, private discussions had been taking place between Young and his counterpart in the Prince of Wales's office, Clive Alderton, on plans for a regency in the event of the Queen being too infirm to perform her duties. 'With the Queen Mother going on past her hundredth birthday, of course we had to think that the Queen would reach the same age. A regency seemed almost inevitable,' explained one member of staff.[16] But how would it work? And what would be the infirmity threshold for a regency? It was suggested that one criterion for a regency might be if the Queen was unable to see or read documents. However, the advisers could now point to the precedent of a blind home secretary. 'No one ever questioned David Blunket's capacity for work,' said a former aide.[17] So, blindness could no longer be grounds for a regency.

Now, the Covid pandemic was throwing up lots of other new precedents and possibilities. What if the monarch was unable to meet the prime minister for the weekly audience? No problem. Under Covid, they could talk remotely. How about receiving credentials from ambassadors? That, too, was now happening remotely via video. A precedent had even been set for remote video meetings of the Privy Council. When Johnson had wanted his prorogation in 2019, he had been forced to send Privy Counsellors up to the Highlands. Now, under Covid rules, it could all be done with people at their desks, albeit with certain challenges. Former Lord Chancellor Sir Robert Buckland recalled one remote video meeting when a fire alarm suddenly went off in his building: 'I said: "I am conflicted, Ma'am, because I am here by command." And she said: "You'd better go."' On another occasion, he was performing his traditional role of introducing new clergy. 'She was very amused when I appeared to have a cupboard full of bishops.'[18] Despite the switch to cameras, the Lord President of the Council, Jacob Rees-Mogg, was still keen to preserve the unique character of the monthly Privy Council meetings. By tradition, the meeting would start with the Lord President's one-on-one audience with the Queen, then a brisk trot through the business of the day and, finally, the monarch's less formal fifteen-minute chat with whichever counsellors were in attendance. This was always an easy-going affair in person. It was stickier when conducted through the artifice of a video link. So Rees-Mogg decided to ask each counsellor present to give the Queen an update on their particular department. She soon came to enjoy these updates so much that her office asked if they could become a regular feature, a reminder that the Queen still liked the human connection to politics. 'She was very, very interested in what was going on. She was engaged,' Rees-Mogg recalled. 'I got this note saying: "Please carry on because the Queen likes this".'[19] She also liked to learn a little about new members of the Council when they were sworn in. In July 2021, a new batch included the new deputy leader of the Labour Party, Angela Rayner. The experience of being installed could often leave even the most experienced politicians lost for words, so Rees-Mogg would always try to help things along. According to another Privy Counsellor, on this occasion, he pointed out to the Queen that Rayner had a claim to fame. 'Oh really? What's that?' asked the monarch. Rees-Mogg explained that she was the youngest grandmother in the Commons. 'Oh, how lovely,' the Queen replied, to which Rayner chipped in: 'I was thirty-seven.' Momentarily digesting this fact, the Queen found herself thinking out loud. 'I suppose mathematically it is possible,' she said brightly.[20]

The Queen's view was that all these things should revert to the correct form, in person, as soon as possible. For now, however, the pandemic had succeeded in greatly reducing any putative mutterings about the need for a regency as she drew closer to her centenary.

There were two happy family distractions. On 17 July, Princess Beatrice married British-Italian property developer Edoardo Mapelli Mozzi in a private ceremony at the Royal Chapel of All Saints in Windsor Great Park. The bride borrowed not only a tiara from the Queen (the same Queen Mary Fringe Tiara worn by Princess Elizabeth in 1947) but also a vintage Norman Hartnell ivory dress, remodelled by Angela Kelly and Stewart Parvin. Though present, the bride's father was omitted from all official photographs. A month later, on 15 August, the Princess Royal marked her seventieth birthday. She chose to spend it with her husband, Sir Tim Laurence, sailing somewhere off the Western Isles. Since the death of the Queen Mother and Princess Margaret, Princess Anne had been an especially important feature in the Queen's life, calling in daily and latterly helping her mother to master the art of Zoom during lockdown. 'The Queen was always very worried about Anne working too hard,' recalled one of her staff from this period. 'She always wanted to know where her children were. "Where's Edward today?" and so on. But she would often say: "Anne's travelling everywhere and she works so hard and I've got to tell her to slow down".'[21] The pandemic would do little to encourage the Princess to take it easy. She was keen to ensure that the Royal Family did not overlook the unsung stalwarts of the Covid campaign. One day, she popped up at a waste depot in Cambridgeshire to pay tribute to binmen and women. At the end of 2020, the Queen spent Christmas away from Sandringham for the first time in decades. It would be the quietest, too, as the family retreated to their various residences, and the monarch spent it with Prince Philip inside 'HMS Bubble'.

Another household generating rather more headlines than most was that of the Duke and Duchess of Sussex. To no one's surprise, they had moved from their temporary home in Canada back to Meghan's native California. Home was a large house in Montecito from where they built up a new media-cum-philanthropy brand, Archewell, with an appropriately Californian mission statement: 'to unleash the power of compassion to drive systemic cultural change'. There were occasional pronouncements on the state of the world, not all of them welcome back in Britain.

Thinly veiled criticisms of Donald Trump and of the imperial roots of the Commonwealth were awkward coming from a couple who still retained ranks and patronages such as Captain General of the Royal Marines (Harry) and vice-president of the Commonwealth Trust (Meghan). These had been untouched by the Queen during the twelve-month review of the Sussexes' new post-royal existence. All of a sudden, on 19 February 2021, a terse statement from the Palace announced that the review had been concluded early and that all the remaining royal patronages would go. Though it was framed as the couple's decision, its speed had clearly surprised them. 'We can all live a life of service,' came a tart response from Sussex HQ. The abrupt decision had been triggered by the news that the couple would be filming an 'intimate conversation' with that unexpected wedding guest, Oprah Winfrey, for the US network, CBS. Her wedding seat in the most exalted section of St George's

2020–21: Recollections

Chapel now made complete sense. Once again, the couple had learned that the Queen could move at great speed when her authority looked as if it was about to be challenged. 'The business of having Oprah at the wedding now made sense,' said one senior aide. 'The Queen had initially been very sympathetic to Meghan and her family problems. I think she saw similarities between Meghan and the young Philip and his chaotic family. But it was now starting to look like the move to California had been a plan all along.' The source added: 'The Queen had seen plenty of narcissists in her life.'[22]

As the interview approached, the Sussexes received another surprise when *The Times* obtained details of a formal complaint of bullying behaviour by the Duchess. It had been nothing to do with Buckingham Palace. Rather, the complaint had come from a Kensington Palace ex-staffer weary of the victim narrative from an ex-boss whose brief royal tenure had evidently not radiated kindness and rose petals for all. The Duchess said she was 'saddened' given that she herself had suffered from bullying.

Just how bad that had been, in her view, was laid bare on the night of 7 March in one of the most coruscating attacks on the Royal Family since Diana's *Panorama* appearance more than twenty-five years before. The worst of the Duchess's charges involved alleged racism. While she had been pregnant with Archie, one member of the family had apparently raised 'concerns and conversations about how dark his skin might be.' His skin colour, she suggested, had denied him security protection and a title. Of equal gravity was her claim that her suicidal pleas for help had gone unanswered.

The Duchess had spoken to Oprah Winfrey alone for most of the interview. Harry was brought on towards the end to amplify and corroborate the stories. In doing so, he swiftly

Elizabeth II

managed to contradict the story about the racist family member (Meghan had said the 'skin' conversation – which she had not heard – had been during her pregnancy, while Harry explained that it had been at the start of their relationship). He also accused his brother of being trapped in a doomed pact with the press and complained that his father had cut him off financially. Some allegations were simply incorrect, such as the claim about Archie's title or the assertion that the couple had already been married by the Archbishop of Canterbury prior to the wedding ceremony at Windsor (which would have been illegal). At other moments, Meghan revisited the bridesmaid dress saga to point out that the Duchess of Cambridge had been the one in the wrong.

In all the reams of global coverage, all the explosive debates and phone-ins and online savagery, the world largely overlooked one genuine fresh and incontrovertible piece of (good) news. The Duchess was expecting a baby girl. Overall, the interview painted a picture of profound misery within the royal fold and liberation in California. To cap it all, the show had aired in Britain on Commonwealth Day.

Once again, the Queen let it be known that this lengthy charge sheet was not to be left dangling unanswered in the court of public opinion. The usual adage of 'never complain, never explain' was not applicable after this sort of assault on the family name. It is not known if the Queen had privately sat through the whole show (Prince Philip certainly did not), though she was fully briefed on the contents. She was, say staff, sad but contained. Having been through the dramas of the nineties and what, at times, felt close to existential threats, this saga had to be taken in context. She asked Sir Edward Young and his team to prepare an appropriate response as a matter of some urgency. Once again, a *Times* editorial had been demanding as much:

2020–21: Recollections

'The allegation of racism is too toxic to ignore.'[23] One member of staff remembers a socially distanced walk with Edward Young through the grounds of Windsor, whereupon a Range Rover pulled up and the Queen wound down the window, asking: 'Have you got anything yet?' Soon enough, Young had come up with an all-encompassing response to the Sussexes' eighty-five-minute tirade in just three words. 'She smiled,' the official recalled. 'She knew exactly what she was doing. What was important is that it changed the mood.'[24]

Less than twenty-four hours after the interview was shown in Britain, the Queen issued a statement saying that the family were 'saddened to learn the full extent of how challenging the past few years have been for Harry and Meghan.' The statement was not long, it acknowledged the gravity of the race issue and promised to address the matter privately. It would always be remembered, however, for those three words, a phrase so quintessentially Elizabeth II that it has been in popular usage ever since: 'Recollections may vary.'

What had infuriated so many of the Queen's family, friends and staff was that, throughout all this, she had quite enough to worry about with the Duke of Edinburgh's declining health. The Sussexes were not to know it when they arranged their CBS interview, but the Duke would be spending several weeks in hospital for an infection and a heart-related procedure. He came home soon after the Oprah Winfrey appearance and the hope was that he might rally in time for his one hundredth birthday in June – not that he was remotely interested in it. The family were starting to wonder what on earth they might get him as a present. The Duke of York was already planning some elm trees for the park.[25] The Prince of Wales even tried to broach the subject of a party. 'We're talking about your birthday – and whether there's to be a reception,' he said. 'Well, I've got to be

Elizabeth II

alive for it, haven't I!' the Duke replied. 'I knew you'd say that,' laughed Prince Charles.[26]

On 9 April, just ten weeks short of what would have been a glorious card from the Queen, he was dead. He had been suffering from a number of increasingly debilitating conditions for some years, and had neither expected nor wished to see his centenary. 'He never wanted to reach a hundred,' one of the close family told this author. 'He ticked the box when he went early.'[27] Theirs had been the longest royal marriage in history. The Queen had been worried about him for years. It was why she had stopped travelling – even forsaking that much-anticipated return trip to Ireland – in case he was taken ill. It was why she had enjoyed the last year inside 'HMS Bubble'. The Queen had been there at the very end, which had been very peaceful – as if 'someone took him by the hand and then he went,' according to the Countess of Wessex.[28]

In the run-up to his funeral, the Queen and all the family were delighted that the tributes focused on the full span of the life of this exceptional man; born royal, raised in chaotic circumstances, shaped by war and destined to be an indispensable consort for longer than anyone in royal history. He had helped to create life-enhancing, life-changing institutions like the World Wildlife Fund and the Duke of Edinburgh's Award. He had even been nominated for a Nobel Prize. He had represented his country at one sport (polo) and invented the rules for another (carriage driving). Above all, he had given the Queen the confidence and strength to be the monarch she was. Of course he could be difficult at times. He could equally be kind and perceptive, spotting those like himself who had come through troubled upbringings, including Diana. The Queen had never wanted anyone else in her life.

Prince Philip had wanted a simple funeral and the diktats

2020-21: Recollections

of Covid ensured he got exactly what he wanted. Under the pandemic rules, there would be room for just thirty mourners, instead of the 600 who would normally fill St George's Chapel. He had been adamant that they should include three German princes, representing the four houses to whom he was related through his sisters.* Those families had been barred from his wedding by the Palace on the basis that the Second World War was too fresh in the mind in 1947. This was atonement.

Everyone processed on foot to the funeral except the Queen, who was driven in the State Bentley with Lady Susan Hussey. The Duke had designed his own hearse, a customized Land Rover, with help from one of his regiments, the Royal Electrical and Mechanical Engineers. He had chosen every element of a service which managed to avoid all mention of himself, except when the Garter King of Arms stepped up to recite his styles and titles, pronouncing him 'Husband of Her Most Excellent Majesty.'

Covid rules had imposed one other restriction which would have amused the Duke no end. Even the thirty mourners, including the Queen, were not allowed to say a word. The ban extended to the national anthem. Only the members of the choir were authorized to sing 'God Save the Queen.' The Queen herself sat in silence throughout, and alone due to the regulations on personal distance. She pointedly placed her handbag on the seat to her left. It was where the Duke used to sit. Afterwards, there was another sight he would have enjoyed. Walking up the hill back to the castle, his grandsons, William and Harry, could be seen talking to one another.

The Queen would cope, of course. 'I don't think she needed

---

* Prince Philipp of Hohenlohe-Langenburg; Bernhard, the Hereditary Prince of Baden; and Prince Donatus, Landgrave of Hesse (the Duke's younger sisters, Cecilie and Sophie, had married into the House of Hesse).

Elizabeth II

a bereavement counsellor,' her old friend Prue Penn observed. As a member of the wartime generation, the monarch would just get through it, soldier on. She had depended so much on Philip for encouragement and moral support through her life – as she memorably acknowledged in that golden wedding anniversary speech – but, of late, he had withdrawn from her official life altogether and that life was carrying on. She was determined to resume regular duties straight away. Within a week of the Duke's death, she held her first engagement, to say farewell to Earl Peel as her Lord Chamberlain. Court mourning was limited to just a fortnight. Within weeks she would be opening Parliament and welcoming the leaders of the G7 nations who were holding their latest summit in Cornwall.

The government had been wary of asking her to get too involved in the summit after all that she had endured. There was a suggestion that she would merely meet one or two visiting world leaders at Windsor. It was the Queen who insisted, via her officials, that she would actually like to play a proper role. She travelled down on the royal train with the Prince of Wales and Prince William. Those on board were delighted to see 'the big three' chatting away happily. As one recalled: 'They had this lovely tea together where they were trying to resolve a few family issues. Prince Charles and the Queen were trying to get Prince William to agree to do something he didn't want to do in a very engaging way. And the Queen was really concentrating on her briefings. You could sense she was thinking "have I still got it?" Then we got in the convoy to this reception at the Eden Project and suddenly the Queen was in this group among Macron, Merkel, Trudeau and Johnson. They were all hovering round her like metal filings reacting to a magnet. And within seconds you could see her shoulders straightening and that sense of "I'm back!" It was a really happy time.'[29]

2020–21: Recollections

At the summit, she helped break the ice as the heads of state stood stiffly in their socially distanced places for the group photo. 'Aren't you supposed to look like you're enjoying yourselves?' she asked, and smiles broke out. Afterwards, she returned to Windsor for a lockdown-compliant reduced Birthday Parade. A day later, she was welcoming US president Joe Biden to Windsor for tea before he left the UK, as she had done with Donald Trump three years before. It was a slower-paced event. Whereas Trump had strolled up the stairs, Biden had needed the old elevator to bring him up to the Oak Room in the private wing of the castle. It was a very cordial tea party as the Queen welcomed the couple to Windsor. 'I loved her sense of independence,' the first lady, Dr Jill Biden, recalled. 'She had a big teapot. And Joe said to her: "Here, let me help you." The Queen had been quite insistent, however. "No, no, no. You sit. I will serve you." Here she was with this big teapot pouring tea and we had the best time because she has such a sense of curiosity. She asked all about American politics and what was going on.' At which point, 'her little dogs came in.'[30]

However, it was not as warm or lively as her first meeting with the ardently Anglophile Donald Trump. He had wanted to celebrate his British connections. Biden, in contrast, always liked to remind people of his Irish ancestry. British government sources later said that they had discreetly sounded out the White House on whether to issue the state visit invitation extended to all US presidents. Biden had shown no great enthusiasm in return.[31]

Biden had been the fourteenth US president she had met, a fact which still astonishes most Americans. It seems impossible to name anyone in history who met so many occupants of the White House. 'It's awesome,' said President George W. Bush, who knew a few, when I asked if he could name anyone with

Elizabeth II

experience of fourteen presidents. 'That's a hard thought.'[32] He believed former Secretary of State Henry Kissinger would be the nearest contender, but that even he would struggle to beat the Queen. The fourteen were every serving president from Harry Truman to Joe Biden, with the exception of Lyndon B. Johnson, plus a retired Herbert Hoover. It now seems the figure may be even higher. In later life, the Queen was going through all her presidential encounters with a private secretary and was asked why she never met Johnson (they would have met if he had attended the funeral of Winston Churchill, but he was ill at the time). 'But I am sure I did meet him at some point,' the Queen replied. 'Because I know I met a lady called "Ladybird". You don't forget a name like that.'*[33]

There was also happy news, for a change, from California. The Duchess of Sussex had given birth to that baby girl. The couple introduced the child to the Queen via video link and she was the first to whom they revealed their choice of name: Lilibet. To some within the family, it was clearly a heartfelt tribute to the Queen. To others, it seemed impertinent to say the least to appropriate the Queen's childhood nickname. The precise chronology of what happened next would be another textbook example of the Queen's post-Winfrey observation that 'recollections may vary'.

The couple were adamant that they had sought the Queen's permission. That was not how the Queen remembered it, said her staff. In her view, it had been presented more as a fait accompli and she had not objected. The result was the same, and the varying recollections might not have mattered until the BBC reported that the Queen had *not* actually been asked.

---

* Texas-born Claudia Johnson was known by her childhood nickname of Lady Bird.

2020–21: Recollections

The Sussexes then instructed lawyers to threaten any publications which repeated the BBC's 'false and defamatory' assertion, whereupon the Palace pointedly refused to back the Sussexes' version of events. 'The Queen was not exactly thrilled about them using her childhood name,' said a close aide, 'but that wasn't what bothered her. What she could not tolerate was being handed a different version of events and then being drawn into legal action to support something she did not recognize.'[34] Years later, in the reign of Charles III, one of the King's officials would point to this row as a reason why the King was so wary of talking to his younger son while Harry was suing the King's ministers in the King's courts over his lack of security. Those recollections just might vary once again.

Chapter Nineteen

2021–22

The 'Too Difficult' Folder

The Queen adjourned to Balmoral for the summer in good spirits. At her urging, her staff prepared for a full autumn programme to reboot the monarch's routine. She was adamant that she was not going to withdraw into what one senior official called 'a cardigan retirement', and had mentally prepared herself for life after Prince Philip. However, the Highland retreat did not start well.

It was her custom to spend the first few days of her holiday with one or two of the family – Lady Sarah Chatto was a regular – at the more homely Craigowan Lodge on the estate before moving in to Balmoral Castle. 'It was a difficult Craigowan,' a friend recalled, explaining that the Queen's insistence on using the stairs rather than a lift had done something to her back. By now, she had also felt that the time had come to give up two things she had always adored. There would be no more riding on Emma, her trusty fell pony. She had also decided to stop drinking alcohol.

She had never much liked wine or champagne, seldom touching either except when a banquet demanded it, but had always loved a gin and Dubonnet or possibly two before and during meals (her staff knew to ensure that the two ice cubes went on top of the lemon to hold it down). 'She never drank too much but there was drink at lunchtime and dinners every evening and that could make her more tired than she used to be,' recalled a veteran of those years.

She was also finding that, as well as reacting with a new medication, the alcohol was starting to affect her feet. Staff avoided using the 'g-word', but she would not be the first monarch to have had some of the symptoms of gout. During that summer, family and friends noticed that she would occasionally decide not to join guests for dinner, which was very unlike her. 'There were fewer house parties and she was not herself,' recalled one member of the Household. 'We'd had that lovely false dawn, but then there seemed to be a decline. I think there's quite a possibility that when she left Balmoral in 2021, she might have thought: "Will I ever see this place again?"'[1]

She returned from Balmoral for that busy autumn reset and staff soon realized that it had been a mistake to load so much into the diary. The Queen had been due to visit all the devolved parliaments, starting with the opening of the Scottish Parliament on 2 October. 'We were thinking how we could "backfix" a lot of stuff which had not happened during Covid and had stupidly planned the sort of programme she might have had two or three years earlier,' acknowledged one aide.[2] And then came a turning point, a moment which some would later point to as the start of her decline. The Queen had delivered her speech in the chamber at Holyrood and was then directed into a reception for politicians and community leaders. It was supposed to be a small event with a few people in horseshoe clusters, as she preferred, but the event had ballooned. More than 150 people were waiting for a handshake. 'She came out and there was this slippery floor and the room was steamy. The Lord Chamberlain's Office, who organized it, were supposed to keep it light, but someone had obviously given in to all the arm-twisting you get with these events,' the aide explained. 'The supposed horseshoe clusters had not been properly supervised and you couldn't see the end of this crowd. I remember the equerry or the protection officer saying, "She's really struggling." On the flight home, she said to her staff: "You've got to push things back." And they did – dramatically.'[3]

To begin with, routes were shortened. A few days afterwards, at a Royal British Legion service at Westminster Abbey, the Queen arrived not at the Great West Door, but through a side door, ensuring a shorter path to her seat. Observers had started to notice that she looked thinner (not, perhaps, unconnected to giving up drink), although what attracted particular attention at the Abbey was that she was using a stick. This was hardly surprising for a woman of ninety-five, particularly among a congregation of veterans, many of whom were in wheelchairs. However, it was the first time she had been seen walking with a stick in eighteen years, and the last time had followed knee surgery. The stick was there again two days later at the Senedd in Wales.

Things briefly seemed to improve when she left the stick behind the following week as she invited delegates from the government's global business summit to a reception at Windsor Castle. Boris Johnson had assembled a stellar cast, including Microsoft founder Bill Gates, and guests remembered the Queen in bright, smiling form. 'Are they spending?' she asked a Foreign Office official. Overseas investment was indeed pouring in, he replied. 'No, I mean here – in the gift shop. We've got to keep the roof on!'[4] After nearly seven decades of hosting grand receptions just like this, it would turn out to be her last. For all the smiles, she was increasingly starting to suffer from what the Palace would call 'mobility issues'.

Just as the Queen was about to head to Northern Ireland on the next leg of this autumn mini-tour came the news that she had cancelled. It emerged, via *The Sun*, that she had spent a night in hospital undergoing 'preliminary tests' for an unspecified condition. The fact that the Palace had tried to keep this quiet, continuing to fly the Royal Standard above Windsor Castle when she was not there, merely amplified the sound of alarm bells. The high point of the autumn programme was to be her appearance at the COP climate summit in Glasgow. At short notice, she cancelled and sent a video message instead. That there was a serious problem became clear on the morning of the most important event in her calendar. With less than two hours to go, she had decided to pull out of the Remembrance Sunday service at the Cenotaph. Since 2017, she had no longer laid a wreath but always watched from a Foreign Office balcony. Now, she would not be there at all, having apparently sprained her back. It was not serious, but it had been what one aide called 'a wobble'.

'There had been a tendency over the years which had served her well of taking a decision to cancel only at the last moment,' said a staffer. That would have to change. From now on, the Queen's planned appearances at events would not be trailed far in advance to avoid constant headlines about another 'cancellation'. Privately, there would be a Plan A for her presence somewhere and a Plan B for a non-appearance, and it then would be a pleasant surprise if her car pulled up. But if she continued to decline at this rate, then her staff would cease Plan A altogether.

With Covid on the rise again and the prospect of more restrictions, the Queen chose to celebrate Christmas once more at

2021-22: The 'Too Difficult' Folder

Windsor with a small family gathering. She did not even attend the Christmas morning service at St George's Chapel. Her Christmas broadcast was unusually personal, with an enchanting tribute to Prince Philip and the same 'mischievous twinkle' he had always had since 'I first set eyes on him'. The Queen and her staff now had two main targets for the year ahead: a national memorial service for Prince Philip and celebrations to mark her Platinum Jubilee. Both would be very much Plan A – with her showing up.

She left for Sandringham in the New Year, in order to be there on Accession Day as always. 'When you look at the record of that place, she might have thought: "Will I ever leave?" It almost feels cursed,' observed a staffer.[5] George VI and George V had indeed died at the family's Norfolk home in the depths of winter. Yet, the Queen enjoyed something of a revival there and was, in the words of one present, 'in bouncy form'. Even when the Covid virus finally caught up with her during her stay, it was a short-lived attack and she was back to normal a few days later. It can now be revealed, however, that the medical events of the previous autumn had focused minds.

Doctors were not giving forecasts, but it was made absolutely clear, said one very close to the Queen, that she would certainly not be emulating her mother by reaching her centenary. Certain decisions, therefore, which had long been kept in what staff called the 'too difficult' folder, really would now have to be addressed as a priority.[6] One of these was the question of the Order of the Garter for Tony Blair, who had by now been out of Downing Street for fourteen years. Aside from royal chums like the Marquess of Salisbury, there had been no career politicians admitted to the Queen's highest order of chivalry since Sir John Major in 2006. The political class had developed a younger complexion since the Blair years, and the Queen had not felt any great urgency in adding him to the Order just yet. However, Blair's omission would look very peculiar if any more recent politicians were added before him.

By far the most important unresolved issue, however, was the Duchess of Cornwall's future title after the accession of Charles III. Every wife of every king in history had been called Queen, yet the current position was that Camilla was due to become the 'Princess Consort'. It was a stop-gap title made up by a courtier at the time of the couple's 2005 wedding, had never been formally endorsed and now seemed out of date, if not redundant. The Queen, said one close to her, had always felt that it was a workable compromise.

However, the private secretaries to the Queen and to the Prince of Wales were united in wanting to resolve the issue, just as the Queen had resolved the question of the future headship of the Commonwealth back in 2018. And it needed to come from her. 'It would have been awful to go into the new reign with a debate going on. But it was all about the timing and the Queen still did not feel the time was right,' said one senior adviser of the period.[7]

One idea had been to make an announcement on the fiftieth anniversary of the Prince of Wales's investiture in 2019, but the Queen had returned it to the 'too difficult' folder. In the run-up to Christmas, Sir Edward Young tried again, suggesting that the best time for an announcement would be a day when the Queen was beyond reproach: Accession Day 2022, the actual seventieth anniversary of the reign, was the obvious moment. But she would lay the groundwork in the New Year Honours List. It was decided that the first step would be to appoint the Duchess of Cornwall to the Order of the Garter at the same time as Tony Blair. There was some low-level sniping from Blair's critics followed by a half-hearted petition against his elevation which fizzled out, but not a squeak about the Duchess.

2021–22: The 'Too Difficult' Folder

On Accession Day itself, the Queen issued a written message using the same language she had adopted over the Commonwealth issue. Thanking her people, and noting how vital her mother and Prince Philip had been as consorts, she said that it was her 'sincere wish that, when the time comes, Camilla will be known as Queen Consort'. Not a murmur could be heard. The timing, again, had been spot on.

The Queen returned from Sandringham ahead of the long-delayed service of thanksgiving for the life of Prince Philip. He had never asked for this service, but there were so many people and organizations who had missed his Covid-compliant funeral that the Queen wanted it to happen. To general astonishment, she arrived escorted by the Duke of York.

Only weeks earlier, the Duke's reputation had sunk even lower following an out-of-court settlement to halt a civil action brought by Virginia Giuffre in the USA. Despite claiming never to have met her, he was paying her a reported £12 million. It was later reported (and not denied) that most of the money had been loaned to Andrew by the late Queen. Ahead of that deal, the Palace had announced that the Duke was relinquishing all remaining patronages and military titles and would no longer use the style 'HRH'.

For all that, no one begrudged him a seat at his father's memorial service. However, he had somehow circumvented the agreed plan, printed in the order of service, that he would arrive in the usual family pecking order. Instead, he had replaced the lady-in-waiting travelling with the Queen and driven up from Windsor alongside his mother. The Queen had acceded to the plan, so the rest of the family had little choice but to accept it. Clearly the Duke had reverted to his 'tea-with-the-Queen' tactic, presumably hoping to show that he continued to have a role to play, that the monarch still had faith in his protestations of innocence. An adviser close to the Queen posited another explanation: 'She was just sorry for him. The others had spouses, duties, respect. He did not.'[8] Nor was she blind to the wider problems raised by his living arrangements.

The Queen had now come to the conclusion that Andrew should no longer live at Royal Lodge. Both his daughters had married and left home and the Queen was now paying the costs of maintenance and security. There could be no use of public funds to secure the home of a man with no public role. The Sussexes were no longer at Frogmore Cottage. William and Catherine were looking to move their children away from school in London to a co-educational prep school, Lambrook, near Windsor, starting in the autumn of 2022. They would hardly want Frogmore Cottage, still gleaming from its Harry and Meghan makeover.

'I remember the Queen looked out of the window and said: "Andrew to Frogmore and William to Royal Lodge". That was the plan,' a lunch guest from that time recalled.[9] She had loved Royal Lodge as a child and wanted a new generation of royal children to enjoy her little Welsh cottage and the swimming pool. The only problem with her plan was that William and Catherine did not want to live there. For now, the Cambridges preferred Adelaide Cottage, a much more modest four-bedroom home often occupied by courtiers and currently used by the Queen's cousin, Simon Rhodes, a great-nephew of the Queen Mother. When Rhodes was informed that the Duchess of Cambridge and her mother would like to come round with a tape measure, say friends, he realized that his days were numbered. It also meant a stay of eviction for the Duke of York.

In years to come, Andrew would put up a fight with his elder brother over Royal Lodge, pointing out that he had a cast-iron lease on the place, before finally giving up and moving to the

2021–22: The 'Too Difficult' Folder

Sandringham estate in even greater disgrace in 2026. Those close to the Queen remain certain that if Prince William had wanted Royal Lodge at the time, and she had sent Andrew to Frogmore, then he would have gone quietly. No amount of furtive lobbying over Sunday tea would have made any difference. Nonetheless, at least the Duke of York had appeared in public at his father's memorial service. The Duke and Duchess of Sussex had declined to return to Britain at all. A spokesperson cited the lack of 'necessary police protection.'

All eyes were now on the Platinum Jubilee in the summer. The Queen would not be undertaking a national tour, let alone an international one. Instead, the family would extend her greetings to her realms. This would prove uncomfortable for the Duke and Duchess of Cambridge, who were despatched to the Caribbean on a troubled tour. In Jamaica, they were accused of 'colonialism' as they inspected troops from the back of the Queen's old open-topped Land Rover and 'segregation' as they met children through a wire-mesh fence in Trench Town. The accusations, which were risible and not made by anyone present, had been stirred up on social media. At the Cambridges' meeting with the Jamaican prime minister Andrew Holness, he launched, without warning, into a homily on the need to abolish the monarchy.

Their experience was a sign of a future problem for the Royal Family. During the Queen's reign, both she and the monarchy had been largely seen as a bulwark of democracy in newly independent ex-colonies like those in the Caribbean. Now, with the passage of time and the rise of identity politics, especially nearby in the USA, the Crown was gradually being painted as a lingering symbol of imperialism. The previous year, the Queen had been deposed, amicably but without a referendum, in Antigua. She was stoical. Through her reign, she had actually lost more thrones than she currently possessed, but she would be glad to leave it to others to lower any more flags.

At home, she continued to pass on more duties to the Prince of Wales. He took her place at the Royal Maundy service, and even opened Parliament on her behalf. They had been getting on better than ever since the death of the Duke of Edinburgh. In part, the Prince was simply being solicitous and mindful of his mother's frailties. However, he had also mellowed himself. There had been plenty of friction in Charles's middle-aged years, when his social agenda was rattling the government. The Queen – and Prince Philip even more so – had frowned on Charles's obsession with his gardens, his messianic belief in organic farming and his fondness for exuberant Queen Mother-style hospitality. They found him spoiled, fussy and extravagant ('you should see her racing bills,' one of the Prince's aides retorted).[10]

Over the previous decade, however, things had moved on, and the Prince had increasingly been positioned as a vice-presidential figure rather than just an experienced apprentice. The Queen was now not merely seeking his help as a stand-in but strategically ensuring that, when the time came, the process of succession (what the Palace liked to call 'transition') seemed as natural as possible. For example, she had even signed new letters patent to ensure that it was Prince Charles who read out the Queen's Speech in Parliament. The historical precedent was for the Lord Chancellor to read it in the absence of the monarch, but she felt that this would marginalize the Prince. She wanted the country to feel used to seeing and hearing him in important regal situations. She was his promoter, just as she had been with those Commonwealth leaders in 2018.

In return, her position appeared unassailable. Historians will look back on this period and note the absence of any calls for

2021–22: The 'Too Difficult' Folder

a regency (even if, as noted, there had been plenty of secret brainstorming). 'There was an inverse rule. The longer the reign went on and the more frail she became, the greater her authority,' said a former private secretary, adding that the credit for that goes as much to Prince Charles as to the Queen.[11] Not once did the Prince or his inner circle give any indication that he was keen for the monarch to move aside, which would swiftly have ignited a debate. That is because, say his closest friends, he was entirely happy to leave the matter in the hands of the Almighty. He would also be the best-prepared (as well as the oldest) new monarch in British history.

Her own engagements were to be kept tightly controlled and extremely short. The greatest fear of the Queen and her officials was some sort of collapse in public or a need for a sudden exit. Although she managed to sit through a full evening performance at the Royal Windsor Horse Show in May, she was not on public display there and also among friends. When she opened the new Elizabeth Line of the London Underground the next week, it was just a ten-minute visit with a tiny media pool to capture the moment. That was all that was needed to produce the appropriate photograph anyway.

The record-breaking £19 billion project might easily have had a different name. When work started, during Boris Johnson's tenure as Mayor of London, it was called Crossrail. Johnson suggested that, when it was finished, it should be called the 'Elizabeth Line'. However, the management were insistent that any name should include 'Crossrail' as well as the Queen. She was not bothered, but her officials let it be known that she would only accept the 'Elizabeth Line' on the basis that another line had been named after a queen. If Victoria could have the 'Victoria Line', why did she have to be immortalized as Elizabeth/Crossrail? The management caved

Elizabeth II

in and the 'Elizabeth Line' it would become. 'We were lucky, as we'd actually got it wrong,' a former private secretary admitted. 'It later turned out the Victoria Line was not named after Queen Victoria at all, but after Victoria Station, which was named after Victoria Street. We got away with it.'[12]

The Platinum Jubilee proper opened with the Queen's annual Birthday Parade. She did not appear at the parade but came out onto the palace balcony at the end, later reappearing at Windsor to light the first in a nationwide chain of beacons. The following day, the Palace said that she was 'too tired' to attend the service of Thanksgiving at St Paul's Cathedral. In fact, it had never been the plan that she would be there at all. Appearing for a few minutes on the palace balcony was fine; a whole church service was not. She would watch it on television, as would the Duke of York, who had miraculously contracted Covid for the entire jubilee weekend. The congregation did include the Duke and Duchess of Sussex, however, who had conquered their fear of flying to the UK and had brought the children, too.

The Queen would finally get to meet Lilibet and was thrilled, say friends, as the one-year-old crawled around her feet. Harry would later paint the scene in his memoir: 'Archie making deep, chivalrous bows, his baby sister Lilibet cuddling the monarch's shins. Sweetest children, Granny said, sounding bemused. She'd expected them to be a bit more . . . American, I think? Meaning, in her mind, more rambunctious.'[13]

The year before, she'd gone all the way to Cornwall to a summit. Now, on Derby day, she was too weak even to go to Epsom for her favourite race or to the jubilee concert at the palace which followed. It did not matter. For most of Britain, the high point of the jubilee weekend was another cameo role, ten years on from her skit with James Bond. As the concert was about to get underway, the television cameras cut away to a scene of the Queen having tea with Paddington Bear. After much slapstick mess, Paddington produced one of his beloved marmalade sandwiches from his hat, whereupon the Queen extracted one of her own from her handbag, saying: 'I keep mine in here – for later.' What gave it even greater emotional impact than the Bond moment were Paddington's final, almost but not quite valedictory words: 'Happy Jubilee, Ma'am – and thank you, for everything.' A beaming Elizabeth II replied: 'That's very kind.'

It struck the perfect note in the midst of this touch-and-go phantom jubilee for a largely absent Queen. The showrunner, as with James Bond, had been her private secretary, Sir Edward Young, but the whole thing nearly did not happen. 'The difference with James Bond was no one thought that was a good idea until it was and then everyone jumped on board,' a member of Young's team recalled. 'With Paddington, it was the other way round. Everyone had been saying for years: "Of course you've got to come up with something". The Queen wanted to do something. But what? They toyed with the idea of another twist on James Bond but that didn't work. So Edward got some top creatives to help him deconstruct the Bond film and work out what was so good about it.'[14]

Young and his team deduced that the essential ingredients were two national treasures, one real and one fictional, playing off the cliche of the fictional character but ensuring the Queen had the upper hand at the end. Finally, someone had the idea of Paddington and the rights holders of the film franchise were happy to be involved. A plotline involving a tea party took shape but, after several months, it still didn't feel quite right. 'Edward was just about to pull it because it just wouldn't be good enough,' the staffer recalled. 'And then at the last minute,

Elizabeth II

someone came up with the Queen pulling out a sandwich "for later" and that was it.' Because of the computer-generated animation involved, the Queen would have to address all her lines to a hat on a stick. 'She loved doing it. She enjoyed the whole process enormously,' said the staffer.[15]

As with her Bond appearance, the Queen had insisted on a tweak to the running order. The original script included a footman, played by actor Simon Farnaby (star of the children's TV series *Horrible Histories*), who brings in the tea and grimaces at Paddington's table manners. He is then splattered by a squashed éclair before the marmalade sandwiches appear. The Queen, however, wanted to include a second footman. The Bond sketch in 2012 had featured her senior page, Paul Whybrew. She thought it only fair that this film should include a walk-on part for her other trusty page, Barry Mitford. The producers initially ruled out the idea, saying that the plot required just one footman and it would be too complicated to tinker with the script. 'They soon got a message passed back: no Barry, no Queen,' recalled one of those on set that day. Sure enough, as well as seeing the scowling Farnaby playing his part with Paddington Bear, viewers worldwide would see (and can still see online) a second footman in attendance – Barry Mitford. The leading lady – as loyal to her staff as they had been to her – had, wisely, been granted her wish. Nor was there any artifice with the marmalade sandwiches. 'They had real marmalade in them,' said the source. 'So Angela Kelly made sure the Queen used an old handbag she would not be using again.'

Filmed in Windsor Castle's Crimson Drawing Room, the sketch would conclude with Elizabeth II and Paddington tapping their teaspoons on their cups in time to the opening bars of 'We Will Rock You', the classic Queen hit kicking off the concert. The action then cut back to the front of the Palace as

2021–22: The 'Too Difficult' Folder

Sir Brian May, the band's peerless lead guitarist, launched into his third successive jubilee concert. The public loved it every bit as much as that Olympic skit a decade before. The James Bond film was funny. So, too, was Paddington, but it also had a deep emotional subtext: adieu . . .

The jubilee concluded the following day with a 7,000-strong rolling pageant meandering the full length of the Mall and past the palace. It featured every decade of the reign through the prism of vehicles, pop stars, music, celebrities and the full tapestry of communities which had evolved through the Queen's reign to create modern Britain. Run by the chairman of the Victoria & Albert Museum, (soon to be Sir) Nicholas Coleridge, and the architect of the Queen's previous two jubilees, Sir Michael Lockett, here was a mix of the Lord Mayor's Show, the Notting Hill Carnival and a sporting victory parade.

Once again, the Queen was watching on television at Windsor until the Prince of Wales felt that she really had to be part of it. Sir Edward Young sped down to Windsor to press the point in person. As the pageant concluded with Ed Sheeran singing in front of the palace, the Royal Standard suddenly appeared on the flagpole above. The Queen had arrived through the back gate. With the Mall now full to capacity with crowds, she emerged on the balcony in dark green, unaided but for her stick. Once again, the royal party alongside her was reduced to the shape of things to come: the Prince of Wales and the Duchess of Cornwall, plus the Cambridges and their three children, George, Charlotte and Louis. Poor weather late in the day had ruled out the usual flypast by the Red Arrows. But no matter. On this occasion, the Queen herself had been the grand finale. Back inside the Centre Room, there would be a small tea party with Louis and Charlotte handing round the sandwiches (no marmalade ones this time).[16]

Elizabeth II

No one had stood on this balcony, waving and being waved at, more often than Elizabeth II. Ninety-five years on from her debut as a tiny child in the reign of George V, she went back through the French windows for the very last time.

Chapter Twenty

Sunset

'Very peaceful'

The Jubilee had exhausted the Queen. For the first time in her reign, she missed every single day of the Royal Ascot meeting, a sure sign something was amiss. As ever, though, there would be a bouncing-back of sorts. At the end of June, she travelled north to Edinburgh for her usual week of official events at the Palace of Holyroodhouse. If the Queen was going to conserve her energies for anything, it was for this traditional reminder of her central role in Scottish life. She had been paying very close attention to the Scottish National Party's latest legal fight to hold another Scottish independence referendum in defiance of the British government, a battle which would end in defeat for the SNP in the Supreme Court five months later. 'The government will win,' the Queen (correctly) predicted to a visitor that week, 'but that won't stop them [the SNP]. They won't stop.'[1] She watched a military parade and held her audiences, but was not strong enough to attend the annual garden party for 10,000 guests. She remained inside the palace with her standard flying to emphasize her presence. The Duke and Duchess of Rothesay, as Prince Charles and the Duchess of Cornwall were known in Scotland, led the royal party into the

Elizabeth II

garden. The Queen looked on from within with some of her officials, who had noticed the SNP leader and First Minister Nicola Sturgeon working her way down the crowd as if it were her own show. 'I see Elsie McSelfie is busy,' the Scottish Secretary of State, Alister Jack, joked, raising a wry royal smile. The monarch then returned to Windsor for the final round of summer engagements ahead of her summer holiday at Balmoral. Though unspoken, many felt a sense of final farewell this time. Perhaps the Queen did too. 'She was so brave,' said an official who saw her regularly over the summer. 'You could tell she was having a lot of treatment from the bruising on her hands where the cannula had gone in. Her hands seemed permanently bruised.'[2]

She went to see her fell pony, Emma, and her other horses for one last time. On the eve of her departure, she held the last round of audiences and meetings for the season, formally saying farewell to the outgoing US ambassador, Jane Hartley, and the outgoing governor of Windsor Castle, Sir James Perowne, before what would be her last Privy Council meeting. 'We had a private chat at the end of it,' said one of those present. 'I felt a bit emotional when I left, because, well, it just felt to me like a goodbye. She had some very clear messages about how she thought things would go in the future. Very clear indeed!'[3]

The Queen wanted all the great-grandchildren to come up to Balmoral at some point over that summer, even if the Sussexes might not be able to make it. 'She wanted to make sure that they all had a really happy memory of her,' explained a friend of the family, acknowledging that there was now a clear sense of loose ends being tied up. The children were not all there at the same time, but the Duchess of Cambridge took an enchanting photograph of the Queen surrounded by eight great-grandchildren (including Catherine's three) and two (Wessex) grandchildren.

Sunset: 'Very peaceful'

Her exact medical condition has never been revealed, though some have attributed her back pain and 'mobility issues' to myeloma, a type of bone marrow cancer. Former prime minister Boris Johnson later stated as a matter of fact that she had been suffering from what he called 'a form of bone cancer', and that remains the consensus view in government circles. Those closest to her will only say that she had 'a number of things' in the late summer of 2022. Whatever the exact cause, she was well aware of her medical prognosis, and it had been enough to encourage her to tie up those loose ends – and to tackle that 'too difficult' folder. She had also given thought to her funeral arrangements – though not much. Some members of the family took great delight in making these plans. The Queen Mother had always wanted to be updated whenever there was a rehearsal for her funeral, while Lord Mountbatten's endless changes to every aspect of his final farewell would exasperate officials. Elizabeth II was well aware that many people had been planning her funeral for decades, but did not dwell on it. Indeed, one member of staff said that she had to be nudged to nominate her choice of hymns after the clergy made a gentle request for guidance.[4] Ever the pragmatist, she was still looking to the present, and had certainly not precluded a sudden return to London at short notice to appoint a new prime minister.

Despite having won a hefty majority at that 2019 election, Boris Johnson's government had become mired in a succession of scandals, many linked to its handling of the coronavirus pandemic. Faced with mass resignations and a report into his personal conduct during Covid lockdowns, Johnson looked ready to fall in July 2022. However, the Palace had not forgotten that failed prorogation stunt in 2019. During Johnson's final days in charge, his former colleagues advised the Queen and her officials that he might make one last-ditch attempt to stay in office by calling a general election. Having just repealed the much-detested Fixed Term Parliaments Act, he would be able to do so, provided he asked the Queen first.

Sir Edward Young and his team warned her that, under no circumstances, should she take any direct calls from the prime minister. She could not risk talking to Johnson until there were officials on both ends of the line to establish exactly what was said. 'Boris had been telling people that he might "go to the palace" but he might have just picked up the phone,' one veteran royal adviser recalled. 'He could have got through to the Queen and said: "Oh, I'm thinking of calling an election." And she'd say: "That's interesting." And he'd take that as a "yes" and before you know it, he's on the steps of Downing Street announcing the country's going to the polls.'[5] While a prime minister can ask the monarch to dissolve Parliament, and thus call an election, it is not automatically granted if the monarch thinks another person might be able to command a Commons majority for a reasonable period. Young's plan, said the adviser, was that the Queen should stall for time until it was quite clear exactly what was being requested. 'Edward told her that it might be necessary for her to be having "some dental work". She loved that,' said the adviser. 'She thought the whole idea was hilarious.'

In fact, she did not really expect Johnson to do any such thing. She knew that, despite the chaos in Downing Street, he was an ardent royalist who disliked upsetting her. One courtier remembered Johnson's 'expression of absolute horror' when he had to explain to her that his progoration had backfired in court.[6] On another occasion, he had come marching out of an audience shouting at staff: 'Why the hell did no one tell me that Randox sponsors the Grand National?' The company had just been involved in a political lobbying scandal.[7] He had learned to shield nothing from her. After she lent him the run of the palace gardens during the pandemic, Johnson was mortified when his wife's Jack Russell, Dilyn, killed a royal gosling. Having made no mention, he was equally mortified at their next meeting when the Queen remarked: 'I gather Jack Russells don't go very well with goslings.'[8] Johnson had never been dull. 'I think she liked him. He was a lot more entertaining than a Royal Variety performance,' Sir Jacob Rees-Mogg recalled.[9] A royal friend confided that the Queen had used the same word to describe both Johnson and Donald Trump: 'amusing'.[10] Johnson was also positively straight-laced compared to some of the prime ministers the Queen had known in her other realms, such as one she entertained in 1977. Her confidential briefing file warned her that this PM was 'unbalanced at times to the point of apparent derangement'.* Not even Johnson's harshest critics had said that of him.

His resignation as Tory leader kickstarted a summer-long Conservative leadership contest which left the country listless for weeks. The Queen had therefore decided that whenever a leader was finally chosen, she would take the royal train down to London to enable Johnson to resign as prime minister, whereupon she could formally ask the winner to form a government. An official told this author that she thought it would look 'selfish' to drag outgoing and incoming prime ministers up to the Highlands with television news cameras following them there and back. Besides, she believed the country needed to resume being governed as quickly as possible.

As the summer wore on, however, she was beginning to feel

---

* Eric Gairy, prime minister of Grenada (FCO 160/26/10).

Elizabeth II

weaker again. In mid-August, she asked her officials if it might be acceptable for her to remain in Scotland. They assured her that it would be and, just to reassure her, they secured the approval of all the leadership candidates too. It was now becoming clear that she might actually never head south again. She discussed it with her children. Typically, her concern was that she might be creating unnecessary problems for everyone else. 'There was a moment when she felt that it would be more difficult if she died at Balmoral,' the Princess Royal told this author. 'And I think we did try and persuade her that it shouldn't be part of the decision-making process. So I hope she felt that that was right in the end.'[11]

On 5 September, Liz Truss was formally declared the new Conservative leader and plans were set in motion for the following day. The Queen was determined to effect the transition with all the dignity and correctness she had observed with all her prime ministers, going back to Winston Churchill. It would require a very great effort, though sadly no one would realize how much effort until later. Johnson arrived at Balmoral shortly before noon on 6 September to resign, stayed for around fifteen minutes and left. An hour later, Truss arrived to be appointed as the fifteenth British prime minister of the Queen's reign. 'She stood up to greet me,' Truss told this author. 'She was clearly physically not very well but we talked for about twenty minutes. She was alert. I would say she was relieved that the thing had actually happened and that we were now moving things forward.'[12] The Queen insisted on sticking to tradition by inviting Truss's husband, Hugh O'Leary, to join the conversation at the end.

The small Truss team then left at speed so that the new PM could address the nation from the steps of Downing Street before the end of the day. The photograph of a beaming Queen,

Sunset: 'Very peaceful'

stick in hand, on her feet, in cardigan and Balmoral tartan in front of the Balmoral fireplace, would be the last image ever taken of Elizabeth II. Later on, sharp-eyed picture editors spotted bruising on her right hand – whether accidental or from a needle, it was unclear. If she had needed some sort of steroidal booster to put on this sort of show, it would not have been surprising. Were an animator to have drawn a bubble emanating from her head, it might have said: 'Job done.'

She had sailed through her jubilee and had now put the country back on an even keel (not for long, though the Queen was not to know it). The Queen still had one more engagement that day, the happy task of investing her outgoing communications secretary, Donal McCabe, as a Lieutenant of the Royal Victorian Order. And there was another matter of great importance to be resolved later in the afternoon at Goodwood, where the Queen had a runner. Her filly, Love Affairs, was in the 3.05. And she won.

There was only a small party in residence at the castle. The Princess Royal was in the area doing engagements and her son, Peter Phillips, had come up for some shooting. The group included the Queen's private secretary, Sir Edward Young, her equerry, Lieutenant Colonel Tom White of the Royal Marines, a lady-in-waiting, Susan Rhodes, and, as ever, the monarch's personal assistant, Angela Kelly. All gathered for early evening drinks where one of those present remembered the Queen buoyed up by her win and 'quite buzzy' as she looked back on some of the prime ministers she had known. The day, however, had taken its toll. She then announced that she would be going upstairs to have dinner alone.

That night, back in London, Boris Johnson confided in friends that he had never seen the Queen look so weak. 'We were helping him to drown his sorrows after resigning, but he said that what really made him sad was that he wouldn't be around as prime minister to give the Queen a really good send-off – which he would have done because he was a wordsmith,' said one of his closest allies. 'He just said, "She looked terribly, terribly frail." He was worried that if she had just one fall and banged her head, that would be it.'[13]

There was, however, no cause for alarm until the following day, when the Queen said that she would be staying in bed. That was unusual, even at this stage of life. The local doctor, Douglas Glass from Ballater, was asked to drop by. He would regularly report in to the Queen's senior doctor, Sir Huw Thomas, the Head of the Royal Medical Household, but at this stage there was no need for medical backup. Plans were put in place for the Queen to attend that evening's meeting of the Privy Council. It was an important one, as these events always are after a change of prime minister and a whole raft of new appointments to the Cabinet and the Privy Council. Given that she was in her bedroom, it would not be conducted on camera. However, it would be acceptable for the Queen to join through an audio link connecting her to the COBRA (Cabinet Office Briefing Room A) conference suite beneath Downing Street. Once again, here was a useful precedent from Covid days. When George V was on his deathbed, a Privy Council meeting had to be held in his bedroom. Now, Elizabeth II could speak down the line. Except that she could not. Suddenly, the politicians in London were told that the meeting was off on 'medical advice'. 'Everyone had gathered for this Privy Council meeting. It was only cancelled at the time when it was meant to go ahead,' Liz Truss remembered. 'So people thought: "This isn't good news."'[14]

The Princess Royal had been keeping her elder brother updated at the other end of Scotland, where he was at Dumfries

Sunset: 'Very peaceful'

House with the Duchess of Cornwall. He had to make a difficult decision. Were he to rip up his schedule and fly to Balmoral, there would inevitably be panic in the corridors of power. How embarrassing if he then arrived to find the Queen on the doorstep asking what the fuss was all about. His private secretary, Sir Clive Alderton, thought it was worth the risk and assured him that it could all be blamed on officials, notably himself. The Princess Royal agreed. 'They were both saying to him: "Think how you would feel if you never said goodbye",' said one member of staff.[15]

The following morning, the Prince and the Duchess boarded a helicopter to fly to Balmoral. Rather than cause a commotion and disturb the Queen at the castle, they landed at their home at Birkhall. It was so last-minute that there was no car waiting for the couple, their two private secretaries and a policeman. The Prince borrowed a Land Rover off a member of the estate staff and got in the driving seat, while the others climbed in for the twenty-minute drive to the castle.

The Prince had already told his brothers and his sons that they should start making their way north. The Queen was fading but, at this stage, they should be thinking in terms of 'a day or two, not an hour or two'. The only difficult discussion was with Prince Harry. By sheer chance, the Sussexes happened to be in Britain in order to carry out some charity engagements. They were making plans to head north when Harry received another call from his father to say that he should come on his own. The family wanted to keep things close and tight. Immediate family only. Instantly sensing another slight to Meghan, Harry exploded. 'Don't ever speak about my wife that way,' he told his father, later writing that Prince Charles had been 'nonsensical and disrespectful'.[16]

Prince Charles patiently explained that he didn't want a

Elizabeth II

circus and that the Duchess of Cambridge was not coming either. 'Then that's all you needed to say,' Harry replied, temper receding. His rage would have continued unabated if he had discovered that the Duchess had not actually been excluded at all. As the future Queen, she was very welcome, but the couple's three children were starting at a new school that very day and she felt her duty was with them. Harry later wrote that he had tried to share a lift with his brother but that his texts went unanswered (a claim queried by Prince William's team, who said that no call came from Harry's side even though they 'had all the numbers'). William and his uncles had secured an RAF Envoy IV to take them from RAF Northolt to Aberdeen at 12.30 p.m. Harry chartered a later private jet from Luton.

By late morning, Prince Charles and the Duchess of Cornwall had arrived at the castle and spent an hour at the Queen's bedside. She had been seen by Dr Glass, who was now in close contact with Sir Huw Thomas and his team. Since word would soon be spreading of all these royal movements, Sir Edward Young knew that a bulletin was needed. Normally, the Palace only issued medical statements if the Queen was hospitalized or missing an engagement. At 12.32, the Palace announced simply that she was 'under medical supervision' while remaining 'comfortable and at Balmoral'. The fact that the bulletin said nothing spoke volumes to those in the know.

Prince Charles and the Duchess decided to leave her to rest for a while. Princess Anne and Angela Kelly ensured that the Queen was never alone. Even at this stage, there was no need for constant medical supervision or intervention. As noted, the current advice was to think in terms of days, perhaps even a week or two. No one was talking hours, let alone minutes. Dr Glass remained at the little staff surgery inside the castle while the Rev. Kenneth MacKenzie, minister at Crathie church and

Sunset: 'Very peaceful'

a chaplain to the Queen, sat at her bedside reading from the Bible. A little after 3 p.m., there was an urgent call for Glass to come upstairs. It appeared that the Queen had now stopped breathing. At the same time, the Princess Royal called Birkhall to alert the Prince of Wales that he needed to return as quickly as possible.

The Prince had been out in the grounds picking mushrooms, as he liked to do in early autumn, while the Duchess was walking the dogs. The couple jumped back in the Land Rover with their tiny team and set off for the castle at speed. The Prince, like his parents, had never been a slow driver anyway. He took the South Deeside Road, between the woods and the river, a route he had known all his life, and then veered off onto an even smaller back road leading into the estate.

Up in the Queen's bedroom, Dr Glass checked and checked again. There could be no doubt. His patient was at peace. Sir Edward Young was waiting outside the room. Glass went outside and confirmed to him that the Queen was dead. Young was now on autopilot. His duty was to tell the new sovereign immediately before telling anyone else. He had been mentally preparing for this moment for years. He had talked through the proposed sequence of events with the Prince of Wales, who had, at one point, hatched a poignant plan by which Young would first inform the Duchess of Cornwall, so that the new Queen Camilla would give her husband the news (just as, in 1952, the new Queen was told of her father's death by Prince Philip). The idea had been gently parked on logistical grounds.

Young called Birkhall to be told that the Prince was on his way. The private secretary asked the Balmoral switchboard to try all the mobile numbers of those in the small entourage in the hope that someone would have a signal. Though phones would probably be in silent mode (as the Royal Family generally

Elizabeth II

preferred), they would still vibrate. The Prince might only be minutes away, but there could be no risk of any delay through a puncture or, worse, some sort of accident. Eventually, one of the party could feel their phone vibrating and could see the call was from the switchboard. The phone was passed to Sir Clive Alderton, who answered, asked his boss to stop the car and handed him the device. For the first time, on a lonely, beautiful Highland roadside sitting in the driving seat of an old Land Rover, King Charles III was addressed as 'Your Majesty'. 'I'm nearly there,' he replied, and put the car in gear.

A handwritten note by Sir Edward Young was immediately agreed with the doctor for clarity and posterity. It would also be very comforting for all who loved her. It stated: 'Dougie [Glass] in at 3.25. Very peaceful. In her sleep. Slipped away. Old age. Death has to be registered in Scotland. Agree 3.10 p.m. She wouldn't have been aware of anything. No pain.'[17]

Three hours later, the bare facts were relayed to the world in a brief statement: 'The Queen died peacefully at Balmoral this afternoon. The King and The Queen Consort will remain at Balmoral this evening and will return to London tomorrow.'

Being monarch carries great responsibility, great privilege, but also a uniquely peculiar dynamic. For anyone else losing a loved one, the instant response from others is sympathy, condolence, plus time and space. However, there cannot be a nanosecond of respite for the holder of a position governed by the statement: 'The Queen is dead. Long live the King'. A monarch has to provide an instant shoulder on which a nation may cry, and also to answer an immediate and constant avalanche of questions. The very first two – while he was still at the wheel of the Land Rover – were the constitutional formalities from Sir Edward Young. By what name would the King

Sunset: 'Very peaceful'

reign? (Charles.) And would His Majesty grant permission to call the prime minister? (Yes.)

Britain had just changed both its head of state and head of government in the space of three days. In some nations, that might trigger civil disorder, if not revolution. Britain simply followed the example of Elizabeth II as it kept calm, carried on and prepared for the greatest farewell in British history.

Codenamed Operation London Bridge, this had been twenty years in the planning under the auspices of the hereditary Earl Marshal, the Duke of Norfolk. A state funeral at Westminster Abbey, attended by the greatest number of heads of state ever assembled in the UK, would be followed by a final service of committal at St George's Chapel, Windsor, attended by friends, staff and family. Before then, Elizabeth II would posthumously unite a fractious nation as people and communities of every faith and political persuasion turned out to pay their respects. The first British monarch to die in Scotland, she would be the first to require a death certificate (Scottish law differs from English law, which exempts the sovereign; Dr Glass recorded 'old age' as the cause of death).

Her final journey across the kingdom would leave so many indelible images; of Aberdeenshire tractors abandoning the harvest to line up scrubbed and solemn, their shovels dipped in homage to their passing neighbour; of ardently nationalist Dundee pouring onto the roads in tribute; of tearful queues through the night down Edinburgh's Royal Mile; of her journey from Edinburgh to London, the last ever flight using her personal call sign, 'Kittyhawk' (which set a new record for the most-tracked air traffic movement in history);[18] of more queues and processions through London; of world leaders filling the Abbey; of the final parade through the park at Windsor; of

Elizabeth II

Emma the fell pony standing to attention on the Long Walk; of the Crown Jeweller removing the Imperial State Crown, Orb and Sceptre from the coffin, before Elizabeth II was lowered slowly beneath St George's to be reunited with Philip, with her mother and with the father in whose revered image she had reigned.

It had been a swift and seamless transition from British history's longest-reigning monarch to its longest-serving heir. She had been writing the diary that she had kept faithfully every day since childhood right up to the last. Its full contents will remain locked away until an official biographer is granted access in the future. However, it can be revealed that the last entry concerned plans for that last Privy Council meeting which never happened, beginning in her customary way: 'Edward came to see me . . .'

In the tumultuous hours immediately after her death, her private secretary, Sir Edward Young, was digesting the enormity of the task ahead with his successor, Sir Clive Alderton, in his Balmoral study when there was a knock on the door. A footman appeared with the Queen's very last Red Box of state papers. She had received one every day for the past seventy years (except birthdays and Christmas Day) and had always worked her way through its contents on time. Young had tried to keep the boxes light in recent days. There had been an agenda for that Privy Council meeting and also a list of names for the Order of Merit. Limited to two dozen exceptionally eminent people of the day, the order has always been in the gift of the monarch and had been long overdue some fresh blood for a while. The Queen had needed to review the list and make some nominations.

Young was not sure what to expect as he slowly unlocked the box. Inside, he found a private letter addressed to himself and another one addressed to Charles. She had known this

Sunset: 'Very peaceful'

would be the last Red Box. There, too, though, was the list of potential 'OMs'. The monarch had read it, had made her choices and had signed it all, while lying on her deathbed. It was the last document she ever handled. Future historians can record that Elizabeth II died as she had always lived – on duty.

The demands of the digital age meant that the new King was expected to speak almost at once. The morning after the Queen's death, he flew from Scotland to London to deliver one of the most emotionally charged and challenging broadcasts of his life. In it, he thanked his beloved mother, reiterated her pledge to a lifetime of service, welcomed the new Prince and Princess of Wales, sent love to the Sussexes and assured his late mama: 'May flights of angels sing thee to thy rest.' Even the naysayers had to concede it was remarkable (the BBC transmitted his first take unedited, while YouGov reported that it had received a dictator-level 94 per cent approval rating).

Chapter Twenty-One

Legacy

'Fresh air'

As her centenary approached in 2026, a plan to erect a national memorial to Elizabeth II started to take shape. The centrepiece would eventually be a statue close to Buckingham Palace in London's St James's Park. Similar memorial projects were also under way, including one in the USA.

Monuments to her had started going up while she was alive; though, unlike Queen Victoria, she was not keen on them (a fine equestrian sculpture presented in 2003 would end up tucked away somewhere in Windsor Great Park). However, inevitably, it is not statues but her stature which will continue to loom in the minds of her heirs and successors, for it will always invoke the question: how can anyone follow in her footsteps? She broke almost every royal record (from the length of her marriage to the number of countries visited). It is hard to envisage anyone in future reigning for seventy years. Nor will any future monarch, surely, enjoy the sort of unquestioning acceptance which greeted her accession. When Elizabeth II was crowned, Britain was a church-going, post-imperial power emerging victorious but battered from war and expecting fresh greatness. Charles III inherited a secular,

Elizabeth II

second-tier, multi-cultural society trying to find its place between Europe and the rest of the world.

Though the new reign would later have to endure serious health setbacks, Charles III was blessed by good fortune in those early days. First, the Queen had died at home peacefully and suddenly, obviating a lingering decline with a protracted, undignified media vigil outside the gates. Yet the heir to the throne was ready, with all his key staff to hand, led by his new private secretary, Sir Clive Alderton. All the years of painstaking funeral planning kicked in instantly. Operation London Bridge was a spectacular success before a global audience. Even the weather was perfect.

From the outset, King Charles's monarchy seemed a paragon of stability compared to the new prime minister, who had taken office just two days before him. Within forty-four days, Liz Truss was out, after a disastrous mini-Budget, and the King was already appointing his second prime minister, Rishi Sunak.

There were two early challenges. The first was a non-stop twelve-week run of negative headlines emanating from a new 'Charles v Diana' strand of the Netflix series *The Crown*, plus a six-part documentary by the Sussexes on their flight from royal life, plus Prince Harry's bracingly candid memoir, *Spare*. The King and the family said nothing, and the polls barely moved. The next test was the Coronation, set for 6 May. Elizabeth II's ceremony in 1953 had been the last imperial Coronation, a replica of her father's crowning in 1937 and of George V's before that. Packed with the nobility, those ceremonies had been conducted entirely by elderly Christian white men. This one would embrace all faiths, all races, both sexes and all sections of society.

With the new reign now firmly established, the King would proceed to embed his new modus operandi. Nine months later,

Legacy: 'Fresh air'

however, two medical bulletins would throw everything into doubt. First, in February 2024, the King announced that he was being treated for cancer (the Palace would not reveal the type but did rule out prostate cancer). Six weeks later, after some lurid and very hurtful online speculation about her disappearance from public view, the Princess of Wales waited until the end of her children's school term to announce that she, too, was undergoing treatment for an unspecified form of cancer. Yet, if 2024 was, in Prince William's words, 'brutal', the monarchy soldiered on – with much heavy lifting from Queen Camilla and the Princess Royal in particular. Both patients responded well to treatment. The King was back to normal duties by the autumn. In January 2025, the Princess announced that she was in remission. The King would continue with his treatment but, by the end of that year, announced that it would soon be reduced.

Of all the questions asked from the start of the reign, the one which recurs most frequently is: what has changed? The short answer is: a lot – and, yet, not much. That is a significant part of Elizabeth II's legacy. The monarchy is an institution which trumpets 'stability and continuity' on its own website (with no mention of 'change'). Set aside, for now, those issues beyond the monarchy's control, and the main alterations have been to do with tone and pace. The court of Elizabeth II was a reflection of her character – dutiful to the memory of her father (for the first part of her reign, at least), pragmatic, reactive and reluctant to interfere on family matters (which would store up problems for the future). The court of Charles III is a reflection of his personality, too. More emotional than his mother, he has sometimes been described as a radical traditionalist and that permeates the way he runs his show.

So visitors from years gone by will still find the same liveried

Elizabeth II

footmen welcoming them into the same state rooms, but they may also sense more of a party atmosphere inside. Guests are now free to roam instead of being pressed into greeting lines and arranged in 'horseshoe clusters', as the late Queen preferred ('They're here to see me but they're here to see each other,' the King likes to say). Those coming to dinner will still find the menus in French but they will be seasonal, local, shorter – and no longer have foie gras on them. Many royal warrants, the badge of honour for those who supply the Royal Household, have continued – from Fortnum & Mason to Bronnley soap – but others have gone (Cadbury's chocolate has lost its crown). Visitors can see places formerly out of bounds. The east wing of Buckingham Palace (behind the balcony), Balmoral Castle and new gardens at Sandringham are open to all. You previously needed an invitation to St James's Palace in order to see where monarchs are proclaimed and royal babies christened. Now everyone can look round, starting and finishing beneath Ralph Heimans' absorbing portrait of Prince Philip shooting the viewer a quizzical sideways look.

For those working inside the Royal Household, the big change has been speed. Long before the King's cancer diagnosis in early 2024, there was a sense of urgency about a seventy-three-year-old King Charles III. When Elizabeth II came to the throne, she waited ten months before speaking to her peoples. In 2022, Charles III was among the crowds and on the airwaves within twenty-four hours.

Court mourning, which lasted for months after the death of George VI, shrank to one week for Elizabeth II. As the oldest new monarch in British history, the King wanted to get on with things. There would be many more of those new-style receptions ('bunfights', as some inside the Palace call them), sometimes two in a day. Presentations of credentials by ambas-

Legacy: 'Fresh air'

sadors used to be done in twos; there would now be three in a morning. Inbound state visits – which involve thousands of people and hundreds of horses – used to happen twice a year. In 2025, there were three. The late Queen would spend long periods at one of her five regular residences for fixed periods of each year. The King likes frequent moves between his considerably larger portfolio of homes (eleven, if the Castle of Mey and his Romanian farmhouse are included). That they have not become a media flashpoint in a time of economic turbulence is largely down to the fact that they all have public use or access. The only exception is Birkhall, the 'marital home' on the Balmoral estate.

The change of reign has seen numerous minor, personal changes. The Queen liked a blanket on her lap even in summer. Charles III likes to lower the temperature wherever he goes. Almost his first remark as monarch at Balmoral, within minutes of becoming King, was: 'Let's get some windows open.'[1] He demands fresh air all year round, whatever the weather. Gone are the dog bowls and ivory tusks which used to greet arrivals through the Buckingham Palace garden entrance. The late Queen disliked rugs at Sandringham, regarding them as a dusty trip hazard. The King likes them and has summoned them up from the cellars.

At some events attended by the King, a small but well-organized protest from the anti-royal pressure group Republic might now appear waving fluorescent 'Not My King' flags and shouting through megaphones. They represent a tiny fraction of any crowd but know how to make a noise and a scene. They rose to prominence at the King's Coronation in May 2023, when eight activists were arrested, though never charged. As the group arrived for the King's 'Scottish Coronation', the Presentation of the Honours of Scotland, two months later, the police allocated the demonstrators a large protest space in a prime position next to St Giles' Cathedral. As a result, chants of 'Not My King' could be heard all through the service. The Secretary of State for Scotland, Alister Jack, claimed that Scotland's nationalist first minster, Humza Yousaf, had sanctioned the anti-royal hecklers: 'I called the chief police officer who said that there had been "operational interference" and that the Scottish government had told them to put the protestors there.'[2] The claim was not denied by Police Scotland, who merely issued a statement saying: 'Safety is our priority.' The noise was somewhat ironic given that Humza Yousaf had been invited to read the first lesson during the service.

This would not have happened under Elizabeth II. Hence, the King's keenness to do more and to do it faster. It is why a certain ruthlessness underpins his court. As previously noted, the issue of family balcony appearances would be a continuous subject for debate during the Queen's reign. For the most part, she liked to have all the family on her balcony and to hell with 'the optics'. The King, however, has now created a two-tier Royal Family. The outward-facing unit on public display is limited to the few who undertake official engagements. The rest are as loved as they have always been but kept out of sight, except on the sort of occasions when any family might gather, like weddings or on Christmas Day. There is no better illustration than photographs of the late Queen's Birthday Parade in 2019, her last 'normal' year before Covid and mobility issues intervened. There are thirty-seven members of the family, including lesser-known Gloucesters and Kents, on public display. Since the accession of Charles III, the number is now just fourteen, including that royal Stakhanovite, Princess Anne, the increasingly busy Duke and Duchess of Edinburgh and the steadfast Duke and Duchess of Gloucester. The only 'non-working' faces

Legacy: 'Fresh air'

on parade will be the three children of the Prince and Princess of Wales plus Princess Anne's husband, Sir Timothy Laurence (a regular quasi-royal presence at so many official engagements anyway). It is all about gently dispelling the (entirely inaccurate) perception of a large, bloated Edwardian-style dynasty of hangers-on. This was equally apparent at the King's Coronation. In 1953, the Mountbattens, Bowes-Lyons and other cousins filled a whole section of Westminster Abbey. In 2023, there were just two of the Bowes-Lyons family and a single Mountbatten. For similar reasons, Queen Camilla has dispensed with the centuries-old tradition of ladies-in-waiting, replacing them with a more informal, occasional system of 'Queen's Companions'. This steeliness is matched by a greater transparency when it comes to official duties and tighter controls in private. So, for the first time, television cameras have captured an Accession Council. The King has helped to produce a feature-length documentary, *Finding Harmony*, exploring his philosophy of living in 'harmony' with nature (for all its earnest, educational content – and the odd harmless revelation, like a Highgrove hen coop called 'Cluckingham Palace' – it was something Elizabeth II would never have done). Medical bulletins are more frank – phrases like 'enlarged prostate' are a world away from the euphemisms like George VI's 'structural changes' – and official briefings are stronger on detail and fact. However, there is fierce opposition to any encroachment on private time. (In 2025, the Prince of Wales won a case against *Paris Match* after it published photographs of a family ski trip.)

As for those who let the monarchy down, the King has shown a surprising capacity for both tolerance and severity. After the death of Elizabeth II, many had expected that the then Duke of York would be ostracized; but the King took a conciliatory approach as he attempted to persuade his brother to downsize,

Elizabeth II

cut costs and move to Frogmore Cottage, former home of the Sussexes. When York refused, the King cut his living allowance. When it transpired that Andrew's account of severing ties with Jeffrey Epstein was manifestly untrue, the King stripped him of all titles and honours and banished him from Royal Lodge to a farmhouse on the Sandringham estate – just as an exhaustive cache of irreparably damning Epstein emails and photos were being released by the US Department of Justice. The decision left other members of the family actually fearing for Andrew's health, especially after one of his final visitors at Royal Lodge found him babbling that being Duke of York had simply been 'an avatar' and that he could now discover 'the real me'. Another visitor was treated to a half-hour lecture from him on how to make the perfect cup of tea. By the spring of 2026, the release of millions more court documents in the USA showed the extent of Epstein's closeness to Andrew, the ex-Duchess and even the couple's daughters. When Andrew – like the disgraced Labour peer, Lord Mandelson – was accused of forwarding confidential UK government reports to Epstein (while he was still UK trade envoy), demands for a full investigation intensified. In February 2026, he was arrested, marking a new low point for the modern monarchy. While it confirmed the King's prescience in defenestrating his brother, it raised more questions about how Andrew had been allowed to behave so badly for so long in the past.

Two things have not changed at all in the new reign. The first is the central importance of the consort. Just as Elizabeth II owed Prince Philip a debt 'greater than we shall ever know' and depended on him in so many ways, so the same has been true of Queen Camilla. The second is the constitutional role. The King's cancer diagnosis in 2024 did not halt a single Red Box – or prime ministerial audience (in the same year, he waved farewell

Legacy: 'Fresh air'

to the Tories and appointed Labour's Sir Keir Starmer as his third prime minister). What has also not changed is the capacity of the monarchy to make Britain interesting and relevant to the rest of the world. Surveys of social attitudes paint a consistent picture (the Palace takes them much more seriously than snap polls). A 2025 Foreign Office case study, conducted in South Korea, showed that 55 per cent of that country viewed the UK favourably, second only to the USA. The biggest influencers behind that sentiment were the Royal Family followed by football.[3]

That is why the British government was quick to send the King on state visits to three key allies: Germany, France and Italy – all fellow G7 nations – in his first three years on the throne. The UK, of course, has no say in the monarch's role as King of fourteen other countries. All his realms wanted a visit, and he started with the two largest. In 2024, he visited Australia. More significant, in May 2025, was a very brief trip to a very worried Canada. Since winning the US election the previous year, Donald Trump had repeatedly expressed a desire to annexe the country, arguing that Canadians were not protecting their borders properly and would be better off if they became the fifty-first state of the USA. As well as threatening tariffs, he had repeatedly mocked Justin Trudeau, the Canadian prime minister, as 'Governor Trudeau'. This went down very badly north of the border. Following a Canadian general election in March, Trudeau's successor, Mark Carney, asked the King of Canada to open the next session of Parliament, a dignified, non-confrontational way of asserting national sovereignty. It was especially challenging for the King since his British prime minister, Sir Keir Starmer, had just invited Mr Trump on a state visit to the UK. However, Charles III could draw on more than half a century of statecraft (he had received his first tutorial on leadership at the White House in 1970, for over an hour, from President Nixon). The King adopted a constructive tone, talking of a 'a new economic and security relationship between Canada and the US rooted in mutual respect', one which would bring 'benefits to both sovereign nations'. The quietly assertive message was clear enough, especially when the King reached his conclusion: 'As the anthem reminds us: "The True North" is indeed strong and free.' A 'speech from the Throne' would not normally generate applause. This one received two standing ovations. The monarch's first trip to Canada as King had left Canadians walking a little taller.

How would President Trump react? Washington would understand that monarchs are not politicians and act on the advice of their prime ministers, yet it had still required very careful calibration. That the King had succeeded was evident four months later, as that US state visit began with a spectacular cavalcade clattering through Windsor Home Park. All state visits are supposed to be equal but some are more equal than others, and this one more so than any. So, while other state visitors to Windsor would be offered a carriage procession through the town, Donald Trump was given a unique one through the park. The Secret Service had never allowed any US president to ride in a public carriage procession on security grounds. However, the King knew that it would mean a great deal to Mr Trump. So he arranged a secure and scenic route through the Home Park without a protestor in sight. It was where the Queen and Ronald Reagan had come riding on Burmese and Centennial in 1982. This time, though, there were 120 horses lined up, along with more than 1,300 troops standing to attention as the presidential helicopter landed next to Windsor's old walled garden. The two heads of state boarded the Irish State Coach; the Queen and First Lady climbed into the Scottish State Coach; and the Prince and Princess of Wales, US Secretary of State Marco Rubio, Treasury Secretary Scott Bessent and US ambassador

Legacy: 'Fresh air'

Warren Stephens, plus the rest of the entourage, were led to a fleet of landaus. Past Prince Albert's dairy and sepulchral Frogmore they rode, up to the top of the Long Walk and through the George IV Gate into the Quadrangle.

There, the largest Guard of Honour ever mounted for a state visit – three companies – awaited the president's inspection. After the welcome lunch and a viewing of the Royal Collection's finest US-related treasures, there was a special Beating Retreat parade by another 200 troops and a Red Arrows flypast. By the end of the day, Mr Trump had been treated to more immaculate drill, trotting and gun salutes than any visitor since the reign of Queen Victoria. All the televisions in the Windsor guest quarters had been tuned into the president's favourite television channels. Staff had even been told which portraits on the walls had a particular Scottish connection, in case it might prove useful, as it did. The President, said one courtier, was delighted when he was shown Thomas Lawrence's portrait of Sir Walter Scott – and then told that his mother would have read Scott's books at school.[4] That evening, in white tie, the president heard the King reflect how far both nations had travelled since the rupture between the two Georges – Washington and his own five-times great-grandfather, George III. 'The ocean may still divide us but in so many other ways, we are now the closest of kin,' the King said. His speech did not actually talk of a 'special relationship' (too boastful, perhaps). President Trump, however, did not hold back. 'The word special does not begin to do it justice,' he declared in the most passionate eulogy from a state visitor for many years. In it, he saluted the King for giving 'everything he's got, to those parts of Britain that are beyond the realm of mere legislation'; he praised Shakespeare, Dickens, Tolkien, Newton, the Magna Carta and the way in which the 'incredible . . . unbelievable . . . lionhearted people

Elizabeth II

of this kingdom defeated Napoleon, unleashed the Industrial Revolution, destroyed slavery and defended civilization in the darkest days of fascism and communism'; he reflected that 'the legal, intellectual, cultural and political traditions of this kingdom have been among the highest achievements of mankind'; he was even a fan of the British Empire, which had 'laid the foundations of law, liberty, free speech and individual rights virtually everywhere... including a place called America.' It was hard to recall the last time that a politician, even a British one, had been so unequivocally generous about the empire. And it came from the leader of the first country to break away from it.

Mr Trump's affection for Britain and, above all, for the monarchy, ran deep. The man who identified and codified the concept of soft power, Harvard professor Joseph Nye, cited the English language and the Royal Family as the UK's two greatest soft power assets.[5] This explained why, three months after that visit, I found myself sitting at breakfast with President Trump at his Florida golf club and then at dinner at his Mar-a-Lago home. I was only there because he had agreed to an informal chat about the monarchy. I had previously interviewed presidents Bill Clinton and George W. Bush about Queen Elizabeth II. Mr Trump, however, was not only the first president to make two state visits to Britain, but retained the distinction of being the last state visitor of Elizabeth II's record-breaking reign. Over seventy years, she had welcomed 112 heads of state, from General de Gaulle to Nelson Mandela, two Popes, three emperors and a Shah. And Mr Trump had been the very last one. He was also an ardent Anglophile, being half-British by descent (his mother was born on the Isle of Lewis). British diplomats often say that, when they are introduced to world leaders, the first thing which invariably comes up is the Royal

Legacy: 'Fresh air'

Family. Mr Trump immediately asked after the King and his health. It was not small talk. 'He's fantastic and he has fought very hard. He's a fighter,' Mr Trump stated. 'We're close. I have a really good relationship with him. Let me just give you the bottom line. He's a great guy and he's grown so much in the last ten years and especially over the last couple of years as King. His fight has shown that.' The King's battle with cancer, he said, was 'something that's taken down a lot of other people'. President Trump looked back very fondly on his recent visit to Windsor. We recalled the fact that he had been the first US president to make two state visits to the UK and the first to enjoy a carriage procession. His breakfast companions, Christopher Ruddy, founder of the Newsmax media empire, and peace envoy Steve Witkoff, had both been guests at the Windsor state banquet too. Ruddy was also at the Queen's state banquet for Mr Trump in 2019. British hospitality had impressed, not least the sight of the table in St George's Hall laid out end to end for 160 guests. Mr Trump joked that his new White House ballroom would be considerably bigger. He was well aware that the King had gone the extra mile to make his welcome an exceptional one. 'He did make it a great state visit,' he recalled. I observed that his speech had been one which no British politician would make these days. 'It came from the heart, right,' he shrugged.

The president had been much impressed by the Waleses. In his Windsor speech, he had praised the King's 'remarkable son'. Shortly after being re-elected in 2024, Mr Trump had met Prince William in Paris at the reopening of the Cathedral of Notre Dame – indeed, the president-elect had travelled to meet the Prince, not the other way round. Their talk had overrun for so long that the Élysée Palace had rung up the British Embassy to see when Mr Trump would be joining President Macron for dinner. Now, the president's mind was on the Princess of Wales. 'How is the Princess doing?' he asked. He had been impressed by her dedication to duty both before and after her cancer diagnosis became known in March 2024. 'She performed so incredibly because that's a very tough position, and you couldn't do better than the way she did,' he reflected. 'And then she became ill and she didn't want to talk about it and wanted to keep it private. And they were so nasty to her – saying that there was something wrong with her.' He shook his head, recalling the spiteful online gossip following her absence from the public gaze in early 2024, prior to her remarkable message to the world, asking for understanding and private time. 'And once they'd found out, she went on.' He wondered about the delay in explaining the situation. 'Why didn't she want people to know?' he asked. 'Were certain people embarrassed?' I explained that the Princess's priority, as ever, was her children and that she had wanted to tell them at the appropriate moment. 'I see. She wanted to wait,' he nodded.

He would not be drawn on prevailing Royal Family dramas, preferring to dwell on the late Queen. Former foreign secretary Jeremy Hunt recalled that, during Mr Trump's visits in 2018 and 2019, the president had behaved impeccably out of respect for the Queen, so much so that he abandoned his social media habit for the entire duration of his time on British soil, as he did in 2025. It was the same now. As noted earlier, he had been very impressed by her steadfast reluctance to be drawn on her 'favourite' presidents and prime ministers. 'I had a really good relationship with her,' he said. 'She was unbelievable and she was ninety-five and she called me a lot.' He was still miffed and rather baffled about an old news report that he had somehow upset the Queen, though he had been assured (via British diplomats) that the opposite was true. 'I'd call her. I liked her,' he told me, 'and she liked me.' This was indeed the case, according to royal staff, who still groan whenever the 2018 story of 'Trump walking in front of the Queen' is recycled, because the president had been doing exactly what he was supposed to do. One senior member of her staff said that she had found him 'charming, tall, tanned, big, courteous, mid-century – not at all how he had been portrayed'. One thing which had particularly struck the late Queen about Mr Trump, according to aides, was his energy, in contrast to the forty-sixth president. Whereas Joe Biden had required the lift during his visit to Windsor in 2021, Mr Trump, said the staffer, had 'bounced' up and down the stairs at both Windsor and the Palace.[6] I asked the president if he remembered all the stairs. 'I had no choice,' he said, 'and there are a lot of stairs at Windsor and the Palace!'

During my visit, I found that all those around the president shared his views on the monarchy. One senior White House aide expressed incredulity that anyone would contemplate getting rid of the first thing most people think about when they think of Britain: 'Are they mad?' Several were puzzled by Britain's reluctance to talk up the benefits of empire, as the president had done at Windsor.

Mr Trump explained that he had wanted a permanent reminder of the Queen and had given the matter a great deal of thought. He had recently acquired a signed reproduction of the last official portrait of Elizabeth II (she had sat for more than 200 during her lifetime). The Polish-British artist Basia Kaczmarowska-Hamilton had painted her at Windsor just four months before her death (the artist had even discussed Mr Trump with the Queen during the session and remembered the monarch remarking that she had enjoyed meeting him). The original painting had been destined for London's Polish Institute, but the Queen had liked it so much that she asked if she could keep it, and it still hangs at Windsor Castle. A quality reproduction went to the institute, and the artist gave another one to Mr Trump when painting his portrait. He had spent a long time discussing with his staff and had only just decided where best to hang it. 'She was so great. I wanted to hang her picture in a room where there is no one else on the wall. You must take a look,' he said. 'I hope you approve.' Later, I looked around Mar-a-Lago, a palatial pink waterfront mansion which dates back to the same year that the late Queen was born. It was built by the richest woman in America at the time, Marjorie Merriweather Post, who wanted a Spanish-Moorish exterior and an interior modelled on an Italian palazzo. After her death, Mr Trump bought it in 1985, turned one wing into the family home and converted the rest into a private members' club. Many of the walls were lined with marble, tapestries or mirrors. The only portraits appeared to be in the bar area, including one of Mr Trump and another of Mrs Post. There was no sign of the Queen in there. I went through to the palatial dining room, Mr Trump's venue for summit meetings. Modelled on Rome's Chigi Palace, this was decorated with frescoes of pastoral and nautical scenes painted by Florentine artists. And there she was. In a neutral patch of the main fresco, high on the wall above a painting of a medieval ship, was the Queen, in pink. Having put a bust of Winston Churchill in his White House Oval Office, Mr Trump now had Elizabeth II in pride of place in his house.

During another conversation, the president asked what I thought of his quest to annexe Greenland. 'Do you think I should go to war with Denmark over Greenland?' he asked mischievously. 'I hear they went from one dog sled to two.' I replied that this would probably destroy NATO and, while we were on the subject, could he please leave Canada alone, too. It had been a

Legacy: 'Fresh air'

staunch ally through history, a gallant D-Day partner and attempting to acquire it would undoubtedly make the King of Canada unhappy. That prompted a slight pause. 'Do they still recognize the King? Or have they stopped that?' he wondered. I said that they did indeed still recognize him as head of state. 'But they have these terrible politicians. They're nice to my face and then they say bad things behind my back,' he replied, adding that the cold weather meant that most Canadians lived in the far south and were only just over the US border anyway. 'The problem is some guy drew that straight line to make a border. He should just have drawn it fifty miles further north and then there wouldn't be a problem.' However, Mr Trump conceded that some things might be beyond even him during the rest of his presidency. 'I suppose the Canadians have got two hundred years of history and all that "Oh, Canada" thing,' he reflected. 'You can't deal with that in three and a half years. I guess it's not going to happen!' This was the closest I had heard to an acknowledgement that, as long as Canada had the King, Mr Trump was not going to usurp him. As he left for his next appointment, I handed him a copy of my biography of the King. 'I hope you gave him good reviews,' he said. 'He's a fantastic guy.'

There could be no doubting the esteem in which the late Queen was held by the most powerful man in the world. He had also voiced the highest praise for her son and heir, who appeared to be the primary reason why he was no longer sabre-rattling at Canada. It might be a very bizarre state of geopolitical affairs. By any metric, however, this was soft power beyond the grasp of any politician and has to be a central element of any assessment of the legacy of Elizabeth II. Mr Trump would continue to test the transatlantic alliance to the limit – not least in January 2026 with his absurd claim that NATO allies including Britain had 'stayed a little back' from

Elizabeth II

the Afghan frontline. He later rescinded the claim, though only with regard to Britain (after royal 'concerns' had been relayed via diplomatic channels).[7] As all European nations and other NATO allies sought to navigate this very uncertain and unsettled outlook, the UK and its politicians did still appear to retain one unique and valuable diplomatic tool. Whatever else the monarchy's critics might say, it remained hard to question its continued relevance.

Elizabeth II's authority had remained undiminished to the very end. That was down to her strength of character and also to the fact that Prince Charles had remained dutifully supportive. There had been no hint of restlessness, let alone impatience. Nor is Prince William keen to trade up a day sooner than he needs to. He voiced his own thoughts about his future reign, telling Canadian actor Eugene Levy in the autumn of 2025 that 'change is on my agenda'.[8] In an unusual interview, the first to feature a future King arriving on an electric scooter and drinking cider in a pub, the forty-three-year-old Prince used the word 'change' six times. Yet those close to him suggest that the 'changes' he has in mind are closer to tweaks than upheavals – trimming the length of certain ceremonies, perhaps, or dispensing with certain royal residences. On becoming Prince of Wales, he had not only ruled out an investiture, like his father's in 1969, but even a church service. A confidential post-accession plan had been drawn up by Prince Charles's staff for Prince William to be welcomed to his new role at an event at St David's Cathedral in West Wales. The government had gone as far as consulting the Welsh nationalist party, Plaid Cymru, to ensure there would be no objection. However, the idea never progressed beyond the desk of Prince William. 'It wasn't ever something that he wanted to do,' said one of his team.[9]

Legacy: 'Fresh air'

From time to time, there have been suggestions that he is a hardliner. Some accounts suggested that he was the driving force behind his Uncle Andrew being stripped of his titles and honours and banished to a house on the Sandringham estate. One friend of the former Yorks, however, reported that on the night they lost their titles, Andrew had been very touched when Prince William was one of the few people to call to offer condolences.

The heir to the throne is less of a traditionalist than his father but he is less of a radical, too. The King is the one who still enjoys sitting up writing letters into the night whereas Prince William's idea of a fun evening, says one of his team, is to 'sit down with the Princess in front of *The Traitors*'.[10] When Prince Charles reached forty-three, he had already picked multiple quarrels with the Establishment over gritty social issues and had earned a complaint from Margaret Thatcher. Prince William has done nothing of the sort. Two things are worthy of note, though. First, in that interview with Eugene Levy, Prince William spoke pointedly of his bond with his grandmother (Prince Harry, too, often speaks of a 'special relationship' with the late Queen).[11] Second, it has now become a Prince William 'tradition' to organize a special engagement on the anniversary of the late Queen's death (in 2025, it was a day out at the Women's Institute, one of her favourite organizations). Just as Prince Charles would so often look to his grandmother for guidance, so Prince William is doing the same.

One of the most important of all of the lessons to be learned from Elizabeth II is that she 'normalized' being monarch without sacrificing her majesty. History shows an almost unbroken line of sovereigns quarrelling with their predecessors or their successors (sometimes both). Unlike those who came before her, Elizabeth II loved – and was loved by – her father

Elizabeth II

and her son. She was not expected to defend an empire but to manage what was left of one and dismantle it amicably. Furthermore, crucially, she was ready. Just over halfway through her reign, she reflected on the key to being a monarch. 'I have a feeling that in the end, probably, that training is the answer to a great many things,' she told Eddie Mirzoeff in 1991. 'You can do a lot if you're properly trained. And I hope I have been.'[12] Indeed she had.

Acknowledgements

I am most grateful to His Majesty The King and to Her Late Majesty Queen Elizabeth II for access, over several years, to material in the Royal Archives which has been invaluable in writing this book. I should also like to thank all those members of the Royal Family who have talked to me for books, articles and documentaries over the course of three decades, starting with His Late Royal Highness The Duke of Edinburgh back in October 1994. Since then, I have been fortunate to interview all the senior members of the family, some of them several times, including His Majesty (as Prince of Wales), Her Majesty (as Duchess of Cornwall), the Princess Royal and the Duchess of Edinburgh (as Countess of Wessex). I am similarly grateful to all the past and present members of the Royal Household who have shared so much of their time and wisdom for no other reason than that they have wanted the story of the modern monarchy to be told fairly and accurately. Some of them remain very much at the heart of current royal operations, while others are enjoying retirement or new careers. A few, sadly, are no longer with us. Equally, I am most grateful for the reflections of all those others who have helped me with previous books and films over the years. They include several friends of the family and many people who have worked with

Elizabeth II

the monarchy in various capacities – not least politicians, diplomats, members of the Armed Forces, writers and filmmakers. All have been acknowledged previously, but this book builds on that body of knowledge, and I remain indebted to all of you.

Since my previous biography of Elizabeth II, written during her lifetime, I have been fortunate to speak to many people who had important new contributions on her final years and on what has happened since. Among those who spoke to me for this book have been the President of the United States, Donald Trump; former Lord Chamberlain Earl Peel; former prime minister Lord Cameron; and former Cabinet ministers Sir Jacob Rees-Mogg, Lord Jack of Courance and Sir Robert Buckland, along with numerous others who have spoken to me privately. My thanks to them all.

I should particularly like to acknowledge the staff of both the Buckingham Palace Press Office and the Royal Archives for doing their best to accommodate my requests in the course of writing this book and those before it. I would also like to thank Barbara Kaczmarowska-Hamilton (known to many as Basia Hamilton), for her kind permission to reproduce her final portrait of Elizabeth II.

For their help in ways too numerous to mention but greatly appreciated, I remain extremely grateful to Sir Rodney and Lady [Sandra] Williams, Lord Janvrin, Samantha Cohen, Christopher Ruddy, Sir William Heseltine, Lord Godson, the Duke of Norfolk, Major General Alastair Bruce of Crionach, Paul Dacre, Simon Heffer, Charles Moore, Will Moore, Garrison Sergeant Major 'Vern' Stokes, Wesley Kerr, Andy Goodsir, Dr David Torrance, Gary Gibbon, Charles Spicer, Ian and Natalie Livingstone, Catherine Ostler, Albert Read, Lord Bethell, Baroness Finn, Sarah Vine, Santa Sebag-Montefiore, Lady [Susan] Roberts, the Duke and Duchess of Beaufort, Anne

Acknowledgements

Somerset, Dr Christopher and Emily Moran, Algy and Blondel Cluff, Sir Francis and Lady Brooke, Patricia Treble, Vere Harmsworth, Dr Amanda Foreman, Jonathan Barton, Katherine and Con Coughlin, Sir Lloyd Dorfman, Zaki Cooper, Nick Loughran, Mike Merritt, James Sproule, Lord Howell, Chris and Natasha Owen, Dan and Todd Daley, Sir Jock Slater, Commodore Anthony Morrow, Octavius and Baroness [Joanne] Black, Jess Pulay, Victor Sebestyen, Nick Boles, Graham Defries, Camilla and Willie Gray Muir, Damian and Pippa Riley-Smith, Mark Foster-Brown, Geoffrey and Jane Gestetner, Rory and Nicky Darling, William Shawcross, Peter Hennessy, Hugo Vickers, Valentine Low, Kate Mansey, Emily Benn, Nicholas Witchell, Simon Perry, Sally Bedell-Smith, Danica Kirka, Ramon Marks, Claire Popplewell, Julia Mizen, David McDonough, John Bridcut, Ralph Isham, Quentin Letts, Marc Roche, Lord Bilimoria, Rawah Badrawi, Emma Hill, James and Tamsin Bruce-Gardyne, Lizzie Pitman, Rosie Glazebrook, Andrew Pierce, Russell Tanguay, Mark Palmer, Jan Moir, Jane Fryer, Guy Adams, Tom Leonard, James Pembroke, Harry Mount, Douglas Murray, Cindy Harvey, John-Paul Evans, Henry Dallal, David Oldroyd-Bolt, George Trefgarne, Dr Annette Prandzioch, Deborah Bonetti, Antonello Guerrera, Natalia Augias, John Bridcut, Nick Kent, Faye Hamilton, Orson Fry and Jack Kelly.

No one has been more patient than the publishing team at Macmillan, led by my editor, Ingrid Connell, together with Rosa Watmough and Kimberley Nyamhondera; also Holly Sheldrake, Lindsay Nash, Neil Lang, Victoria Denne, Ross Jamieson and Caroline Jones. My thanks, too, to Jessica Case and Clairborne Hancock at Pegasus Books in the USA. I am extremely thankful to have as my agent Georgina Capel, together with Simon Shaps, Irene Baldoni, Polly Halladay, Rachel Conway and the rest of the team at Georgina Capel Associates who are always

Elizabeth II

there (even at the most antisocial times) with sound advice and a plan of action. Once again, it has been a pleasure to record the audio version of this book with Nicholas Jones and his team at Strathmore Publishing.

Like all my books and documentaries, this has been written in parallel with the job of roving journalist and broadcaster. As a reporter, my work has always depended to a great extent on the photographers with whom I have been fortunate to work. My thanks to them all, especially Murray Sanders (whose book, *Live Aid Relived*, is a study of the resourcefulness of a great photographer) and Ian Jones, with whom I covered some of the most important royal tours of modern times. His pictures have long outlasted the words. My thanks, too, to Kirsten Sanders and Licky Jones for their forbearance. I am always fortunate to be able to draw on the thoughts of *Daily Mail* colleagues Richard Kay, Rebecca English, Richard Eden and Sam Greenhill on all things royal, along with the editorial support of Ted Verity, Liz Hunt, Andrew Morrod, Oliver Thring, Andrew Yates, Dominic Midgley, Clara Gaspar, Lily Amory, Nick Pyke, Ulla Kloster, Peter Knight, Charlotte Ambrose, Sue Connolly, Alex Bannister and Tara Eude. I am equally thankful to Professor Kate Williams, my podcasting co-presenter of *Queens, Kings & Dastardly Things*, a constant source of fresh royal perspectives, and to Ben Devlin and Bella Soames who do their best (mostly successfully) to keep us both on track and on time.

Having been asked to distil one of the one most astonishing lives in modern history into a book that is 'fresh', 'personal', 'accessible' and 'authoritative', there have been so many occasions when I have been grateful for the triumviral wisdom of Simon Sebag-Montefiore, Andrew Roberts and Michael Gove. Likewise, I am, once again, indebted to Melanie Johnson for

Acknowledgements

her astute editorial observations and unfailing eye for the *mot juste* (or absence of one). This book is all the better as a result. Equally invaluable has been the help of my sister, Harriet Hewitson, on so many fronts, not least in mastering the social media side of things and having a solution to almost any seemingly insurmountable problem.

None of this could have happened without the love and support of my wife, Diana. As ever, writing a book encroaches greatly on time which should be spent with her and with our children, Matilda, Phoebe and Hal. I cannot thank them enough. We have been greatly aided by the wider family, especially Richard and Dinah Hardman, Johnny Hewitson, Hugo and Victoria Hardman, Victoria and Justin Zawoda, Fleur and Alex Evans, Michael Cowley and Richard and Amanda Cowley. Always there, uncomplainingly ready to take up the slack at so many moments ever since I started writing my first book, twenty years ago, has been Diana's mother, Marion Cowley. This book is dedicated to her, with love and heartfelt thanks.

Notes

CHAPTER ONE: A PERSONAL VIEW: 'OH, REALLY?'

1. Interview with author; Robert Hardman, *Our Queen* (Arrow, 2012), p. 38.
2. *Elizabeth at 90*, BBC/John Bridcut, 2016.
3. Interview with author.
4. Private information.
5. Private information; Robert Hardman, *Queen of Our Times: The Life of Elizabeth II, 1926–2022* (Macmillan, 2022), p. 604.
6. Interview with author.
7. Interview with author.
8. Interview with author.
9. Interview with author; *Our Queen*, p. 64.
10. Private information.
11. Interview with author.
12. Robert Lacey, *Royal* (Little, Brown, 2002), p. 399.
13. Private information.
14. Interview with author; Robert Hardman, *Queen of Our Times*, p. 449.
15. Churchill Archives/Lascelles to wife, 30 April 1947.
16. Private information.
17. Interview with author; Robert Hardman, *Queen of the World* (Century, 2018), p. 204.
18. Interview with author.
19. Graham Turner, *Elizabeth: The Woman and the Queen* (Macmillan, 2002), p. 70.
20. Tony Blair, *A Journey* (Hutchinson, 2010), Kindle edition.
21. Interview with author.
22. Private information.

Elizabeth II

23 Interview with author.
24 Private information.
25 Private information.
26 Ingrid Seward, *Majesty* magazine, September 2025.
27 Turner, *Elizabeth*, p. 70.
28 Private information.
29 Interview with author.
30 *Hansard*, 7 March 2012.
31 Gresham lecture, 'The Queen at 90', 18 April 2016.
32 Private information.
33 Interview with author.
34 Interview with author.
35 Marion Crawford, *The Little Princesses* (Orion, 2011), p. 168.
36 Turner, *Elizabeth*, p. 5.
37 Private information; *Queen of Our Times*, p. 546.
38 Elizabeth Longford, *Elizabeth R* (Weidenfeld & Nicolson, 1983), quoted in Turner, *Elizabeth*, p. 15.
39 Interview with author.
40 Interview with author.
41 Interview with author.
42 Interview with author.
43 *Hansard*, 6/8 November 1961.
44 Ben Pimlott, *The Queen: Elizabeth II and the Monarchy* (HarperCollins, 1996), p. 454.
45 Hardman, *Queen of the World*, pp. 308–9.
46 Hardman, *Our Queen*, p. 60.
47 Interview with author.
48 Interview with author.
49 Interview with author.

CHAPTER TWO (1926-39): NUMBER THREE

1 Simon Heffer (ed.), *Henry 'Chips' Channon: The Diaries (Volume 1): 1918-38* (Hutchinson, 2021), 21 April 1926.
2 William Shawcross, *Queen Elizabeth the Queen Mother* (Pan, 2010; Kindle edition), p. 322.
3 Duff Hart-Davis (ed.), *King's Counsellor: Abdication and War - The Diaries of Sir Alan Lascelles*, p. 105.

Notes

4 Ibid.
5 Marion Crawford, *The Little Princesses* (Orion, 2011), p. 24.
6 Ibid., p. 25.
7 Kenneth Rose, *King George V* (Papermac, 1984), p. 392.
8 Philip Ziegler, *King Edward VIII: A Biography* (HarperCollins, 2012), p. 209.
9 Ibid.
10 *British Medical Journal*, May 1994
11 Crawford, *The Little Princesses*, p. 53.
12 Ibid., p. 59.
13 John W. Wheeler-Bennett, *King George VI: His Life and Reign* (Macmillan, 1958), p. 286.
14 Private information.
15 Crawford, *The Little Princesses*, p. 73.
16 Ibid., p. 74.
17 Shawcross, *Queen Elizabeth the Queen Mother* (Kindle edition), p. 497.
18 RA/QEII/PRIV/PERS; Pam Clark, Julie Crocker, Allison Derrett, Laura Hobbs and Jill Kelsey, *Treasures from the Royal Archives* (Royal Collection Trust, 2014), pp. 38–9.
19 Kenneth Rose, *The Journals*, Vol. II (Weidenfeld & Nicolson, 2019), p. 27.
20 Shawcross, *Queen Elizabeth the Queen Mother* (Kindle edition), p. 596.
21 Crawford, *The Little Princesses*, p. 98.
22 Wheeler-Bennett, *King George VI*, p. 749.
23 Crawford, *The Little Princesses*, p. 115.
24 RA/GVI/PRIV/DIARY/WAR King's War Diary, 7 October 1939.
25 Interview with author; Robert Hardman, *Queen of Our Times: The Life of Elizabeth II, 1926–2022* (Macmillan, 2022), p. 345.
26 *Daily Mail*, 11 March 2016.

CHAPTER THREE (1939–47): 'PEOPLE WILL SAY WE'RE IN LOVE'

1 Marion Crawford, *The Little Princesses* (Orion, 2011), p. 124.
2 RA/GVI/PRIV/DIARY/WAR King's War Diary, 13 May 1940.
3 *Desert Island Discs*, BBC, 1981.

Elizabeth II

4   William Shawcross, *Queen Elizabeth the Queen Mother* (Pan, 2010; Kindle edition), p. 643.
5   Crawford, *The Little Princesses*, p. 137.
6   King's War Diary, 13 September 1940.
7   Ibid., 19 September 1940.
8   Crawford, *The Little Princesses*, p. 133.
9   Wartime broadcast, 1940. Accessed via www.royal.uk.
10 Private information.
11 Alathea Fitzalan Howard, *The Windsor Diaries 1940–45* (Hodder & Stoughton, 2020), 6 March 1941.
12 King's War Diary, 18/19/20 October 1941.
13 Fitzalan Howard, *The Windsor Diaries*, 15 November 1941.
14 Shawcross, *Queen Elizabeth the Queen Mother* (Kindle edition), p. 692.
15 Fitzalan Howard, *The Windsor Diaries*, 18 December 1943.
16 Crawford, *The Little Princesses*, p. 160.
17 Basil Boothroyd, *Philip: An Informal Biography* (Longman, 1971), p. 150.
18 Duff Hart-Davis (ed.), *King's Counsellor: Abdication and War – The Diaries of Sir Alan Lascelles*, p.189.
19 Shawcross, *Queen Elizabeth the Queen Mother* (Kindle edition), p. 720.
20 John W. Wheeler-Bennett, *King George VI: His Life and Reign* (Macmillan, 1958), p. 602.
21 Shawcross, *Queen Elizabeth the Queen Mother* (Kindle edition), p. 726.
22 Fitzalan Howard, *The Windsor Diaries*, 15 February 1945.
23 Margaret Rhodes, *The Final Curtsey* (Umbria, 2011), p. 69.
24 King's War Diary, 8 May 1945.
25 RA GVI/PRIV/DIARY/1945, 26 July 1945.
26 Duff Hart-Davis (ed.), *King's Counsellor*, p. 342.
27 King's War Diary, 21 May 1945.
28 Crawford, *The Little Princesses*, p. 173.
29 Boothroyd, *Philip: An Informal Biography*, p. 24.
30 Shawcross, *Queen Elizabeth the Queen Mother* (Kindle edition), p. 778.
31 Interview with author.
32 Crawford, *The Little Princesses*, p. 197.
33 RA/F&V/VISOV/SA/1947, 13 April 1947.

Notes

34 Lascelles' letter to Dermot Morrah, 10 March 1947, Churchill Archives Centre; Robert Hardman, *Queen of Our Times* (Macmillan, 2022), p. 90.
35 Ibid.
36 Lascelles' papers, 23 April 1947, Churchill Archives Centre; Hardman, *Queen of Our Times*, p. 91.
37 Crawford, *The Little Princesses*, p. 184.

CHAPTER FOUR (1947-52): DUCHESS DAYS

1 William Shawcross, *Queen Elizabeth the Queen Mother* (Pan, 2010; Kindle edition), p. 783.
2 Ibid.
3 Ibid., p. 784.
4 *Daily Express*, 10 September 2012.
5 Michael Thornton, *The Daily Telegraph*, 25 September 2012.
6 Ibid.
7 Gyles Brandreth, *Philip: The Final Portrait* (Coronet, 2021), pp. 298-9.
8 Gyles Brandreth, *Elizabeth: An Intimate Portrait* (Penguin Michael Joseph, 2022; Kindle edition), p. 411.
9 Private information.
10 Tim Heald, *Philip: A Portrait of the Duke of Edinburgh* (Hodder & Stoughton, 1991), p. 113.
11 Richard Mead, *General 'Boy': The Life of Lieutenant General Sir Frederick Browning* (Pen & Sword Military, 2017), p. 343.
12 Marion Crawford, *The Little Princesses* (Orion, 2011), p. 209.
13 Ibid., p. 208.
14 Cynthia Jebb's diaries, Churchill Archive Centre, Churchill College, Cambridge, 19 February 1949.
15 Ibid.
16 Hugo Vickers, *Elizabeth, the Queen Mother* (Hutchinson, 2005), p. 433.
17 Robert Lacey, *Royal: Her Majesty Queen Elizabeth II* (Little, Brown, 2002), p. 161.
18 John Wheeler-Bennett, *King George VI: His Life and Reign* (Macmillan, 1958), p. 294.
19 Shawcross, *Queen Elizabeth the Queen Mother* (Kindle edition), p. 805.

Elizabeth II

20 Ben Pimlott, *The Queen: Elizabeth II and the Monarchy* (HarperCollins, 1996), p. 171.
21 Private information.
22 *Daily Mail*, 4 February 1952.
23 Interview with author.
24 Jim Corbett, *Tree Tops* (Oxford University Press, 1955), pp. 22–3.
25 Shawcross, *Queen Elizabeth the Queen Mother* (Kindle edition), p. 813.
26 William Shawcross, *Queen and Country* (BBC Books, 2002), p. 16.
27 Shawcross, *Queen Elizabeth the Queen Mother* (Kindle edition), p. 814.
28 Pimlott, *The Queen*, p. 176.
29 Pimlott, *The Queen*, p. 179.

CHAPTER FIVE (1952–55): A RELUCTANT GLORIANA

1 Ben Pimlott, *The Queen: Elizabeth II and the Monarchy* (HarperCollins, 1996), p. 179.
2 Gyles Brandreth, *Elizabeth: An Intimate Portrait* (Penguin Michael Joseph, 2022; Kindle edition), p. 323.
3 Andrew Roberts, *Churchill: Walking with Destiny* (Allen Lane, 2018), p. 929.
4 Pimlott, *The Queen*, p. 180.
5 Sarah Bradford, *Elizabeth: A Biography of Her Majesty the Queen* (William Heinemann, 1996), p. 168.
6 Interview with Peter Hennessy for *What Has Become of Us*, Channel 4, 1994.
7 William Shawcross, *Queen Elizabeth the Queen Mother* (Pan, 2010; Kindle edition), p. 661.
8 Jock Colville, *The Fringes of Power: Downing Street Diaries 1939–1955* (Weidenfeld & Nicolson, 2004); quoted in Pimlott, *The Queen*, p. 184.
9 Tim Heald, *Philip: A Portrait of the Duke of Edinburgh* (Hodder & Stoughton, 1991), p. 12.
10 Valentine Low, *Courtiers* (Headline, 2022), p. 106.
11 Shawcross, *Queen Elizabeth the Queen Mother* (Kindle edition), p. 728.

Notes

12 Gyles Brandreth, *Philip and Elizabeth: Portrait of a Marriage* (Century, 2004), p. 209.
13 PREM 11/320, 3 April 1952.
14 BBC website, 30 May 2013.
15 Coronation Joint Committee (CJC) minutes, 7 July 1952.
16 PREM 11/34, 7 July 1952.
17 *The Daily Telegraph*, 24 October 1952.
18 PREM 11/34 Memo, 24 October 1952.
19 RA/F&V/COR/1953.
20 *Queen of the World*, Oxford Films/ITV, 2018.
21 Richard Johnstone-Bryden, *The Royal Yacht* Britannia*: The Official History* (Conway Maritime Press, 2003) p. 33.
22 Author interview with former private secretary.

CHAPTER SIX (1955–60): RIFTS

1 Ben Pimlott, *The Queen: Elizabeth II and the Monarchy* (HarperCollins, 1996), p. 186.
2 Andrew Roberts, *Churchill: Walking with Destiny* (Allen Lane, 2018), p. 948.
3 Pimlott, *The Queen*, p. 230.
4 Duff Hart-Davis (ed.), *King's Counsellor: Abdication and War – The Diaries of Sir Alan Lascelles*, p. 430.
5 PREM 11/1565.
6 Sarah Bradford, *Elizabeth: A Biography of Her Majesty the Queen* (William Heinemann, 1996), p. 209.
7 Interview with author.
8 Interview with Peter Hennessy for *What Has Become of Us*, Channel 4, 1994.
9 Interview with author.
10 Interview with author.
11 Interview with author; Robert Hardman, *Queen of Our Times: The Life of Elizabeth II, 1926–2022* (Macmillan, 2022), p. 145.
12 *Baltimore Sun*, 8 February 1957.
13 Gyles Brandreth, *Elizabeth: An Intimate Portrait* (Penguin Michael Joseph, 2022; Kindle edition), p. 394.
14 Interview with author.

Elizabeth II

CHAPTER SEVEN (1960-69): MOUNTBATTEN-WINDSOR

1. Ben Pimlott, *The Queen: Elizabeth II and the Monarchy* (HarperCollins, 1996), p. 287.
2. Michael Farebrother's letter to his father, 2 January 1956.
3. Harold Macmillan, *Pointing the Way* (Macmillan, 1972), p. 472.
4. Interview with Peter Hennessy for *What Has Become of Us*, Channel 4, 1994.
5. BBC, 14 January 2025.
6. Sarah Bradford, *Elizabeth: A Biography of Her Majesty the Queen* (William Heinemann, 1996), p. 325.
7. Interview with author.
8. FO 371/183178.
9. Interview with Hennessy, Channel 4, 1994.
10. Interview with author.
11. Interview with author.
12. Interview with author.
13. Interview with author.
14. Private information.

CHAPTER EIGHT (1970-79): WALKABOUTS AND MONSTERS

1. Interview with author.
2. *Daily Mail*, 13 March 1970.
3. FCO 57/405, 28 April 1972.
4. PREM 15/1880.
5. Interview with Peter Hennessy for *What Has Become of Us*, Channel 4, 1994.
6. Interview with author.
7. *The Guardian*, 10 November 1969.
8. *Hansard*, 14 December 1971.
9. Michael Bloch, *The Secret File of the Duke of Windsor* (Corgi, 1989) p. 301-2, quoted in Robert Hardman, *Queen of the World* (Century, 2018), p. 288.
10. Sarah Bradford, *Elizabeth: A Biography of Her Majesty the Queen* (William Heinemann, 1996), p. 412.
11. Interview with author.

Notes

12 Interview with author.
13 Ben Pimlott, *The Queen: Elizabeth II and the Monarchy* (HarperCollins, 1996), p. 420.
14 Interview with author.
15 Interview with author.
16 Arnold Smith, *Stitches in Time: The Commonwealth in World Politics* (General Publishing, 1981), p. 248.
17 Interview with author; Robert Hardman, *Our Queen* (Arrow, 2012), p. 137.
18 Interview with author.
19 Interview with author.
20 Interview with author.
21 PREM 16/1349
22 Ibid.
23 Interview with author.
24 Interview with author.
25 *Reuters*, 13 May 1991.
26 Interview with author.
27 Interview with author; Robert Hardman, *Queen of Our Times: The Life of Elizabeth II, 1926-2022* (Macmillan, 2022), p. 260.
28 Interview with author; Hardman, *Queen of the World*, p. 104.
29 *Daily Mail*, 3 March 1979.
30 Interview with author; Hardman, *Queen of the World*, p. 52.

CHAPTER NINE (1979-82): 'DON'T LOOK BACK'

1 Elizabeth Longford, *Elizabeth R* (Weidenfeld & Nicolson, 1983), pp. 278-9.
2 Interview with Peter Hennessy for *What Has Become of Us*, Channel 4, 1994.
3 Ibid.
4 Interview with author; Robert Hardman, *Queen of Our Times: The Life of Elizabeth II, 1926-2022* (Macmillan, 2022), p. 266.
5 Interview with author.
6 Hardman, *Queen of Our Times*, p. 266.
7 Keating State Library talk, 3 November 2025.
8 Interview with author; Hardman, *Queen of Our Times*, p. 176.
9 Andrew Marr, *The Diamond Queen* (Macmillan, 2011), p. 289.

Elizabeth II

10 Interview with author.
11 Interview with author.
12 Interview with author.
13 Interview with author; Hardman, *Queen of Our Times*, p. 323.
14 Charles Moore, *Margaret Thatcher: The Authorized Biography*, Vol. II, *Everything She Wants* (Allen Lane, 2016), p. 577.
15 Interview with author.
16 *Daily Mail*, 3 July 1979.
17 Arnold Smith, *Stitches in Time: The Commonwealth in World Politics* (General Publishing, 1981), p. 270.
18 FCO 105/26; Robert Hardman, *Queen of the World* (Century, 2018), p. 336.
19 BBC Radio 5, 5 June 2012.
20 Andrew Morton, *Diana: Her True Story – In Her Own Words* (Michael O'Mara Books, 1992), p. 51.
21 *Daily Telegraph*, 4 February 2024.
22 Interview with author.
23 *Daily Mail*, 29 October 1980.
24 Interview with author.
25 Interview with author.
26 Hardman, *Queen of Our Times*, p. 278.
27 Interview with author.
28 Graham Turner, *Elizabeth: The Woman and the Queen* (Macmillan, 2002), p. 133.
29 Private information.
30 Turner, *Elizabeth*, p. 134.
31 Robert Hardman, *Our Queen* (Arrow, 2012), p. 56.
32 Interview with author.
33 Private information.
34 *Elizabeth at 90*, BBC/John Bridcut, 2016.
35 Morton, *Diana: Her True Story*, p. 63.
36 Interview with author; Hardman, *Our Queen*, p. 239.
37 FCO 82/1217.
38 William Shawcross, *Queen and Country* (BBC Worldwide, 2002), p. 195.
39 Morton, *Diana: Her True Story*, p. 71.
40 Sarah Bradford, *Elizabeth: A Biography of Her Majesty the Queen* (William Heinemann, 1996), p. 447.

Notes

41 Douglas Hurd, *Elizabeth II* (Penguin, 2018), p. 48.
42 Interview with author; Hardman, *Queen of Our Times*. p. 292.

CHAPTER TEN (1983-91): 'LET'S HAVE HIM'

1 Interview with author.
2 Interview with author.
3 Interview with author.
4 Interview with author.
5 *Elizabeth: Our Queen*, Channel 5, 2018.
6 Interview with author.
7 Charles Moore, *Margaret Thatcher: The Authorized Biography*, Vol. II, *Everything She Wants* (Allen Lane, 2016), p. 583.
8 Interview with author.
9 FCO 21/3475.
10 Interview with author.
11 Andrew Morton, *Diana: Her True Story – In Her Own Words* (Michael O'Mara Books, 1992), p. 82.
12 Andrew Lownie, *Entitled* (HarperCollins, 2025; Kindle edition), p. 73.
13 Interview with author.
14 Interview with author.
15 Moore, *Margaret Thatcher: The Authorized Biography*, Vol. III, *Herself Alone*, p. 725.
16 Interview with author.
17 Interview with author.
18 Interview with author.
19 Interview with author.
20 *The Sunday Times*, 10 February 1991.
21 Interview with author.

CHAPTER ELEVEN (1992-95): 'HORRIBILIS'

1 Private information.
2 Interview with author.
3 Interview with author.
4 Interview with author.
5 Interview with author.

Elizabeth II

6   Interview with author.
7   Interview with author.
8   Graham Turner, *Elizabeth: The Woman and the Queen* (Macmillan, 2002), p. 9.
9   Ibid.
10 Interview with author; Robert Hardman, *Queen of Our Times: The Life of Elizabeth II, 1926-2022* (Macmillan, 2022), p. 342.
11 Interview with author; Robert Hardman, *Our Queen* (Arrow, 2012), p. 91.
12 Interview with author.
13 William Shawcross, *Queen Elizabeth the Queen Mother* (Pan, 2010; Kindle edition) p. 1111.
14 Interview with author
15 Interview with author; Hardman, *Queen of Our Times*, p. 345.
16 Hardman, *Queen of Our Times*, p. 344.
17 Shawcross, *Queen Elizabeth the Queen Mother* (Kindle edition), p. 1113.
18 Interview with author.
19 Private information.
20 Peter Townsend, *Time and Chance: An Autobiography* (Collins, 1978), p. 198.
21 *Mirror*, 12 February 1993.
22 Interview with author.
23 Interview with author; Hardman, *Queen of Our Times*, p. 349.
24 Private information.
25 Hardman, *Our Queen*, p. 84.
26 Interview with author; Hardman, *Our Queen*, p. 38.
27 Interview with author; Robert Hardman, *Queen of the World* (Century, 2018), p. 61.
28 Interview with author; Hardman, *Queen of the World*, p. 452.
29 Interview with author.
30 Interview with author.
31 *Daily Telegraph*, 2 July 2014.
32 *Daily Telegraph*, 12 July 1996.
33 Interview with author.
34 Private information.
35 Interview with author.
36 Private information.

Notes

CHAPTER TWELVE (1996-97): 'THESE ARE FOR YOU'

1. Graham Turner, *Elizabeth: The Woman and the Queen* (Macmillan, 2002), p. 54.
2. Interview with author.
3. Private information.
4. Interview with author.
5. Prince Harry, *Spare* (Penguin Random House, 2023), p. 11.
6. Tony Blair, *A Journey* (Hutchinson, 2010), p. 139.
7. Interview with author.
8. Private information.
9. Interview with author; Robert Hardman, *Queen of Our Times: The Life of Elizabeth II, 1926-2022* (Macmillan, 2022), pp. 384-5.
10. Interview with author.
11. Alastair Campbell, *The Alastair Campbell Diaries,* Vol. II (Hutchinson, 2011), p. 187.
12. Hardman, *Queen of Our Times*, p. 386.
13. Interview with author; Hardman, *Queen of Our Times*, pp. 384-5.
14. Blair, *A Journey*, p.147.
15. Interview with author.
16. *The Times*, 6 September 1997.
17. Blair, *A Journey*, p. 147.
18. *The Times*, 6 September 1997.
19. Prince Harry, *Spare*, p. 24.
20. Private information.
21. Prince Harry, *Spare*, p. 25.

CHAPTER THIRTEEN (1998-2002): 'WE MUST SPEAK OF CHANGE'

1. Interview with author.
2. Interview with author.
3. Interview with author.
4. Interview with author.
5. Robert Hardman, *Queen of Our Times: The Life of Elizabeth II, 1926-2022* (Macmillan, 2022), p. 418.
6. *The New Statesman*, 7 August 2000.

7 Ibid.
8 Interview with author.
9 Hardman, *Queen of Our Times*, p. 412.
10 Private information.
11 Interview with author.
12 Interview with author.
13 Sarah Bradford, *Elizabeth: A Biography of Her Majesty the Queen* (William Heinemann, 1996), p. 251.
14 Interview with author; Hardman, *Queen of Our Times*, p. 423.
15 Angela Kelly, *The Other Side of the Coin* (HarperCollins, 2019), p. 56.
16 Interview with author; Hardman, *Queen of Our Times*, p. 423.
17 *The Times*, 22 January 2002.
18 Hardman, *Queen of Our Times*, p. 428.
19 Interview with author.
20 Prince Harry, *Spare* (Penguin Random House, 2023), p. 73.
21 Andrew Morton, *Diana: Her True Story – In Her Own Words* (Michael O'Mara Books, 1992), p. 86.
22 Private information.
23 Interview with author.
24 William Shawcross, *Queen Elizabeth the Queen Mother* (Pan, 2010; Kindle edition), p. 1160.
25 Interview with author; Hardman, *Queen of Our Times*, p. 433.
26 Interview with author.
27 Interview with author.

CHAPTER FOURTEEN (2003-11): THE WINNERS' ENCLOSURE

1 Interview with author; Robert Hardman, *Our Queen* (Arrow, 2012), p. 52.
2 Interview with author; ibid., p. 50.
3 Interview with author; Robert Hardman, *Queen of Our Times: The Life of Elizabeth II, 1926-2022* (Macmillan, 2022), p. 439.
4 Interview with author.
5 Private information.
6 Interview with author.
7 Graham Turner, *Elizabeth: The Woman and the Queen* (Macmillan, 2002), p. 141.

Notes

8 Private information.
9 Interview with author; Hardman, *Queen of Our Times*, p. 442.
10 Interview with author
11 Private information.
12 Interview with author
13 Interview with author.
14 Interview with author.
15 Interview with author; Hardman, *Queen of Our Times*, p. 451.
16 Interview with author; ibid., p. 453.
17 Robert Hardman, *Monarchy: The Royal Family at Work* (Ebury Press, 2007), p. 9.
18 Interview with author; Hardman, *Our Queen*, p. 163.
19 Interview with author.
20 Interview with author.
21 Interview with author.
22 *The Daily Telegraph*, 29 April 2011.
23 Private information.
24 Private information
25 Interview with author; Hardman, *Our Queen*, p. 55.
26 Ibid.
27 Jonathan Dimbleby, *The Prince of Wales: A Biography* (William Morrow & Co., 1994), p. 214.
28 Interview with author; Hardman, *Our Queen*, p. 55.
29 Interview with author.
30 Michelle Obama, *Becoming* (Penguin, 2018), p. 318.
31 Interview with author
32 Ben Rhodes, *The World As It Is: Inside the Obama White House* (Bodley Head, 2018), p. 150.
33 Interview with author.

CHAPTER FIFTEEN (2012-16): DIAMOND DAYS

1 Interview with author.
2 Private information.
3 Private information.
4 Private information.
5 Private information.
6 Interview with author.

Elizabeth II

7   Interview with author; Robert Hardman, *Queen of Our Times: The Life of Elizabeth II, 1926-2022* (Macmillan, 2022), p. 466.
8   Interview with author.
9   Interview with author.
10 Interview with author.
11 Interview with author.
12 Interview with author.
13 Interview with author.
14 Interview with author; *Our Queen*, ITV, 2013.
15 Angela Kelly, *The Other Side of the Coin* (HarperCollins, 2019), p. 168.
16 Private information.
17 Interview with author.
18 Interview with author.
19 Private information.
20 Robert Hardman, *Charles III: New King. New Court. The Inside Story* (Macmillan, 2024), p. 80.
21 Interview with author.
22 Private information.
23 Interview with author.
24 Interview with author.
25 Interview with author.
26 Richard Crossman, *The Diaries of a Cabinet Minister*, Vol. II (Penguin, 1976), 11 January 1967.
27 Interview with author; Hardman, *Queen of Our Times*, pp. 603-4.
28 Interview with author.
29 *The Cameron Years*, BBC, 2019.
30 Interview with author; Hardman, *Queen of Our Times*, p. 517.
31 Interview with author; ibid.
32 Private information.
33 Interview with author.
34 Angela Kelly, *The Other Side of the Coin*, p. 137.

Notes

CHAPTER SIXTEEN (2016-18): 'MY SINCERE WISH'

1. Interview with author.
2. Interview with author.
3. Interview with author.
4. Interview with author.
5. Private information.
6. Private information.
7. Interview with author.
8. Private information.
9. Private information.
10. Private information.
11. Interview with author.
12. Prince Harry, *Spare* (Penguin Random House, 2023), p. 296.
13. Private information.
14. Prince Harry, *Spare*, p. 335.
15. Ibid., p. 336.
16. Omid Scobie and Carolyn Durand, *Finding Freedom* (HQ, 2020), p. 256.
17. Private information.
18. Private information.
19. Private information.
20. Prince Harry, *Spare*, p. 336.
21. Private information.
22. Prince Harry, *Spare*, p. 341.
23. Private information.
24. Private information.
25. Interview with author.
26. Scobie and Durand, *Finding Freedom*, p. 161.
27. Interview with author.
28. Interview with author.

CHAPTER SEVENTEEN (2019): 'ONE HELL OF A LADY'

1. Private information.
2. Interview with author.
3. *Sunday Times*, 8 December 2018.
4. Private information.

Elizabeth II

5 Prince Harry, *Spare* (Penguin Random House, 2023), p. 350.
6 Ibid., p. 345.
7 Private information.
8 Interview with author; Robert Hardman, *Queen of Our Times: The Life of Elizabeth II, 1926-2022* (Macmillan, 2022), p. 543.
9 Interview with author.
10 Interview with author.
11 Interview with author.
12 Interview with author.
13 *The Times*, 26 January 2019.
14 Private information.
15 Interview with author.
16 Interview with author.
17 Interview with author.
18 Interview with author.
19 Interview with author.
20 Interview with author.
21 Interview with author.
22 Interview with author.
23 Interview with author.
24 Interview with author.
25 Private information.
26 Interview with author.
27 Private information.
28 Private information.
29 Private information.
30 Interview with author.
31 Private information.
32 Epstein Library, US Department of Justice, 2 January 2011.
33 Interview with author.

CHAPTER EIGHTEEN (2020-21): RECOLLECTIONS

1 Valentine Low, *Courtiers* (Headline, 2022), p. 306.
2 Private information.
3 Private information; Robert Hardman, *Queen of Our Times: The Life of Elizabeth II, 1926-2022* (Macmillan, 2022), p. 564.
4 Interview with author.

Notes

5   Interview with author.
6   Valentine Low, *Power and the Palace* (Headline, 2025), p. 320.
7   *Hansard*, 28 November 2024.
8   Private information.
9   *Hansard*, 28 November 2024.
10 Private information.
11 Robert Hardman, *Our Queen* (Arrow, 2023), p. 44.
12 Private information.
13 Interview with author.
14 Interview with author.
15 Private information.
16 Robert Hardman, *Charles III: New King. New Court. The Inside Story* (Macmillan, 2024), p. 89.
17 Interview with author.
18 Interview with author.
19 Interview with author.
20 Private information.
21 Interview with author.
22 Private information.
23 *The Times*, 9 March 2021.
24 Private information.
25 Private information.
26 Interview with author for *Prince Philip: The Royal Family Remembers*, BBC/Oxford Films, 2021.
27 Private information.
28 *Daily Mail* and others, 11 April 2021.
29 Interview with author.
30 Interview with author for *Charles III: The Coronation Year*, BBC/Oxford Films, 2023; quoted in Hardman, *Charles III*, p. 112.
31 Private information.
32 Interview with author; Hardman, *Queen of Our Times*, p. 624.
33 Private information.
34 Private information

Elizabeth II

CHAPTER NINETEEN (2021-22): THE 'TOO DIFFICULT' FOLDER

1. Private information.
2. Private information.
3. Private information.
4. Private information.
5. Private information.
6. Private information.
7. Private information.
8. Private information.
9. Private information.
10. Private information.
11. Private information.
12. Private information.
13. Prince Harry, *Spare* (Penguin Random House, 2023), p. 405.
14. Interview with author.
15. Private information.
16. Private information.

CHAPTER TWENTY: SUNSET: 'VERY PEACEFUL'

1. Private information.
2. Interview with author.
3. Interview with author.
4. Private information.
5. Private information.
6. Interview with author.
7. Robert Hardman, *Charles III: New King. New Court. The Inside Story* (Macmillan, 2024), p. 58.
8. Hardman, *Charles III*, p. 58.
9. Interview with author.
10. Private information.
11. Hardman, *Charles III*, p. 88.
12. Ibid.
13. Interview with author.
14. Hardman, *Charles III*, p. 60.
15. Ibid., p. 62.

Notes

16 Prince Harry, *Spare* (Penguin Random House, 2023), p. 403.
17 Private information; Hardman, *Charles III*, p. 68.
18 Hardman, *Charles III*, p. 100.

CHAPTER TWENTY-ONE: LEGACY: 'FRESH AIR'

1 Interview with author; Robert Hardman, *Charles III: New King. New Court. The Inside Story* (Macmillan, 2022), p. 127.
2 Interview with author.
3 Written evidence to Foreign Affairs Committee, 3 March 2025.
4 Private information.
5 Interview with author; Robert Hardman, *Queen of Our Times: The Life of Elizabeth II, 1926–2022* (Macmillan, 2022), p. 623.
6 Interview with author.
7 Private information.
8 *The Reluctant Traveller*, Apple TV, 2025.
9 Interview with author.
10 Private information.
11 Prince Harry, *Spare* (Penguin Random House, 2023), p. 406.
12 *Elizabeth R*, BBC, 1992.

Selected Bibliography

Allison, Ronald and Riddell, Sarah, *The Royal Encyclopaedia* (Macmillan, 1991)
Bedell Smith, Sally, *Elizabeth The Queen* (Penguin, 2016)
———, *Charles: The Misunderstood Prince* (Michael Joseph, 2017)
Blair, Tony, *A Journey* (Hutchinson, 2010)
Bloch, Michael, *The Secret File of the Duke of Windsor* (Corgi, 1989)
Boothroyd, Basil, *Philip: An Informal Biography* (Longman, 1971)
Bradford, Sarah, *Elizabeth: A Biography of Her Majesty the Queen* (William Heinemann, 1996)
Brandreth, Gyles, *Elizabeth: An Intimate Portrait* (Penguin Michael Joseph, 2022)
———, *Philip: The Final Portrait* (Coronet, 2021)
———, *Philip and Elizabeth: Portrait of a Marriage* (Century, 2004)
Brown, Tina, *The Diana Chronicles* (Arrow, 2017)
Cameron, David, *For the Record* (William Collins, 2019)
Campbell, Alastair, *The Alastair Campbell Diaries*, Vol. II (Hutchinson, 2011)
Channon, Henry 'Chips', *The Diaries 1918-38*, Vol. I, edited by Simon Heffer (Hutchinson, 2021)

Elizabeth II

——, *The Diaries 1938-43*, Vol. II, edited by Simon Heffer (Hutchinson, 2021)

——, *The Diaries 1943-57*, Vol III, edited by Simon Heffer (Hutchinson, 2022)

Clark, Pam, Crocker, Julie, Derrett, Allison, Hobbs, Laura and Kelsey, Jill, *Treasures from the Royal Archives* (Royal Collection Trust, 2014)

Colville, Jock, *The Fringes of Power: Downing Street Diaries, 1939-1955* (Weidenfeld & Nicolson, 2004)

Connors, Jane, *The Glittering Thread* (University of Technology, Sydney, 1996)

Corbett, Jim, *Tree Tops* (Oxford University Press, 1955)

Crawford, Marion, *The Little Princesses* (Orion, 2011)

Crossman, Richard, *The Diaries of a Cabinet Minister*, Vol. II (Penguin, 1976)

Dimbleby, Jonathan, *The Prince of Wales: A Biography* (Little, Brown, 1994)

Eade, Philip, *Young Prince Philip* (HarperPress, 2011)

Fitzalan Howard, Alathea, *The Windsor Diaries 1940-45* (Hodder & Stoughton, 2020)

Gillard, Julia, *My Story* (Transworld, 2014)

Glenconner, Anne, *Lady in Waiting* (Hodder & Stoughton, 2019)

Hardman, Robert, *Monarchy: The Royal Family at Work* (Ebury, 2007)

——, *Our Queen* (Arrow, 2012)

——, *Queen of the World* (Century, 2018)

——, *Queen of Our Times: The Life of Elizabeth II, 1926-2022* (Macmillan, 2022)

——, *Charles III: New King. New Court. The Inside Story* (Macmillan, 2024)

Harris, Kenneth, *The Queen* (Weidenfeld & Nicolson, 1994)

Selected Bibliography

Hart-Davis, Duff (ed.), *King's Counsellor: Abdication and War, The Diaries of Sir Alan Lascelles* (Weidenfeld & Nicolson, 2006)

Heald, Tim, *Philip: A Portrait of the Duke of Edinburgh* (Hodder & Stoughton, 1991)

Hennessy, Peter, *The Prime Minister* (Allen Lane, 2000)

——, *The Secret State* (Penguin, 2010)

Hoey, Brian, *Anne: The Princess Royal* (Grafton Books, 1989)

——, *Anne: The Private Princess Revealed* (Sidgwick & Jackson, 1997)

Jay, Antony, *Elizabeth R* (BBC Books, 1992)

The Diaries of Cynthia Gladwyn (Constable, 1995),

Johnstone-Bryden, Richard, *The Royal Yacht* Britannia*: The Official History* (Conway Maritime Press, 2003)

Junor, Penny, *The Firm* (HarperCollins 2011)

Kelly, Angela, *Dressing the Queen* (Royal Collection Trust, 2012)

——, *The Other Side of the Coin* (HarperCollins, 2019)

Lacey, Robert, *Royal: Her Majesty Queen Elizabeth II* (Little, Brown, 2002)

——, *The Crown* (Blink Publishing, 2019)

——, *Battle of Brothers* (William Collins, 2020)

Longford, Elizabeth, *Elizabeth R* (Weidenfeld & Nicholson, 1983)

Low, Valentine, *Courtiers* (Headline, 2022)

——, *Power and the Palace* (Headline, 2025)

Lownie, Andrew, *Entitled* (HarperCollins, 2025)

Luce, Richard, *Ringing the Changes* (Michael Russell, 2007)

Lumley, Joanna, *A Queen for All Seasons: A Celebration of Queen Elizabeth II* (Hodder & Stoughton, 2021)

Macmillan, Harold, *Pointing the Way* (Macmillan, 1972)

Marr, Andrew, *The Diamond Queen* (Macmillan, 2011)

McKinnon, Don, *In the Ring* (Elliott and Thompson, 2013)

Mead, Richard, *General 'Boy': The Life of Lieutenant General Sir Frederick Browning* (Pen & Sword Military 2010)

Elizabeth II

Moore, Charles, *Margaret Thatcher: The Authorized Biography*, Vol. I, *Not For Turning* (Allen Lane, 2013)

———, *Margaret Thatcher: The Authorized Biography*, Vol. II, *Everything She Wants* (Allen Lane, 2016)

———, *Margaret Thatcher: The Authorized Biography*, Vol. III, *Herself Alone* (Allen Lane, 2019)

Morton, Andrew, *Diana: Her True Story – In Her Own Words* (revised 25th anniversary edition, Michael O'Mara Books, 2017)

Murphy, Professor, *Philip, Monarchy and the End of Empire* (Oxford University Press, 2013)

Nye, Joseph S., *Do Morals Matter?* (Oxford University Press, 2020)

Obama, Barack, *A Promised Land* (Viking, 2020)

Obama, Michelle, *Becoming* (Penguin, 2021)

Owen, David, *Time to Declare* (Michael Joseph, 1991)

Pimlott, Ben, *The Queen: Elizabeth II and the Monarchy* (HarperPress, 2012)

Prince Harry, *Spare* (Penguin Random House, 2023)

Ramphal, Shridath, *Glimpses of a Global Life* (Hansib Publications, 2014)

Rhodes, Ben, *The World As It Is: A Memoir of the Obama White House* (Bodley Head, 2018)

Rhodes, Margaret, *The Final Curtsey* (Umbria, 2011)

Ridley, Jane, *George V – Never A Dull Moment* (Vintage, 2023)

Roberts, Andrew, *House of Windsor: A Royal History of England* (Weidenfeld Nicolson Illustrated, 2000)

———, *George III: The Life and Reign of Britain's Most Misunderstood Monarch* (Allen Lane, 2021)

———, *Churchill: Walking with Destiny* (Allen Lane, 2018)

Roche, Marc, *Elizabeth II: Une Vie, Un Règne* (Tallandier, 2016)

Rose, Kenneth, *King George V* (Papermac, 1984)

Selected Bibliography

——, *Kings, Queens and Courtiers* (Weidenfeld & Nicolson, 1985)
——, *The Journals,* Vol. I (Weidenfeld & Nicolson, 2018)
——, *The Journals,* Vol. II (Weidenfeld & Nicolson, 2019)
Scobie, Omid and Durand, Carolyn, *Finding Freedom* (HQ, 2020)
Sebag Montefiore, Simon, *The Romanovs* (Weidenfeld & Nicolson, 2016)
Shawcross, William, *Queen and Country* (BBC Worldwide, 2002)
——, *Queen Elizabeth the Queen Mother* (Macmillan, 2009)
Smith, Arnold, *Stitches in Time: The Commonwealth in World Politics* (General Publishing, 1981)
Stock, Victor, *Taking Stock* (HarperCollins, 2001)
Townsend, Peter, *Time and Chance: An Autobiography* (Collins, 1978)
Turner, Graham, *Elizabeth: The Woman and the Queen* (Macmillan, 2002)
Vickers, Hugo, *Alice: Princess Andrew of Greece* (Hamish Hamilton, 2000)
——, *Elizabeth, the Queen Mother* (Arrow, 2006)
——, *Coronation: The Crowning of Elizabeth II* (The Dovecote Press, 2023)
Wheeler-Bennett, John, *King George VI: His Life and Reign* (Macmillan, 1958)
Williams, Kate, *Young Elizabeth* (Phoenix, 2013)
Wilson, A. N., *Victoria: A Life* (Atlantic, 2015)
——, *The Queen* (Atlantic, 2016)
Windsor, Duke of, *A King's Story* (Cassell & Co., 1951)
Ziegler, Philip, *King Edward VIII* (HarperPress, 2012)

Sources

With the kind permission of Her Late Majesty The Queen and His Majesty The King, I have previously been granted access to a number of files and boxes held in the Royal Archives (RA) at Windsor. I have drawn on some of these for this book, including:

RA/GVI/PRIV/DIARY/WAR/Volumes I–XI (The War Diary of King George VI)

RA/F&V/VISOV/SA/1947 (Official Diary of the 1947 Tour of Southern Africa)

RA QEII/ADD/COPY/MISC – Recollections of guests and onlookers at the Coronation of Queen Elizabeth II

RA F&V/COR/1953 – Lists of the Royal Family and of Royal and Foreign guests for the Coronation; 'Ceremonial to be observed', 1953

Under the Open Government Licence, I have drawn extensively on the files held (both physically and digitally) by The National Archives (TNA) at Kew. They include papers from:

The Cabinet Office (CAB)

Elizabeth II

The Foreign Office (prior to its merger with the Commonwealth Office) (FO)

The Lord Chamberlain's Office (LCO)

The Prime Minister's Office (PREM)

I am grateful to the staff at the Churchill Archives Centre, Churchill College, Cambridge for access to their extensive collections including the papers of Sir Alan Lascelles and Cynthia Jebb, later Lady Gladwyn.

I am very grateful to those who have kindly shared diaries, albums, scrapbooks and family archives with me. In the course of writing this book, I have also drawn on my own interviews (for books, newspaper articles and documentaries), notes, cuttings and news archive material. Some have been gathered for this book. Other material has been accumulated in the course of more than thirty years of covering this subject. I have also used official records such as the Court Circular, *Hansard* and the *London Gazette*. However, new material continues to emerge all the time. Elizabeth II was the most famous woman of her era and the most widely travelled monarch in history. At every talk or event I have attended in relation to my previous books and documentaries on the subject, someone always appears with a story, a vignette, a memento or just a memory of her. They are always interesting, enjoyable and appreciated. There can be no last word on someone who lives on so clearly in the minds of so many.

Picture Credits

SECTION ONE

1 The Duke and Duchess of York at Princess Elizabeth's christening in 1926 © Universal History Archive/Universal Images Group via Getty Images.
2 Princess Elizabeth and her grandparents in 1932 © Topical Press Agency via Getty Images.
3 Princesses Elizabeth and Margaret with their governess, Marion Crawford © Bettmann / Contributor via Getty Images.
4 Princesses Elizabeth and Margaret with the Prince of Wales at Balmoral in 1935 © Popperfoto via Getty Images.
5 Princess Elizabeth with two corgis at 145 Piccadilly in 1936 © Lisa Sheridan / Studio Lisa / Hulton Archive via Getty Images.
6 Princess Elizabeth with her father, King George VI, at Windsor in 1942 © ibid.
7 A young Elizabeth and Philip at Britannia Royal Naval College, Dartmouth, in 1939 © The Britannia Museum and Archive.
8 Princess Elizabeth records her twenty-first birthday broadcast from South Africa in 1947 © Topical Press Agency / Hulton Archive via Getty Images.
9 The Duke and Duchess of Edinburgh on their wedding day in 1947 © Hulton-Deutsch Collection / Corbis via Getty Images.
10 Queen Mary, King George VI, Queen Elizabeth and the Duke and

Elizabeth II

Duchess of Edinburgh at the christening of Princess Anne in 1950 © Popperfoto via Getty Images.

11 Princess Elizabeth dances with the Duke of Edinburgh at a Royal Navy ball in Malta, 1950 © AFP via Getty Images.

12 The new Queen, Elizabeth II, lands on British soil for the first time and is greeted by Winston Churchill and Clement Attlee © Popperfoto via Getty Images.

13 Queen Elizabeth II's Coronation day, 2 June 1953 © Chronicle via Alamy.

14 The Queen and the Duke of Edinburgh with Queen Sālote Tupou III at the royal palace at Tonga in 1953 © Esten / Popperfoto via Getty Images.

15 The Queen dances with President Kwame Nkrumah of Ghana at the State House in Accra in 1961 © CENTRAL PRESS / AFP via Getty Images.

16 The Queen and the Duke of Edinburgh with their children in 1965 © Keystone via Getty Images.

17 The new Prince of Wales leaves Caernarvon Castle with the Queen following his investiture in 1969 © Ray Bellisario / Popperfoto via Getty Images.

18 The Queen and the Duke of Edinburgh with their children at Buckingham Palace on their silver wedding anniversary in 1972 © George Freston / Fox Photos / Hulton Archive via Getty Images.

19 The Prince of Wales and Lady Diana Spencer with the Queen at Buckingham Palace in 1981 © Fox Photos via Getty Images.

20 The Queen and President Ronald Reagan on horseback at Windsor Castle in 1982 © Tim Graham Photo Library via Getty Images.

SECTION TWO

1 The Queen and Prince Philip in China in 1986 © Forrest Anderson via Getty Images.

2 The Royal Family on the balcony at Buckingham Palace at

Picture Credits

Trooping the Colour in 1992, the Queen's 'annus horribilis' © Patrick Durand / Sygma via Getty Images.

3 The Queen and Prince Philip among the mourners at Buckingham Palace following the death of Diana, Princess of Wales, in 1997 © PA Images via Alamy.

4 The Queen at the decommissioning of the Royal Yacht in 1997 © Tim Graham Photo Library via Getty Images.

5 The Queen and Prince Philip progress down the Mall in an open-top vehicle during the Golden Jubilee in 2002 © Anwar Hussein via Getty Images.

6 The Prince of Wales and the new Duchess of Cornwall leaving St George's Chapel, Windsor in 2005 © Tim Graham Photo Library via Getty Images.

7 The Queen greets former IRA commander Martin McGuinness in Northern Ireland in 2012 © PAUL FAITH / AFP via Getty Images.

8 Members of the Royal Family on the balcony at Buckingham Palace following the Queen's ninetieth Birthday Parade in 2016 © Zak Hussein – Corbis via Getty Images.

9 The Queen with the new Duke and Duchess of Sussex at the Queen's Young Leaders Awards in 2018 © John Stillwell – WPA Pool via Getty Images.

10 The Queen and US president Donald Trump at a state banquet at Buckingham Palace in 2019 © Dominic Lipinski / POOL / AFP via Getty Images.

11 The Queen and Prince Philip opening cards together at Windsor in 2020 © Chris Jackson / Getty Images for Buckingham Palace.

12 Members of the Royal Family in Cornwall in 2021 © Jack Hill – WPA Pool via Getty Images.

13 The Queen and the then Duke of York at the memorial service for Prince Philip at Westminster Abbey in 2022 © RICHARD POHLE / POOL / AFP via Getty Images.

Elizabeth II

14 Members of the Royal Family on the balcony at Buckingham Palace for the Queen's Platinum Jubilee in 2022 © Chris Jackson via Getty Images.

15 The Queen prepares to appoint her last prime minister shortly before her death in September 2022 © Jane Barlow / POOL / AFP via Getty Images.

16 Members of the Royal Family walk behind the late Queen's coffin at the procession to her Lying-in-State © Karwai Tang / WireImage via Getty Images.

17 Portrait of Queen Elizabeth II by artist Basia Hamilton © Basia Hamilton.

18 A copy of Basia Hamilton's portrait of the Queen at President Donald Trump's home in Mar-a-Lago © Robert Hardman.

Index

9/11 terrorist attacks, USA 223, 224
17 Bruton Street, London 27
145 Piccadilly, London 29–30, 33, 34

Abercorn, Alexandra Hamilton, Duchess 60
Aberfan disaster, Mid Glamorgan 110
Adeane, Sir Michael 89, 90, 94, 107
Airlie, David Ogilvy, 13th Earl 164–6, 178–9, 180, 206–7, 208–9, 215, 256
Albert, Prince, Duke of York *see* George VI, As Duke of York
Alderton, Sir Clive 309, 317, 354–5, 358, 360, 364
Alice of Battenberg, Princess 50, 51, 54, 55
Altrincham, John Grigg, 2nd Baron 99
Amin, Idi 126–7
Anderson, Mabel 64, 193
Andrew of Greece, Prince 50, 51
Andrew, Prince, Duke of York (now Andrew Mountbatten-Windsor)
  birth 101
  births of children 160
  character 160, 164, 253–5, 260–1, 303, 304–5, 305–6
  childhood 108
  confrontation with Master of the Household 304–5
  daughters' weddings 287, 338
  Epstein scandal 253, 301–2, 305–6, 337, 370
  Falkland Islands War 151, 152–3
  father's memorial service 337–8
  Giuffre's (née Roberts) allegations 302, 337
  It's a Knockout (BBC) 163
  loss of titles 102
  made Duke of York 160
  mother's indulgence of 25, 160, 303, 305, 337
  Newsnight interview 302
  Pitch at the Palace 301, 303, 304
  'Randy Andy' image 159
  removal from public life 303–5
  removal of HRH 337
  Royal Lodge 338–9, 370
  and Sarah 158–60, 175, 199–200
  stripped of all titles and honours 370, 381
  as trade envoy 233, 253–4
  Way Ahead Group 185
  Windsor Castle fire 178

Elizabeth II

Angola 200, 307
Anne, Princess Royal
  aiding Charles III 365, 368–9
  birth 67
  births of children 61, 134
  childhood 67–8, 71, 86, 88, 101
  education 102–3
  interests/pursuits 124
  kidnap attempt 124–5
  and Mark Phillips 124, 175
  mother's declining health 352, 353, 354, 355, 356
  Olympic Games 131, 261
  seventieth birthday 319–20
  and Tim Laurence 175, 182–3, 319
Anson, Charles 156, 178, 179, 184
Antigua 339
Archie of Sussex, Prince 283–4, 296, 307, 321, 342
Argentina 151, 152–3, 195
Armstrong-Jones, Anthony (Lord Snowdon) 104, 128–9
Armstrong-Jones, Lady Sarah (Chatto) 129, 227, 235, 331
Attlee, Clement 49, 70, 119, 203
Audience, The (Morgan) 269
Australia 28, 86–8, 106, 117, 120, 125, 131–2, 160, 196–7, 201, 218–19, 227, 257–8, 261, 371

Baldwin, Stanley 32, 33, 35
Ball, Ian 125
Balmoral Castle, Aberdeenshire
  after Diana's death 17, 203–5, 207, 208
  afternoon tea 15
  Anne and Tim's wedding reception 183
  appointment of Liz Truss 352–3
  Diana's first visit to 145
  Knatchbull children's stay at 144
  last Red Box 360–1
  open to public 366

Philip's post-war visit 50
prime minister visits to 18, 128, 139–40, 197
Privy Council meeting on prorogation 298–301
Queen's last illness and death 348–9, 351–8
during Second World War 37
shooting weekends 8–9, 13–14
summer breaks 92, 176–7, 202, 264, 270, 331–2
trapped butterfly 9
Baltimore Sun 97
Barzun, Matthew 273–4
Bashir, Martin 198
BBC
  Children's Hour 42
  Desert Island Discs 40
  Elizabeth at 90 5–6, 129
  Elizabeth R 173–5
  It's a Knockout 162–3
  Monarchy 241
  Newsnight 302
  Panorama 198–9, 301–2
  Princess Lilibet's name 328–9
  Queen Mother's centenary 219–20
  Queen's Coronation 84
  Queen's COVID broadcast 314–16
  Queen's Middle East tour 136
  Royal Family 113–14, 129, 174–5
  Sports Personality of the Year award 124
Beaton, Jim 125
Beatrice, Princess 160, 177, 338, 370
Bellaigue, Antoinette 'Toni' de 48
Bellisario, Ray 112
Biden, Dr Jill 327–8
Biden, Joe 327–8, 377
Birkhall Estate, Aberdeenshire 37, 314, 355, 357, 367
Blair, Sir Tony 9, 13, 108, 192,

424

Index

202–3, 204, 206, 208, 209, 217–18, 232, 239, 240–1, 335–6
Blunt, Sir Anthony 106–8
Bogdanor, Professor Sir Vernon 17
Bosnia 200
Boyle, Danny 261–3
Brabourne, John Knatchbull, Baron 80–1
Brazil 130
Brexit 270–2, 291, 296–7, 298, 299, 300, 301
Britannia, HMY 10–11, 88, 95, 104, 129, 133, 146–7, 186–7, 187–8, 190–2, 203
British Empire 20, 52, 53
Brooksbank, Jack 287–8
Brown, Gordon 241, 250
Browning, Lieut Gen Sir Frederick 'Boy' 62
Bruce, Maj-Gen Alastair 300
Bryan, John 176–7
Buckingham Palace, London
  after Diana's death 206, 207–8, 208–9
  balcony appearances 36, 48, 56, 150, 185, 260, 342, 344, 368
  birth and christening of Prince Charles 60–1
  christening of Princess Elizabeth 28
  Churchill's resignation 90
  Commonwealth Summit (2018) 288–9
  Diana's funeral 210
  Edinburghs' offices 57
  Elizabeth II and family's move to 79–80
  Fagan's appearance in bedroom 153–4
  flag policy 207
  garden parties 3–4, 98
  George VI and family's move to 34
  Golden Jubilee 229
  hosting state visitors 9–10, 103, 126–7, 134–5, 232–3, 250–1, 294–6
  James Bond skit 261–3
  luncheons 98
  open to public 366
  Platinum Jubilee 342–4
  post-war return to 49
  prime minister meetings 8, 140
  during Second World War 37, 41–2
  Sussex's office 292–3
  terrorist threats and attacks 22–3, 148–9
Buckland, Chris 8
Buckland, Sir Robert 13, 14, 318
Bush, George H. W. 169, 232
Bush, George W. 169, 222–3, 232, 327–8
Butler, R. A. 'Rab' 101, 104
Butler, Sir Robin, Baron 157, 205

Cabinet Manual 242
Callaghan, Jim 131, 134, 137
Cameron, David 8, 14, 18, 24, 98, 243, 251, 253–4, 257–8, 260, 261–2, 264, 268–9, 270–1, 272, 316
Camilla, Duchess of Cornwall (now Queen) 143, 183, 196, 233–7, 260, 275, 281, 336, 344, 347, 355, 356, 357–8, 365, 369, 370
Campbell, Alastair 206–7
Canada 22, 36, 70–1, 99, 119, 131, 186, 258, 261, 280–1, 371–2, 378–9
Carmichael, Ian 299
Carnarvon, Henry Herbert ('Porchie'), 7th Earl 223–4
Carney, Mark 371
Catherine (Kate), Duchess of Cambridge (now Princess of Wales) 244–8, 274–5, 282, 292,

425

Catherine (Kate) (*cont.*)
  311, 322, 338, 339, 345, 348, 356, 365, 376
Ceaușescu, Nicolae and Elena 134–5, 168
Chamberlain, Neville 35–6, 40, 180
Channon, Henry 'Chips' 28
Charles, Prince of Wales (now Charles III)
  As Prince
    Andrew problem 303–4
    attack in Sydney 196, 197
    birth 60–1
    births of children 152, 159
    Camilla's future title 336
    childhood 64, 67–8, 71, 86, 88
    christening 61
    Commonwealth 288–9
    Covid infection 314
    Diana's death and funeral 204–11
    Dimbleby project 197–8
    education 102–3
    Harry and Meghan's wedding 286
    investiture 113, 114–15
    liaising with mother and William 312, 326
    meeting Meghan 281
    mother preparing for succession 340
    mother's Jubilees 260, 345
    mother's last illness and death 354–5, 356, 357–8
    Prince's Trust 196
    royal duties and state visits 160, 175, 177, 196–7, 203, 236, 259, 266, 275, 326, 339–40, 347
    supportive of Queen 380
    Sussexes' resignation from public duties 308–9, 309–10
    Way Ahead Group 185

Elizabeth II

  As King
    accession 358, 364
    Andrew problem 369–70
    broadcast after mother's death 361
    cancer 365
    changes to balcony appearances 368–9
    changes to royal court and lifestyle 365–9
    constitutional role 370–1
    Coronation 81–2, 364, 367, 369
    Head of Commonwealth 289
    homes 367
    and President Trump 23, 371–5, 379
    private time 369
    regnal name 358
    Republic protest group 367–8
    'Scottish Coronation' 367–8
    'slimmed-down' monarchy 368–9
    speeding things up 366–7, 368
    state visits 370–2
    transparency 369
  and Camilla 143, 183, 196, 233–7, 370
  and Diana 144–5, 147–8, 149–50, 162, 175, 177–8, 182, 197, 198, 199–200
  relationship with grandmother 148
  relationship with Harry 329
  relationship with nanny 193
  relationship with parents 247
  relationship with Uncle Louis 247
Charlotte of Wales, Princess 265, 282, 345, 369
Charteris, Martin
  Blunt spy scandal 107–8
  consensus politics 137
  Duke of Rutland offending Princess 19
  Queen–Thatcher relationship 138

Index

Queen's 1972 Christmas broadcast 120, 121
Queen's accession 74, 75, 76–7
Queen's character 14, 16, 110–11
Queen's friendship with Douglas-Home 105
retirement 133–4
Sekos' stay at Palace 127
sense of humour 133–4
Silver Jubilee 132
the 'smiling problem' 70
Suez Canal crisis 93–4
Chatto, Lady Sarah (Armstrong-Jones) 129, 227, 235, 331
Children's Hour (BBC) 42
China 161, 201, 203, 261
Chirac, Jacques 239
Churchill, Sir Winston
  pre-War 36
  Second World War 40–1, 47, 48, 55
  post-War 49, 53, 55, 69, 70, 73, 75–6, 78, 79, 81, 82, 88, 89–90, 91, 109
Clarence House, London 57, 61–2, 67, 76, 79–80, 91, 191
Clark, Helen 13
Clegg, Nick 243, 244
Clifton, Bill 186–7
Clinton, Hillary 251
Coe, Sebastian, Baron 263
Cohen, Samantha 267, 289
Colville, Cmdr Richard 87, 97, 112–13
Colville, Jock 62, 78, 84, 89, 90
Commonwealth; *see also specific country*
  and EU 120
  London Declaration 65
  reforms to the monarchy 257–8
  representatives at Coronation 84–5
  and South Africa 53, 103–4, 156–8, 188

Study Conferences 94–5
Suez Canal crisis 93
summits 8, 118–19, 142–3, 156–7, 167, 227, 233, 238, 257, 266, 268, 288–9
Connors, Dr Jane 87, 88
Corbett, Jim 72–3
corgis 31, 56, 127, 192, 234, 300
Covid-19 pandemic 312–19, 324–5
Crawford, Marion 'Crawfie' 30–1, 34, 35, 37, 39, 40, 42, 45, 47, 49, 52, 62–3, 66–7
Crown Jewels 41
Crown, The (Netflix) 21, 95, 139, 275–6, 364
Cummings, Dominic 313

D-Day anniversaries 186–7, 267–8, 294, 296
Daily Mirror, The 132, 176–7, 184
Dawson of Penn, Bertrand, 1st Viscount 32–3
Diana: Her True Story (Morton) 176
Diana, Princess of Wales
  births of children 152, 159, 160
  and Charles 144–5, 147–8, 149–50, 162, 175, 177–8, 182, 197, 198, 199–200
  death and funeral 203–11
  Dianamania 160, 195–6, 200–1
  divorce 199–200
  eating disorders 148, 149–50, 162, 176
  family background 144–5, 145–6
  first Balmoral visit 145
  Morton's biography 176
  in Nepal 195
  Panorama (BBC) 198–9
  post-royal life 200–1, 201–2
  royal duties and state visits 160, 177
Dimbleby, Jonathan 162, 197–8

427

Elizabeth II

Dipendra of Nepal, Crown Prince 195
Douglas-Home, Sir Alexander 105, 108
Duke of Edinburgh's Award 94, 95, 216–17, 324
Dunblane Primary School massacre, Stirling 214

Eden, Sir Anthony 89, 90, 92, 93–4, 104
Edward, Prince, Earl of Wessex (now Duke of Edinburgh) 108, 129, 162–3, 216–17, 259, 310, 368
Edward, Prince of Wales/Edward VIII/Duke of Windsor 27, 29, 31, 32, 33–4, 36, 55, 123–4, 260
Egypt 93–4
Elizabeth at 90 (BBC) 5–6, 129
Elizabeth Cross 240
Elizabeth II
  As Princess Elizabeth
    pre-War
      birth 27–8
      birth of Margaret 29
      childhood 28–9, 29–30, 30–1
      christening 28
      corgis 31
      education 30, 35
      father's accession 34
      first meeting Philip 31
      grandfather's death 33
      Heir Presumptive 35
      move to Buckingham Palace 34
      nickname 'Lilibet' 29
      parents' Coronation 35
      with Philip at Dartmouth 36–7
      Uncle David's abdication 34
      Uncle George's wedding 31
    Second World War
      Auxiliary Territorial Service (ATS) 48
      bombing raids at Windsor 42
      Children's Hour broadcast 42
      life at Windsor 42–3
      made Colonel of the Grenadier Guards 44
      made Counsellor of State 18, 68
      move to Royal Lodge 39
      move to Windsor Castle 40
      patronages 44
      Philip's photograph 48
      Philip's visits 43–4, 45, 46
      remaining in Britain 40–1
      royal duties 47
      in Scotland 37
      sinking of *Royal Oak* 38
      suitors 43–4
      VE Day 48–9
      Windsor Horse Show 46–7
    post-War
      engagement 50, 51, 53–4
      horse racing 49
      Philip's courtship 50
      Philip's photograph 49
      return to Buckingham Palace 49
      state visit to southern African countries 51–2
      twenty-first birthday broadcast 52–3
      wedding 54–6
  As Duchess of Edinburgh
    births of children 60–1, 67
    corgis 56
    family homes 57–8, 61–2
    father's final farewell 71
    horse racing 64
    learning of father's death 74
    on Malta 64, 67–8
    Philip's driving 62, 63
    'smiling problem' 70
    standing-in for King 68–9
    state visits 58, 69, 70, 71–3
    training for monarchy 68

Index

As Queen
9/11 terrorist attacks, USA 224
1966 World Cup 110
abdication in Fiji 161
Aberfan disaster 110
accession 74, 75–6
Airlie's changes to Household 165
Andrew and Royal Lodge 338–9
Andrew's engagement and wedding 158–60
Andrew's removal from public life 303–5
Andrew's wartime service 151, 152–3
Anne's first wedding 124
Anne's second wedding 182–3
'annus horribilis' speech 171, 172–3, 180
appointment of Liz Truss 352–3
'Are you sure?' response 20–1, 241, 299, 300
Audience, The (Morgan) 269
authority 380
avoidance of family showdowns 24–5, 92, 181, 255, 304, 305
Balmoral, love of 202
Beatrice's wedding 319
Birthday Parade balcony photo (2019) 368
Birthday Parade shooting 148–9
births of children 101, 108
Blair appointed to Order of the Garter 335–6
Blunt spy scandal 106–8
'Bobo' MacDonald's death and funeral 192–3
California visit 152
Camilla appointed to Order of the Garter 336

Camilla's future title 237, 336
ceasing long-haul travel 258, 266
Charles and Camilla's marriage 235–7
Charles and Diana's engagement 147–8
Charles and Diana's marital breakdown 162, 182, 199–200
Charles' first wedding 150
Charles' second wedding 236–7
children's education 102–3
Christian faith 23–4
Christmas broadcasts 23, 77, 98, 120–1, 182, 291, 335
Churchill's death and funeral 109
Churchill's resignation 90
Commonwealth summits 8, 118–19, 142–3, 156–7, 167, 227, 233, 238, 257–8, 268, 288–9
Coronation 80, 81–5
Covid-19 broadcast 314–16
Covid-19 impacts 312–19, 324–5
Covid infection 335
D-Day anniversaries 186–7, 267–8, 296
death and funeral 356–60, 364
declining health 331–4, 347, 348–9, 351–2, 353–6
decreasing/delegating duties 258–9, 266, 280, 332–3, 334, 339–40, 341, 347
Diamond Wedding on Malta 238
Diana's death and funeral 204–11
diary 360
Dimbleby project 197–8
'double eyebrow' response 20, 270

Elizabeth II

Elizabeth II (*cont.*)
  Dunblane, visit to 214
  Eastern Europe 185–6
  Edward's wedding 216
  eightieth birthday 237–8
  Elizabeth Cross 240
  Elizabeth R (BBC) 173–5
  EU 119–21, 176, 270–2, 297
  Eugenie's wedding 287–8
  Fagan's appearance in
    bedroom 153–4
  family surname 78–9, 101–2
  father's influence 38, 77, 79, 181
  Freud painting 222–3
  funeral arrangements 349
  G7 summit, Cornwall (2021)
    326–7
  giving up alcohol 331–2
  against 'Gloriana' idea 76–7
  grandmother's death 81
  Gulf War broadcast 168
  Harewood's request to remarry
    19, 111
  Harry's wedding 286–7
  helicopters, fear of 22, 133
  helping Meghan 289–90
  HMY *Britannia* 190–2
  horse racing 49, 82–3, 224, 353
  hosting global business
    summit reception 333
  hosting state visitors 5, 9–10,
    103, 126–7, 130, 134–5, 151–2,
    232–3, 250–1, 274–5, 294–6,
    327–8, 374, 377
  investiture of Prince of Wales
    114–15
  James Bond skit 261–3
  Johnson's prorogation stunt
    298–301
  Jubilees 5, 9, 13, 131–4, 171,
    223, 224, 227, 228–9, 258–60,
    335, 336–7, 339, 341–2, 342–5
  Kaczmarowska-Hamilton
    portrait 377, 378
  keeping abreast with news
    17–18
  Kentucky holiday 156
  kidnap attempt on daughter
    125
  Knatchbull children, caring for
    144
  last Red Box 360–1
  leaving Windsor for last time
    348
  Leibovitz photographs 11
  liaising with Charles and
    William 312, 326
  Lilibet of Sussex's name 328–9
  'the look' of displeasure 12–13
  Lord Mountbatten's murder 144
  love of animals 16, 21, 31
  Macmillan's replacement
    104–5
  on Malta (2015) 268
  Margaret's death and funeral
    224–6
  McCabe's investiture 353
  meeting Pope John Paul II 146
  Meghan's wedding tiara 282–4
  Millennium New Year's Eve
    217–18
  modernizing monarchy 97–8,
    112, 113–14
  'Mother of the Nation' 232
  mother's death and funeral
    227–8
  move to Buckingham Palace
    79–80
  negative media attention 96–7,
    98–9, 105–6, 122, 157–8,
    168–9, 177, 180, 182, 183–4,
    207–8, 218, 297
  nervous breakdown 115
  ninetieth birthday 273
  normalizing monarchy 381–2
  Northern Ireland visit 132–3
  number of US presidents met
    327

Index

'Oh, really?' response 20
Olympic Games, 1976, Montreal 130–1, 261
Olympic Games, 2012, London 261–4
Paddington Bear sketch 342–4
Panorama show's impact on 198–9
Philip's death and funeral 323–5
Philip's declining health 258, 260, 277, 298
Philip's memorial service 337–8
preparing Charles for succession 340
Privy Council meetings 13, 17, 75–6, 239–40, 298–301, 317–19, 348, 354
remembering small, personal details 17
Royal Family (BBC/ITV) 113–14
royal finances 121–2
Scottish independence referendums 269–70, 347–8
Scottish Parliament (1999) 214–15
'smiling problem' 106, 231
Snowdons' separation 128–9
state visits
    Australia 86–8, 106, 117, 125, 131–2, 160, 218–19, 227
    Baltic states 238
    Brazil 130
    Canada 22, 99, 258
    Caribbean 86
    China 161
    Fiji 86
    France 99, 119–20, 123, 267–8
    Germany 109–10, 268
    Ghana 22, 103–4
    India and Pakistan 103
    Indonesia 125
    Italy 220–1, 266–7
    Jamaica 227
    Middle East 136
    Morocco 146–7
    New Zealand 13, 86, 106, 117–18, 227
    Republic of Ireland 248–50
    Russia 187–8, 188–9
    South Africa 188, 189
    Thailand 200–1
    Tonga 86
    USA 99, 130, 169, 238, 258
    Zambia 22
Suez Canal crisis 93–4
Supreme Governor of the Church of England 24
Sussexes withdrawal from royal duties 308–11
Sussex's allegations, response to 322–3
tax question 176, 177, 179–81, 183–4
terrorist threats and attacks 22–3, 154
Thatcher's funeral 265–6
Thatcher's Order of Merit 166
Uncle David's death and funeral 123–4
understanding British public 17, 269
'walkabouts' 117–18
Way Ahead Group 185
William's wedding 246–8
Wilson's social reforms 110–11
Windsor Castle fire 171, 178–9
centenary celebration plans 363
character
    authenticity 8
    bravery 22–3, 103, 133, 189
    canniness 141, 142–3
    constancy 14, 25
    emotional reticence 16, 75
    equanimity and sangfroid 3–4, 13–14, 19, 148–9, 153–4, 184

Elizabeth II

Elizabeth II (*cont.*)
  frankness 6–8, 239–40
  kindness 10–11, 15, 19, 124, 144
  moderation and temperance 14–15
  pragmatism 4–5, 6, 77, 110
  public versus private 6–7, 21–2
  self-confidence 222–3, 238–40, 242, 264
  sense of duty/purpose 12, 52, 63, 103, 154, 326, 360–1
  sense of humour 3, 5–6, 8–10, 13, 130, 140–1, 169, 239, 268–9
  shyness 21, 43–4, 45
  relationships
    Andrew 25, 160, 303, 304, 305, 337–8
    Bobo 192–3
    Charles 247
    Edward 162–3, 216–17
    grandparents 28–9
    Harry 264, 381
    Margaret 91, 129, 225
    mother 57, 77, 102, 231
    Nelson Mandela 167, 189, 266
    niece Sarah 129
    parents 57, 63
    Patrick Plunket 127–8
    Philip 60, 87, 94, 97, 101–2, 238, 258, 277, 314, 324, 335
    'Porchie' Carnarvon 223–4
    prime ministers 105, 108, 109, 118, 119, 126, 137–43, 156–8, 166, 298–301, 350–1
    Uncle David 123–4
    William 246–7, 312, 326, 381
Elizabeth Line, London Underground 341–2
Elizabeth, Princess *see* **Elizabeth II, As Princess Elizabeth**
Elizabeth R (BBC) 173–5
Elizabeth R (Jay) 184

Elizabeth the Queen Mother
  as Duchess of York 27–8, 29, 30, 33
  as Queen Consort 34, 35, 36, 37, 39, 40, 41, 44, 47, 51–2, 54, 67, 73, 80
  as Queen Mother 15, 77, 79–80, 102, 148, 181, 204, 226, 231–2
  centenary 219–20
  death and funeral 81, 227–8
  relationship with Elizabeth 57, 77, 102, 231
Emma, the fell pony 331, 348, 360
Epstein, Jeffrey 253, 301–2, 303, 305, 306, 370
Eugenie, Princess 160, 177, 245, 287–8, 370
European Economic Community (EEC)/European Union (EU) 119–21, 176, 270–2, 296, 297
Euston, Hugh FitzRoy, Viscount 43
Evening Standard 34

Fagan, Michael 153–4
Falkland Islands War 151, 152–3
Fall, Sir Brian 189
Farebrother, Michael 102–3
Fayed, Dodi 202, 204
Fayed, Mohammed 201–2
Fellowes, Sir Robert 147, 167, 172, 176, 182, 193, 199, 205, 215, 218, 225, 235
Ferguson, Sarah *see* Sarah, Duchess of York (now Ferguson)
Fiji 86, 161
Finding Freedom (Scobie and Durand) 283, 289–90, 293
Fisher, Archbishop Geoffrey 57, 61, 83, 85
Fitzalan Howard, Alathea 43–4, 45, 48
Fixed Term Parliaments Act (2010) 244

Index

Ford, Gerald 130
Ford, Sir Edward 73, 94, 172
France 36, 37, 47, 58, 93, 99, 119–20, 123, 135, 186–7, 239, 267–8, 371, 375
Francis, Mary 213–15, 235
Francis, Pope 267
Freud, Lucian 222
Frogmore Cottage, Windsor Home Park 292, 338, 370
Frost, Sir David 213

G7 summit, Cornwall (2021) 326–7
Gandhi, Indira 23
Geidt, Sir Christopher 242, 244, 257, 279
general elections 8, 49, 70, 108, 118, 122, 125–6, 155, 162, 175, 176, 202, 203, 241–3
George of Wales, Prince 264, 265, 274, 345, 369
George, Prince, Duke of Kent 31, 45
George V 28–9, 30, 31–3, 79
George VI
  As Duke of York 27–8, 29, 30, 32, 33, 34
  pre-War 34, 35–6, 80, 180
  Second World War 18, 37, 38, 39, 40–1, 41–2, 43, 46–7, 48–9
  post-War 49, 51–2, 53, 54, 57, 58, 62, 65, 68–9, 70–1, 73–4, 261
  influence on Elizabeth 38, 181
Germany; *see also* Second World War 36, 37, 50, 55, 109–10, 221, 268, 371
Ghana 22, 103–4
Gillard, Julia 219, 257
Giscard d'Estaing, Valéry 130, 135
Giuffre (née Roberts), Virginia 301–2, 337
Glass, Dr Douglas 354, 356–7, 358, 359
Glenconner, Anne, Baroness 226
Gloucester, Brigitte, Duchess 368
Gloucester, Prince Richard, Prince, Duke 368
Greenland 378
Grenada 155–6
Guardian, The 106
Gulf Wars 168, 169, 232

Harewood, George Lascelles, 7th Earl 19, 111
Harris, Kenneth 138
Harry & Meghan (Netflix) 364
Harry, Prince, Duke of Sussex
  Angola visit 307
  Archewell brand 320
  Balmoral summer break 202
  birth 159, 160
  births of children 293–4, 328
  children meeting great-grandmother 342
  closing 2012 Olympic Games 264
  Commonwealth tour 290
  Commonwealth Youth Ambassador 289
  grandfather's funeral 325
  grandmother's Jubilees 259, 260, 263, 342
  grandmother's last illness and death 355–6
  on great-Aunt Margaret 225
  Harry & Meghan (Netflix) 364
  hosting the Obamas 274–5
  Invictus Games 275, 280–1
  lawsuits 329
  loss of patronages 320
  made Duke of Sussex 286
  and Meghan 280–7
  mother's death and funeral 204, 210, 211
  offices 245–6, 292–3
  Oprah Winfrey interview 320–3
  problems with the media 293–4, 307, 328–9
  relationship with grandmother 264, 381

433

Elizabeth II

Harry, Prince (*cont.*)
  relationship with William 66, 292, 311, 325
  resignation from royal life 308–11
  Spare 66, 283, 284–5, 293, 310, 364
Hassan II of Morocco 146–7
Heath, Edward 118, 119–20, 121, 122, 125–6, 142–3
Hennessy, Prof Peter, Baron of Nympsfield 77, 121, 242, 244, 271
Heseltine, Sir William
  appointments 112
  Bobo MacDonald 193
  Ceauşescus' visit 135
  China visit 161
  George VI's influence on Queen 38
  It's a Knockout (BBC) 163
  Jubilees 131
  modernizing the monarchy 112, 113
  Northern Ireland visit 133
  paparazzi 112–13
  Queen's international pulling power 130
  Queen's relationships with prime ministers 126, 141, 157, 158
  Royal Family (BBC/ITV) 114, 174
  tax issue 180–1
  walkabouts 117–18
Higgins, Michael D. 250
Hitler, Adolf 36, 40
Hollande, François 267–8
Hong Kong 201, 203
Hunt, Jeremy 294, 376
Hurd, Douglas 6–7, 12, 146, 147, 173, 188, 216, 239
Hussein, Saddam 168, 232

Independent, The 177
India 53, 65, 103, 175
Indonesia 125

Invictus Games 275, 280–1
IRA 22, 135, 144, 154, 156, 183, 220, 250
Iraq 168, 232, 238
Ireland, Republic of 144, 248–50, 297–8
Israel 93
Italy 160, 220–1, 236, 266–7, 371
It's a Knockout (BBC) 162–3
ITV 113–14, 129, 174–5, 197–8, 201, 220, 307

Jack, Alister 367–8
Jamaica 86, 227, 339
James Bond skit 261–3
Janvrin, Sir Robin 184–5, 203–4, 205, 207, 215–16, 235, 241, 242
Jay, Sir Anthony 23, 109, 113, 135, 174, 184
Jebb, Cynthia 63
Jebb, Sir Gladwyn 63
John Paul I, Pope 8
John Paul II, Pope 146, 151, 236
Johnson, Alan 95, 239–40
Johnson, Boris 7, 298–9, 300, 301, 313, 316, 317, 333, 341, 349–51, 352, 353–4
Johnstone-Burt, Vice Admiral Tony 304–5, 314
Jones, Kathryn 209
Judd, Alan 136

Kaczmarowska-Hamilton, Basia 377, 378
Kaufman, Sir Gerald 17
Kaunda, Kenneth 143
Keating, Paul 139, 197
Kekkonen, Sylvi 9–10
Kelly, Angela 221–2, 263, 267, 272, 283, 284–5, 344, 353, 356
Kennedy, John F. 23, 103, 110, 115
Kensington Palace, London 57, 66, 196, 200, 207, 210, 274–5, 285, 292

Index

Kenya 71–2, 74, 75
Kerr, Sir John 131–2
Khan, Hasnat 200, 202
Kinnock, Neil 165, 175
Kirkwood, Pat 58–9
Knatchbull, Tim and Amanda 144
Knight, Clara ('Alah') 29–30, 42
Korea 70, 177
Kuwait 168, 169, 232

Lascelles, Sir Alan 'Tommy' 10, 29, 46, 47, 49, 52–3, 73, 79, 80, 83, 89, 90, 91, 183
Laurence, Cdr Sir Timothy 175, 182–3, 319, 369
Leibovitz, Annie 11
Lilibet of Sussex, Princess 328–9, 342
Little Princesses, The (Crawford) 66–7
Llewellyn, Roddy 128, 226
Lockerbie, Dumfries and Galloway 164
Longford, Elizabeth 20
Louis of Wales, Prince 265, 345, 369
Luce, Richard, Baron 10, 140–1

McCabe, Donal, MVO 353
McCulloch, Bishop Nigel 23
MacDonald, Margaret ('Bobo') 30, 64, 192–3
McGuinness, Martin 135, 250
MacKenzie, Rev. Kenneth 356
Macmillan, Harold 97, 101, 103, 104–5
Magpie, HMS 67, 69
Mail on Sunday, The 253, 307
Major, Sir John 166, 176, 180, 181–2, 186–7, 191–2, 202, 203, 232, 246, 335
Malta 64, 67–8, 233, 238, 268
Mandela, Nelson 5, 167, 188, 189, 266

Manning, Sir David 245–6
Mar-a-Lago, Florida, USA 374, 378
Margaret, Princess, Countess of Snowdon
  pre-War 29–30, 30–1, 34, 35, 36–7
  Second World War 37, 40, 41, 42–3, 44–5, 46–7, 48
  post-War 6, 51–2, 66, 67, 81, 122, 158
  character 45
  death and funeral 224–6
  and Peter Townsend 90–2
  and Roddy Llewellyn 128, 226
  and Tony Armstrong-Jones 104, 128–9
Marina of Greece, Princess, Duchess of Kent 31, 45
Markle, Thomas 285–6
Marten, Sir Henry 35, 91
Martin, Chris 11–12
Mary, Queen 28, 30, 35, 55, 73–4, 76, 78, 81
May, Sir Brian 229, 345
May, Theresa 291, 293, 294, 298
Meet the Press (NBC) 121–2
Meghan, Duchess of Sussex 280–7, 289–90, 292–4, 296, 307–11, 320–3, 328, 342, 364
Middle East 135–6, 168, 169
Millennium Dome, Greenwich 217–18
Mirzoeff, Edward 173–5, 382
Mitterrand, François 186–7
monarchy
  Australia's referendum on 196–7, 218–19
  finances 121–2, 165–6, 176, 179–81, 183–4, 255–6
  and imperialism 339
  laws of succession 27–8, 35, 256–8
  modernizing 97–8, 112, 113–14

Elizabeth II

monarchy (*cont.*)
  Monarchy: The Nation Decides (ITV) 201
  normalization 381–2
  popularity 371
  post-Diana evolution 213–14, 215–16
  regency questions 265, 317
  relevance today 379, 380
  repeal of Royal Marriages Act 257
  'slimmed-down' 260–1, 368–9
  stability and continuity 365
  transition 358–9
  Way Ahead Group 184–5
Monarchy (BBC) 241
Monarchy: The Nation Decides (ITV) 201
Moore, Charles 7, 139, 158
Moran, Charles Wilson, Baron 69, 89
Morgan, Peter 269, 275–6
Morocco 146–7
Morrah, Dermot 52–3
Morton, Andrew 149, 176
Mountbatten, Louis, 1st Earl Mountbatten of Burma 45, 46, 51, 62, 64, 78, 102, 144, 247
Muggeridge, Malcolm 99
Mureithi, Nahashan 72

Napolitano, Giorgio 266–7
Nasser, Gamal Abdel 93
National and English Review, The 98
NATO 378, 379–80
Neil, Andrew 157, 168–9
Nepal 195
New Statesman 218
New Zealand 13, 28, 77, 86, 106, 117–18, 160, 227, 247, 303
Newsnight (BBC) 302
Nkrumah, Kwame 103–4
Northern Ireland 115, 132–3, 249

Obama, Barack and Michelle 250–1, 273–5
O'Connell, Pat 250
Olympic Games 93, 95, 131, 218, 261–4
Oprah Winfrey Show, The (CBS) 320–3
Osborne, George 250–1, 256
Owen, David, Baron 24, 135–6

Paddington Bear 342–4
Pakistan 53, 103
Panorama (BBC) 198–9, 301–2
paparazzi 112–13, 176–7, 195–6, 207
Paris Match 369
Parker Bowles, Camilla *see* Camilla, Duchess of Cornwall (now Queen)
Parker Bowles, Lieut Col Andrew 143, 150, 154, 234
Parker, Maj Sir Michael 220
Parker, Mike 60, 61, 74, 96, 97
Paul VI, Pope 8
Payne, Keith 12
Peat, Michael 165
Peel, William, 3rd Earl 3–4, 7, 17, 19–20, 251, 296, 302, 304, 326
Penn, Prue 6, 9, 126, 134, 204, 225, 227, 325
'People Will Say We're In Love' (Rogers and Hammerstein) 50, 268
Philip, Prince, Duke of Edinburgh
  pre-marriage as Prince of Greece
    at Britannia Royal Naval College 36–7
    childhood and education 50–1
    engagement 50, 51, 53–4
    family background 50–1
    first meeting Elizabeth 31
    post-war courtship 50
    sending photo to Elizabeth 48

Index

wartime service 46
wartime visits 43-4, 45, 46
achievements 94-5, 324
Andrew's confrontation with Master of the Household 304-5
Birthday Parade shooting 149
births of children 60-1, 67
Britannia, HMY 191
ceasing long-haul travel 258
character 9, 277-8, 278-9
children's education 102, 103
Commonwealth Study Conferences 94-5
D-Day anniversaries 187
death and funeral 323-5
Diamond Wedding on Malta 238
Diana's death and funeral 204, 208-9, 210
Dimbleby project 197-8
driving 62-3, 291-2
Duke of Edinburgh's Award 94, 95, 216-17, 324
and Elizabeth 60, 87, 94, 97, 101-2, 238, 258, 277, 314, 324, 335
Elizabeth R (BBC) 174-5
Elizabeth's Christmas broadcast tribute to 335
Elizabeth's concern for health of 258, 260, 277, 298
engagement of Charles and Diana 147-8
Establishment's hostility towards 78-9, 80-1, 94
family homes 61-2
family surname 78-9, 101-2
gaffes 278-9
Golden Jubilee tour 228-9
gossip about 58-60, 96-7
hosting state visitors 274, 275
interests/pursuits 54, 59-60, 63, 95-6
kidnap attempt on daughter 125
learning of George VI's death 74
leaving Royal Navy 69
made Duke of Edinburgh 54
made Prince of the United Kingdom 97
on Malta (2015) 268
Melbourne Olympics and South Seas adventure 93, 95
memorial service 337-8
Millennium New Year's Eve 217-18
moderation and temperance 15
modernizing Court 97-8
opening 1956 Olympic Games 261
Operation HMS Bubble 314
opinion polls 215-16
Order of the Garter 54
posted to Malta 64, 67-8
Queen's Diamond Jubilee 259-60
Ranger of Windsor Great Park 95
retirement 276, 279, 296, 314
royal finances 121-2
state visits 58, 69, 70, 71-3, 86-8, 117-18, 125, 136, 146, 161, 219, 238, 267
staying out of things 236, 279, 314
wanting Edward to follow as Duke 216-17
wedding 54-6
Windlesham Moor 58
Windsor Castle 80
World Wildlife Fund (WWF) 96, 324
Phillips, Capt Mark 124, 175
Phillips, Peter 61, 134
Plunket, Patrick, 7th Baron 127-8
Poland 37, 185
Prince of Wales, The (Dimbleby) 197-8

Elizabeth II

Privy Council meetings 13, 17, 75–6, 239–40, 298–301, 317–19, 348, 354
Profumo Affair 105–6
Pun, Tul Bahadur 241
Putin, Vladimir 232–3

Ragland, Doria 281, 293, 294
Rayner, Angela 318–19
Reagan, Ronald 151–2, 155–6
Rees, Merlyn 132–3
Rees-Mogg, Sir Jacob 271–2, 298–300, 318, 351
Republic protest group 367–8
Rhodes, Ben 251, 274–5
Rhodes, Margaret 38, 43, 48
Rhodes, Simon 338
Rhodesia 52, 53, 142
Rifkind, Sir Malcolm 8
Roberts, Andrew 75
Roberts (later Giuffre), Virginia 301–2, 337
Romania 134–5
Romsey, Penelope Knatchbull, Viscountess 60
Roosevelt, Eleanor 44
Rose, Kenneth 12, 22, 278
Ross, Lieut Col Sir Malcolm 206, 266
Royal Family (BBC/ITV) 113–14, 129
Royal Lodge, Windsor Great Park 30, 39, 40, 80, 179, 180, 227, 338–9, 370
Royal Maundy ceremony 24, 339
Royal Oak, HMS 38, 39
Runcie, Archbishop Robert 150
Russell, Ron 125
Russia 28, 187–8, 189, 195, 233
Rutland, Charles Manners, 10th Duke 18–19, 43

Sālote of Tonga, Queen 6, 85, 86
Sandringham House, Norfolk 6, 17, 39, 60, 64, 98, 177, 226, 310, 335, 337, 339, 366
Sarah, Duchess of York (now Ferguson) 158–60, 162, 163, 175, 176–7, 199–200, 255, 281, 370
Sarjeant, Marcus 149
Saturday Evening Post 99
Scottish independence referendums 269–70, 347
Scottish Parliament 214–15, 332–3
Second World War
  bombing raids 41–2, 47
  D-Day 47, 186
  German advances 40
  protection of Royal Family 40
  sinking of *Royal Oak* 38, 39
  start 37
  VE Day 48–9
Seko, Mobutu Sese and Marie-Antoinette 127
Sentamu, Archbishop John 244
Shea, Michael 158
Simpson, Wallis Warfield *see* Windsor, Wallis (Simpson), Duchess of
Slater, Sir Jock 12, 139
Smuts, Jan 51, 53
Snowdon, Anthony Armstrong-Jones, 1st Earl 104, 128–9
Snowdon, David Armstrong-Jones, 2nd Earl 129, 227
Soames, Sir Christopher 123
Sophie, Countess of Wessex (now Duchess of Edinburgh) 216, 259, 282, 310, 324, 368
South Africa 51–2, 53, 103–4, 119, 156–8, 167, 188, 189
Spare (Sussex) 66, 202, 211, 283, 284–5, 293, 310, 364
Spencer, Charles, 9th Earl 210–11
Sri Lanka 266
St James's Palace, London 366
Starkey, David 24
Starmer, Sir Keir 371

Index

Stock, Victor 15
Strathmore, Claude Bowes-Lyon, 14th Earl 27
Suez Canal crisis 93-4
Sullivan, Martin 20-1
Sullom Voe oil terminal, Scotland 22
Sun, The 172, 177, 182, 208, 271, 333-4
Sunak, Rishi 364
Sunday Times, The 157-8, 168-9, 176, 197

terrorist threats and attacks 22-3, 103, 115, 132-3, 142, 144, 148-9, 154, 156, 164, 196, 197, 223, 224, 249
Thailand 200-1
Thatcher, Margaret 137-43, 148, 150, 151, 155-8, 161, 162, 165, 166, 232, 265-6
Thin, Dr Jean 123
Thomas, Sir Huw 354, 356
Times, The 32-3, 180, 209-10, 224-5, 297, 314, 321, 322-3
Tonga 86
Townsend, Group Capt Peter 90-2, 183
Trudeau, Justin 371
Trudeau, Pierre 119
Truman, Harry 70
Trump, Donald 23, 294-6, 371-80
Truss, Liz 352, 354, 364
Turner, Graham 16, 19, 177

Uganda 7, 126-7, 238
United States (USA)
　9/11 terrorist attacks 224
　Bicentennial 130
　D-Day anniversaries 186-7
　Gulf Wars 168, 169, 232
　invasion of Grenada 155-6
　Queen's California visit 152
　Queen's Kentucky holidays 156
　'special relationship' 373-4
　state visits to 36, 70, 99, 130, 160, 169, 238, 258, 275
　Suez Canal crisis 93
　as threat to Canada 371, 378-9

Vanguard, HMS 6, 51
Vickers, Hugo 66-7
Victoria and Albert, HMY 36, 37

Way Ahead Group 184-5
Wedgewood-Benn, Anthony 108-9
Welby, Archbishop Justin 322
Whelp, HMS 46, 51
William, Prince, Duke of Cambridge (now Prince of Wales)
　Adelaide Cottage 338
　Balmoral summer break 202
　birth 152
　and Catherine 244-8
　childhood 160
　grandfather's funeral 325
　grandmother's Jubilees 260, 263, 345
　grandmother's last illness and death 356
　as heir 380-1
　hosting the Obamas 274-5
　made Duke of Cambridge 247
　mother's death and funeral 204, 210, 211
　relationship with grandmother 246-7, 312, 326, 381
　relationship with Harry 66, 292, 311, 325
　royal duties 247, 259, 339
　state visit to Caribbean 339
　Sussexes' resignation from public duties 308-9, 309-10
　and Trump 375
　and Uncle Andrew 381
Wilson, Harold 19, 76, 108, 109,

Elizabeth II

Wilson, Harold (*cont.*)
  110–11, 118, 122, 125, 126, 128, 139, 192
Windlesham Moor, Surrey 57–8
Windsor Castle, Berks.
  Diamond Jubilee lunch 5
  fire 171, 178–80
  global business summit 333
  hosting state visitors 151–2, 250, 273, 274, 327–8, 372–4, 375, 376–7
  Operation HMS Bubble 314, 320, 323
  Paddington Bear sketch 342–5
  Platinum Jubilee 342, 344–5
  Privy Council meetings 239–40
  Queen's COVID broadcast 314–16
  Queen's eightieth birthday 237–8
  Queen's last Christmas at 334–5
  royal funerals 124, 225–6, 227–8, 324–5, 359–60
  as royal home 80
  royal weddings 216, 237, 286–7
  during Second World War 40, 42–3, 45, 46, 47–8
Windsor, Edward, Duke of *see* Edward, Prince of Wales/Edward VIII/Duke of Windsor
Windsor, Wallis (Simpson), Duchess of 31, 33–4, 36, 123, 124
Winfrey, Oprah 286, 287, 320–3
Woodard, Sir Robert 12–13, 188, 189, 190
World Wildlife Fund (WWF) 96, 324

Yeltsin, Boris 187–8
Young, Sir Edward
  background 279–80
  Brexit 272
  Covid-19 313, 315–16, 316–17
  James Bond skit 263
  Johnson 350
  last Red Box 360–1
  Paddington Bear sketch 343
  planning Ireland visit 297–8
  Platinum Jubilee 342–3, 345
  Queen's death 357, 358
  Queen's failing health 353, 356
  Queen's response to Sussexes' allegations 323
  Sussexes' resignation 309
Yousaf, Humza 368

Zaire 127
Zambia 22, 52, 142–3
Zimbabwe 52, 53, 143, 167, 195, 234